WITHDRAWN

IDOLS OF THE MARKETPLACE

IDOLATRY AND COMMODITY FETISHISM IN ENGLISH LITERATURE, 1580–1680

David Hawkes

palgrave

IDOLS OF THE MARKETPLACE
Copyright © David Hawkes, 2001.
All rights reserved. No part of this book may be used or reproduced in any manner whatsoever without written permission except in the case of brief quotations embodied in critical articles or reviews.

First published 2001 by
PALGRAVE™
175 Fifth Avenue, New York, N.Y. 10010 and
Houndmills, Basingstoke, Hampshire, England RG21 6XS.
Companies and representatives throughout the world.

PALGRAVE™ is the new global publishing imprint of St. Martin's Press LLC Scholarly and Reference Division and Palgrave Publishers Ltd. (formerly Macmillan Press Ltd.).

ISBN 0–312–24007–4

Library of Congress Cataloging-in-Publication Data
Hawkes, David, 1964-
Idols of the marketplace : idolatry and commodity fetishism in English literature, 1580–1680/ David Hawkes.
   p. cm.—(Early Modern Cultural Series)
Includes bibliographical references and index.
ISBN 0–312–24007–4
1. English literature—Early modern, 1500–1700—History and criticism. 2. Idolatry in literature. 3. Christianity and literature—Great Britain—History—17th century. 4. Christianity and literature—Great Britain—History—16th century. 5. Economics and literature—Great Britain—History—17th century.
6. Economics and literature—Great Britain—History—16th century.
7. Protestantism and literature—History. 8. Consumption (Economics) in literature. 9. Materialism in literature.
10. Fetishism in literature. I. Title. II. Series.

PR438.I36 H39 2001
820.9'38291218—dc21
                                                              2001021548

A catalogue record for this book is available from the British Library.

Design by Letra Libre, Inc.

First edition: October 2001
10 9 8 7 6 5 4 3 2 1

Printed in the United States of America.

To my parents

CONTENTS

Series Editor's Foreword		vii
Preface		ix
Introduction		3
Chapter One	Idolatry and Political Economy	27
Chapter Two	Commodity Fetishism and Theology	49
Chapter Three	Idolatry and Commodity Fetishism in the Antitheatrical Controversy	77
Chapter Four	Sodomy, Usury, and the Narrative of Shakespeare's *Sonnets*	95
Chapter Five	Typology and Objectification in George Herbert's *The Temple*	115
Chapter Six	Alchemical and Financial Value in the Poetry of John Donne	143
Chapter Seven	The Politics of Character in Milton's Divorce Tracts	169
Chapter Eight	Thomas Traherne: A Critique of Political Economy	191
Chapter Nine	John Bunyan's One-Dimensional Man	213
Notes		231
Index		289

SERIES EDITOR'S FOREWORD

Once there was a time when each field of knowledge in the liberal arts had its own mode of inquiry. A historian's labors were governed by an entirely different set of rules than those of the anthropologist or the literary critic. But this is less true now than it has ever been. This new series begins with the assumption that, as we enter the twenty-first century, literary criticism, literary theory, historiography, and cultural studies have become so interwoven that we can now think of them as an eclectic and only loosely unified (but still recognizable) approach to formerly distinct fields of inquiry such as literature, society, history, and culture. This series furthermore presumes that the early modern period was witness to an incipient process of transculturation through exploration, mercantilism, colonization, and migration that set into motion a process of globalization that is still with us today. The purpose of this series is to bring together this eclectic approach, which freely and unapologetically crosses disciplinary, theoretical, and political boundaries, with early modern texts and artifacts that bear the traces of transculturation and globalization.

This process can be studied on a large as well as on a small scale, and this new series is dedicated to both. It is just as concerned with the analyses of colonial encounters and native representations of those encounters as it is with representations of the other in Shakespeare, the cultural impact of the presence of strangers/foreigners in London, or the consequences of farmers' migration to that same city. This series is as interested in documenting cultural exchanges between British, Portuguese, Spanish, or Dutch colonizers and native peoples as it is in telling the stories of returning English soldiers who served in foreign armies on the continent of Europe in the late sixteenth century.

Positing a strong connection between economic formations and shifts in English cultural life, David Hawkes's *Idols of the Marketplace: Idolatry and Commodity Fetishism in English Literature, 1580–1680* explores the responses of a number of late-sixteenth and seventeenth-century writers to the philosophical and theological implications of the nascent market economy. The authors Hawkes treats here approach the phenomenon of the market economy from various angles, but all are deeply troubled by the market's penchant for elevating an object's exchange-value over its use-value, resulting in an ethically unacceptable fetishization of commodities. This fundamentally Aristotelian viewpoint is supplemented by the religious conviction that the market economy trespasses on the Biblical dictates against idolizing "the works of men's hands." *Idols of the Marketplace* painstakingly examines the presence of both the religious and the classical objection to the market place in the writings of William Shakespeare, George Herbert, John Donne, Thomas Traherne, John Milton, and John Bunyan. What emerges is a rich tapestry of connections that links charges of idolatry and commodity fetishism to a wide range of issues such as anti-theatricalism, divorce, sodomy and usury, typology and carnality, alchemy and capital, all of which reveal important stress points in early modern English culture. Hawkes argues forcefully that the success of the market "produces a carnal consciousness which ultimately causes the death of the human soul."

Ivo Kamps

Preface

Many of the ideas in this book first occurred to me in the late 1980s, while I was a graduate student at Columbia University. The guidance I received there from mentors such as Jean Howard and Victoria Silver was inspirational and remains incalculably influential on my work. The privilege of studying under teachers like John Archer, David Kastan, Edward Said, and Jim Shapiro is one for which I shall always be grateful. My colleagues in the English department at Lehigh University have been remarkably good-humored over the years, and it is hard to imagine my endeavors bearing any fruit without the affable ambience of Drown Hall. The intellectual comradeship of Scott Gordon and Barbara Traister has been especially valuable to me, Barry Kroll is a hugely supportive head of department, and nothing at all would get done without Carol Laub, Viv Steele, and Donna Warmkessel. In the fall of 1999 I had the wonderful and frightening experience of teaching a faculty seminar in the Philosophy Department, where the cogent criticisms of Gordon Bearn, Steve Goldman, Alex Levine, Ralph Lindgren, and their colleagues roughly licked many of my arguments into shape. I owe Jim Holstun special gratitude for his meticulous and brilliant critique of this book. Kristi Long and Ivo Kamps are helpful and perceptive editors, and it has been a refreshing pleasure to work with them. Earlier versions of chapters 3, 4, and 9 appear respectively in *Studies in English Literature* 39 no.2 (spring 1999), *Renaissance Studies* 14 no.3 (fall 2000), reproduced by permission of Oxford University Press, and *The Eighteenth Century: Theory and Interpretation* 41 no.1 (spring 2000), reproduced by permission.

If, in conclusion, you ask me for any conceivable cause or meaning of these things—I can tell you none, according to your modern beliefs; but I can tell you what meaning it would have borne to the men of old time.

—*John Ruskin,*
The Storm-Cloud of the Nineteenth Century*

INTRODUCTION

And the merchants of the earth shall weep and mourn over her; for no man buyeth their merchandise any more.

—*Revelation 18:11*[1]

And now the Hireling Teachers of all sorts, the Merchants of Mystery Babylon, shall cry, Alas! alas! that great City, People begin to see us, and they will not trade with us, nor buy our Merchandize, as in former dayes, but declare against it.

—Thomas Taylor, To the People at and about Stafford[2]

That which we call national economy today is built up on premises that are openly and specifically English. Credit-money, in the special form imparted to it by the relations of world-trade and export-industry in a peasantless England, serves as the foundation whereupon to define words like capital, value, price, property....

—Oswald Spengler, The Decline of the West[3]

I

Shortly after the Restoration, Lucy Hutchinson composed a lengthy memorial to her husband, the regicide Colonel John Hutchinson, who had died in a Royalist prison in 1664. Describing the nature of her late husband's love for her, she wrote "never was there a passion more ardent and less idolatrous."[4] What did she mean? What is this "idolatrous" passion that Hutchinson evidently regards as not merely distinct from, but opposite to, healthy, "ardent" affection? Are we to imagine that the Hutchinsons held conversations about their feelings for each other in which the need to eschew idolatry figured prominently? If so, how typical were they in this? What connections, if any, did they perceive between this idolatrous passion and the idolatry of priest and king, against which John Hutchinson spent his life fighting? These are the kinds of questions this book seeks to address.

I believe that, when Lucy Hutchinson writes with pride that her husband did not, and would never, idolize her, she means that he did not "objectify" her. A modern woman making the same point would probably intend it in a specifically sexual sense. She would be indicating that her husband did not regard her as a "sex object." Hutchinson probably does mean that, but I think that her use of the term "idolatrous" extends beyond the physical plane. She means, I think, that her husband's love for her was not an end in itself but a means to a higher end. Idolatry, she assumes, consists in a confusion of ends and means, which is simultaneously an act of objectification. And objectification is a process with ramifications far beyond the sexual sphere. Elsewhere in her memoir, Hutchinson expands:

> Yet even this, which was the highest love he or any man could have, was yet bounded by a superior: he loved [me] in the Lord as his fellow-creature, not his idol, but in such a manner as showed that an affection, bounded in the just rules of duty, far exceeds every way all the irregular passions in the world.[5]

John Hutchinson's love for his wife, it seems, was not "idolatrous" because it was continually referred to a higher end. It was not an end in itself; it was "bounded" by virtue of its reference to the Creator. John Donne expresses a similar idea when he recalls his love for his dead wife: "Here the admyring her my mind did whett / To seeke thee God; so streams do shew their head."[6] The wives of Hutchinson and Donne were not loved for themselves; that would have been, in the words of George Herbert's God, to "adore my gifts in stead of me / And rest in Nature, not the God of Nature."[7] They were loved, rather, for what the love which they provoked in their husbands was seen to *represent*.

I have argued elsewhere that twenty-first century society is characterized by the autonomy of representation.[8] In linguistics and philosophy, the media of representation are increasingly afforded determining power over the reality they once claimed to represent. In politics and culture, image and presentation overwhelm content. The economy is guided by fluctuations between various forms of money, and money is pure representation. In the twenty-first century, corporations such as Nike and McDonald's do not sell material products so much as "brands," which is to say, images. The sign, the simulacrum, the icon: These are the postmodern currency of debate in every field of intellectual endeavor, and they are also fast becoming the stuff of everybody's everyday experience. In this book, I draw attention to a mode of thought that condemns the autonomy of representation in the strongest possible terms. Many such modes of thought have existed throughout history. But here, broadly speaking, I will concentrate on the ideas of Protestant English people from the late sixteenth until the late seventeenth centuries. These people called the autonomy of representation "idolatry." They detected "idolatry" in every area of life and thought, and they tended to blame it for every psychological and social ill they encountered.

Because of this capaciousness, the chronological limitations of my project are balanced by the breadth of topics addressed in the texts I discuss. Despite this variety in their subject matter, however, the works studied here are united by their common response to the issues with which they deal. When, in 1583, Phillip Stubbes looked at the London playhouses, he saw "idolatry." When, in 1643, John Milton considered the divorce laws, he found "idolatry." When, in 1680, John Bunyan examined the workings of retail trade, he discovered "idolatry." The strain of thought that unites these visions might be said to dominate the intervening century, and it will be my subject here.

My primary thesis is that Lucy Hutchinson's connection of idolatry with a confusion of means and ends—that is to say with a violation of "natural teleology"—was typical, indeed axiomatic, in sixteenth- and seventeenth-century England. As far as I have been able to tell, the evidence indicates that literate English people of this period were aware, at many levels of articulacy and with regard to many areas of experience, that the core assumptions of natural teleology were being undermined. There is, furthermore, a striking degree of consensus among them regarding the consequences of this development. The general feeling seems to have been that, once natural teleology is abandoned, it tends to be replaced by human custom. This custom then comes to appear as a "second nature" that displaces authentic nature and is frequently mistaken for it. In Greek terms, the people of Renaissance England were concerned that *phusis* was being occluded and *telos* eclipsed by the *eidola* of *nomos*.

Under the influence of the Reformation, however, Protestant English people tended to syncretize these Greek concepts with Biblical ideas. In the Bible, the replacement of nature by custom is called "idolatry." It amounts to a fetishization of the merely human; an adoration of "the works of men's hands." The Septuagint translates "torah" as "nomos," so that in Christianity "custom" is identified with the carnal "law" of the old dispensation. For Protestants of the

Reformation period, the concept of *nomos* is further associated with the idolatrous rituals and fleshly traditions of Catholicism. And in fact, for the Judeo-Christian tradition as a whole, idolatry is not merely a theological problem but rather an all-encompassing view of the world. It involves a fatal materialism—an unhealthy, irrational orientation toward the things of this world and the pleasures of the flesh—and it fosters the twin addictions of covetousness and sensuality. Ultimately, the idolatrous will receive chastisement, quite probably in the form of a global conflagration preceded by large-scale climactic change, but in any case through the eternal damnation of their immortal souls. In the century discussed here these beliefs were not peripheral but central; they were not eccentric but conventional. It should not be surprising, therefore, that anti-idolatry permeated the culture of early modern England with such profundity that it transcended the distinction between the personal and the political, shaping the erotic relations of couples like the Hutchinsons while simultaneously providing the intellectual framework for their regicidal politics. It *should* not be surprising, but perhaps it is. Perhaps this is because the condition of mind that these people called "idolatry" has, in our time, achieved a triumph so complete as to render itself imperceptible.

My secondary thesis is that the people of Reformation England recognized an analogous, or rather an homologous, violation of natural teleology in the growing influence of the market economy. On the basis of Aristotle and the Bible, they generally thought that exchange for profit, and the making of money with money—what we call "capitalism"—reflected a confusion of means with ends. This transgression against *telos* was, by their logic, idolatrous. It was idolatrous in the widest sense: It both exemplified and encouraged a materialist or "fleshly" approach to life and a "carnal" view of the world. When we study idolatry in this period, then, we are dealing with a process of *objectification*. A concern with objectification is the common element among the authors discussed here. I hope to show first that they discuss the process of objectification under the rubric and using the concepts and vocabulary of "idolatry," and second that they habitually, and, as it were, automatically, associate objectification with capitalism and the market economy.

With the exceptions of Milton and Bunyan, the major authors discussed here were neither committed iconoclasts nor opponents of capitalism. Shakespeare and Milton were the sons of money-lenders;[9] Donne, Herbert, Traherne, and most of the antitheatricalists were Anglican priests. Indeed, the canonical writers of the English Renaissance are interesting in this context precisely because they did not, as a rule, adopt radical theological or economic positions. Taken as a group, they could almost be said to represent the mainstream opinion of the privileged classes and gender. And yet, despite this, we find in their work a general agreement that seems to reflect a fundamental set of shared assumptions, on a point that might seem quite radical to us, since in our society it is made almost exclusively by political radicals. This is the claim that the market economy and the worship of idols are similar (we might say "homologous") forms of psychological fetishism that result from the displacement of *telos* by "the works of men's hands."

It also seems interesting that this logic is applied to what we might regard as a wide variety of "spheres." It is applied, in other words, to the totality of life. William Prynne finds in the theater an infernal conglomeration of idolatry and commodity fetishism, while Shakespeare's *Sonnets* are guided in their reflections on homoerotic love by the conviction that sodomy and usury are homologous violations of natural teleology. The assumption that idolatry results from a confusion of means and ends is the common thread uniting Milton's arguments for divorce with his politics and theology. Bunyan's *Mr. Badman* portrays *homo economicus* as idolatry personified. In Herbert, the typological movement from the idol of the law to the spiritual gospel is conceived in terms of financial redemption from debt. So powerful is the logic of this homology that it leads Herbert, like Shakespeare, into what is for us the most egregious antisemitism. Donne and Jonson delineate the demise of the Elizabethan world picture in the figure of the deluded or dishonest alchemist whose Aristotelian art is incompatible with financial value. Traherne, writing amid and perhaps in response to the earliest rationalizations of political economy, still sees the Fall repeated in the child's first recognition of exchange value.

Insofar as I concentrate on these canonical writers, I have eschewed the principle of "history from below," according to which the voices of subaltern social groups are especially deserving of attention. This decision does not spring from any sense that such research is unimportant or unfruitful. There is no doubt that, as James Holstun's *Ehud's Dagger* has recently reminded us, all of the theological and economic opinions I discuss in this book were voiced, perhaps even formulated, and certainly translated into practice by many less socially and literarily exalted figures than the ones treated here.[10] In my opinion, however, the facts that the connection between idolatry and commodity fetishism seems to have been taken for granted by people with nothing practical to gain from this theoretical weapon, and that this connection is evident even when they are not primarily discussing issues of theology or economics, make these texts more, rather than less, eloquent of the spirit of their age. We can readily understand why a leader of a plebeian social movement such as Gerrard Winstanley would associate idolatry with the market and assert that it is "the power and government of the Beast" that draws "the people into the way of buying and selling."[11] It is less obvious, although equally instructive, to consider how arcane quibbles over usury legislation could come to shape the intrigues of Shakespeare's boudoir or how the crisis of Aristotelian teleology could come to mar the delight of Milton's marriage bed.

II

One of the attractions of early modern England to left-wing historians is the fact that it displays the capitalist world system in embryonic form. This system first took shape in fifteenth-century England, with the beginnings of the mass expropriation of the peasantry, a process which was not completed for three hundred years. Expropriated peasants became proletarians, at first rural and later urban, who sold the commodity of their labor power on the market in exchange for money.[12] Having been deprived of the resources to produce their own subsistence, they used this money to purchase food and other commodities on the market. By the nineteenth century this process had been replicated on a global scale, and today capitalism has extirpated every other way of life from the world. For this reason it is difficult for us to evaluate, or even accurately to perceive, its psychological consequences. This is why it is interesting to study the reactions of the first people to be fully exposed to this system, which is to say the inhabitants of early modern England.

It may be appropriate at this stage to offer some clarification regarding my methodology. I use many terms and concepts—exchange value, labor power, commodity fetishism—which may be associated with the philosophy of Karl Marx, although they actually originate in Aristotle and the Bible. I do not, however, use the main interpretative tools usually employed by Marxist critics and historians—the class struggle, the mode of production, materialism. This book thus departs from, though it remains obviously and heavily indebted to, the venerable tradition of British socialist histories of early modern England. Perhaps significantly, this tradition was inaugurated by a Christian, rather than a Marxist, work: R. H. Tawney's *Religion and the Rise of Capitalism,* which was first published in 1926. Having surveyed early modern Protestant condemnations of the market economy, Tawney concludes that: "Compromise is as impossible between the Church of Christ and the idolatry of wealth, which is the practical religion of capitalist societies, as it was between the Church and the state idolatry of the Roman empire."[13]

Tawney wrote in reaction to Max Weber's famous thesis that the Protestant Reformation created a psychological orientation favorable to the development of capitalism. He pointed out that, while Weber was correct to note that Protestant injunctions to hard work and frugality were conducive to the accumulation of worldly goods, the writings of Protestant theologians, scholars, poets, playwrights, and pamphleteers very frequently denounced such phenomena as trade, usury, and covetousness, and that they usually did so in overtly religious terms.[14] Tawney thus prepared the way for an entire school of historians who were interested in the relations between religious and economic radicalism during the English Renaissance and Reformation.

However, the British Marxists brought to their task two doctrinaire assumptions that strongly influenced, and perhaps prejudiced, their interpretation of the period. Both of these assumptions can be traced to Marx's writings of the 1840s, and especially to the *Communist Manifesto,* a polemical tract written for a specific occasion and composed in collaboration with the less acute Engels. The first assumption is that the movement from feudalism to capitalism constituted a form of progress; the second is that this progress, like all of history, was driven forward by the material engine of the class struggle. The English revolution, in this view, was the work of a progressive bourgeois class pursuing their economic interests by means of a radical Protestant ideology. As Christopher Hill put it, "an old order that was essentially feudal was destroyed by violence, and a new and capitalist social order was created in its place."[15] From this perspective, the decline of Aristotelian teleology and the rise of Baconian empiricism must be positive developments, because they accompany the tide of progress. In fact, according to the breathtakingly ironic logic of orthodox Marxism, the rise of capitalism itself must be adjudged a "progressive" development. In 1951, the admittedly youthful Hill opined that:

> Bacon inaugurated the bourgeois epoch in science as Lysenko and his colleagues are inaugurating the new epoch today. In the Soviet Union the obstructive dogmas of bourgeois science have to be brushed aside, to the indignation of the logic-choppers, if socialist science is to devote

itself whole-heartedly to the relief of man's estate: so Bacon was fighting against the prejudices and dogmas of an effete civilization, dogmas which a priestly academic caste continued to preach although they manifestly impeded the development of industrial science.[16]

Hill's belief in historical progress thus leads him to side with the Baconians against the Aristotelians. In fact, Hill believes that one of Bacon's own greatest achievements was to popularize the idea that history is progressive. Elsewhere he writes:

> When Karl Marx held forth hopes of an egalitarian classless society to the exploited, the idea of progress had already become a commonplace. But Bacon spoke to men for whom, for centuries, the dogma of fallen humanity had been axiomatic.... Bacon gave them a theory which united a coherent optimism for humanity with a critique of Aristotle and the Schoolmen on grounds not only of their uselessness but also of their wickedness.[17]

The conviction that ideas are in the last instance determined by economic factors leads Hill to connect Baconian science to emergent capitalism[18] and also to "a powerful Puritan tradition, which was equally . . . opposed to Aristotle and the Schoolmen."[19] This putative triple alliance of puritanism, empiricism, and capitalism sits awkwardly with Hill's own discovery of a copious anticapitalist literature among seventeenth-century Protestant radicals, but it is forced upon him by his dogmatic presupposition that these three movements constitute historically "progressive" forces.[20]

It is hard, after the fall of the Soviet bloc, to imagine how socialists could ever have viewed capitalism as progressive. Such a position could only be justified on the assumption that capitalism was an intermediate stage in the progress from feudalism to socialism. Now that this assumption has been comprehensively demolished by history, it may again be possible to acknowledge what was obvious to most people in the sixteenth and seventeenth centuries: that the conquest of the world by capital was an unmitigated disaster, an irremediable injustice, and an unadulterated tragedy—the fatal, and probably the terminal, error of human history.[21] Today, the Protestant Reformation's attacks on "idolatry" may look less like the "ideology" of the "bourgeoisie" with which Weberians and Marxists have identified it, and more like an accurate, objective diagnosis of the material and psychological condition toward which early modern society was visibly lurching and at which postmodern society has shudderingly arrived.

The contention that material forces determine the movement of history assumes that it is possible to distinguish and separate a "material" sphere of life from a sphere of "ideas." The dialectical response has always been to point out that the concepts "material" and "ideal" constitute a mutually definitive binary opposition, that they interpenetrate, so that each term of the polarity depends on the other for its existence. The question of historical causality thus takes on a rather different form. Historical change must be understood as being caused by the interaction of different elements within an overarching totality. This in no way diminishes the argument that the course of history is determinate, but it does suggest that no single element of the totality can be promoted to the status of determining factor.

Although the British Marxist historians are often credited with having emolliated the dry economic determinism of orthodox Marxism, they were usually compelled by their commitment to the class struggle to retain a materialism of the last instance. Thus, so subtle an economist as Maurice Dobb wrote, concerning the crisis of feudalism, that "in deciding the outcome economic factors must have exercised the deciding influence,"[22] while so erudite a historian as Christopher Hill claimed that "the economic stage of development determines ultimately both the political superstructure and the ideology of that society."[23] During the 1970s the doctrine of materialism in the last instance gained theoretical credibility from the work of Louis Althusser, and consequently it won a new lease of life among historians. In *Lineages of the Absolutist State*, Perry Anderson argued that Renaissance England exhibited a system of government called "Absolutism," which represented an intermediate stage of development between what he calls "feudalism" and "capitalism." His premise is that "The rule of the Absolutist State was that of the feudal nobility in the epoch of transition to capitalism. Its end would signal the crisis of power of its class: the advent of the bourgeois revolutions, and the emergence of the capitalist state."[24]

Anderson's argument has received support from historians such as Robert Brenner, who wish to distinguish "absolutist" commercial activity from full-blown "capitalism."[25] It seems, however, that by the *economic* terms "feudalism" and "capitalism," Anderson really intends the *political* dominance of the aristocracy and bourgeoisie respectively. Thus he writes "The Absolute monarchies introduced standing armies, a permanent bureaucracy, national taxation, a codified law, and the beginnings of a unified market. All these characteristics appear to be preeminently capitalist."[26] With the exception of the last, it is hard to see how these examples can be described as "preeminently capitalist." It is true that, in their modern forms, they originate in and accompany the rise to political power of the bourgeoisie, but that does not qualify them as "capitalist." In fact, Anderson frequently elides the distinction between "capitalist" and "bourgeois," both of which he assumes are progressive forces battling against the conservative tendencies of aristocracy and feudalism. The contradictory imperatives of these "progressive" and "conservative" forces led, according to Anderson, to the breakdown of the absolutist state:

> English Absolutism was brought to crisis by aristocratic particularism and clannic desperation on its periphery: forces that lay historically behind it. But it was felled at the center by a commercialized gentry, a capitalist city, a commoner artisanate and yeomanry: forces pushing beyond it.[27]

However, as Anderson's own research amply demonstrates, there is no practical reason why the landed aristocracy should not also engage in capitalist enterprise.[28] The political dominance of the bourgeoisie, in other words, may or may not have been a characteristic of late seventeenth-century England, but it is neither a definitive nor a universal characteristic of capitalism.

Why, in that case, has radical critique of capitalism become so closely associated with the notion of class struggle? The answer is that in nineteenth- and early twentieth-century Europe, where such critique acquired its characteristic modern dimensions, the forces of capital and labor power were indeed embodied, or incarnated, in two distinct and easily recognizable social classes. A proletarian revolution against the bourgeoisie would thus have constituted the overthrow of capital by labor. By taking a wider perspective, however, we can see that this situation was merely a temporary phase in the history of capitalism. The categories "bourgeois" and "proletariat" refer not to empirically observable social classes but to positions within the mode of production: The proletarian sells his or her labor power for wages, and the bourgeois receives his or her income from capital investments. In postmodern Western economies, however, most people simultaneously exchange their labor power for wages *and* receive some income in the form of interest, if only through a savings account or a pension plan. They thus, to varying degrees, simultaneously occupy the positions of "bourgeoisie" and "proletariat." Despite this, of course, postmodern Western societies remain as deeply divided as ever along class lines. But today's class divisions boil down to disparities in wealth. In contrast, the opposition between the bourgeoisie and the proletariat is not always or necessarily a conflict between the rich and the poor—it is perfectly possible for a proletarian to be richer than a bourgeois. The division between the bourgeoisie and the proletariat is rather a logical opposition, a *contradiction*. It is the material manifestation of the contradiction between labor power and the objectified form of labor power, which is financial value. In postmodern society, as in early modern society, the contradiction between value and labor power is experienced not so much as a struggle between opposed social classes as a struggle between opposed psychological forces. In early modern society, and again in postmodern society, the opposition between value and labor power does not appear only as a conflict *between* individuals but also as a conflict *within* individuals.

The marriage of convenience between Marxist philosophy and the labor movement set the agenda for anticapitalist theory and practice from the late nineteenth through the mid twentieth centuries. As it became clear that capital was a more durable force than had been hoped, *clercs* and *ouvriers* began accusing each other of *trahison* with the vehemence once reserved for the class enemy. But the truth is that both partners paid a price for this alliance. The main philosophical damage was suffered by the labor theory of value. Due to the political imperative that labor power should remain identified with the industrial proletariat, the notion became widespread that the price of commodities, and thus the profit of capitalists, was created by the material acts of labor performed by individual workers. This is, in fact, the labor theory of value as it is found in the classical political economy of Adam Smith and David Ricardo. But Marx saw his refinement of this simplistic version of the theory as his most important advance on his predecessors.[29] As he explains in *Capital,* the source of economic value for him is precisely the *abstraction* from concrete, material acts of individual labor into the generalized form of "socially necessary average labor time," or "labour-power":

> ... the labour that forms the substance of value is equal human labour, the expenditure of identical human labour-power. The total labour-power of society, which is manifested in the values of the world of commodities, counts here as one homogeneous mass of human labour-power, although composed of innumerable individual units of labour-power.[30]

It is labor per se, labor conceived in the abstract, labor as a totality, whose objectified form is financial value: "the value of a commodity represents human labour pure and simple, the expenditure of human labour in general."[31] This is because the function of value is to provide a common denominator that renders distinct objects equivalent for the purposes of exchange, and discrete acts of individual labor cannot fulfill that function. Only labor conceived in the abstract can provide the medium in which different things can become commensurable, and labor so conceived is able to carry out this role even for those commodities—an untilled field, for instance, or a human being—that are obviously not the products of labor.

Marx defines labor power, then, precisely by its distinction from individual acts of labor. His concept of labor power is the direct descendent of Feuerbach's "species-being," which is the generalized form of human subjective activity. Labor power is thus not a narrowly economic category: It cannot even be identified with wage labor in total. It is, rather, human subjective activity considered as a whole. In fact, Marx's concept of "labor power" is coterminous with human life itself. The process of labor power's objectification is emphatically brought home on a daily basis to anyone who works for a wage. What the worker sells for money is neither the product of his or her labor nor the material act of labor. Workers sell their labor power, which is to say their time, which is to say their lives. In the *Economic and Philosophical Manuscripts* Marx refers to

> ... the relation of the worker to his own activity as an alien activity not belonging to him ... the worker's *own* physical and mental energy, his personal life indeed, what is life but activity?—as an activity which is turned against him, independent of him and not belonging to him.[32]

And this equation of labor power with "life activity" is no less pronounced in *Capital*, where Marx insists that the term refers to "labour as such, in its simple capacity as purposive productive activity."[33] Every day, virtually everyone in a capitalist society exchanges a portion of their lives for an objectified representation of life. It follows that financial value, the objectified form of labor power, is nothing more than the objectified form of life itself. Human societies have historically developed many cogent ways of understanding the psychological struggle of the forces of subjective life against the forces of objectification. Most such systems of thought belong to the category that we would call "religion." Our modern use of this term, however, tends to be unnecessarily restrictive. We associate religion with the organized worship of God, or of gods, but in most historical periods, and certainly in sixteenth- and seventeenth-century England, people would not so rigorously have cordoned off "religion" from the rest of their lives. One of the purposes of this book is to demonstrate the impact of "religion" on the area of life which we think of, in equally restrictive fashion, as "economics."

In order to do this, we must first rid ourselves of any notion that capitalism can be equated with the political dominance of the bourgeoisie. According to Marx, capitalism is simply the system that results from a global market in commodities:

> The circulation of commodities is the starting-point of capital. The production of commodities and their circulation in its developed form, namely trade, form the historic presuppositions under which capital arises. World trade and the world market date from the sixteenth century, and from then on the modern history of capital starts to unfold.[34]

As Paul Sweezy points out in his critique of Maurice Dobb, the British Marxist school's emphasis on the class struggle between the aristocracy and the bourgeoisie leads them to miss the true economic causes of feudalism's decline: The growth of a large-scale commodity economy, the expropriation of the peasantry, the influx of gold and the expansion of trade consequent upon the discovery of America, and the world system of international commerce thus produced. In Sweezy's view, it is above all the rise of this global market economy that brought about the demise of the feudal order and the emergence of a system of "pre-capitalist commodity production."[35] According to Sweezy, capitalism is to be distinguished from feudalism not because it involves the dominance of the bourgeoisie as opposed to that of the aristocracy, but because it is a system of production for exchange rather than for use—it is, in other words, a commodity-based economy. Immanuel Wallerstein concurs with Sweezy regarding the determining importance of the global market, and he is willing to identify this system with capitalism as such: the "full development and economic predominance of market trade emerged in sixteenth-century Europe. This was the system called capitalism."[36]

Their adherence to a class-based model of society also means that the British Marxists must view the English revolution of the seventeenth century as somehow unfinished or incomplete. Christopher Hill sometimes suggests that there were actually two revolutions: an aristocratic-bourgeois revolution, which largely succeeded, and a subaltern plebeian revolution, which was defeated. For Perry Anderson and Tom Nairn, the English revolution was premature compared to the continental revolutions of the eighteenth and nineteenth centuries, since capitalism had not developed to the extent of producing a unified and self-conscious bourgeoisie capable of seizing state power without aristocratic assistance. In *The Pristine Culture of Capitalism*, Ellen Meiksins Wood takes issue with this "Nairn–Anderson thesis." Wood concedes the point that early modern England was in no sense bourgeois, but she argues convincingly that it was nevertheless aggressively and increasingly capitalist. In fact, far from being premature or anomalous, the capitalism of the English Renaissance (rather than, say, that of the French Enlightenment) was the prototype of the modern market economy:

> ... this commercial system had more in common with the modern capitalist market than with "classical" commerce; and its movements were increasingly determined not by the ancient principle of "profit on alienation," typically in transaction between markets, but by the imperatives of productivity and competition within a single market. Inserted in a distinctive framework of social relations of production, the market was ceasing to be simply a more or less cyclical mechanism of circulation and was becoming the driving force of a self-sustaining economic growth.[37]

For Nairn and Anderson, however, the continued power of aristocratic politics and ideology disqualifies early modern England from counting as a truly capitalist society.[38] This adherence to a class-based materialism of the last instance has also prevented many historians from noticing the *critique* of capitalism that was articulated in early modern England. Inevitably, this critique was couched in the terms and concepts of religion, and it may not sound to twentieth-century ears as though it has anything to do with economic matters. If, however—contra Anderson—a capitalist market economy did take identifiable form in Renaissance England, we might expect that an intellectual response to that economy, whether analytical or critical, would emerge around the same time. In fact, historians such as Neal Wood argue that the theory as well as the practice of capitalism as we know it today originates in sixteenth-century England, so that "The intellectual foundations of political economy ... were laid in early Tudor times."[39] Once again, this conclusion conflicts with the British Marxist school, for whom the plethora of literature denouncing trade, usury, fetishism and avarice that was produced in this period must be, so to speak, premature anticapitalism, mistakenly criticizing economic phenomena in obsolescent theological discourse. This notion haunts even the work of Christopher Hill, who has done more than anyone else to bring sympathetic attention to this literature.

The problem, from the perspective of twentieth-century materialist Marxists, is that in Renaissance England the critique of capitalism did not take a primarily economic form. It took, rather, a form that we would call "religious." But the idea that economy and religion are distinct areas of experience would have been alien to the people of the sixteenth and early seventeenth centuries. This idea emerges after the Restoration and is itself testimony to the dissociation of sensibility that is among the most profound consequences of the rise of capitalism. My working assumption here will be that, from the late sixteenth century onwards, England evinces an embryonic form of the same capitalist market economy that now dominates the entire world, and that, in the words of Wallerstein, "By 1650, the basic structure of historical capitalism as a viable social system had been established and consolidated."[40] The fact that the most famous and canonical writers of the era do not discuss capitalism in economic terms alone but also in the vocabulary of religion, which is to say also in terms of ethics, aesthetics, and hermeneutics, means only that we must rethink our understanding of the relation between these "spheres" in the early modern period.

III

How, then, should we understand this relation? More specifically, to move on to the particular concerns of this book, what is the precise relation of idolatry to commodity fetishism? Clearly these phenomena are not identical, but I have found that their liaison is too intimate to be merely analogous. The most accurate way of describing their relationship, I think, is as a *homology*. However, idolatry and commodity fetishism do not necessarily or always stand in homologous relations to each other. As far as we know, for example, there was no protest against commodity fetishism in iconoclastic Byzantium, and nor was iconoclasm a burning issue in capitalist Venice. This provokes the question of why this homology took shape under the specific conditions of sixteenth- and seventeenth-century England, and this is one of the problems this book will attempt to solve.

Over the last 15 or 20 years, many literary critics have come to believe that their discipline has much in common with economics.[41] The rise of this belief was no doubt facilitated by the "linguistic turn" taken by post-Saussurean continental philosophy. Saussure's structural linguistics laid the foundations for an expansion of linguistic techniques into the study of signifying systems in general, a discipline that has become known as "semiotics." Once people grew accustomed to analyzing, say, an advertisement or a fashion show in terms similar to a literary text, it was a short step to acknowledge that economics is also a "discourse" that utilizes signs, figures, and tropes to construct and analyze its subject matter, and that it too could be studied on that basis. By the 1990s, this convergence of economics and literary criticism was sufficiently prominent to be given a name and anointed as a movement. The appearance in 1999 of Martha Woodmansee and Mark Osteen's edited collection of essays, entitled *The New Economic Criticism,* delineated the counters of this eponymous phenomenon with appropriate gravitas. In their introduction, the editors raise an interesting question: " . . . the first wave of economic criticism, which appeared during the late 1970s and early 1980s, has given way to a second, seemingly tidal wave of scholarship investigating the relations among literature, culture and economics. Why this explosion of new work?"[42]

Woodmansee and Osteen suggest several possible answers, based mainly on developments within various academic disciplines and in the publishing industry. However, they also venture beyond the confines of the academy to offer what seems to me a more convincing explanation: " . . . the political economy of the 1980s thrust economics and its discussion of interest rates, stock market speculation, takeovers, leveraged buyouts, and so on, into the public attention as never before since the 1930s."[43] One might, perhaps, take issue with the final qualification: It is unclear that economic concepts occupied as exalted a place in the public consciousness in the thirties as they have since the eighties. The main point, however, seems indisputable. Over the last 20 years, people have become much more aware of the influence of "the economy" over their lives, and much more knowledgeable about, and involved in, the workings of "the market." In a recent issue of *New Literary History* devoted to "Economics and Culture," the economist Gregory LaBlanc observed that "As money comes to dominate the material world of exchange, so too does an economic way of thinking gain common currency in the culture."[44] Amy and Douglas Koritz neatly frame the central question raised by this interpenetration: "Does culture, when understood as a symbolic economy, become economic, *tout court?*[45]

The historian cannot but perceive a remarkable irony in this convergence, for the belief that the economy is the most important factor in determining people's lives was once, quite recently, identified with that politico-philosophical school whose tenets are popularly believed to have been unanswerably refuted by recent history. Of course, it is not immediately obvious how a traditional Marxist analysis of the market (fraught as it is with a set of premises—the economic primacy of the mode of production, the social primacy of the class struggle, the philosophical primacy of materialism—that have evidently been superseded in the Western world) might be of value to an "economic criticism" that, perhaps to avoid any such unfashionable associations, ostentatiously brands itself as "new." In fact, the precise nature of their departures from Marxism has become a fertile field for debate among new economic critics. The relationship between money and language is conceived of by some, for example Ferruccio Rossi-Landi, as *analogous*. In that case, the old debate about which of the elements of the analogy is prior to and determines the other retains its central importance. For others, such as Marc Shell, the relationship between money and language is conceived of as *homologous*. In that case, it would be otiose to quibble about the nice issue of which is the "base" and which the "superstructure."[46] The mutations of economic and cultural history would then be viewed as elements within a greater, total history of representation. Advocates of this latter position can bolster their case by pointing out that the Western consumer economies are no longer visibly based upon material production but upon market exchange (production having been shunted out of sight and mind, into the southern hemisphere). The economy, which for traditional Marxism is the material base of the ideological superstructure, can no longer function as such when it has ceased to manifest itself as a material phenomenon.

This "de-materialization" of the Western economy has produced among some economists an interest in the ways that language, and rhetorical figures and tropes, influence their discipline. Such practitioners of the "rhetoric of economics" are increasingly happy to discuss the economy as a structure of signs that lack any necessary referent in the material process of production. The best-known exponent of this approach, Deirdre McClosky, declares that her work "takes the order of the economy to be the same as the order of speech."[47] This, however, remains a minority opinion among economists. Jack Amariglio and David F. Russo offer a salutary reminder:

> Symbolic Economy? Libidinal Economy? General Economy? Political Economy of the Sign? The Economy of Desire? These and other current formulations appear to be extremely popular and productive in the broad fields of literary theory and cultural studies.... [However] these terms have not, and we believe would not, be treated as deserving of serious attention by most professional economists.[48]

Amariglio and Russo offer as verification an anecdote recalling how, when asked to peruse and give their opinion of Lyotard's *Libidinal Economy,* most members of an economics department could not get past the *title.* Much the same response was heard 20 years ago from traditional literary critics when semiotics first began to demonstrate that the boundaries of their discipline were no longer tenable. The truth, surely, is that neither literature nor the economy is any longer defensible as an essential, definitely delineated field of inquiry. It is obvious that the belief that "economics" and "culture" occupy distinct and separable "fields" depends on a metaphor. Of course, this does not invalidate that belief: It is a metaphor that seemed to make sense while the economy of the Western world was tangibly based on material production. However, its validity is much less obvious once the economy seems to be based on market exchange. Market exchange appears, at a naively empirical level, to be powered not by the physical energy of workers but by the psychic energy of consumers, as that energy is produced and directed by advertising and market research. There is thus a strong case to be made for a semiotic approach to economics. Unlike Enlightenment political economy, the current economic orthodoxy of neoclassicism views human beings as consumers by nature, and it assimilates the psychology of the individual *qua* consumer into the discipline of economics. The result is that, whether it likes it or not, neoclassical economics is inexorably impelled toward engagement with the mode of contemporary philosophy that sees individual psychology as mediated through systems of representation.[49]

As we are about to see, the people of the early modern period regarded economics and culture as elements within a greater totality, and it did not occur to them to consider the economic domain in isolation from the cultural, aesthetic, or ethical aspects of life. The best of the new economic critics have demonstrated this fact with admirable clarity. For example, Marc Shell's *Money, Language and Thought* shows how economic and linguistic theory, and semantics in general, have historically developed in lockstep, moving away from intrinsic and toward nominal modes of evaluation. The history of representation, Shell claims, is characterized by the progressive independence of signs—whether words, money, or visual images—from things. In his incisive studies of the historical relationship between language and money, which he calls "complementary or competing systems of tropic production and exchange,"[50] Shell observes that the Greek "seme" means both "word" and "coin," and he makes the case that these two forms of "semantics" follow a continuous and parallel historical trajectory. He particularly notes the attention paid in the past to the theological implications of money, observing that for many medieval thinkers "money, like the Verbal Eucharist, seems to constitute a common or architectonic denominator for all things."[51]

Jean-Joseph Goux has also remarked upon "the profoundly theological character of the monetary system,"[52] and he further concurs with Shell in viewing the joint history of money and language as a march towards "the *operative and autonomous signifier*,"[53] claiming that "The history of value in the West is the inexorable shift *from Archetypes to tokens*."[54] Over the course of this process, Goux notes subtle distinctions between the semiotic implications of various forms of money. For example: "The type of language that could be compared to *gold money* would be a full, adequate language. In it, and through it, the real would be conveyed without mediation, both as the objective reality of the external world and as the subjective reality of the internal world."[55] However, by the end of the seventeenth century, the new science of political economy had reached the understanding that value did not reside in the matter of gold, but that it could be expressed just as effectively in a *sign* of gold—this advance eventually resulted in the introduction of paper money. As a result, according to Goux:

> ... the relationship between language and being begins to be problematic. Just as in the economic sphere there arises the question of *convertibility*, that is, the existence or not of a deposit serving to back the tokens in circulation, likewise in the domain of signification the truth value of language will become a crucial concern. Language will no longer be conceived as fully expressing (or as being *capable* of adequately expressing) reality or being; it will necessarily be conceived as a means, a relatively autonomous instrument, by which it is possible to represent reality to varying degrees of exactitude.[56]

Until the twentieth century, the myth that all the money in circulation could theoretically be converted into gold was held to be indispensable for economic confidence. Once the gold standard was abandoned, however, financial value was no longer supposed to refer to any external or material substance. Money was finally conceded to be pure signification and this, according to Goux, was accompanied by "the moment of true crisis of confidence in the value of language."[57] The nonreferential linguistics of Saussure, for example, his "affirmation that linguistic value has no root in things and their natural relationships,"[58] is based upon the same principle of the "inconvertibility" of signs into referents. The postmodern era is characterized by what Goux calls "the despotism of the empty signifier"[59] and "the 'bankerization' of life itself"[60]—the autonomous, unaccountable, tyrannical power of financial and linguistic media of representation. Goux concludes that: "The parallel between language and money, literature and political economy, is not a mere juxtaposition, but is made possible and operative by processes at work simultaneously in both economies."[61]

This raises another interesting question. Generally speaking, the philosophers, economists, and literary scholars who practice this kind of criticism regard the growing autonomy of representation within their disciplines as ethically neutral. Where they do not, they frequently applaud its liberation of humanity from teleology and logocentrism, in terms notably similar to their closest philosophical allies, the American neopragmatists and antifoundationalists. And it is indeed true that the global market is an implacable enemy, in theory and in practice, of *telos* and *logos* in all their forms. The cumulative effect of Saussurean linguistics, Foucauldian historiography, and Derridean philosophy has been to launch a massive, sustained, and largely successful intellectual assault on teleology, logocentrism, and totalization. What the postmodern era conspicuously lacks, however, is any ethical criteria for evaluating either the decline of such modes of thought or the emergence of autonomous, fetishized representation as their heir.

This is why it is salutary to consider the alarm, fury, and righteous indignation with which the people of the early modern era viewed the germinal stages of these phenomena. Between 1580 and 1680 the population of England had to come to terms with the existence of financial value as an independent force. During this century, the economic attitude known to posterity as "bullionism" was challenged and defeated by thinkers who achieved the conceptual breakthrough of separating financial value from gold bullion. At the beginning of our period, it was generally assumed that gold *was* financial value; by its end this position had become empirically and theoretically untenable. Value had escaped from its physical prison like the genie from the bottle. However (and it is impossible to emphasize this too strongly) this was not necessarily thought of as an "economic" development. For most literate Englishmen, the autonomy of value was one manifestation of the same tendency that could be observed in religious idolatry and carnal sensuality in all its forms. It is this totalizing perspective that allows the thinkers of the early modern period an insight into the spiritual and ethical implications of commodity fetishism that has largely been lost to our own epoch.

For hundreds of years, the Christian world debated the ethical implications of semantic questions through the paradigm of religious iconography, particularly the Eucharist. But that does not mean that people were blind to the relevance of semantic ethics in what we might consider other areas of life. In the case of economics, for example, we find money consistently denounced as a carnal invention that obscures and distorts the divinely ordained natural order and that tends to provoke undue awe and adoration in fallen humanity. Financial value is an alien meaning imposed upon nature; like Aristotle's "custom" it constitutes a kind of "second nature." As Martin Luther put it: "Money is the word of the devil, through which he creates everything in the world, just as God creates through the true word."[62] We are dealing here with what Shell calls an "internalization of economic form,"[63] in which external forms of representation are subjected to ethical judgment on the basis of their effect on the spiritual condition of humanity.

I have found that in post-Reformation England, the connection between idolatry and commodity fetishism was virtually axiomatic, a commonplace regarded as obvious by everybody. Often, this means that its expression seems trite or cliched. But the most tenacious cliches are truisms, and I hope to show that this connection rests upon an ancient, complex, and profound heritage of philosophical and religious belief. The specific vocabulary in which commodity fetishism was discussed during our century is already firmly in place in canto 5 of *The Faerie Queene,* where Guyon dismisses the temptations of Mammon:

> Suffise it then, thou Money God (quoth hee)
> That all thine idle offers I refuse.
> All that I need I have; what needeth mee
> To covet more, then I have cause to use?
> With such vaine shews thy worldlings vile abuse . . . [64]

As we will see, Spenser's contemporaries would have recognized significances lost to us in the way these lines deploy such terms as "idle," "use," "abuse," "covet," "vaine," and "worldlings." Similarly, Spenser may be repeating a set of commonplaces in his depiction of "Avarice," but his audience would have noticed the precise, specific ways in which they were intended: " . . . of his wicked pelfe his God he made, / And unto hell him selfe for money sold; / Accursed usurie was all his trade, / And right and wrong ylike in euqall ballaunce waide." (1.4. 27. 6–9). The same is true of Ben Jonson's portrait of Volpone:

> Good morning to the day; and next, my gold!
> Open the shrine that I may see my saint.
> Hail the world's soul, and mine....
> ... let me kiss
> With adoration, thee, and every relic
> Of sacred treasure, in this blessed room....
> ... Riches, the dumb god, that giv'st all men tongues:
> That canst do nought, and yet mak'st men do all things[65]

Spenser and Jonson wrote near the beginning of the period under discussion in this book, but this diagnosis of money fetishism is repeated incessantly until late in the seventeenth century. Robert Burton's *Anatomy of Melancholy* (1621) states the equation between the departure from *telos*, commodification, and idolatry in a straightforward, matter-of-fact tone, which indicates that he finds in it nothing controversial, or even contestable: "In a word, every man for his own ends. Our Summum bonum is commodity, and the goddess we adore Dea Moneta, Queen Money, to whom we daily offer sacrifices...." By the time William Clark trotted out the argument in *The Grand Tryal* (1685) it had become weary through overuse:

> To Gold, why there too is a boasting Ore,
> Though in its Veins it signifies no more
> Then other Mettals, yellow Earth at best,
> Meer coloured Dust, but once brought to the Test,
> 'Tis no more dust, 'tis no more simple Ore,
> No more a heap of Sand, as't was before:
> But now a most illustrious name it bears,
> Beyond all Mettals, and indeed appears
> To be the Worlds Idol. (155–63)[66]

Gold, observes Clark, has two forms of signification; a natural one, whereby "it signifies no more / Then other Mettals," and a nominal one, an "illustrious name" imposed upon it by custom. The adoration of this human, arbitrary mode of significance was understood by educated English people of the seventeenth century to be the very definition of idolatry.

In itself, that might not sound like a very important point. But this union of Hebraic aniconism and Hellenic teleology, which allowed the people of three and four hundred years ago to make sense of the local and specific changes taking place around them, has no less profound implications for subsequent epochs. It is at least worth considering the possibility that the writers studied here, from Gosson to

Bunyan, had a sound point when they claimed that the abandonment of teleology is the cause of what they called "idolatry." Again, this might not seem a particularly pressing issue in a secular age, until one pauses to consider the precise valence acquired by the concept "idolatry" in post-Reformation England. That valence was certainly very wide. However the multifarious meanings attached to the term are consistent in one respect: They all involve the reduction of spirit to matter. Idolatry is an act, to repeat, of *objectification*. The psychological tendency to objectification can manifest itself in any area of experience—in sexuality, for instance, or in hermeneutic literalism, as well as in the pursuit of riches and the worship of icons. My aim here is to delineate the structural parallels perceived by the people of the early modern epoch between such ostensibly diverse areas of human experience.

Chapter One

Idolatry and Political Economy

> *The balance-sheet of historical capitalism ... is perhaps complex, but the initial calculus in terms of material distribution of goods and allocation of energies is in my view very negative indeed. If this is so, why did such a system arise? Perhaps, precisely to achieve this end. What could be more plausible than a line of reasoning which argues that the explanation of the origin of a system was to achieve an end that has in fact been achieved? I know that modern science has turned us from the search for final causes and from all considerations of intentionality (especially as they are so inherently difficult to demonstrate empirically). But modern science and historical capitalism have been in close alliance as we know; thus, we must suspect the authority of science on precisely this question: the modality of knowing the origins of modern capitalism.*
>
> —Immanuel Wallerstein, Historical Capitalism[1]

I

This chapter examines the historical process whereby financial value became separated from its physical incarnation in precious metals and came to be acknowledged as a purely nominal, legal, and customary mode of representation. It also shows that this change demanded the elevation of the nominal to the status of the real. Nominal and customary though it was, during the sixteenth and seventeenth centuries financial value strongly asserted its claims to ontological and ethical equality with the essential, the natural, and the teleological. At the end of the sixteenth century, Aristotelian teleology retained the dominant place in Western philosophy that it had occupied throughout the middle ages. As Christianized by Thomistic scholasticism, the teleological habits of thought formed by the disciples of the Stagirite remained deeply ingrained in the minds of English people. By the end of the seventeenth century, however, such ancient rivals of teleology as materialism, skepticism, and empiricism had enjoyed a dramatic resurgence, which fatally impaired Aristotle's intellectual hegemony. The impact of this development was by no means limited to the academy; on the contrary, as the following chapters will show, it was experienced and remarked upon in every area of human life, from the most mundane to the highly exalted. One of my aims here is to study the death throes of "natural teleology" as they are reflected in a variety of sixteenth- and seventeenth-century texts. These texts are concerned with a diverse range of fields that are not, today, thought of as specifically philosophical, such as economics, sexuality, aesthetics, and religion. The eclipse of teleology did not take place in libraries and debating chambers only, but also and simultaneously in the spirits, perceptions, desires, and actions of individuals. It is my intention here to draw out the implications of *telos*' philosophical obsolescence for everyday life. This seems to me an important project, partly because it sheds light on several interesting conflicts and quarrels of four hundred years ago, but also because (although we are no longer so clearly aware of it) we are still living with those implications today.

Teleology is the branch of philosophy which deals with *telos:* the end, or final cause, of any thing. In *On the Generation of Animals,* Aristotle summarizes his four-fold division of causality into final, formal, material, and efficient causes: "There are four causes: first, the final cause, that for the sake of which; secondly, the definition of essence (and these two we may regard pretty much as one and the same); thirdly, the material; and fourthly, that from which the sense of movement comes."[2] In the *Metaphysics,* he elaborates on his understanding of *telos:* "the *final cause* is an end, and that sort of end which is not for the sake of something else, but for whose sake everything else is."[3] And in the *Nicomachean Ethics* and the *Magna Moralia,* this final end is identified with the "good": "What then is the good of each [art]? Surely that for whose sake everything else is done,"[4] "every science and capacity has an end, and that too a good one."[5] For man, concludes Aristotle, the good or *telos* is "an activity of soul in accordance with virtue,"[6] which is to say a life of "intellectual speculation." The Christian interpretation of Aristotle's causality, which through Aquinas became canonical doctrine by the thirteenth century,⁷ is illustrated with admirable clarity by the *Catholic Encyclopedia*, using the example of a ball of wax that has been molded into a sphere:

> The wax, as permanent substratum of the change of figure, is considered to be the matter, or material cause. The spherical figure supervening upon that of the cubical, is the induced formal cause. The moulder, or fashioner of the sphere, is the efficient cause. The final cause is to be sought for in the intention of the moulder.⁸

The final cause, then, actually has two kinds of existence. It exists outside and beyond the ball of wax, "in the intention of the moulder." But that intention, and thus the final cause, can also be perceived *within* the ball of wax. Without this intention, the ball of wax would not be what it is. The intention, the *telos*, is in this sense immanent and inherent in the ball of wax.⁹ And, according to Aristotle, this is true of everything that exists.

Many philosophers of our period, such as Francis Bacon and Rene Descartes, claimed that knowledge of any such final causes was impossible for human beings. Instead, they concentrated either on Aristotle's "formal" or "efficient" cause. This latter is a clearly perceptible, often mechanical, cause of an effect, such as the physical act of molding the wax in the above example. Post-teleological thought usually regards the efficient cause as the true, or even the only, cause of a material effect. To point away from the mechanical action of molding to some thought or intention in the molder's mind, as Aristotle or Aquinas would have done, is from this perspective to lapse into the most nebulous of speculation. How, Bacon would ask, can we know, and what does it matter, what was going through the molder's mind? Why is this relevant to our knowledge of the ball of wax?¹⁰

In scientific endeavor, Baconian empiricism produces an instrumental view of reason, whereby effects are studied and sought after to the exclusion of the reasons for producing them. The Greeks called this kind of merely technical knowledge *banausic* and considered it inferior and servile; today technical knowledge is frequently equated with knowledge per se. This shift of attention from the final to the efficient cause has, since the seventeenth century, taken place in many fields of human activity. The people of the period studied here noticed it, above all, in the attention paid to signs (whether linguistic, financial, or iconic) as opposed to the referents they were supposed to signify. This, they thought, was at once a confusion of means with ends, a substitution of custom for nature, and the replacement of God's work with "the works of men's hands." This adoration of the signifier they held to affect the most intimate and personal minutiae of everyday life, just as it affected weighty matters of church and state. It is impossible, for example, to follow the argument of Milton's divorce tracts without understanding the connection he assumes between Papist "idolatry," carnal sensuality, Judaic "legalism," and hermeneutic literalism. We think of these errors (if we consider them errors at all) as utterly different in kind. For Milton, in contrast, they are essentially manifestations of the same fundamental error: the mistaking of the sign for the referent. And this, in turn, is one aspect of the displacement of final by efficient cause. Thus the material shape of the ball of wax, from the Baconian perspective, is to be understood as an end in itself. From the Aristotelian perspective, by contrast, it is to be regarded as a *sign,* an indication of an anterior, ultimate cause—the intention of the molder—which, while not material or empirically perceptible, is nonetheless immanent within the waxen orb.

Over the last three or four centuries, human experience has been characterized by a gradual displacement of things by signs, of reality by representation. The history of the economy provides a lucid example. As soon as groups of hunter-gatherers began to engage in the barter of goods with their neighbors, a conceptual revolution occurred that is second in importance only to the development of language. In order for two different things, say a chicken and a goat, to be exchanged for one another, it is necessary to conceive of an *equivalence* between them. These two things are not, of course, *identical;* if they were, there would be no point in exchanging them. A chicken and a goat are different from each other in nature, in essence. Nevertheless, they can be made equivalent by an act of human conception. Human beings have the ability to impose equivalence upon things that are essentially and naturally different.[11] In the very act of imposing this equivalence, however, the notion of essence, of nature, simultaneously comes into being. If things are equivalent they are not identical; if they are not identical then there must be some essence or nature that each possesses and that differentiates them from each other.

The simplest act of barter thus assumes that an object has two distinct identities—a natural essence and a customary value. In Greek philosophy this is expressed as the opposition between nature, or *phusis,* and custom, or *nomos.* As Aristotle writes in the *Politics:* "Every possession has a double use. Both of these uses belong to it as such, but not in the same way, the one being proper and the other not proper to the thing. In the case of footwear, for example, one can wear it or one can exchange it."[12] Here, the true nature of the shoe is identified with its final cause, or *telos*. The shoe fulfills its inherent *telos*—it realizes its natural "shoe-ness"—by being worn. The shoe can also be traded for something else, but this use of it is "not proper to the thing," because it involves the imposition on the shoe of a human concept that does not naturally belong to it. So the shoe has two different values for human beings: a natural, intrinsic "use value," and a merely conventional "exchange value."

In societies that have developed beyond a simple barter economy, the exchange value of objects is expressed in money. Money is a *general* equivalent, in which the exchange value of any thing may be expressed.[13] Thus, in the *Nicomachean Ethics,* Aristotle notes that "money has not a natural but a conventional existence."[14] Whereas use value is natural and belongs to the realm of *phusis,* exchange value is a human imposition on natural objects and so it belongs to the sphere of *nomos*. Aristotle gives a strong ethical priority to use value over exchange value. Commerce is necessary, he concedes, to provide the comforts of civilized life, but it must always remember, and be reminded, of its subsidiary role. Money's proper purpose, its *telos,* is to facilitate the exchange of goods that are useful in themselves. It is, properly speaking, a *sign*. It is not, then, an end in itself, and to regard it as such is to reverse the ethical hierarchy of custom and nature. To adopt the terminology of modern economics, Aristotle looks benignly on the exchange cycle C-M-C, whereby commodities (C) are exchanged for one another through the medium of money (M). He is opposed, however, to the cycle M-C-M, whereby money is used to purchase a commodity, which is then sold for more money.[15] He opposes this because it is a violation of natural teleology: Such a transaction erroneously views exchange value as an end in itself. The most unnatural economic activity of all, by this logic, is usury, which actually makes money "breed" as if it were a natural creature instead of a customary convention:

> Expertise in business relative to crops and animals is thus natural for all. But since it is twofold, as we said, part of it being commerce and part expertise in household management, the latter necessary and praised, while expertise in exchange is justly blamed since it is not according to nature but involves taking from others, usury is most reasonably hated because one's possessions derive from money itself and not from that for which it was supplied. For it came into being for the

sake of exchange, but interest actually creates more of it.... So of the sorts of business this is most contrary to nature.[16]

A mercantile society, for Aristotle, is an unnatural society. To manufacture something for the purpose of exchanging it, rather than of using it, is already a violation of natural teleology. To elevate the medium of exchange into an end in itself exacerbates this violation, and the belief that the medium of exchange is autonomous and self-generating is its monstrous apotheosis. An English gloss on the *Politics* published in 1598 summarizes the Renaissance understanding of these distinctions. The author distinguishes three kinds of exchange:

> ... first of ware for ware; as of wheate for wooll, wine for oyle: which way being plainely used for the remedy of mens wantes, is agreeable to nature. Secondly of wares for money, which might also be said to be agreeable to nature, in case it were practiced for none other purpose, but for the necessarie and plentifull provision of mans life. But when it is put in use for the getting of needlesse gaine, as in ingrossing up of commodities to utter them againe at high prices, then it is no longer naturall but artificiall. ... the other kind of exchange [is] by mony, which Marchants and Brokers use for gaines sake only, and differeth from the former, as being against Nature and endlesse, and therefore blame worthy.[17]

According to this schema, clearly, the history of capitalism, and especially its recent history, constitutes the most convincing empirical refutation imaginable of Aristotle's teleology. No one would dispute that the last three hundred years of history have rendered Aristotelian natural teleology empirically false. It is less clear, however, that they have either refuted its logic or superseded its ethics.

II

It will, I hope, soon become obvious that in England between 1580 and 1680, people were acutely conscious of the encroachments of exchange value upon use value and of the growth in the power of money.[18] They interpreted this as the economic manifestation of a wider, deeper phenomenon that involved every aspect of individual and social experience. The "rise of capitalism" was certainly a highly visible and acutely symptomatic part of this development, but it occurred to few people to claim for it a determining role. The change in the attitude toward money that we will observe in this period was part of a shift in the status of representation in general, and it was understood as such by the people of the time. Most of the writers analyzed here (who represent a confident consensus at the beginning of this period but an embattled rearguard by the end) follow Aristotle in his teleological approach to representation. They deplore the autonomous power of the signifier, whether they find it in the Catholic Mass or in the power of money to reproduce. Such an attitude is by no means wholly conservative. In many cases, it exists alongside a strong commitment to radicalism and innovation in other areas, and in some cases this produces contradictions.[19]

For example, Francis Bacon is deeply suspicious of the human tendency to "idolize" financial or linguistic signifying systems. He advocates an empirical approach to knowledge, which assumes that the world as it is given, or immediately represented to us is the closest approximation to truth that fallen human beings can attain. Bacon's empiricism therefore abandons the search for final causes, and Bacon is thus the central English figure in the philosophical movement away from Aristotelian teleology. For Bacon, Aristotle was nothing less than "the highest deceiver of all ages."[20] Bacon did not, however, attempt to refute Aristotle's logic; rather, he argued that the investigation of final, as opposed to efficient, causes was, pragmatically speaking, useless. In the *Novum Organon* he declares that "the final cause rather corrupts than advances the sciences,"[21] and when he refers below to "the ignorance of causes," he intends a mistaken view as to which cause is important and useful, rather than any mere absence of knowledge:

> For man is but the servant and interpreter of nature: what he does and what he knows is only what he has observed of nature's order in fact or in thought; beyond this he knows nothing and can do nothing. For the chain of causes cannot by any force be loosed or broken, nor can nature be commanded except by being obeyed. And so those twin objects, human knowledge and human power, do really meet in one; and it is from ignorance of causes that operation fails. And all depends on keeping the eye steadily fixed upon the facts of nature and so receiving their images simply as they are. For God forbid that we should give out a dream of our own imagination for a pattern of the world, rather may he graciously grant to us to write an apocalypse or true vision of the footsteps of the Creator imprinted on his creatures. (1:53)

Bacon makes three grave charges against teleology here. First, he asserts that knowledge of final causes is impossible, because such knowledge cannot be derived from empirical observation alone, and in Bacon's view empirical observation is the only legitimate route to knowledge. Second, the pursuit of final causes is a distraction from the true purpose of knowledge, which is instrumental. Third, to perceive final causes in the material world is to impose a human concept on a divine creation.[22] It is, in other words, a species of idolatry.

Bacon does not claim that the human mind enjoys unmediated access to the objective world; he was as well aware as Descartes that sense perception is unreliable. He does, however, claim that (following the eradication of certain obstacles to clear perception) human beings can experience "a true vision of the footsteps of the Creator." In other words, Bacon believes that it is in principle possible for the human mind to attain an accurate knowledge, not of the external world in itself, but of the external world as it is represented or "given" to us by Providence. We find the same line of reasoning in aphorism 23: "There is a great difference between the Idols of the human mind, and the Ideas of the divine; That is to say, between certain empty dogmas, and the true signatures and marks set upon the works of creation, as they are found in nature." (1:72) The dichotomy is not between image and reality but between an idolatrous, human image and a natural, divine image—the "true signatures and marks" that Bacon identifies with our experience of reality. The world as we perceive it, as it is represented to us, is for Bacon an immediately legible sign; it is the seal or "impression" of God. Among the humanly erected barriers to our knowledge of the world, which Bacon calls the "idols," we find "the idols of the market-place," which arise inevitably "from the intercourse and association of men with each other" (1:78):

> ... the Idols of the Market-place are the most troublesome of all, idols which have crept into the understanding through the alliances of words and names. For men believe that their reason governs words, but it is also true that words react upon the understanding; and this it is that has rendered philosophy and the sciences sophistical and inactive. (1: 86)[23]

There is, in Bacon's view, a systematic and ineradicable disjunction between words and things. Hence the absurdity of speculation as to final causes. A final cause is not an empirically perceptible thing; it consists merely in "words." In what sense then, asks Bacon, can it be said to exist? Rather than idolatrously rely on our own system of signification, he argues, we should pay attention to the divine system of signification, which is manifested to us in our direct experience of the material world. In other words, we should pursue the efficient cause, which is empirically perceptible, and abandon our pursuit of the final cause, which is not, on the grounds that this final cause is simply a human invention: an "idol."

For Bacon then—unlike, for example, Calvin[24]—human experience as such is not *necessarily* idolatrous. Rather, idolatry arises in the signifying systems through which we "express" that experience. These include language, which produces figurative "idols of the market-place," and also money, which produces literal "idols of the market-place." Hence Bacon's casual assumption that "No man can be ignorant of the idolatry that is generally committed in these degenerate times to money, as if it could do all things public and private."[25] In fact, despite his innovations in natural science, Bacon's understanding of money was entirely typical of his time, as we can see from his essay "Of Usury." Bacon believed that: "The discommodities of usury are, first, that it makes fewer merchants; for were it not for this lazy trade of usury, money would not lie still but would in great part be employed upon merchandising, which is the *vena porta* of wealth in a state."[26] The first point to note here is that Bacon does not understand that usury *is* a form of "merchandising" that trades in the commodity of money. This is because he does not conceive of money as a commodity, like bread or eggs, but as the medium that facilitates the exchange of commodities other than itself. To treat money as a commodity is, for Bacon, both idolatrous and usurious.

Second, as a logical consequence of this position, Bacon holds what modern economists call a "bullionist" view of wealth: He identifies financial value with physical, literal, gold bullion. He therefore assumes that the wealth of a nation is assured by a favorable balance of trade, since this will bring about a net influx of specie into the kingdom. Since value *is* specie in the bullionist view, the more gold a nation physically possesses, the richer it will be. Bacon does not perceive the possibility that financial value may be autonomous and non-referential, so that it can exist apart from the physical body of gold. If, however, one does assume this possibility, then usury (which involves an expenditure of specie) is by no means a "lazy trade" but on the contrary one that puts money itself to work. To conceive of money in this way, as an active, subjective force, was a violation of teleology so fundamental that even Bacon, the greatest opponent of teleology of his day, finds it unthinkable. Barely a century later, however, Isaac Gervaise presents the view that value is independent of specie as the "generally received Opinion," albeit one with which he conservatively and ineffectually disagrees: "Having, for a long time since, looked upon Gold and Silver, as the Design or End of Commerce; I never could reconcile myself, to that generally received Opinion, that they increase it, and that by consequence, Credit also does the like; for how to imagine the End to be the Cause?"[27]

Gervaise is here lamenting the inversion of Aristotelian teleology. What Aristotle called an end has become a means, and what Aristotle called an object has become a subject. Money, which Aristotle said was not alive, has, to the dismay of Gervaise and many of his contemporaries, become animate. It was not so much that economic theory lagged behind economic practice as it was that a specifically economic theory, in the sense of a theory that limited itself to the economy, only became possible with the recognition of financial value's autonomy. For Bacon, and still even for Gervaise, the empirical fact of this autonomy is obviated by its philosophical falsehood. The power of value was unmistakably and increasingly *real* throughout this period, but only toward the end of the seventeenth century did it become possible to regard it as *true*.[28]

III

The belief that value is somehow literally incarnated in the physical matter of gold cannot be called a theory. It is rather in the nature of a popular superstition, the most tenacious remnant of primitive animism, and perhaps the only one to survive until the Enlightenment.[29] In *A Discourse of Trade* (1690), Nicholas Barbon still feels it necessary to refute this fetishism:

> Some Men have so great an Esteem for Gold and Silver, that they believe they have an intrinsick value in themselves, and cast up the value of every thing by them: The Reason of the Mistake is, Because Mony being made of Gold and Silver, they do not distinguish betwixt Mony, and Gold and Silver.[30]

Despite its universality until the modern era, economic historians only bother to give a name to this superstition in the sixteenth and seventeenth centuries, when its fallacy was in the process of being demonstrated: As I mentioned above, it is known to economics as "bullionism." By definition, a bullionist must conceive of the potential volume of trade as finite.[31] There can only be a certain amount of value in the world, because there can only be so much gold and silver in the world. The object of commerce, it follows, is to obtain as large a proportion of the precious metals as possible, and this holds true for a nation as much as for an individual. This doctrine thus led to protectionism, tariffs, and other restrictions on free trade, which by the 1620s led many mercantilist thinkers to dispute its veracity. The monetarization of the European economy began before Columbus. The silver mines of central Europe quintupled their production of money between 1460 and 1530,[32] Portuguese explorations of Africa introduced unprecedented amounts of precious metals into circulation,[33] and early banking houses such as the Fuggers, founded in 1487, grew up in the interstices of the land-based feudal economy. However, the process by which financial value was liberated from referentiality was given massive impetus by the sudden influx of American gold and silver into Europe. From 1500 to 1540, between 1,000 and 1,500 kilograms of American gold reached Spain every year,[34] and consequently between 1540 and 1640, Europe experienced what has come to be known as the "Price Revolution." This inflation meant that, for the first time, gold coins became part of commerce at a local and humble level. Instead of occupying a sacred realm, far removed from the prosaic transactions of the marketplace, gold, the source of all value, descended and walked among men.

Once in circulation, however, the general equivalent inevitably lost something of the superstitious reverence in which it had customarily been held. Gold coins often suffered physical as well as financial debasement, as criminals "clipped" them for their specie—a clearly visible humiliation for a metal that had once been considered divine.[35] But what really diminished gold's sacred aura was the increasingly evident fact that the physical condition of the coin and its financial value were not necessarily correlated. Between 1530 and 1650 European prices approximately tripled,[36] while between 1500 and 1640 English food prices rose by 600 percent.[37] It thus penetrated the mind of the simplest peasant that the value of gold fluctuated according to criteria other than weight. It took a long time for the lesson to sink in, but it was clear enough: Gold was not the literal embodiment of value, but its *sign*.

In England, the destabilizing effects of this inflation (R. H. Tawney famously described it as "an acid dissolving all customary relationships"[38]) were compounded by the "Great Debasement" of 1542–1551, when Henry VIII lowered the specie content of England's coins as a means of raising revenue,[39] and then by Elizabeth's "Great Re-coinage" of 1560. Similar measures in Poland had, in 1526, inspired the astronomer Copernicus to compose his *Treatise on Debasement*, which has a good claim to be the first theoretical recognition of autonomous financial value. Copernicus suggested that the amount of gold or silver contained in coins is irrelevant to their value, which he believed to be determined according to the market fluctuations of supply and demand.[40] We can see in this argument the first stirrings of monetary value as an independent power, and as Hermann van der Wee puts it, by the end of the sixteenth century, "everywhere money was on the march."[41] This is true partly in the familiar sense that money was increasingly used in transactions from which it had been absent before: Feudal dues were commuted from kind to cash, cash replaced barter in the local economy, small-scale credit became widely available, and so on. It is also true in the sense that financial value—the true essence of money—was freeing itself from the restrictions of referentiality, although this process took place at a more subterranean, subliminal level. In addition to unprecedented inflation and debasement, the sixteenth century experienced enormous fluctuations in price ratios *between* the precious metals. First, the initial influx of gold drove up the price of silver; then, after the discovery of the silver mountain of "Peru," the process was reversed. The early banking houses made their fortunes by speculation on these differences. Their money, apparently, was not identical with gold or silver but rather with the play of difference between them. It could be, and often was, said that such money was purely imaginary, that it did not really exist: That it was, like St. Paul's description of an idol, "nothing in the world" (1 Cor. 8:4).

The people who said this did not mean that capital did not empirically exist; they meant that it did not *truly* exist. When Thomas Violet observes that "Spain, that is, according to a wel-regulated Trade, the Fountain of Gold and Silver, is filled only with black money, copper money, going at ten times the true value"[42] he differentiates between the "true value" of the debased coinage and its actual, empirical value, which he assumes to be false. Such value was inauthentic because it was no part of nature, not being identical with natural objects like gold or silver. Clearly, then, it existed only in the sphere of custom, of *nomos*. To people who believed this, the most prominent social and economic developments of the late sixteenth century must have seemed like the triumphant conquest of nature by custom. The first English joint stock company was founded in 1553, the Royal Exchange was built in 1566, and by 1587 Sir Thomas Gresham could wage effective economic warfare on Spain by cornering the market in Genoan bank bills in order to delay supplies to the Armada.[43] A few more dates must suffice to show the phenomenal vigor and exponential growth in the power and influence of capital in this period: The London East India Company was founded in 1600 and the Dutch in 1602. In Holland and Germany, large public banks were springing up, founded on the model of the Italian city states, in Amsterdam (1609), Middleburg (1616), Hamburg (1619), Delft (1621), Nuremberg (1621), and Rotterdam (1635). In England, the goldsmiths profited from the increased opportunities in foreign exchange and money lending, evolving into something resembling modern bankers. They began issuing notes in 1633, printed the earliest known check in 1659, and during the civil war they functioned as secure safe deposits for the nervous rich. By the Restoration, goldsmith's receipts were fully functioning banknotes. This was a big step on the road toward paper money, and it strongly implied that financial value has a purely nominal, or imaginary, existence. On February 29, 1668, Samuel Pepys records, with no evident misgivings, sending his father the enormous sum of six hundred pounds in the form of a goldsmith's banknote. In 1698, George Davenant estimated that more than half of the English money supply existed in paper form.[44] The following year, in an event of epochal symbolic significance, the alchemist Isaac Newton became Master of the Mint.

IV

By the end of our period, then, it was pretty obvious that financial value, which had once been identified with the physical matter of gold and silver, was in fact the "money of the mind."[45] The expansion in the quantity, power, and influence of capital led to an enhanced degree of theoretical sophistication regarding money. By the 1620s, leading merchants like Gerard de Malynes, Edward Misselden, and Thomas Mun were engaged in a lively and innovative debate over the nature of financial value. The only people in this period who wrote about finance from any other than a violently hostile perspective were merchants. Consequently, the earliest tracts that today are considered part of the science of "economics" (which, of course, excludes the thousands of impassioned denunciations of trade and usury which constantly streamed from the presses throughout the seventeenth century) are concerned to advance and protect the interests of merchants, usually by arguing that a favorable balance of trade is identical with national wealth and by appealing for government intervention to ensure such a balance.[46]

All that the "mercantilists" really had in common was their desire to boost the mercantile interest.[47] Nevertheless, over the course of the hundred years we are dealing with here, it is possible to discern a definite shift in their view of how this ought to be done. At first, the equation of money with bullion is virtually universal. By the end of the seventeenth century, in sharp contrast, it is widely accepted that financial value is nonmaterial. Some of the more ingenuous mercantilists happily proceeded from this conclusion to the opinion that value is imaginary, or fictional. More canny heads, however, perceived that such a conclusion might easily threaten their own interests. By the end of this period we find economists making the innovative, and to conservative contemporaries astonishingly counterintuitive, argument that, although financial value was admittedly (indeed undeniably) imaginary, *it was nonetheless real for that.*

Bullionist trade policy was entirely logical, once one granted its initial premise. If financial value really were identical with gold and silver, then it would make perfect sense to pursue riches by attempting to acquire and retain precious metals. Thomas Violet indicates the practical implications of this theory when he laments the supposed effects of the export of precious metals: "let the transporters of Gold and Silver, and the cullers and melters of the heavie coin of this Nation, run their cours a little longer (which God defend) they will leave no Monie in the Nation."[48] What is remarkable about the first generation of thinkers to challenge this opinion is that, while understanding that financial value is a relative and fluctuating notion that cannot be identified with any species of matter, they nevertheless continued to believe that a favorable balance of trade would make a nation wealthy. They assumed, that is to say, that the purpose of trade is to amass a hoard of money, and they still equated wealth with the actual possession of money. In other words, they merely separated the fetish of value from its material incarnation in a physical thing; the fetish itself remained inviolate. They still believed that money, whether in the form of gold or banknotes, *was* value. They did not fully understand (although experience had convinced them of this with regard to precious metals) that value is not an essence, but is produced by the fluctuations and differences *between* essences.

We can observe this reasoning in Edward Misselden's *Free Trade, or The Meanes To Make Trade Flourish* (1622). Misselden unquestioningly adopts the Aristotelian view of money as custom:

> ... the riches of former ages did not consist *re pecuniaria* but *pecuaria* ... But when Immooveable and Immutable things came also to be in Commerce amongst men, as well as those things which were mooveable and fit for change, then came money in use, as the rule and square whereby things might receive estimation & value. Therefore the Civilians affirme that *Numus est dictus, quod instiu-*

tum sit Civile. According to that of Aristotle: *Numus non est a natura sed a lege.* And thence it is that money in our tongue is derived of *moneta, quasi numi nota.*[49]

Misselden is in no doubt that money is not natural but artificial. However he acknowledges that, in contemporary practice, the traditional hierarchy of nature and custom has been overturned. His tract therefore announces a contradiction between philosophical and empirical modes of investigation:

> The matter of Trade, is either Naturall or Artificial. The Natural matter of Commerce is Merchandize: which Merchants from the end of Trade have stiled Commodities. The Artificial matter of Commerce is Money, which hath obtained the title sinews of warre and of State. Old Jacob blessing his Grandchildren, crost his hands; and laide his right hand on the yonger, and his left hand on the elder: And Money, though it be in nature and time after Merchandize, yet forasmuch as it is now in use become the chiefe, I will take leave of Method, to handle it in the first place.[50]

In his response to Misselden, *The Maintenance of Free Trade* (1622), Gerard de Malynes criticizes his predecessor for failing to distinguish between money and foreign exchange. Malynes tells his readers that he has "lately perused a Treatise intituled *Free Trade, or the Meanes to Make Trade Flourish;* wherein the Author, either ignorantly or willfully, hath omitted to handle The Predominant Part of Trade, namely, the Mystery of Exchange."[51] Misselden, in Malynes's view, has correctly deduced that money dictates the flow of commodities, rather than the other way around, but has failed to draw out the implications of this position:

> Now even as monyes were invented to bee coyned of the purest mettals of silver and gold to bee the Square and Rule to set a price unto all commodities and other things whatsoever within the Realme, and therefore called Publica Mensura: even so is exchange of monyes by Bills, The Publike Measure between us and forraine countries, according to which, all commodities are bought and sold in the course of Traffique; for this exchange is grounded upon the weight, fineness and valuation of the money of each countrey: albeit the price thereof in exchange doth rise and fall according to scarcity and plenty of money, and the few or many deliverers and takers thereof.

Malynes's epiphany is his realization that foreign exchange stands in relation to money as money does to commodities. With regard to foreign exchange, he has understood, money *is* a commodity. This recognition entails a further departure from the natural hierarchy of things, adding another layer to the process by which commodification evades natural teleology:

> For even as Commodities being the Body of Trafficke, draw unto them moneys, and therein may seem to be Active; yet money (being the right judge or Rule which giveth or imposeth a price unto Commodities:) is the Thing Active, and Commodities become the thing Passive: Even so, although money is the Subject whereupon exchanges are made: yet still th'exchange is made to Rule moneys . . .

Money, claims Malynes contra Aristotle, is the active and subjective force in commodity exchange. However, claims Malynes contra Misselden, this is not due to any intrinsic qualities of money in itself. This can be seen from the fact that, in foreign exchange, money itself becomes a commodity with a fluctuating, as opposed to an inherent, value. The commodification of money, or rather the theoretical awareness of this process, is a momentous occasion in the history of economics. Henceforth, the *medium* of exchange becomes an *object* of exchange. The intellectual consequence was that the most advanced economic thinkers of the time were eventually able to make three logically progressive breakthroughs. They realized (a) that value did not reside in the physical substance of gold; (b) that value was not inherent in the medium of exchange at all; and (c) that value was not in fact an essence at all, but a *sign*. Armed with this knowledge, the merchants of seventeenth-century England were ready to defend the legitimacy of making money breed on purely empirical grounds: Money, after all, clearly *did* breed. They made no attempt, however, to do the impossible—that is, to defend financial speculation by the standards of Aristotelian philosophy. They were, always, forced to concede that according to those standards their practice reversed the natural relationships of use and exchange, things and signs, reality and representation. Rice Vaughan's *A Discourse of Coins and Coinage* (published in 1675, but written decades earlier) follows Malynes's three-fold distinction of commodities, money, and the trade in money, or "exchange":

> The first use of Money was then by it to supply every man's particular wants. This introduced a second use of Cauponation, when men did by the Pledge of Money procure not only those things which they themselves wanted, but which they might sell to others for more money: and under that kind is all Trades comprehended, whether it be

grose sale, or retale; and this use hath brought in a third use of Money, for the gain of cauponation did give a Colour to those that lent Money to such as did encrease it by Trade, to take usury for it, which is therefore termed the most unnatural use of Money, because it is most remote from the natural Institution. Of this there are many kinds of which the most refined is that of Exchange, which is mix'd with an usury of place, as that is of time.[52]

In defiance of their own logic (but in defense of their own interests), the mercantilists continued to believe in the *reality* of this admittedly "unnatural," purely symbolic value. We can see this from the instance of Thomas Mun's *England's Treasure by Foreign Trade* (written circa 1630). In this tract, Mun sets out to demonstrate what for a bullionist is logically impossible; namely that "The Exportation Of Our Moneys In Trade Of Merchandize Is Means To Encrease Our Treasure."[53] In essence, Mun argues that true wealth consists in money invested at profit (that is, in capital) rather than in money simply hoarded. One does not have to physically, literally possess money in order to be wealthy. Mun is aware that this view will seem odd to his audience, since it contradicts the inherited philosophical assumptions of his age:

> This Position is so contrary to the common opinion, that it will require many and strong arguments to prove it before it can be accepted of the Multitude, who bitterly exclaim when they see any monies carried out of the Realm; affirming thereupon that wee have absolutely lost so much Treasure, and that this is an act directly against the long continued laws made and confirmed by the wisdom of this Kingdom in the High Court of Parliament, and that many places, nay Spain it self which is the Fountain of Mony, forbids the exportation thereof, some cases only excepted.[54]

In their naive view that Spain is "the Fountain of Mony," Mun's opponents ("the Multitude") betray their ingenuous equation of money with literal, material gold. If gold is an end in itself, the logical thing to do with it, having acquired it, is to hoard it. For Mun, on the contrary, gold is a means to an end, an instrument to be employed in investment. It is, or should be, a commodity:

> we have no other means to get Treasure but by forraign trade, for Mines wee have none which do afford it, and how this mony is gotten in the managing of our said Trade I have already shewed, that it is done by making our commodities which are exported yearly to over

ballance in value the forraign wares which we consume; so that it resteth only to shew how our moneys may be added to our commodities, and being jointly exported may so much the more encrease our Treasure.[55]

The idea, so familiar to us today, that it is possible to get rich through capital investment here acquires its earliest theoretical expression. Money, Mun understands, is fungible. It is a quantity not a quality, a sign rather than a referent. It has no essential identity but can instantly be transformed into anything:

> For it is in the stock of the Kingdom as in the estates of private men, who having store of wares, doe not therefore say that they will not venture out or trade with their mony (for this were ridiculous) but do also turn that into wares, whereby they multiply their Mony, and so by a continual and orderly change of one into the other grow rich, and when they please turn all their estates into Treasure; for they that have Wares cannot want mony.[56]

This argument soon becomes a mercantilist commonplace, as in Nicholas Barbon's observation that "It is the denomination and currency of the money that men regard in bargaining, and not the quantity of silver."[57] It is stated with great clarity and assurance by Sir Dudley North in his *Discourses of Trade* (1691). Because, says North, "Money is a Merchandize"[58]:

> No Man is richer for having his Estate all in Money, Plate, etc. lying by him, but on the contrary, he is for that reason the poorer. That man is richest, whose Estate is in a growing condition, either in Land at Farm, Money at Interest, or Goods in Trade: If any man, out of an humour, should turn all his Estate into Money, and keep it dead, he would soon be sensible of Poverty growing upon him, whilst he is eating out of the quick stock.[59]

North's point, like Mun's, is that money should be treated as "Ware," that is, as a commodity to be traded like any other. Like any other commodity, then, money acquires an exchange value, which is grafted onto its use value (which is to function as the medium of exchange). As John Locke put it: "Money has a Value, as it is capable by Exchange to procure us the Necessaries or Conveniencies of Life, and in this it has the Nature of a Commodity; only with this difference, That it serves us commonly by its Exchange, never almost by its Consumption."[60] According to traditional economic and semiotic morality, this opinion is fetishistic. The natural body of money is abandoned and so is its natural function, which is to act as a common denominator facilitating the exchange of useful objects. Money attains a purely imaginary, fetishistic status at the same moment that it departs from its natural *telos* and becomes an end in itself.

We should remember, however, that the mercantilists still believed that a favorable balance of trade is the way to enrich a nation. In the well-known words of Mun, "The ordinary means therefore to increase our wealth and treasure is by Forraign Trade, wherein wee must ever observe this rule; to sell more to strangers yearly than wee consume of theirs in value."[61] This opinion contradicts the belief that money has not an intrinsic but a nominal value. But Mun and his mercantilist successors remained blind to this contradiction. Having removed the physical body of the idol gold, they replace it with the nonmaterial, interior, psychological fetish of financial value. The spiritual tendency to fetishism that this contradiction reveals and the criticisms that contemporaries leveled against that tendency will be the concerns of the following chapters. But we may get a firmer grasp on the nature of this fetishism if we first briefly extend our view beyond the seventeenth century to examine the arguments of mercantilism's later critics. Adam Smith, whose work represents at once the culmination and the supersession of mercantilism (its dialectical *aufhebung*), saw the fetishistic nature of the mercantilist view of money just as clearly as Barbon or North saw the fetishistic nature of the bullionist view of gold:

> Money is neither a material to work upon, nor a tool to work with; and though the wages of the workman are commonly paid to him in money, his real revenue, like that of all other men, consists, not in the money, but in the money's worth; not in the metal pieces, but in what can be got for them.[62]

Money, for Smith and the "Classical" school of economics, is pure representation. David Hume explains the implications of this discovery pithily in his essay "Of Interest": "Money having chiefly a fictitious value, the greater or less plenty of it is of no consequence if we consider a nation within itself."[63] Statements such as these blur the distinction between fiction and reality. If money is a fiction, then surely fiction is real. This was, in fact, precisely the conclusion arrived at by John Law, the man behind the first European attempt to introduce a paper currency, in France in 1714. In the following passages from *Money and Trade Considered* (1705), Law expresses more clearly than his predecessors the idea that money is a commodity of which the use value is its function as the medium of exchange. This function is only made possible by the customary value that human convention agrees to ascribe to money. But Law ostentatiously refuses to admit that such value is "fictitious":

> It is reasonable to think Silver was Barter'd as it was valued for its Uses as a Mettal, and was given as Money according to its Value in Barter. The additional Use of Money Silver was apply'd to would add to its Value, because as Money it remedied the Disadvantages and Inconveniences of Barter, and consequently the demand for Silver encreasing, it received an additional Value equal to the greater demand its Use as Money occasioned.[64]

Law here describes the genesis of exchange value, which, he suggests, was originally an "additional value" attributed to silver because of its double usefulness as a metal and as a medium of exchange. As we saw at the beginning of this chapter, Aristotle believes that this kind of value is "not proper to the thing"—it has nothing to do with the natural properties of silver but belongs exclusively to the realm of custom, of *nomos*. This value cannot, therefore, be the *telos* of silver, because an object's *telos* is immanent within it. Aristotle concludes that this kind of value is therefore (a) less real, and (b) ethically inferior to the natural kind of value that resides in *telos*. It is these conclusions that Law denies. The passage cited above continues:

> And this additional Value is no more Imaginary, than the Value Silver had in Barter as a Mettal, for such Value was because it serv'd such Uses, and was greater or lesser according to the demand for Silver as a Mettal, proportioned to its Quantity. The additional Value Silver receiv'd from being used as Money, was because of its Qualities which fitted it for that Use; And that Value was according to the additional demand its Use as Money occasioned.

For Law, then, the exchange value of money *is* its use value. Just as the use value of Aristotle's shoe consists in being worn, so the use value of money consists in its having exchange value. Law has thus *fetishized* exchange value. He views it, like the shoe, as an end itself. He does not view it as a *sign* that points to a referent beyond itself; he views it as having immanent, inherent value. He has made money into an idol. Or rather, he has succeeded in giving theoretical expression to a fetishism that had long pertained in practice. As he goes on to observe, "If either of these Values are Imaginary, then all Value is so." Of course, in the teleological view, all customary value is indeed imaginary. Law, however, is facing a situation in which imaginary value had empirically replaced natural *telos*. We face a highly exacerbated form of the same situation today. The following chapters discuss some ways in which people of the sixteenth and seventeenth centuries responded to its earliest manifestations.

Chapter Two

Commodity Fetishism and Theology

> *Let this be our principle, that we err not in the use of the gifts of Providence when we refer them to the end for which their author made and destined them, since he created them for our good, and not for our destruction. No man will keep the true path better than he who shall have this end carefully in view. Now then, if we consider for what end he created food, we shall find that he consulted not only for our necessity, but also for our enjoyment and delight. Thus, in clothing, the end was, in addition to necessity, comeliness and honour; and in herbs, fruits, and trees, besides their various uses, gracefulness of appearance and sweetness of smell.... Has he not given qualities to gold and silver, ivory and marble, thereby rendering them precious above other metals or stones? In short, has he not given many things a value without having any necessary use?*
>
> —*Calvin*, Institues[1]

I

In his studies of the early political economists, Karl Marx often draws the analogy between Adam Smith's "Classical" critique of the mercantilists' money fetishism and the Protestant critique of religious idolatry. In the *Economic and Philosophical Manuscripts* of 1844, he writes:

> To this enlightened political economy, which has discovered—within private property—the *subjective essence* of wealth, the adherents of the

monetary and mercantile system, who look upon private property only as an *objective* substance confronting men, seem therefore to be *fetishists, Catholics*. Engels was therefore right to call *Adam Smith* the *Luther of Political Economy*.[2]

And he repeats the observation in the *Grundrisse*:

> In so far as bourgeois political economy did not simply identify itself with the past in a mythological manner, its criticism of earlier economies—especially of the feudal system against which it still had to wage a direct struggle—resembled the criticism that Christianity directed against heathenism, or which Protestantism directed against Catholicism.[3]

Marx is also quite explicit about the iconoclastic heritage of his own ideas. In *Comments on James Mill* he discusses the same problem faced by the political economists we discussed in the last chapter: What happens when the proper *telos* of money (its role as a sign of other things, as the medium of exchange) is obscured and, instead, money is regarded as an end in itself? His answer is that this produces idolatry:

> It is clear that this *mediator* thus becomes a *real God*, for the mediator is the *real power* over what it mediates to me. Its cult becomes an end in itself. Objects separated from this mediator have lost their value. Hence the objects only have value insofar as they *represent* the mediator, whereas originally it seemed that the mediator only had value insofar as it represented *them*. (3:212, emphases in original)

Marx broadly concurs with the Classical critique of mercantilism. But he subjects Adam Smith's description of financial value to the same iconoclastic criticism that Smith employs against his seventeenth-century predecessors. From Mun through Smith to Marx, the history of political economy moves through successive diagnoses, and denunciations, of money fetishism. Mun derides the bullionists for their superstitious belief that gold is value incarnate; Smith points out that Mun holds the same belief with regard to money in the abstract; and Marx attacks Smith and his followers for their insistence that, despite the acknowledged fact that it is an empty sign, money nonetheless has an objective, "real" existence. Marx expresses this through a predictable analogy:

> The monetary system is essentially Catholic, the credit system essentially Protestant. "The Scotch hate gold." As paper, the monetary ex-

istence of commodities has a purely social existence. It is faith that brings salvation. Faith in money value as the immanent spirit of commodities, faith in the mode of production and its predestined disposition, faith in the individual agents of production as mere personifications of self-valorizing capital. But the credit system is no more emancipated from the monetary system as its basis than Protestantism is from the foundations of Catholicism.[4]

Between 1620 and 1867, the history of political economy forms a continuous, evolving pattern of protest against two superstitious errors that each successive generation perceives in its predecessors: the attribution of subjective agency to an object, and the mistaking of the sign for the referent. These charges are made by mercantilism against bullionism, by the Classical school against mercantilism, and by Marxism against the Classical school. The aim of this book is to investigate the connection (which seemed obvious to the people of the seventeenth century but is rather obscure today) between these two criticisms. How was the objectification of the subject related to the autonomy of representation? One way to approach this question is to examine the striking analogies between the discourses of political economy and theological iconoclasm. The economists' critique of money fetishism is, in its logical argument and its ethical assumptions, the same case that successive forms of iconoclastic religion have made against idolatry. As we saw in the introduction, this similarity was revealed to Marx by his reading of Ludwig Feuerbach's *The Essence of Christianity*. Feuerbach claims that:

> ... the historical progress of religion consists in this: that what by an earlier religion was regarded as objective, is now regarded as subjective; that is, what was formerly contemplated and worshipped as God is now perceived to be something *human*. What was at first religion becomes at a later period idolatry; man is seen to have adored his own nature.[5]

The critiques of money fetishism and of religious fetishism are made on grounds that are fundamentally similar. What they criticize is the hypostatization of the human, the mistaking of *nomos* for *phusis*, and the substitution of the sign for the referent. As he freely admits, Marx simply transfers Feuerbach's analysis of religion to the "sphere" of economics. Discussing the concept of commodity fetishism in *Capital*, Marx observes:

> In order ... to find an analogy, we must take flight into the misty realm of religion. There the products of the human brain appear as

autonomous figures endowed with a life of their own, which enter into relations both with each other and with the human race. So it is in the world of commodities with the products of men's hands. This I call the fetishism which attaches itself to the products of labor as soon as they are produced as commodities, and is therefore inseparable from the production of commodities.[6]

Marx here refers to an "analogy" between idolatry and commodity fetishism, but this assumes a relationship between distinct "spheres" of experience, and this assumption is anachronistic for the seventeenth century (as well as distinctly dubious in the twenty-first). It might be more accurate to speak of a *homology* between idolatry and commodity fetishism, insofar as they represent the same tendency of human thought applied to different objects.

Today, value in the Western world appears, falsely, to arise from circulation rather than from production. It may be that this development has made the semiotic implications of monetary theory more visible than they were in the nineteenth or early twentieth centuries. It may also be that the ethical implications of various forms of representation will soon become an important factor in economic thought (or rather, given the nature of the discipline currently known as "economics," in the *critique* of economic thought). If this is the case, philosophers of the economy will inexorably be led to attack the fetishism of the sign after the manner of theological iconoclasm. As Jacques Derrida has recently noted:

> ... Marx always described money, and more precisely the monetary sign, in the figure of appearance or simulacrum, more exactly of the ghost. He not only described them, he also defined them, but the figural presentation of the concept seemed to describe some spectral "thing," which is to say "someone." What is the necessity of this figural presentation? What is its relation to the concept? Is it contingent? That is the classic form of our question.[7]

Derrida here raises the issue of the objectification of the subject. Money, for Marx, is objectified human activity, objectified subjectivity, and in this regard it resembles—effectively it *is*—a "ghost" and a "spectral 'thing.'" This constitutes Marx's ethical case against money; as we shall see below, it also constitutes the iconoclastic case against idols. Today, that case seems to many to have been refuted by events. Is there really any room for an ethical critique of autonomous representation, or of the objectification of the subject, in a world that daily demonstrates the empirical reality of both these phenomena?

What if representation really *is* autonomous; what if the subject really *is* merely an object? These are some of the most pressing philosophical questions raised by postmodernism. As Jean Baudrillard has pointed out, however, they are hardly new questions:

> This is precisely what was feared by the Iconoclasts, whose millennial quarrel is still with us today. Their rage to destroy images rose precisely because they sensed the omnipotence of simulacra, this facility they have of effacing God from the consciousness of men, and the overwhelming, destructive truth which they suggest: that ultimately there never has been any God, that only the simulacrum exists, indeed that God himself has only ever been his own simulacrum.[8]

It seems to me extremely plausible that "the omnipotence of simulacra" would indeed bring about an epochal alteration in human consciousness, and especially that it would tend to erase any notion of an ultimate referent or *logos*. But it also seems worth raising the possibility that this is not, as Baudrillard assumes, an "overwhelming, destructive truth" but an overwhelming, destructive *lie*.

II

In the Christian tradition, the critique of idolatry has generally been made on Aristotelian grounds. Idolatry transgresses against natural teleology because it misconstrues the *telos* of the material sign, mistaking it for the spiritual referent. Such a misconstruction is symptomatic of a more general misunderstanding of the proper relationship between spirit and matter, and thus of the psychological tendency we would call "objectification." Idolatry is a fetishism of the sign, which is a synecdoche and paradigm of a more general tendency to pay attention to mere appearance, to the material world as it is empirically given to us. It makes little theoretical or ethical difference whether the fetishized sign is financial, linguistic, erotic, or iconic. The argument against fetishism is identical in each of these "spheres," and we must suspend our conception of these "spheres" as separate and distinct. The writers studied here extended the valence of the term "idolatry" far beyond the discourse of theology; they discerned and deplored its baleful influence in every aspect of psychological and social existence. What was it about the concept of "idolatry" that made it seem so relevant and useful to the thinkers of the early modern period?[9]

The prohibition of idolatry is Yahweh's first concern in the decalogue. In the first two commandments the Israelites are warned not to raise up a "graven image," and the fact that the image is the product of human labor—that it is "graven"—is of paramount significance. Shortly after enumerating the decalogue, Yahweh elaborates on the nature of proscribed worship: "Ye shall not make with me gods of silver, neither shall ye make unto you gods of gold" (Exod. 20:23). "And if thou wilt make me an altar of stone, thou shalt not build it of hewn stone: for if thou lift up thy tool upon it, thou hast polluted it" (Exod. 20:25). Two distinct kinds of icons are specifically banned here: those made of precious metals and, more generally, those that have been manufactured by human hands. Idolatry is defined as: (a) the worship of gold and silver, and (b) the worship of the products of labor. These definitions remain constant throughout the Hebrew Bible. They are repeated in Isaiah:

> The workman melteth a graven image, and the goldsmith
> spreadeth it over with gold, and casteth silver chains.
> He that is so impoverished that he hath no oblation chooseth
> a tree that will not rot; he seeketh unto him a cunning
> workman to prepare a graven image, that shall not be
> moved. (40:19–20)

The most extended discussion of idolatry in the Hebrew Bible occurs in Psalms. Psalms 115:4–8 and 135:15–18 use virtually the same words to justify opposition to idols:

> The idols of the heathen are silver and gold, the work of men's
> hands.
> They have mouths, but they speak not; eyes have they, but
> they see not;
> They have ears, but they hear not; neither is there any breath
> in their mouths.
> They that make them are like unto them: so is every one that
> trusteth in them. (135:15–18)

The first point to note here is that, as in the decalogue's prohibition of graven images (Exod. 20:25; Deut. 5:7–8), and also in the anti-iconic satire of the Babylonian captivity (Isa. 40:19 and 46:6), the idols are specifically said to be the products of human labor. The ban on idolatry is a ban on hypostatizing human works: it is a ban on elevating *nomos* above *phusis*. Secondly, the Psalmist emphasizes that idols are dead, purely material things; they are objects, not subjects, and they are therefore powerless to assist their supplicants in any way. The *Wisdom of Solomon* repeats the essential points: "The really degraded are those whose hopes are set on dead things, who give the name of gods to the works of human hands, to gold and silver fashioned by art into images of living creatures, or to a useless stone carved by a craftsman long ago" (13:10).[10]

Nevertheless, the idols *look* like living creatures, and the idolatrous heathen, being unable to distinguish appearance from reality, accord them the veneration that they intend to direct toward the god they represent. This idolatry of representation exacts a psychological price on its practitioners. That price, according to the Psalmist, is objectification. The idolater becomes "like" the idol he worships, and the idol's most salient characteristic is that it is an object, as opposed to a subject. The idolater was understood to be spiritually dead, although physically alive, as in Augustine's exegesis of Psalms 135:18: "there is a likeness to these idols expressed not in their flesh, but in their inner man."[11] Reformation commentators on this text, writing when Europe was suddenly awash in literal gold and silver from America, tended to emphasize the material substances the Psalmist attributes to the idols. According to Calvin, for instance, in this Psalm "Man is forced to confess that he is but the creature of a day, and yet would have the metal which he has deified to be regarded as God."[12] We can perceive the influence of Old Testament aniconism on our period's understanding of commodity fetishism in this famous passage from John Wheeler's *A Treatise of Commerce* (1601):

> ... all the world choppeth and changeth, runneth and raveth after Marts, Markets and Merchandising, so that all things come into Commerce, and pass into traffic.... this man maketh merchandise of the works of his own hands, this man of another man's labor, one selleth words, another maketh traffic of the skins and blood of other men, yea there are some found so subtle and cunning merchants, that they persuade and induce men to suffer themselves to be bought and sold, and we have seene in our time enowe, and too manie, which have made merchandise of mens soules ... [13]

The New Testament's references to idolatry occur mostly in Paul, and are dominated by two seemingly unambiguous definitions:

> Mortify therefore your members which are upon the earth; fornication, uncleanness, inordinate affection, evil concupiscence, and covetousness, which is idolatry. (Col. 3:5)
> For this ye know, that no whoremonger, nor unclean person, nor covetous man, who is an idolater, hath any inheritance in the kingdom of Christ and of God. (Eph. 5:5)

However, these texts are susceptible to a certain elision, which we will meet again, between the cardinal sins of avarice and lust. By "covetousness," Paul does not mean greed for money alone, but the generalized desire of carnal goods and pleasures that is prohibited by the tenth commandment. As is his practice, Paul gives a figurative or "spiritual" rendering of the Old Testament's letter: He reads the literal "gold and silver" of Exodus and Isaiah as a metonym for the things of this world. It is this "covetousness," in the general sense of "fleshly desire," that Paul, in his comment on Jesus' interpretation of the decalogue, calls the unavoidable sin, the sin that is part of the ontological condition of humanity. In Matthew 5, Jesus stresses the fact that covetousness, which is an interior sin, a sin of desire only, is yet a sin of the same order as an external sin manifested in action: "Ye have heard that it was said by them of old time, Thou shalt not commit adultery: But I say unto you, That whosoever looketh at a woman to lust after her hath committed adultery already with her in his heart" (Matt. 5:27–28). In Romans, Paul concludes from this that the purpose of the tenth commandment is to indicate the ontological, inevitable nature of sin. The prohibition against covetousness, understood as carnal lust in general, is not intended to be kept. To keep it is impossible for a fallen, fleshly creature. It is intended, rather, to establish the fact that fleshly desires are sinful: "Nay, I had not known sin, but by the law: for I had not known lust, except the law had said, Thou shalt not covet" (Rom. 7:7). Paul announces that an orientation toward what he calls the "flesh" must be understood in the spiritual sense, as an inescapable element of the human mind, just as the literal flesh is the element of the human body.[14] Augustine's gloss on Paul emphasizes the connection, which is taken for granted by Herbert and Milton but largely forgotten today, between carnality and literalism, the fleshly law and the dead letter. The literal letter of the law convicts us of sin and condemns us to death, while the spirit of the gospel redeems us and thus gives us life:

> But this is not the only meaning of the apostle's saying: "the letter killeth, but the spirit giveth life." There is also, and perhaps more important, the sense which he clearly indicates elsewhere, in the words: "I was unaware of concupiscence, did not the law say; 'Thou shalt not covet.'" And a little further on: "Sin, taking occasion by the commandment, deceived me, and through it slew me." There is the real killing! . . . The apostle has purposely chosen a general all-embracing precept, to convey the voice of the law, forbidding all sin; for there is no sin whose commission does not begin with coveting . . .[15]

It is this generalized sense of covetousness as a "carnal" orientation that, in Colossians 3:5 and Ephesians 5:5, Paul identifies as idolatry. Thus, "idolatry" for Paul involves more than icon worship; it signifies a general tendency of postlapsarian human perception. This is the source of such Patristic opinions as that of Tertullian: "All sins are found in idolatry and idolatry in all sins,"[16] and Aquinas: "idolatry is stated to be the cause, beginning and end of all sin, because there is no kind of sin that idolatry does not produce."[17]

In Renaissance Europe, all sides of the Protestant theological spectrum agreed on this point. This is what Calvin means when he declares that "the human mind is, so to speak, a perpetual forge of idols,"[18] just as it is what Arminius means when he observes:

> Idolatry ... according to the etymology of the word, is "service rendered to an idol;" but, with regard to fact, it is when divine worship is paid to any other than the true God.... In proof of this, the belly, covetousness, and idolatry, are severally said to be the god of some people, and covetous men are called "idolaters."[19]

However, just as the term "idolatry" was obviously also used in a specifically religious sense, so the term "covetousness" was very often employed to mean specifically the desire for money. The greed of "Mr. Covetousness" in Richard Bernard's *The Isle of Man* (1627) is entirely financial. "Master Common-Weal" complains that "Covetousness"

> hath entred so farre into al businesses, as hee hath almost utterly undone mee. Hee propounded Offices to sale, and so maketh the buyers to sell their duties for profit to make up their monies. He hath monopolized commodities into his hands, inhaunced the prizes of things, to the great grievance of the Kings Subiects ...[20]

And so forth. It is significant, however, that this narrow use of the term does not lead to any diminution of the traditional identification of covetousness with idolatry. Thus, in Bernard's trial scene, when "Covetousness" and "Papistry" are indicted together, we are instructed that "Covetousnes was ioyned with Idolatry, because he is also called Idolatry."[21] In fact, this period continued to understand the desire for money as one among many forms of carnal concupiscence that, like all fleshly desire, does violence to natural teleology by mistaking the proper end, or "use," of worldly things. Nicholas Bacon's "Agaynste Covetousness" compares the vice with other forms of carnal desire, such as gluttony. Having established the homology,

Bacon interprets it in classically Aristotelian terms, pointing out that covetousness transgresses against natural teleology:

> What is the cause the gredye manne
> With care to gett waxethe pale and wanne?
> Haueinge enoughe whye craues he more?
> Whye dothe desier growe with his store?
> A like disease to my thinkeinge
> As where thirste growes by muche drinkeinge.
> Whye makes he wante where plentye is
> And haueinge thinges their use doe misse?
> Hee seekes with payne and keepes with care,
> Hee hordes and hydes and makethe rare.
> Thinges of that kynde shoulde common bee,
> Changeinge nature in hur degree.[22]

The essence of covetousness, as of idolatry, is objectification, or "carnality." The pursuit of fleshly pleasures or worldly goods indicates a misconstrual of the *telos* of the human being. To be carnal is to forget that the body is a means to a spiritual end. Such a fleshly consciousness will systematically reduce the spiritual to the material and the subjective to the objective. It is, in other words, a *fetishistic* consciousness.

A fetish is an objective representation of something that is, in reality, subjective. It is therefore a radically false object: It cannot possibly be what it claims to be. This is what Paul means when he observes "We know that an idol is nothing in the world" (1 Cor. 8:4). The Greek word used here is not "eikon," which refers to the material object of the fetish, and thus obviously does have a real, worldly existence. It is "eidolon," which refers to the false mental image that the idolator imposes upon the material icon.[23] This image, while real enough to the idolator, does not have a material existence. In the Septuagint, *eidolon* translates the Hebrew *a ven*, which literally designates various forms of nonexistence: "nothing," "vanity," "lie," "iniquity," and so on. *Eidolon* is also the Homeric word for "ghost," "phantom," or "hallucination," as in Agamemnon's "lying dream." It is best understood as an *unreal objective representation of a real subjective phenomenon*. This definition, which applies equally well to such seemingly disparate concepts as ghosts, religious idols, and money, will be our working understanding of the term "idolatry."

This Pauline critique of idolatry was vulnerable to a Platonic attack. Defenders of icons in all ages draw inspiration from Plato's theory of the prototype, as expressed in such texts as the *Symposium* and the *Timaeus:* "For an image, since the reality, after which it is modeled, does not belong to it, and it exists ever as the fleeting shadow of some other, must be inferred to be in another."[24] For Plato, the image actually participates "in" the prototype, and it cannot be conceived of separately from its original. Thus for Neoplatonists, whether pagan like Plotinus or Christian like Dionysus Areopagita, the visible universe was a chain of images that both emanated from and led toward the Absolute. In this view, an icon becomes not only a legitimate but even a necessary link in the golden chain connecting the human mind to divinity. From here it was a short step to perceiving the *pneuma* of divinity inhabiting the *eikon*. In fact, "eikon" is the word used by the Septuagint for "image," in the sense in which man is said to be made in the "image" of God, and in this sense the Son himself could be conceived of as an *eikon* of the Father.[25] The *eikon* exists in a relation of kinship, or *oikeiosis,* with the prototype. For millennia, advocates of Platonic emanation, for whom the sign participates in its referent, have fought theoretical and literal battles with the followers of Aristotle, for whom the sign enjoys a purely immanent teleology, so that its relationship to any external referent must be merely customary. In order to grasp the practical implications of this highly theoretical dispute, it will be useful to turn to a concrete historical example.

III

There are two periods of Christian history in which the debate over the status of iconic representation ceases to play its usual significant but largely academic role in the lives of nations and becomes instead a matter of pressing urgency and popular partisanship, bringing in its wake war, tumult, and revolution. One, which will be our main concern, took place in western and central Europe between 1517 and 1660. The other took place in the Byzantine empire between 726 and 843. Because the fundamental arguments used by advocates of Reformation and Counter-Reformation alike derive, in large part, from those developed in the earlier controversy, the colorful history of Byzantine iconoclasm demands some attention here.

A visit to a restored ancient city such as Ephesus or the forum at Rome can still give some sense of the pervasive, ubiquitous presence of representations of the gods in the pagan metropolis. The psychological effects of living constantly surrounded by hordes of icons are harder to recapture, but they can be inferred from Alain Besancon's observation that the ancient Greek god "was not really distinguishable from his representation."[26] Even once discredited among post-Orphic philosophers, this elision of sign and referent often characterized the piety of the uneducated. What does this imply about their conduct in day-to-day life? Perhaps we catch a glimpse of the answer in Augustine's citation of Seneca:

> But go into the Capitol, and you will be ashamed of the folly there disclosed, and of the duties which a deluded madness has assigned itself. One servant informs Jupiter of the names of his worshippers, another announces the hours; one is his bather, another his anointer, that is, he gestures with empty hands to imitate the act of anointing. There are women who are hairdressers for Juno and Minerva: while standing far away from the temple as well as from the image they move the fingers as if they were dressing the hair, and there are others who hold a mirror. There are men and women who summon the gods to give bond for them, and some who offer them lawyers' briefs and explain their case. . . . Still, these men, though they offer useless service to the god, offer no base or indecent service. But there are women who sit in the Capitol, who imagine that Jupiter is their lover. . . . [27]

While primitive Christianity deplored such fetishism, this rigor was gradually relaxed following the donation of Constantine, and early Byzantine Christianity readily adopted an attitude toward icons that it inherited from Hellenistic polytheism. Until the eighth century, the iconodule spirit permeated Byzantine society with a profundity that is hard for the modern world to fathom. A fragment of the true cross stood on a column of porphyry in the center of the capital; Constantine himself rode into battle using a bridle-bit made out of nails from the cross; Byzantine military manuals contained detailed analyses of the tactical deployment of icons on the battlefield.[28] In urban centers, life-size icons filled the public spaces; Byzantium must have contained many more icons than people. It was reported, and believed, that certain of the icons would walk the streets among their human compatriots; the enormous figure of Christ that stood over the entrance to the Chalke was wont to descend and fight on the battlements during sieges. Some people ate parts of icons along with the Eucharist. There were allegations of sexual liaisons between people and icons. On one occasion, a court jester is reported to have glimpsed the empress Theodora embracing an icon in her bedroom; she assuaged her husband's fury with the assurance that she had merely been kissing her own image in a mirror.[29]

The people of eighth century Byzantium thus inhabited an environment which can accurately be described as "hyper-real." Theirs was a world in which simulacra really were tangible, animate, virtually subjective forces and influences in the minds and everyday lives of the general population.[30] Hence both the remarkably intense resentment the icons occasioned in some and the peculiarly fierce devotion they inspired in others. The iconoclasts and the iconodules fought and killed each other for over a century because of their differing interpretations of iconic representation, but to the modern observer those beliefs that they held in common may appear more striking than those that divided them. Neither side would have dreamed of questioning the practical power of the icons. Both sides agreed that the issue of the icons was of absolutely fundamental importance to the health of the state and the individual alike. Both sides, in other words, saw fairly abstract and arcane questions as to the phenomenological status of images as matters of life and death.

Byzantine iconoclasm (and thus also Reformation iconoclasm) is born of antimaterialism, and the nucleus of the case made by the iconodule Council of 787 was that its heretical iconoclast predecessor was guilty of "taking matter as evil."[31] It originates in the systematic denigration of matter elaborated by the Gnostics and Manichees, and the iconoclasts were often accused of monophysitism, which denied the independence of Christ's human nature and thence inferred that his human form could not be represented without simultaneously representing his divine form, which would be blasphemous. The defenders of icons, on the other hand, were vulnerable to charges of two separate heresies: Nestorianism and Arianism. The Nestorians argued that the Incarnation had redeemed matter, so that it was legitimate to represent the human *hypostasis* of divinity in the form of an icon. The Arians, in contrast, divided the divine from the human at the level of nature, or *phusis*. Their claim that the Son is not coeternal with the Father also renders iconography acceptable, since it is legitimate to make an image of a mere creature, as opposed to the Creator. The favorite argument of the iconoclasts, which they called the "disjunctive syllogism," was that the iconodules must logically be guilty of one or the other of these heresies:

> From those, therefore, who think that they are drawing the icon of Christ, it must be gathered either that the divinity is circumscribable and confused with the flesh, or that the body of Christ was without divinity and divided. . . . Let them be far from us—Nestorius' division and Arius's . . . confusion—two evils diametrically opposite to each other, but equal in impiety. (90)

The implications of this abstruse dispute for individual piety are clarified by a fourth-century letter from Eusebius, bishop of Cesarea, refusing a request from the sister of emperor Constantine that he should send her an image of Christ:

> What sort of Christ are you seeking? Is it the true and unalterable one which bears His essential characteristics, or the one which He took up when He assumed the form of a servant? . . . Granted He has two forms, even I do not think that your request has to do with His divine form. . . . Surely then, you are seeking His image as a servant, that of the flesh He put on for our sake. But that too, we have been taught, was mingled with the glory of His divinity so that the mortal part was swallowed up by Life. . . . How can one paint an image of so wondrous and unattainable a form—unless, like the unbelieving pagans, one is to represent things that bear no possible resemblance to anything?[32]

Not surprisingly, iconoclasm was closely connected, theologically and politically, with the other, more overtly iconoclastic religions of the book that rubbed shoulders with Christianity in the Byzantine middle ages. Iconoclasm emerged out of the eastern provinces of the empire, where Muslim influence was strong, and the immediate cause of its outbreak was said to be the influence of a Jew over Caliph Yazid, whose edict against Christian icons shortly preceded that of the first iconoclast emperor, Leo III "the Isaurian" (717–41). Leo's iconoclastic proclamation was issued around 726, and the emperor wrote to Pope Gregory II, to inform him that "one should not venerate things made with hands. . . . let me know who has taught us to venerate things made with hands, while God legislates not to do so" (27). Under Leo and his son Constantine V (741–75), known to history by the iconodules' affectionate epithet "Copronymus" (i.e., "also called Shit"), the iconoclast policy was pursued with great vigor, and Constantine convened what claimed to be a general council of the church in 754, in order to codify and canonize the iconoclasts' case. The icons were reinstated by the empress Irene (780–802), under whom the second council of Nicea met to anathematize the iconoclasts and their dogma in 787. Irene seized power from her iconoclast son under circumstances described with Gibbonian ingenuousness by Luther's Catholic opponent, Johannes Eck. For theological reasons, Eck considers Irene "a most pious woman," and "a most religious empress," but he is forced to admit that "impelled by the nobility of her character, [she] had her son seized, blinded, and thrown into prison, where he suffered the just punishment of his impiety and sacrilege."[33] But opposition to icons must have remained fervent, and political instability and military defeat precipitated a second period of iconoclast ascendancy under Leo V "the Armenian" (813-20). The bitter struggle then continued for two more decades, until the empress Theodora finally restored the icons in 843.

We know the arguments of the iconoclast council of 754 only through the acts of the iconodule council of 787, which reproduced them for the purposes of mockery and refutation. As far as one can tell from this source, the iconoclastic case was made on christological grounds. The council of 754 used the disjunctive syllogism to argue that the iconodules must be either Arians or Nestorians (83), citing in support of this argument Gregory of Nyssa:

> ... with the pretext of Christianity [Satan] reintroduced idolatry unnoticeably by convincing, with his subtleties, those who had their eyes turned to him not to relinquish the creation but rather to adore it, and pay respect to it, and consider that which is made as God, calling it with the name "Christ." (62)[34]

We know rather more than this about the arguments made by the defenders of the icons. These were various; they might be based on the notion derived from Pope Gregory the Great that icons were *biblia pauperum*, on the distinction between veneration (*dulia*) and worship (*latria*) which was known as the "relative cult," or on the idea that the Incarnation had permanently redeemed and sanctified all matter.[35] But, as we have seen, the most interesting and sophisticated iconodule argument was based on the Platonic metaphysics of ascending images that participated in the prototype. Theodore the Studite assumes this understanding of *mimesis* when he argues that "the prototype and the image have their being, as it were, in each other."[36] The iconic sign, he claims, stands in the same necessary relation to the divine referent as a shadow does to the body that casts it.

The iconodules' argument is very subtle. They are not, of course, suggesting that the sign is *essentially* the same as the referent. They deplored any such suggestion with as much vehemence as the iconoclasts. What they claim is that the sign is *nominally* the same as the referent. Thus, the iconodule council of 787 declared that "The icon resembles the prototype, not with regard to the essence, but only with regard to the name" (77); that "what the icon has in common with the archetype is only the name, not the essence" (84); and that "In the icon the true discourse knows nothing else but how to communicate in name, not in essence, with the one who is in the icon"

(89). The emphatic repetition of this point shows that the council considered it a strong one, for the iconoclasts were forced to concede that the icon is indeed *nominally* similar to its referent. The difference is that the iconodules claimed, on Platonic grounds, that this merely nominal identity is a *true* identity; while the iconoclasts used immanent teleology to argue that no merely nominal identity can be true. The most sophisticated of the iconodules, Theodore the Studite, bluntly equates the nominal with the real and thus arrives at what, from the iconoclast perspective, is the most egregious possible idolatry—he orders that the words "image of Christ" should be erased from the icons and replaced with "Christ":

> Christ is one thing and the icon of Christ another, according to nature. But there is an identity as to the name, which is undivided. And when one considers the nature of the icon, one should not call what one sees "Christ," or even "image of Christ." For it should be called "wood," "paint," "gold," "silver," or any of the different material. But when one looks at its likeness to the archetype depicted, it should be called "Christ."[37]

It is on this point that the phenomenology of the iconodules converges with that of the Classical political economists whom we studied in the last chapter. John Law and Adam Smith believe that money is valuable in itself, despite the fact that its value is purely nominal. It was this belief in the *reality* of merely nominal value that inspired Law to attempt the introduction of paper money in 1714. The iconodule case rests upon the claim that the iconic sign is efficacious in itself, despite the fact that its relationship to the Divinity is purely nominal. This efficacy is doubtless by virtue of its participation in the prototype, but it is nevertheless located within the material sign itself. The efficacy of the sign is thus at once nominal and intrinsic. The council of 787 proclaimed that:

> many of the sacred things which we have at our disposal do not need a prayer of sanctification, since their name itself says that they are all-sacred and full of grace.... when we signify an icon with a name, we transfer the honour to the prototype; and by embracing it and offering to it the veneration of honour, we share in the sanctification. (99)

As Theodore the Studite put it, using a favorite iconodule metaphor: "It is not the essence [*ousia*] of the image which we venerate, but the form [*character*] of the prototype which is stamped upon it."[38] A seal stamped in wax, he points out, leaves its formal impression behind, and this form of the seal can be said to be "in" the wax, even though the material body of the seal is different in substance from that of the wax. According to Theodore, a similar process takes place in the icon. For example, "Crosses can be seen small and large, wider and narrower, with blunt or sharp ends, with or without inscription.... Nevertheless, in spite of such great differences, there is one veneration of the symbol and the prototype; so evidently the same likeness is recognised in both."[39] As Moshe Barasch has noted, the idea of the cross is here conceived Platonically, as existing entirely separately from any actual, material crosses. It is not, and could not be, conceived in terms of Aristotelian teleology, whereby the form of the cross would be understood as immanent within any actual, material cross, for such a conception would indisputably be idolatrous.[40] The Council of 787 expressed the reality of *mimesis* by analogy with Byzantine imperial iconography:

> When one looks at the icon of a king, he sees the king in it. Thus, he who bows to the icon bows to the king in it. ... And as he who reviles the icon of a king is justifiably subject to punishment for having actually dishonored the king—even though this icon is nothing but wood and paints mixed and blended together with wax—so does he who dishonours the figure of any of these [saints] transfer the insult to him whose figure is [on the icon]. (101)

According to the imperial cult of Rome (which many would find resurgent in the monarchical idolatry of seventeenth-century England), the power of the emperor was omnipresent. Since the emperor was not physically omnipresent, imperial power was represented by images of the emperor which must, by law, be revered and obeyed as though they were literal incarnations of the emperor's body.[41] The cult of the emperor seemed to primitive Christianity to be the veritable apotheosis and epitome of idolatry. With the conversion of the emperors, however, the church gradually withdrew its opposition, eventually concluding with Athanasius that

> The likeness of the emperor in the image is exact, so that a person who looks at the image sees in it the emperor; and he again who sees the emperor recognizes that it is he who is in the image. And from the likeness not differing, to one who after the image wished to view the emperor, the image might say, "I and the emperor are one; for I am in him, and he is in me. " ... Accordingly, he who worships the image, in it worships the emperor also; for the image is his form and appearance.[42]

Form, in this view, is more important than substance, appearance overrides essence, ideal representation overcomes material reality, and *nomos* displaces *phusis*. This is the same approach to representation that sees nominal, financial value actually resident in the physical body of money. Nor is this similarity coincidental. The single most important instance of the literal presence of imperial power in a figurative representation of the emperor is found in coinage. In order for coins to be valuable, the image of Caesar that they bear must be acknowledged as a literal incarnation of imperial power. Christ's reply to the tempting Pharisees can be interpreted as ascribing the idolatrous financial power of the image to Caesar, while reserving the natural body of the metal to God: "And he saith unto them, Whose is this image and superscription? They say unto him, Caesar's. Then saith he unto them, Render therefore unto Caesar the things which are Caesar's; and unto God the things that are God's. (Matt. 22:20–21) As the iconodules were not slow to point out, there was no logical reason why iconoclasm should confine itself to ecclesiastical affairs, and the iconodule Stephen attempted to demonstrate the implications of iconoclasm to Constantine by trampling on a coin bearing the emperor's image.[43] Unfortunately, we lack the historical documents to conclude much about the psychological, personal, or sexual implications of Byzantine iconoclasm. It is extremely tempting, for example, to infer from the fact that the leading royal iconodules (Irene and Theodora) were women while the iconoclast emperors were men, from what we know of the sympathies and influence of the palace eunuchs, and even from the language of the respective councils, that the debate was, as we might put it, "gendered." But the loss of so much of the relevant documentation means that any such inference must remain conjectural. Fortunately, we are better informed regarding the second great age of Christian iconoclasm, and it is to that era that we now turn our attention.

IV

To an extent that is often forgotten outside Germany, the Marxian critique of political economy is the direct philosophical inheritor, via Hegel and Feuerbach, of the theological thought of Martin Luther. The Reformation began as a protest against the fetishization of alienated labor. A papal "indulgence" was a sign that represented a particular quantity of human penitential labor, or "works." As Luther saw it, the Papacy had, out of base covetousness, encouraged the popular mind in a fetishized understanding of these certificates, so that they were widely believed to possess the power to liberate the souls of the dead from purgatory.[44] An indulgence was thus a fetishized sign, representing in falsely objective form a determinate amount of subjective activity, and it was believed to be valuable and efficacious in itself. It was, that is to say, a form of *paper money*. Luther's revelation that religious and financial fetishism follow an identical, deluded logic was deeply and thoroughly assimilated by the collective consciousness of Protestant Europe. In fact, it was taken for granted throughout the sixteenth and seventeenth centuries. A century and a half after Luther's *Theses*, the Earl of Rochester casually observed that "If Rome can pardon sin, as Romans hold, / And if these pardons can be bought and sold, / It were no sin t'adore, and worship gold." Rochester can hardly be accused of excessive Protestant zeal, and he obviously feels that he is repeating a suave truism rather than engaging in theological controversy.[45] Alexander Cooke's address to a "Masse Priest" (1630) adopts a tone of amused incredulity:

> I reade in your bookes, that as in the old law there was a Treasury to keepe money in for the use of the poore; so now there is in the Church a treasurie to keepe spitituall commodities in for the use of such, who having their sinnes forgiven them, are yet liable to great punishments, either here or in Purgatorie. Which spirituall commodities are raised (as you tell us) of the surplussage of Christ's sufferings . . . [46]

In his Germanic naivete, Luther was shocked and outraged to discover that the indulgence system was no temporary aberration of papal policy, but merely an especially egregious abuse of an ecclesiastical system that was, as he saw it, openly run on market principles. This commodification of religion is the crux of Luther's case against Rome. In his *Appeal to the Ruling Class of the German Nationality* (1520) he informs his audience of

> . . . a state of affairs in Rome that beggars description. You can find there a buying and selling, a bartering and a bargaining, a lying and trickery, robbery and stealing, pomp, procuration, knavery, and all sorts of stratagems bringing God into contempt, till it would be impossible for the Antichrist to govern more wickedly. There is nothing in Venice, Antwerp, or Cairo to compare with the fair which traffics in Rome. . . . the pope has built a market-house for the convenience of all this refined traffic, viz.: the house of the *datarius* in Rome. This is where all those resort who deal in this way in benefices and livings . . . if you bring money to this ecclesiastical market, you can buy any of the

goods.... Indeed, here the devil becomes a saint and a god: what cannot be done anywhere else in heaven or earth, can be done in this house.[47]

Luther's work evinces an intense, visceral revulsion from all forms of the market, whether ecclesiastical or secular.[48] In fact, he does not thoroughly differentiate between the "ecclesiastical market" described above and the worldly operations of capital's early concentrations. It did not escape his attention that the Papacy was deeply in debt to the Fuggers and that, in order to protect their investment, these capitalists were orchestrating the Papacy's commodification of salvation (including, although Luther was unaware of this at the time, the visit of Tetzel to Wittenberg, which provoked the 95 theses). In fact, the transfer of indulgence moneys was the first large-scale international operation carried out by the Fuggers, and the foundation on which they built their fortune.[49] In Luther's opinion, things had reached the point at which the "ecclesiastical market" and the financial market can be said to have undergone a merger:

> ... the business is now to be transferred, and sold to Fugger of Augsburg. Henceforward bishoprics and livings for sale or exchange or in demand, and dealings in the spiritualities, have arrived at their true destination, now that the bargaining for spiritual or secular properties has become united into a single business. But I would like to hear of a man who is clever enough to discover what Avarice of Rome might do which has not already been done. Then perhaps Fugger would transfer and sell to someone else these two lines of business which are now to be combined into one. (430)

Luther described the effects of this commodification on every aspect of dogma and liturgy;[50] but for brevity's sake we must confine our discussion to the paradigmatic instance of the Mass. As is well known, Luther did not object to the doctrine of the Real Presence. He was quite convinced that the bread and wine were literally the body and blood of Christ. His difference with the Catholic church lay in his understanding of how this was possible. The Catholics used Aristotle to argue that the substances of the sacraments were transformed, while their accidents remained the same, and that this "transubstantiation" was effected by the ritualistic actions of the priest. The Mass, in this view, was something that the priest *did,* it was a "finished work," or *opus operatum*.[51] The consequence of this doctrine was that the priestly labor of the mass was rendered efficacious, and thus valuable, in itself. It became a *thing,* a commodity that could be bought and sold. In the *Commentary on Galatians* (1531), Luther observes that

> ... the more we know the profanation of the papistical Mass, so much the more we abhor and detest the same, and embrace the true use of the Mass, which the Pope hath taken away, and hath made merchandise thereof, that being bought for money, it might profit others. For he saith that the massing priest, an apostate denying Christ and blaspheming the Holy Ghost, standing at the altar, doth a good work, not only for himself, but also for others, both quick and dead, and for the whole Church, and that only by the work wrought, and by no other means. (114)

The Mass thus functions as a synecdoche for every kind of "works righteousness." By this term, Luther means the belief that fleshly, human actions can be efficacious in the justification of the soul. To Luther, such "works righteousness" was idolatry—it was the fetishization of "the works of men's hands." In contrast to this opinion, Luther claims that the transformation of the sacrament, and thus its salvationary power, is effected through the word of God's promise, which is received with faith by the communicant. Since this is so, there is no need for the hair-splitting distinction between substantial and accidental change, for the miraculous power of Christ is bound by no such distinctions. Luther thus advances the theory of the Mass which has become known as "consubstantiation":

> Why could not Christ maintain His body within the substance of the bread as truly as within its accidents? Iron and fire are two substances which mingle together in red-hot iron in such a way that every part contains both iron and fire. Why cannot the glorified body of Christ be similarly found in every part of the substance of the bread? (267–8)

In Luther's view, the only obstacle to universal recognition of this truth is the fact that it would refute the doctrine that the priest's actions effected a transubstantiation and thus make impossible the commodification of fetishized ecclesiastical labor against which he protests:

> ... there is no belief more widely accepted in the church today, or one of greater force, than that the mass is a good work and a sacrifice. And this abuse has brought in its train innumerable other abuses; and these, when faith in the sacrament has completely died away, turn the holy sacrament into mere merchandise, a market, and a business run for

profit. This is the origin of the special feasts, the confraternities, intercessions, merits, anniversaries and memorial days. Things of this kind are bought and sold in the church, dealt in and bargained for, the whole income of priests and monks depending on it. (271)

Luther describes these commodified services as "Specters" (282) because, like the *eidola*, they are objectified representations ("works") of a properly subjective activity ("faith"). As we have seen, this is the universal definition of an idol, and Luther clearly understands the Catholic Mass as idolatrous. But what it truly significant for our project is the clarity with which Luther also understands that this process of idolatrous fetishization is the direct result and necessary consequence of commodification. One further example will have to suffice to establish this point. In the treatise usually translated as *The Babylonian Captivity of the Church*, Luther bluntly equates this "captivity" in the land of idols with the commodification of salvation:

> But, you will say: What is this? Surely your contentions will overturn the practices and purposes of the all churches and monasteries, and destroy those by which they have waxed rich for many centuries, since they have been founded on masses at anniversaries, intercessions, "applications," "communications." You will deprive them of their largest incomes. My answer is: That is the very thing which led me to write that the church has been taken prisoner. (284)

In Luther's critique of the Mass, then, we encounter a highly developed account of commodity fetishism as the adoration of the sign and the objectification of the subject. It is a sophisticated point, but it was confirmed by empirical observation, and so amenable to general comprehension. The popular Protestant literature of the Reformation era teems with doggerel condemning the Mass as commodification, as in Hugh Hilarie's "The Resurreccion of the Masse" (1554), where the Anglican "Communion" accuses the Catholic "Mass":

> The Sacrament of Christes body and bloud
> By you Antichristes is defyled vtterly
> Marchandyse ye make of it as ye were woode
> And dayly to your chapmen ye sell it for monye (557–60)[52]

The violence of Luther's reaction against Aristotle, whom he calls a "beast" and a "wretched man," is almost Oedipal in its neurotic vehemence. The Aristotelian–Thomistic interpretation of the Eucharist drew a distinction between appearance (the "accidents") and essence (the "substance"). Luther was appalled by this, because he could not accept that Christ would present himself under a form of appearance other than his own. Christ did not hide his substance beneath an accidental disguise of bread and wine. The lack of change in the empirical appearance of the bread and wine thus did not refute the accidental manifestation of Christ, it simply meant that the distinction between "substance" and "accidents" was a human illusion.

V

If this distinction was an illusion, however, it was an extremely widespread and strongly tenacious one. The Catholic Mass demanded that the communicant accept that the bread and wine cease to be what they appeared to be. This was easy enough for a mind brought up on Aristotelian distinctions. But Luther asked his followers to believe that the bread and wine ceased to *appear* to be what they appeared to be. Luther demanded that the communicant perceive Christ in the accidents, in the empirical manifestation of the bread and wine, just as much as in its spiritual significance. For Luther, the empirical appearance of the bread and wine *was* God. Like Bacon's epistemology, Luther's Eucharistic doctrine boils down to an assertion of the sacredness of surfaces, of the holiness of the given, of the Real Presence in the sign. What Luther found idolatrous was not the adoration of the sign but the belief that the sign was made sacred by the fetishized actions of the priest.

The subtlety of Luther's critique is clearly revealed when we compare his notion of idolatry with that of the more radical Protestant "fanatics," or *Schwarmer*, whom he soon came to view as more dangerous enemies than the Pope. The most prominent of these was Andreas Karlstadt, who evaded the intricacies of Luther's sacramental doctrine by simply denying the Real Presence altogether.[53] For Karlstadt, the Eucharist was only a sign that indicated and commemorated, but did not contain, its divine referent. Karlstadt and his followers thus espoused a nominalist view of the sacrament, and they extended this view to any kind of material representation of the Divinity. Their argument was monophysite: They denied the efficacy of the flesh. Images, in Karlstadt's view, "do not lead further than the flesh . . . from the image of Christ you learn only about the suffering of Christ in the flesh, how his head hung down and the like. Now Christ says that his own flesh is of no use but that the spirit is of use and gives life (John 6:63)."[54] All images are thus inherently evil, so that "God prohibits any kind of image because men are frivolous and are inclined to worship them,"[55] and "When God rises up, all likenesses fall. Where images sit, God cannot be."[56]

As his Lutheran and Catholic opponents alike immediately remarked, Karlstadt has an almost Manichean fear of images and their power. For Luther, images are essentially things indifferent; he does not ascribe to them any real power, and he therefore does not object to their existence. It does not matter to God whether or not human beings look at images, and to pretend that it does bespeaks a faith in the importance of human actions that falls under the definition of "works righteousness." Karlstadt, in Luther's opinion, puts his faith in works of the flesh, and is therefore more of an idolater than those who venerate images: "[The *Schwarmers*'] idea that they can please God with works becomes a real idol and a false assurance in the heart. Such legalism results in putting away outward things while filling the heart with idols."[57] For Karlstadt, images were active, dangerous forces that must be physically destroyed like an invading army. Not only Lutheran, but also Catholic opponents of Karlstadt, such as Hieronymous Emser, saw this attitude as idolatrous:

> If one has never trusted someone, then that person cannot deceive him. Now we Christians seek no solace in images or place any trust in them. Therefore, they are not able to deceive us. But Karlstadt not only says that images are deceitful, he also calls them scoundrels and murderers and says that they bring death to those who worship them.[58]

In fairness, however, Karlstadt often analyses his own psychological reaction to images, and he freely confesses that this reaction is idolatrous in character. By Karlstadt's logic, however, the idolatrous reaction images provoke—whether that reaction is worshipfully reverent or, as in his own case, violently hostile—is a further argument in favor of destroying them:

> But (I lament to God) from my youth onward my heart has been trained and grown up in the veneration and worship of pictures. And a harmful fear has been bred into me from which I would gladly deliver myself and cannot. As a consequence, I stand in fear that I might not be able to burn idols. I would fear that some devil's block of wood [i.e., an idol] would do me injury.[59]

During the early years of the Reformation, as in the Byzantine controversy, the fiercest opponents of icons and images tended to be those who believed most strongly in their power. The sacramental hermeneutics of John Calvin, however, ameliorated the heretical tendencies of the radicals and provided a dialectical synthesis that reconciled the incarnationalism of Luther with the nominalism of Karlstadt. As Calvin himself stated his dilemma:

> ... two faults are here to be avoided. We must neither, by setting too little value on the signs, dissever them from their meanings to which they are in some degree annexed, nor by immoderately extolling them, seem somewhat to obscure the mysteries themselves.[60]

On the one hand, the Catholics "who devised the adoration of the sacrament ... forsook the living God, and fabricated a god for themselves, after the lust of their own hearts. For what is idolatry if it is not to worship the gifts instead of the giver?"[61] From this perspective, Luther remains "half-papist" because of his belief that the Real Presence inhered in the empirical, accidental qualities of the bread and wine: "He has sinned ... from ignorance and the grossest extravagance. For what absurdities he pawned upon us ... when he said the bread is the very body! ... a very foul error!"[62] Luther has lapsed into literalism, which is the hermeneutic form of objectification. Calvin claims that the earlier reformer is unable to conceive that the Real Presence may be "spiritual" in nature. For Luther, notes Calvin, the Presence is material or it is nothing:

> Some, who see that the analogy between the sign and the things signified cannot be destroyed without destroying the truth of the sacrament, admit that the bread of the Supper is truly the substance of an earthly and corruptible element, and cannot suffer any change in itself, but must have the body of Christ included under it. ... Because they cannot conceive any other participation of flesh and blood than that which consists either in local conjunction and contract, or in some gross method of enclosing.[63]

On the other hand, Calvin is equally scathing with regard to those who claim that the sacrament is merely a sign: "In the Supper it is not presented as an empty symbol, but, as the apostle testifies, we receive the reality."[64] Karlstadt and his fellow radicals claimed that, when Christ commanded his disciples to "eat" his body, he was speaking metaphorically, using the term to indicate the figurative "eating" of faith. Calvin agrees with them, against Luther, that Christ could not possibly have meant the word "eat" literally. But he also denies that the term is metaphorical:

> Meanwhile, we admit that this is nothing else than the eating of faith, and that no other eating can be imagined, but there is this difference between their mode of speaking and mine. According to them, to eat is merely to believe; while I maintain that the flesh of Christ is eaten by believing, because it is made ours by faith, and that that eating is the effect and fruit of faith; or, if you will have it more clearly, according to them, eating is faith, whereas it rather seems to me to be a consequence of faith. The difference is little in words, but not little in reality.[65]

In the Calvinist view, the bread of the sacrament is neither the literal body of Christ nor a mere sign of that body. For him, the bread is really the body, and it is *also* figuratively the body. Calvin's epochal breakthrough in the Sacramentarian Controversy was his realization that a figurative presence could be real. The fact that Christ is present in the bread only nominally, and not essentially, is for Calvin no obstacle to the belief that he is really present within it. The words of Christ at the Last Supper are to be read neither literally nor metaphorically, but *metonymically:*

> It remains, therefore, to hold, that on account of the affinity which the things signified have with their signs, the name of the thing itself is given to the sign figuratively, indeed, but very appropriately. . . . I say that the expression which is uniformly used in Scripture, when the sacred mysteries are treated of, is metonymical. . . . For although the sign differs essentially from the thing signified, the latter being spiritual and heavenly, the former corporeal and visible,—yet, as it not only figures the thing which it is employed to represent as a naked and empty badge, but also truly exhibits it, why should not its name be justly applied to the thing?[66]

This became the official Eucharistic doctrine of the Calvinist churches including, most importantly for our purposes, the Anglican. Number 28 of the 39 Articles declares that "The body of Christ is given, taken, and eaten in the Supper, only after an heavenly and spiritual manner. And the means whereby the body of Christ is received and eaten in the Supper is faith." The body of Christ is really consumed by the communicant, but this reality is not physical. This kind of reality occupies a level above the physical, it is a "heavenly and spiritual" reality, a reality that consists in the recognition of the real power of a sign. It is, in the strictest sense, a "hyper-reality." This concept, then as now, was arrived at through a process of abstruse reasoning, but Anglican propagandists were adept at simplification. Gregory Scott's *Against the Sacrifice of the Masse* (1574) expresses the basics in accessible form:

> Therfore the bread and wyne do beare
> (we neede not thinke it straunge)
> The names of thynges they signifye,
> yet substance doth not chaunge.
> The outwarde visible Sacramentes,
> the mouth doth taste alone,
> But spirituall foode is geuen therby,
> which faith must feede vpon.[67] (177–84)

Let us recall again the difference between this Calvinist reading of the sacrament and that of Karlstadt. Both agree that the bread and wine do not contain the body and blood in any literal sense—the sacrament is a sign. For Karlstadt, however, it follows that the body and blood are not really present in the sacrament at all, and the purpose of the sacrament is merely to remind us of Christ's sacrifice. For Calvin, on the other hand, the tropological significance of the sacrament is a *reality*. Calvin's sacramental theory is a portentous occasion in the history of semiotics; it represents the moment at which the distinction between literal and symbolic signification no longer holds. As we saw in chapter one, this is the same conclusion to which the early political economists were led when they argued that the reality of exchange value was undiminished by the fact that it had only an imaginary existence. For Calvin, the Eucharist was admittedly a mere sign, but it was an efficacious sign. This is precisely the opinion of John Law with regard to money. The people of the sixteenth and seventeenth centuries were more cognizant of the consequences prophesized by this development than are the people of the third millennium. But it is worth bearing in mind during the following chapters that this blindness has not fallen upon us because those prophecies have been falsified, but because they have been fulfilled.

Chapter Three

Idolatry and Commodity Fetishism in the Antitheatrical Controversy

> *Let us suppose the existence of two objects: one of them shall be Cratylus, and the other the image of Cratylus; and we will suppose, further, that some God makes not only a representation such as a painter would make of your outward form and colour, but also creates an inward organization like yours, having the same warmth and softness; and into this infuses motion, and soul, and mind, such as you have, in a word copies all your qualities, and places them by you in another form; would you say that this was Cratylus and the image of Cratylus, or that there were two Cratyluses?*
>
> —*Plato*, Cratylus

> *The "difference" from the model, which Plato and Dionysus the Areopagite judged necessary, has now been erased, and hyperrealism produces a "Mme. Tussaud" version of our world, which is frightening because nature returns like the ghost of a murder victim.*
>
> —*Alain Besancon*, The Forbidden Image[1]

I

In the preceding chapters we have tried to establish the theological and philosophical bases for the early modern homology between idolatry and commodity fetishism. Clearly, disputes between Baconians and Aristotelians, and even those between Calvinists and Lutherans, remained largely academic. However, I believe that this homology was also detectable at less rarified altitudes. This chapter examines its influence on a practical issue that affected the everyday lives of all Elizabethan and Jacobean Londoners and that is known to posterity as the antitheatrical controversy. The dispute over the early modern English theater turned on the distinction between the "use" and the "abuse" of plays. The antitheatricalists generally claimed that they were not opposed to the theater per se, but only to its "abuse." John Northbrooke explains that:

> As farre as good excercises and honest pastimes & plays doe benefit the health of manne, and recreate his wittes, so farre I speake not against it, but the excessive and unmeasurable use thereof, taketh away the right institution thereof, and bringeth abuse and misuse . . . and therefore they are rather chaunged into faults and transgressions, than honest exercises for mans recreation.[2]

Stephen Gosson cautions his readers that "I touche but the abuses. . . . When we accuse the Phicition for killing his patient, we finde no faulte with the Arte itselfe, but with him that hath abused the same,"[3] while Thomas Nashe denies that the antitheatricalists have truly made this distinction: "[they] extend their invectives so farre against the abuse, that almost the things remaines not whereof they admitte anie lawfull use."[4] Thomas Heywood makes the same point in 1612, when he writes of acting:

> I hope there is no man of so unsensible a spirit, that can inveigh against the true . . . use of this quality: Oh but say they, the Romanes in their time, and some in these days have abused it, and therefore we volly out our exclamations against the use. Oh shallow! . . . The use of any generall thing is not for any one particular abuse to be condemned.[5]

Francis Rous concedes this tendency in some antitheatricalists but ascribes it to the enormity of the abuse. Acting is lawful in itself, he notes, "But such great abuses, have defiled this kind of Representation, that it hath not onely left the true and naturall profit of it, but it hath seemed to many grave and godlie men rather fit to be taken away than hopefull to be cured."[6] Even supporters of the stage are at pains to note that they are not defending the "abuses" to which, they confess, that medium can be subjected. John Taylor concluded that "Playes are good or bad, as they are us'd, / And best intentions often are abus'd"[7] and Thomas Lodge's position is typical: "I wish as zealously as the best that all abuse of playing weare abolished, but for the thing, the antiquitie causeth me to allow it, so it be used as it should be."[8]

How can we define this all-important "abuse" of the theater? After all, most writers are quite willing to allow religious and educational drama, and private performances or court masques rarely draw antitheatrical fire. The main objection, it seems, is not to the theater per se but to the startlingly new form taken by the theater in Elizabethan London. The most conspicuous novelty to scandalize puritan opinion was the fact that the playing companies had become commercial enterprises, selling a product for a fee. Again and again, the tracts deplore the fact that the public playhouses charge admission, and they decry the aesthetic effect of the consequent need to pander to popular taste. The "abuse" of the theater, in short, involved its *commodification*, and to "abuse" poetry was to transform it into a commodity to be traded on the market.[9]

In Elizabethan England, the term "abuse" referred to various forms of the subversion of natural teleology. Puttenham's *English Poesie* (1589) uses it to translate "catachresis," which is "the Figure of abuse ... if for lacke of naturall and proper terme or worde we take another, neither naturall nor proper and do vntruly applie it to the thing which we would seeme to expresse."[10] In 1598, an English gloss on Aristotle observed that exchange value "appertaine not to the proper use of a shoe, which is to be worne, and for that purpose it is made, and not to be exchanged, though the shoemaker abuse it to exchange."[11] The anonymous author of this pamphlet comments that usury "abuseth naturall vertues, and also both sciences and faculties, which it maketh mercenary and ministers to get money; as though such were their end."[12]

The taboo against commercialism is evident throughout the antitheatrical controversy. The first act passed against plays by the London City Council in 1574 specifically exempted from its ban all performances "withowte publique or Common Collection of money of the Auditorie or behoulders thereof."[13] Northbrooke makes a point of noting that he supports plays, so long as they are not performed "publicly for profit and gain of money, but for learning and excersise sake"; however "prodligalitie is to bestow money and goods, in suche sort as is spent, either in banqueting, feasting, rewardes to plaiers of Enterludes ... to give thy goodes to Enterlude and Stage players is a great vice and sinne."[14] Anthony Munday summarizes the case concisely: "Who writeth for reward, neither regardeth virtue, nor truth; but runs unto falsehood, because he flattereth for commoditie."[15]

John Gager denied that actors are infamous in themselves: "they are not all, but only such as play for gaine," and in reply John Rainoldes grumbled, "Doe we not see before our eyes, howe he that can hardly be drawn to spare a penie in the Church, can yet willingly and chearfullie afoord both pence and teasters enow for himself and others at a play?"[16] For Dudley Fenner, "abuse" involved the sin of prodigality: "he which doth play more away then he may well without any doubt or scruple bestow upon honest delight ... doeth abuse his recreation,"[17] and William Prynne confirms that "the very giving of money to Players as Players; that is, for the exercising of their lewde lascivious art, is prodigality."[18] Henry Chettle (1592) merrily imagines the ghost of the actor Richard Tarleton parodying the antitheatricalists in the same terms: "Fie uppon following plaies, the expence is wondrous. . . . Is it not lamentable that a man should spende his two pence on them in an after-noone . . . ?"[19] William Rankins carefully limits "abuse" to the public, commercial theater, thus tactfully exempting court entertainments: "that is poison to some, which is medicinable to others, and of a particular good, by abuse may spring a generall evill."[20]

The very existence of the public theater obviously presupposed a consumer economy.[21] Because they had to appeal to popular taste—to the market—in order to turn a profit, the playing companies were indeed rather vulnerable to charges that they diluted, degraded, or "abused" the gifts of the Muses, subordinating aesthetic purity to financial gain.[22] Even those generally well disposed toward the stage draw this connection. Thus Thomas Dekker notes that

> The Theater is your poets' Royal Exchange upon which their Muses (that are now turned to merchants) meeting, barter away that light commodity of words for a lighter ware then words—plaudites and the breath of the great beast; which (like the threatnings of two cowards) vanish all into air.[23]

In sixteenth- and seventeenth-century England, the rise of a consumer culture, the growth in the power of money, the exaltation of the mercantile classes, and the new social mobility combined to produce a crisis in traditional understandings of hierarchy and order. The antitheatricalists find this phenomenon exemplified in the "shape-shifting" on the stage, and they rail against the theater's explicit violation of stable identity, which they connect with its commercialism. "A Player," writes Gosson in 1582, "is like to a Marchant's finger, that standes sometime for a thousande, sometime for a cypher."[24] In his view, playhouses were "the very markets of bawdry, where choise without shame hath bene as free, as it is for your money in the royall exchaung, to take a short stocke or a longe, a falling bond, or a french ruffe."[25]

Several critics have recently analyzed the relations between the Elizabethan public theater and the rapidly growing consumer economy.[26] Jean-Christophe Agnew argues persuasively that the stage provided "an intelligible, formal analogue of the increasingly fugitive and abstract social relations of a burgeoning market economy"[27] while Jean Howard observes that the playhouses functioned as an "instructive synecdoche"[28] for the social dislocation which characterized an increasingly commercial milieu. In the rest of this chapter, I want to suggest that, just as the plays performed in the theaters reflected and analyzed the effect of market relations on subjectivity, so the critics of the theater elaborated a coherent and sophisticated critique of the ideological and psychological effects of a commodity culture. I will argue that even those who wrote for the theater themselves recognized similar effects of commercialization on their medium, and I will illustrate this through a reading of John Marston's *Histrio-Mastix*. The key to this critique of commodification lies in the concept of "abuse," and I intend to trace the genealogy of that concept in order to show how it came to describe the psychological consequences of large-scale commodity exchange.

It might perhaps be objected at this point that my reading of the antitheatrical literature is selective and tendentious. While it is obviously true that the pamphleteers attack the commercialization of the stage, are they not finally more concerned with its supposedly Satanic, pagan and papist origins? Is not the major objection against the stage that it fosters idolatry? In fact, is not idolatry, rather than commodification, the usual significance of the word "abuse"?[29] It is certainly true that the antitheatricalists emphasize the idolatrous nature and ancestry of stage-plays; John Stockwood is typical is his claim that "they were first instituted in the honor of the vile idols, and filthy Gods of the Gentiles."[30] Equally certainly, the term "abuse" could and did refer to idolatry. Rous notes that, although the painting of religious images is good per se, "It hath been abused to Idolatry, eyther while that which is worshipped is painted, or that which is painted is worshipped"[31] while, considering the question of whether the use of religious images led inevitably to idolatry, John Donne concluded that "if the true use of pictures bee preached unto them, there is no danger of an abuse."[32] In 1636, John Weemse recalled that the "Ephod which Gideon appointed for an holy use, was afterwards abused, and turned into an Idoll,"[33] and in 1659 Henry Clarke reminded his audience of Edward VI's command that "such feigned Images . . . which were abused by pilgrimage and offerings, were to be taken down without delay."[34] However, my claim is that the valence given to the word "abuse" by the antitheatricalists *combines* the senses of commodification and idolatry, and that this combination gives the concept its explanatory and rhetorical power.[35]

One important source of the antitheatrical concept of "abuse" is Augustine's *Christian Doctrine*. In that work, a distinction is made between those things that are intended for our "use" and those that are intended for our "enjoyment." Augustine constructs this polarity along Aristotelian lines:

> Those things which are objects of enjoyment make us happy. Those things which are objects of use assist, and (so to speak) support us in our efforts after happiness, so that we can attain the things that make us happy and rest in them. We ourselves, again, who enjoy and use these things, being placed among both kinds of objects, if we set ourselves to enjoy those which we ought to use, are hindered in our course, and sometimes even led away from it; so that, getting entangled in the love of lower gratifications, we lag behind in, or even altogether turn back from, the pursuit of the real and proper objects of enjoyment.[36]

Happiness is produced in the pursuit of virtue, which is the proper *telos* of man, and Augustine reserves the term "enjoyment" for experiences that produce this end. Things that are merely means to this end we ought to "use." When we confuse the means with the ends, we run into "abuse," which, from Augustine's Christian perspective, consists in worldliness and sensuality, which he calls "the love of lower gratifications." The abusive consciousness pursues an inappropriate end, attempting to find happiness in the things of this world: "For to enjoy a thing is to rest with satisfaction in it for its own sake. To use, on the other hand, is to employ whatever means are at one's disposal to obtain what one desires, if it is a proper object of desire; for an unlawful use ought rather to be called an abuse."[37]

The contemporaries of the antitheatricalists habitually remarked that idolatry and commodity fetishism were complementary forms of this worldly "abuse." Thomas Cooper, writing in 1621, intends both of these senses when he observes that "by the gathering and abusing of these earthly things, it is more manifest that Worldlings engage their soules for them."[38] The section of the *Book of Common Prayer* entitled "Of Ceremonies" uses "abuse" to refer to fetishism in general, whether avaricious or iconic:

> ... the most weighty cause of the abolishment of certain Ceremonies was, That they were so far abused, partly by the superstitious blindness of the rude and unlearned, and partly by the unsatiable avarice of such as sought more their own lucre, than the glory of God, that the abuses could not well be taken away, the thing remaining still.[39]

The anonymous author of *The Massacre of Money* (1602) encapsulates the popular understanding of "abuse's" financial effects. Addressing money, he remarks

> Though in thy selfe lyes no disaster crosse,
> Yet in thy usage stands or good, or losse.
> We neuer knew that Natures holy Nature
> Created ought to a prepost'rous end,
> Good in it selfe we know is euery creature,
> And from it selfe doth good effects intend.
> Yet using vertue in an euill cause,
> We guiltie are of breaking vertues lawes.
> Siluer is framed to a good entent,
> To be reducted to the shape of coine,
> So to buy corne, land, houses, nutriment,
> If any man bribe with it or purloine,
> Turning th'good creature to a wicked use,
> The creature's blameles: t'is the mans abuse.[40]

It seems to me that the notion of "abuse," as it is employed in the antitheatrical pamphlets, mingles an attack on idolatry with a critique of commercialization to produce a sophisticated diagnosis of the psychological tendency we know as "commodity fetishism." But the antitheatricalists are also concerned with one particularly egregious and symptomatic instance of "abuse," which they identify specifically with the visual spectacle of the theater. To understand how this became possible, we will need to return to another patristic source of their arguments: the early polemical diatribes of Tertullian.[41]

II

Writing in Carthage around the end of the second century A.D., the newly converted Tertullian was preoccupied with the problem of how to live as a Christian in a pagan state. To what degree could a Christian compromise with and participate in the rituals and customs of Rome? Tertullian devoted three treatises to this question—*Idolatry*, *Spectacles* and *The Apparel of Women*. As his modern editors note, the first of these might seem rather redundant. Its purpose is to forbid Christians from practicing idolatry, a prohibition surely obvious to all and clearly stated in the first two commandments. Tertullian's point, however, is that "idolatry" means far more than the worship of idols. As he puts it:

> Idolatry is the chief crime of mankind, the supreme guilt of the world, the entire case put before judgement. For even if every sin retains its own identity and even if each is destined for judgment under its own name, each is still committed within idolatry . . . all sins are found in idolatry and idolatry in all sins.[42]

Everything, in fact, can be regarded in an idolatrous light, and idolatry is a psychological habit rather than an external form of worship. In *Spectacles,* this provides Tertullian with his refutation of the argument that attendance at the Roman games and theaters was permissible for a Christian, because the creatures and people exhibited therein have been created by God. It is true, concedes Tertullian, that animals and actors are created by God and thus good in themselves, but "the real issue is idolatry."[43] Since the Fall, Satan has perverted the good things of this world away from their proper uses, so that postlapsarian humanity is under a constant temptation to turn things away from their God-given purpose. This is what happens when animals and people are exhibited for gain and pleasure by the theaters. His opponents, proclaims Tertullian

> must be unaware of the rival power that by its hostile actions seeks to pervert to wrong uses the things of divine creation. . . . We must, then, consider not only by whom all things were created, but also by whom they were perverted. For in this way it will become clear for what use they were created, once it is evident for what use they were not.[44]

So human beings may "use" the things of creation properly or, led astray by Satan, they may use them improperly. This improper usage involves a fetishization that is analogous to the adoration of an object which takes place in idolatry. In *The Apparel of Women,* Tertullian gives as an example of this "abuse" the fetishistic financial value that human beings impose upon gold, and that has therefore become known as *valor impositus.* Tertullian contrasts this value with natural, God-given use value:

> But the basic nature of iron and brass and of other metals, including the cheapest, is the same [as that of gold and silver], both as to their

earthly origin and manufacture in the mines, and hence, according to nature itself, the substance of gold and silver is no more noble than theirs. Should, however, gold and silver derive their estimation from the quality of being useful, then certainly the value of iron and brass is higher. . . . Certainly you will never plow a field with a golden plow nor will any ship be held together with silver bolts. . . . The only thing that gives glamour to all these articles is that they are rare and that they have to be imported from a foreign country. In the country they come from they are not highly priced. When a thing is abundant it is always cheap. . . . Therefore, those things cannot be the best by nature which do not come from God, who is the Author of nature. Hence, they must be understood to be from the Devil, who is the corrupter of nature.[45]

Exchange value, according to Tertullian, is idolatrous and Satanic, but the sin lies in the adoration, not in the idol adored.[46] Consequently, anything could be an idol if it was regarded in an idolatrous manner. It is the duty of a Christian, therefore, to "safeguard ourselves against the abundance of idolatry by not only recognizing it in its conspicuous manifestations,"[47] but by also rooting out the temptation to idolatry, which is offered even by seemingly innocuous institutions such as the theater.

Tertullian is thus of the view that everything in the world partakes of two quite distinct epistemological conditions: a proper, Godly use and an idolatrous, Satanic abuse. The influence of this notion on the Renaissance debate over the stage is obvious; all of the participants accept and repeat this assumption. Northbrooke is typical: "There is nothing used, but that also maye be abused. For God in mercie giveth us nothing (be it never so good) but the devil is presently busie to draw us to the abuse thereof."[48] Like most of the antitheatricalists, Gosson approvingly cites

> Tertullian, who noteth verie well that the Devill foreseeinge the ruine of his kingdome, both invented these shewes, and inspired men with devises to set them out the better to enlarge his dominion and pull us from God. . . . [Plays were] suckt from the Devill's teate to nurce us Idolatrie.[49]

The idea that a thing may be either "used" or "abused" rests upon Aristotelian teleology, which holds that any thing is "used" properly when it is directed towards its natural *telos* or "end." When it is directed towards an end that is not proper to it, a thing is said to be perverted away from its natural condition. The Aristotelian understanding of "abuse" can be summarized in the words of John Howson, castigating the unrighteous in 1597 for their inability

> to discerne between the true use of that which is good, and the abuse of it; nor betweene that fault that proceedeth *ex natura facti*, out of the nature of the fact it selfe, because it is *malum simpliciter*, simply evill, and that which proceedeth *ex abusu boni*, from the abuse of that which is good, which is *malum per accidens*, evill but by an accident . . . [50]

What is important for our purposes is the fact, which we noted in the introduction, that Aristotle identifies this unnatural use of an object with commodity exchange. This, I think, is what the antitheatricalists mean when they say that the commercial theater is an "abuse" of poetry. It is art designed with the primary end of making money. But making money is not the natural *telos* of art. Therefore, according to Aristotelian teleology, the commercial theater is bad art. This, it seems to me, is the philosophical heritage of Renaissance antitheatricalism.[51]

The clearest departure of the puritan antitheatricalists from Aristotle involves their use of a Christian vocabulary. Here they draw on Augustine's concept of *abusus*, and on Tertullian, who describes the perversion of things away from their natural essences as "idolatry" and ascribes it to the devil. Whereas Aristotle calls the values that human convention attaches to things over and above their teleological essences "unnatural," Tertullian calls this kind of value Satanic. The grafting of conventional exchange value onto natural use value was a kind of re-creation, a twisting and distorting of things away from their proper condition. This Satanic creation takes place within the minds of fallen humanity, and its viewpoint is idolatrous and fetishistic. Here, I think, we can see why the antitheatricalists of early modern London could equate "abuse" simultaneously with commodification and idolatry. We have seen how during this period idolatry and commodification could both be designated by the term "abuse." The public stage provided a nexus in which this solicitation to psychological abuse in the audience neatly converged with the exhibition on the stage of the kind of mercurial shifts in social identity that characterize a market society. Such social mobility also represents a departure from natural, divinely ordained identity and it seems to offer yet another instance of "abuse." The concatenation of idolatry, commodification, and "shape-shifting" on the stage and in the antitheatrical literature produced a clear and specific critique of the ideological effects of a commodity culture.

What are those effects? The antitheatricalists argue that the idolatrous commodification of the theater produces a fleshly, carnal mode of perception—a thoroughgoing *objectification* of consciousness. They all remark, for example, that the theater relies on a visual, sensual, medium of signification, which is intrinsically corrupting. As Prynne notes, "It is marvelous to consider how the gesturing of a plaier, which Tullie termeth the eloquence of the bodie, is of force to move, and prepare a man to that which is ill."[52] Once again, this results in a fetishized or "idolatrous" sensibility, and the adoration of human figures upon the stage leads to a correspondingly objectified view of human beings in general. Thus Anthony Munday declares that "None delight in those spectacles, but such as would be made spectacles . . . harlots, utterlie past all shame: who presse to the forefrunt of the scaffoldes, to the end to show their impudencie, and to be as an object to all mens eies."[53]

For Francis Rous, the transvestism of the boy actors provided a similar temptation: "[I] wish that there were not so much merchandize of Play-boyes, nor so much counterfeiting intisement to that trafficke."[54] The sensual vices that accompany the public stage are similar in kind to the action performed on that stage: They are fleshly pleasures and thus intimately connected to the carnal (and papist) hermeneutic that the theater also allegedly inculcated. This argument finds patristic inspiration in Tertullian's strictures, and also in Augustine's observation that "it is a servile infirmity to follow the letter and to take signs for the things they signify."[55] In its "puritan" form the argument connects play-acting to the Catholic doctrine of the Eucharist. As we saw in chapter two, the notion that the bread and wine are literally transubstantiated into the body and blood of Christ was held, by Protestants, to be the paradigmatic instance of idolatry. The antitheatricalists were not slow to point out that the drama presupposes a similarly iconic identity of sign and referent. As early as 1558, Bartholomew Traheron referred to the Mass as "the popes toiysh apes plaie."[56] Gosson emphasizes the historical and hermeneutical connections between the Mass and the drama when he cites

> Naziancen detesting the corruption of the Corpus Christi Playes that were set out by the Papistes, and inveighing against them, thought it was better to write the passion of Christ in numbers him selfe, that all such as delight in numerositie of speach might read it, not beholde it upon the Stage, where some base fellowe that plaide Christe, should bring the person of Christ into contempt.[57]

Fifty years later, William Prynne declares of the Catholic Eucharist: "Loe here a Roman Masse-priest becomes a Player, and in stead of preaching, of reading, acts Christ's Passion in the Masse, which this Author stiles, a Tragedy."[58] To Gosson and Prynne, it is clear, the incarnational understanding of the Mass links it irrefutably with the drama, in which the audience must pretend that the character being represented is incarnated in the material body of the actor. This common hermeneutic means that the Mass and stage-plays are fundamentally similar, as Prynne emphasizes:

> . . . as they have turned the Sacrament of Christ's body and blood into a Masse-play; so they have likewise transformed their Masse it-selfe, together with the whole Story of Christ's birth, his life, his Passion, and all other parts of their Ecclesiastical service into Stage-playes.[59]

Prynne's conclusion, reached by logical deduction about the nature of stage-plays rather than by empirical verification, is that "Papists are much addicted to Playes, many of our Players being such."[60] We can thus see that one of the fundamental charges against the stage was that it inherited a papist model of iconic representation. It collapsed the sign into the referent, thereby denying the proper mediating role of signification, as exemplified in the Calvinist reading of the Eucharist as merely symbolic of Christ. The theater, like the mass, fostered an idolatry of the sign and a fetishistic objectification of the media of signification.[61]

III

In addition to inculcating this idolatrous hermeneutic, the theater was also portrayed as a metonym for the market economy and therefore as complicit in the destruction of the feudal order and the "natural" social relations it supported. The argument that the theater was Satanic seems almost comical today. However, if we remember the specific sense in which this term was used—as a fetishistic psychological perversion of things away from their natural conditions—then the charge comes to seem less far-fetched. It has become a critical commonplace that the concern with shifting identities and "self-fashioning" that characterizes the drama of the period somehow reflects the breakdown of stable feudal relations and the sense of a natural, God-given order in the world, which such relations foster. The fact that many late twentieth-century critics tend to applaud this development as ludic and liberatory does not rob the antitheatricalist criticisms of their coherence. Indeed, these criticisms were accepted as substantially true by all contemporaries, including many playwrights. Antitheatrical arguments are frequently echoed from the stage itself, and many plays take up positions that themselves seem antitheatrical.[62] For example, the combatants in the "War of the Theaters" enlisted many antitheatrical arguments in the effort to denigrate the theatrical techniques of their enemies. In Ben Jonson's work this frequently shades into a marked suspicion of the public stage in general; a suspicion that is no less dark for the fact that it was loudly declaimed from that very forum. In *Bartholomew Fair,* the puritan identification of idolatry and commodity fetishism is satirized in Zeal-of-the-land Busy's diatribes. Busy informs a bemused market trader that: "Thy hobby-horse is an idol, a very idol, a fierce and rank idol; and thou the Nebuchadnezzar, the proud Nebuchadnezzar of the Fair, that set'st it up for children to fall down and worship" (3.6.52–55). Busy goes on to rail against "this wicked and foul Fair . . . the abuses of it, the foul abuses of it . . . the merchandise of Babylon . . . this idolatrous grove of images, this flasket of idols" (3.6.79–90). Jonson's exquisite awareness of the paradox involved in preaching against the theater and the market from the commercial stage, and his subtle sense of complicity in the processes he deplores, prevent his work from acquiring the contours of an antitheatrical diatribe.[63] The same cannot be said of the play that fired the opening shot of the War of the Theaters, John Marston's *Histrio-Mastix.*

Marston's play endorses the arguments of the antitheatricalists and it does so in insouciant disregard of the fact that it is itself a piece of theater.[64] An analysis of the play will show, however, that under the rubric of the "theater," Marston intends a great deal more than the playhouses. Because Marston writes in the very genre he attacks, the true target—for which the theater is a metonymical surrogate—is necessarily brought into sharper focus. *Histrio-Mastix* unequivocally identifies "playing" with the breakdown of feudal relations, the rise of a mercantile, money-based economy, and the disastrous ideological effects that are perceived to follow thereon.

Throughout the play, Marston links the fortunes of the aspiring merchants with the vogue for the buffoonish commercial playing company. We are introduced to a drunken company of rude mechanicals—a beard-maker, a peddler, and so on. They are weary of these occupations:

> INCLE: This Peace breeds such Plenty, trades serve no turns.
> BELCH: The more fooles we to follow them.

> POSTE-HASTE: Lett's make up a company of Players. (B)

The group of merchants and lawyers that enters next debates the relative merits of the "liberall Arts" and the plebian playhouses. They conclude in favor of the latter and soon begin to mock the scholarly labors of Chrisoganus—Marston's Jonsonesque protagonist. The plebeian players, now "Sir Oliver Owlet's Men," entice them further away from highbrow pursuits with some drunken cavortings, which prompt a passing Italian to sneer:

> Most ugly lines and base-browne-paper-stuffe
> Thus to abuse our heavenly poesie
> That sacred off-spring from the braine of Jove
> Thus to be mangled with prophane absurds,
> Strangled and chok't with lawlesse bastards words. (C3)

This violation of pristine poesie is an "abuse"—the universal antitheatrical term for degraded theatricality. Once again, we should note that poetry and theater are not condemned as such. It is the particularly disorderly and anarchic manifestation of the theater represented by the strolling company of players that is criticized. This, we are to understand, represents a new phenomenon, and its rise to prominence takes place amid the complete collapse of society. Act 3 introduces the allegorical figure of Pride, whose first act is to tempt the lawyers and merchants to break the sumptuary laws. The language of the ensuing debate is strikingly reminiscent of Northbrooke and Gosson, and it is clear that the violation of the dress code is equivalent to social mobility:

> VOUCHER: But wee have Lawes to limitte our attire.
> PRYDE: Broke with the least touch of a golden wyer.
> . . . .
> FOURCHER: Is not ambition an aspiring sinne?
> PRYDE: Yes for blind batts and birds of lazy wing.
> LYON-RASH: Me seemes tis good to keepe within our bounds
> PRYDE: Why beasts themselves of bounds are discontent (D2)

The imagery dwells on excess, superfluity, aspiration, just as in the antitheatrical literature.[65] But in Marston's play, the socially destructive impact of theatricality is even more clearly defined. Following the temptation of the ambitious middling sort detailed above, we encounter Mavortius, a noble, dismissing his feudal retainers. To their complaints that "For service, this is savage recompence. / Your fathers bought lands and maintained men:/ You sell your lands and scarce keepe rascall boyes," his Steward replies that this is a sign of the times: "all the Lords have now cashierd their trains" (D2). The reasons Mavortius gives to his friends to encourage them to follow suit are instructive:

> MAVORTIUS: My Lord Philarchus, follow all my course,
> I keepe a Taylor, Coach-man, and a Cooke,
> The rest for their boord-wages may goe looke,
> A thousand pound a yeare, will so be sav'd
> For revelling, and banquetting and playes.
> PHILARCHUS: Playes, well remembred, we will have a play.
> STEWARD: Lets have Sir Olliver Owlets men. (D3)

Feudal service is thus ousted by a debased, bastardized form of feudalism, in which "Sir Olliver Owlets men" (owlets were proverbial figures for poverty) negotiate the price of their services in the market economy. Marston's point here recalls Anthony Munday's *A Second and Third Blast of Retrait from Plaies and Theaters* (1580):

> but since the reteining of these Caterpillers, the credite of Noble men hath declined, and they are thought to be covetous by permitting their servaunts, which cannot live of themselves, and whome for neerenes they wil not maintaine, to live at the devotion or almes of other men, passing from once countrie, from one Gentlemans house to another, offering their service, which is a kind of beggarie.[66]

It is this exposure of theatrical art to the demands of the market—rather than that art itself—which is derided and blamed in Marston's *Histrio-Mastix*. We soon encounter Chrisoganus, turned playwright through poverty and reduced to hawking his works to the disreputable company of mechanicals. When they scorn his price as too high, he launches into a Jonsonian tirade—"O age when every Sriveners boy shall dippe / Prophaning quills into Thessaliaes Spring"—and condemns them to "yawle on to the common sort / Of thickskin'd auditors" (D3). Once again, it is the degradation consequent upon commercialism that is criticized, not the theater itself, for which the wise Chrisoganus is perfectly willing to write.

In *Histrio-Mastix*, then, Marston endorses the central point of the antitheatrical pamphlets: He uses the theater as a metonym for the market. The mercantile classes rise, the lower classes become wage-laborers instead of feudal retainers, the nobility feels threatened. It is noble Mavortius who first initiates the conflict into which *Histrio-Mastix*'s society degenerates, when he refuses to pay the players the price they demand, preferring to get drunk and pass out. On waking, he begins to decry the decline of the aristocracy, deploring the new state of affairs

> When broad-cloathd tradesman and what lack you sir
> Is wrapt in riche habilement of silke,
> Whilst urgent need makes Princes bend their knee
> As servile as the ignobilitie
> To crouch for coyne, whilst slaves tye fast our lands
> In Statute Staple, or these Marchants bands. (E2)

This hostility is returned with interest by the merchants. One of them, Velure, declares that

> My entrailes burn with Scorne, that Merchandize,
> Should stand and lick the pavement with his knee,
> Bare-head and crouching to Nobility
> Though forfeited to us be all their State. (E3)

And he vows that soon "All, all, is ours, Jewells, plate and lands, / All take cariere into the Marchants hands." The act concludes with another clownish performance from the players and a lengthy diatribe from Chrisoganus bemoaning the lack of respect afforded "Art."

In act 5, civil war breaks out between the nobles and the merchants. Chaos soon ensues, and the stage is held by a crowd of nameless "Russetings and Mechanicalls," who vow to kill all the nobles and middle classes alike:

> 4. . . . All shall be common.
> 1. Wives and all: what, Helter, skelter.
> 2. Slid, we are men as well as they are.
> 3. And we came all of our Father Adam.
> 2. Goe to then, why should we be their slaves?
> OMNES: Liberty, liberty, liberty. (F2)

Once the string of degree is untuned, discord inevitably follows. The players, who metonymically embody this social breakdown, also fall victim to the anarchy as they are pressed into the army. As in the scornful rhetoric of Prynne, they are addressed in terms that make endless, heavy-handed play on their profession, being exhorted to "play the Tamburlain," and enduring many such jibes until the war ends in mutual destruction. Chrisoganus is permitted a gloating speech about the dangers of the limbs making war on the head before his opponents, the players, are banished from the realm. The scene is thus set for the re-accession of Peace, who accompanies the liberal arts in a triumphal congress around the throne of Queen Elizabeth, symbolized in the person of Astrea.

IV

In *Histrio-Mastix,* theatricality is unequivocally associated with the rise of commerce and the consequent breakdown of social order. In *Timon of Athens,* Shakespeare makes a similar point, attributing to money precisely the same transformatory power that the antitheatricalists blame on the theater. In his exile from Athens, Timon discovers gold:

> Thus much of this will make
> Black white, foul fair, wrong right,
> Base noble, old young, coward valiant.
> Ha, you gods! why this? what this, you gods? Why, this
> Will lug your priests and servants from your sides,
> Pluck stout men's pillows from below their heads.
> This yellow slave
> Will knit and break religions, bless th'accursed,
> Make the hoar leprosy ador'd, place thieves,
> And give them title, knee, and approbation
> With senators on the bench. (4.3.28–38)

Money, in other words, allows one to change one's identity. Its Protean nature makes possible the kind of social mobility and identity confusion that is frequently exhibited on the Renaissance stage. Shakespeare, like Marston, understood that money fetishism was incompatible with the older forms of reverence that it would soon displace. In *King John,* Philip the Bastard describes commodification as a generalized perversion, or "bias," of the world away from its natural, harmonious condition:

> That smooth-fac'd gentleman, tickling commodity,
> Commodity, the bias of the world—
> The world, who of itself is prized well,
> Made to run even upon even ground,
> Till this advantage, this vile-drawing bias,
> This sway of motion, this commodity,

> Makes it take head from all indifferency,
> From all direction, purpose, course, intent—
> And this same bias, this commodity,
> This bawd, this broker, this all-changing word . . .
> (2.1.573–83)

The Bastard's speech concludes with a neat prediction of the displacement of monarchical by financial idolatry: "Since kings break faith upon commodity, / Gain be my Lord, for I will worship thee." (2.1.597–98) The influence of such early modern accounts of commodity fetishism on Karl Marx was immense and direct. He was sufficiently impressed by the accuracy of the above passage from *Timon* to cite it in four separate works.[67] In his commentary in the *Economic and Philosophical Manuscripts,* Marx notes that

> Shakespeare stresses especially two properties of money:
>
> 1. It is the visible divinity—the transformation of all human and natural properties into their contraries, the universal confusion and distortion of things; impossibilities are soldered together by it.
> 2. It is the common whore, the common pimp of peoples and of nations. . . . Money as the external universal *medium* or *faculty* . . . for turning an *image into reality* and *reality into a mere image.*[68]

It is this power of money that made possible the social mobility and the transforming of identity that we find displayed in the Renaissance theater. We should note, however, that for Marx this is no ludic, transgressive self-fashioning. Rather, it is the replacement of the authentic human subject with an alien, reified parody of subjectivity. The primary ideological effect of a market economy, according to Marx, is the objectification of the subject. The Renaissance antitheatricalists appear to recognize this phenomenon, and to find it exemplified in the exchange of false identities that took place on the stage, and playwrights such as Marston, Jonson, and Shakespeare appear to concur. The antitheatricalists and their ostensible opponents alike bear witness to the birth of the Society of the Spectacle.[69]

CHAPTER FOUR

SODOMY, USURY, AND THE NARRATIVE OF SHAKESPEARE'S *Sonnets*

> *Usury kills the child in the womb*
> *And breaks short the young man's courting*
> *Usury brings age into youth; it lies between the bride*
> *and the bridegroom*
> *Usury is against Nature's increase.*
>
> —*Ezra Pound*, Canto LI[1]
>
> *Can the grand enemie erect up any yoke-fellow to match with Idolatrie, but only Usurie.... Doe [usurers] not cherish Idlenesse in their Debtors, by lending to all idle uses? And doe they not maintayne themselves by Usurie in idlenesse; yea with the abuse of those Talents which God hath lent them for honest employment...*
>
> —*Anon*, Usurie Araigned and Condemned *(1625)*[2]

I

It seems clear that the men and women of early modern London would have had their attention drawn to the homology between idolatry and commodity fetishism as they engaged in such ordinary activities as going to the theater. The antitheatrical controversy was a good deal more accessible, and its practical implications were much clearer, to ordinary people than was the academic quarrel between scholasticism and empiricism. But the argument over the theaters remained nevertheless a public debate. In this chapter, by contrast, I propose to study the effects of the decline of natural teleology on the private sphere. In his widely influential *History of Sexuality*, Michel Foucault challenges the "repressive hypothesis" that claims that the seventeenth century inaugurated an age of sexual conservatism:

> By placing the advent of the age of repression in the seventeenth century, after hundreds of years of open spaces and free expression, one adjusts it to coincide with the development of capitalism: it becomes an integral part of the bourgeois order.... A principle of explanation emerges after the fact: if sex is so rigorously repressed, this is because it is incompatible with a general and intensive work imperative. At a time when labor capacity was being systematically exploited, how could this capacity be allowed to dissipate itself in pleasurable pursuits, except in those—reduced to a minimum—that enabled it to reproduce itself?[3]

Foucault has in his sights Whigs, Weberians, and Marxists, for whom the thesis of a bourgeois suppression of nonreproductive sexuality conveniently converges with the onset of wage labor and the consequent need to discipline the body.[4] He objects that the precapitalist world already imposed a strict taboo on nonprocreative sexual acts, which were collectively known as "sodomy." He also argues that, far from instigating the repression of deviant sexualities, the capitalist era has witnessed their definitive emergence into public discourse. The modern age is characterized by "a multiple implantation of 'perversions.' Our epoch has initiated sexual heterogeneities."[5] Since the Renaissance, power has been deployed in such a way as to identify, and thus to provoke, an enormous range of "unnatural" sexual orientations:

> since the end of the sixteenth century, the "putting into discourse of sex," far from undergoing a process of restriction, on the contrary has been subjected to a mechanism of increasing incitement.... the techniques of power exercised over sex have not obeyed a principle of rigorous selection, but rather one of dissemination and implantation of polymorphous sexualities...[6]

In this chapter I consider Shakespeare's *Sonnets* in the light of Foucault's provocative suggestion that the capitalist era has encouraged and fostered "perverse" forms of sexuality. During the early modern period, capital and "unnatural" sexuality were often conceptually united because of their common violation of natural teleology. The official Aristotelian–Thomistic morality of precapitalist Europe condemned as unnatural those sexual acts that do not result in reproduction, on the grounds that reproduction is the natural *telos* of sex. Similarly, teleological objections to usury—the reproduction, or "breeding," of money—formed the major ideological obstacle to the accumulation of capital. Aristotle and Aquinas hold that money cannot breed because it is naturally barren, its natural *telos* being merely to facilitate exchange. The capitalist challenge to this assumption involved the gradual abandonment of natural teleology as a basis for ethics, and this was a development the implications of which reached far beyond economics.[7]

Of course, Shakespeare was writing poetry rather than political economy, and his references to usury are punning and paradoxical, not logical or discursive. Nevertheless, his deployment of usury as a pivotal metaphor in the *Sonnets* and his sophisticated treatment of the theme in *The Merchant of Venice* indicate a high degree of familiarity with this highly topical issue. Shakespeare's father was twice charged with usury before the Royal Exchequer,[8] and during this period the traditional conception of money-lending as a criminal vice was being publicly contested in a variety of contexts.[9] Between the usury bill of 1571 (which banned interest of over 10 percent) and that of 1624 (which effectively legalized most forms of interest), a fierce battle was fought in parliament, press, and pulpit over the precise nature of usury. There were major parliamentary debates on the subject, with attendant pamphlet wars, in 1571, 1604, 1606, 1614, 1621, and 1624, and such men as Martin Bucer, Francis Bacon, and Lord Burghley made public their opinions on the matter. Neal Wood notes that cases of civil litigation, "a very large number of them concerned with indebtedness,"[10] increased ten-fold over the sixteenth century.

This was not merely a technical economic dispute. The critique of scholastic usury doctrine was by extension an attack on the entire edifice of Aristotelian teleology, and it had particularly direct implications for its understanding of sexuality. My hypothesis is that an analysis of the connections between early modern conceptions of "usury" and "sodomy" can shed significant light on the *Sonnets*, which consistently employ the imagery and logic of the usury debate in a sustained meditation on the ethical status of homoerotic desire. While not wishing to claim that any unitary narrative of events runs through the sequence, or that Shakespeare intended to explore any particular strand of imagery to the exclusion of others, I would suggest that a familiarity with the issues surrounding usury may offer clues to the mysterious and elusive pattern of relationships that the *Sonnets* seem to describe.

Aristotelian-Thomistic thought presupposes close conceptual and metaphorical connections between usury and sodomy. In the sixteenth and seventeenth centuries, we often also find sodomy identified with Catholic "idolatry." In Hugh Hilarie's *The Resurrecion of the Masse* (1554), the personified Mass announces that: "To stincking Sodomites and adulterers / To pollers, pyllers and usurers / Am I louing / kynde and gentle euers."[11] In *A Warning to England to Repente* (1558) Bartholomew Traheron demands, concerning papists: "what idolatrie, what pride, what covetousness, what crueltie, what lecherie, what sodomitrie, was ever heard of in anie age, that they have not far exceeeded?"[12] Writing in 1636, John Weemse remarks:

> ... how easie a thing it is for men to fall from bodily whoredome to spirituall, and what great affinity is betwixt the two, the breaking of the seventh commandment by bodily adultery, and the second, by spirituall adultery ... men fall easily from Idolatry to whoredome, and from whoredome to Idolatry. ... Great is the affinitie betwixt these two sorts of whoredomes; and therefore it is, that Antichirsts seate, Rev.11.8 is called spirituall Sodome.[13]

The paradigmatic instance of this genre is John Bale's *Comedy Concernynge thre lawes, of Nature, Moses and Christ, corrupted by the Sodomytes, Pharysees and Papystes*, in which the character Sodomismus vows: "I wyll corrupt Gods Image / With most unlawfull usage, / And brynge [man] into dottage, / Of all concupyscence."[14] His partner, Idololatria, describes herself as sodomy's spiritual equivalent: "Within the flesh thou art, / But I dwell in the hart, / And wyll the sowle pervart ..." A third villain, Infidelity, predicts that "These two wyll hym so use, / Ich one in their abuse," while Natural Law laments "that false Idolatrye / Hath hym perverted by slayghtes dyabolycall, / And so hath Sodomye through hys carnall abuses."

The vices of idolatry, usury, and sodomy thus follow an homologous pattern. For Bale, clearly, the vices of idolatry and sodomy were different manifestations of the same fundamental confusion of means and ends, which in chapter three we identified as "abuse." Usury and sodomy share the further similarity of confusing what is fruitful with what is barren. As a result of this confusion, usury and sodomy violate natural law, employing sex and money toward ends that do not naturally belong to them. Sodomy devotes sexual acts, the natural *telos* of which is reproduction, to the unnatural end of carnal pleasure, or "concupiscence." Usury takes money, whose natural *telos* is to facilitate exchange, and uses it for the unnatural end of reproduction—it makes money "breed." Thomas Bancroft's epigram "Money, a fruit-full commodity" (1639) milks this commonplace for sarcastic humor:

> As with coyn'd Metalls we our Trades maintaine,
> So th'Indians Trafficke with their fruits for gaine:
> Yet doe our dealings no lesse fruite inferre
> Than theirs; How comes that? Aske the Usurer.[15]

The sins of sodomy and usury are mirror images: Sodomy is sinful because it makes what is properly generative sterile, while usury is sinful because it makes what is properly sterile generative. Elizabethan moralists could thus draw on a long heritage that associated usury and sodomy. According to scholastic theology, any erotic act that was not performed with the aim of reproduction could be condemned under the rubric of "sodomy,"[16] following Aquinas's teleological condemnation of the "sin against nature":

> The end, however, which nature intends in copulation is offspring to be procreated and educated, and that this good might be sought, it has put delight in copulation. . . . Whoever, therefore uses copulation for the delight which is in it, not referring the intention to the end intended by nature, acts against nature; and this is also true unless such copulation is had as can be appropriately ordered to that end.[17]

The emphasis on reproduction in sexual ethics emerged out of the struggles of the early Catholic church against heretical movements such as the Manicheans, who refused to accord an ethically superior status to reproductive intercourse.[18] In fact, Catholic propagandists claimed that these heretics believed that any sexual act was permissible *except* those aimed at reproduction. In reaction the Church Fathers, led by the repentant former Manichee Augustine, insisted that *only* acts intended to cause reproduction were allowed—indulgence in any sensual pleasure as an end in itself was "concupiscence."

The teleological ethic invoked against sodomy logically condemns usury too, and on analogous grounds. In the *Politics*, Aristotle refers to usury by the Greek word "tokos," or "birth." It is, he explains, an unnatural form of birth, since the *telos* of money is to be a sign facilitating the exchange of useful objects, and not to function as an end in itself, through self-reproduction. Money, says Aristotle, does not naturally reproduce because it is not a natural, living creature, but an artificial human invention. Thus usury, like sodomy, violates the law of nature. The traditional view of sodomy was expressed succinctly in the first century by Philo of Alexandria: "Like a bad husbandman [the sodomite] spends his labor night and day on soil from which no growth at all can be expected."[19] Augustine and Chrysostom gave Patristic sanction to this line of reasoning. The latter remarks, of the biblical cities of the plain, that

> ... the very nature of the punishment was a pattern of the nature of the sin. Even as [the Sodomites] devised a barren coitus, not having for its end the procreation of children, so did God bring on them such a punishment as made the womb of the land forever barren and destitute of all fruits.[20]

The connection remained commonplace throughout the middle ages. In the *Inferno,* Dante has Virgil explain why sodomites and usurers are imprisoned together:

> Puossi far forza ne la Deitade,
> Col cuor negando e bestemmiando quella,
> E spregiando natura e sua bontade:
> E pero lo minor giron suggella
> Del segno suo e Soddoma e Caorsa ... [21]

Boccaccio makes the same point in the first story of the *Decameron,* which describes the death of Ser Ciapelletto, who "was as fond of women as a dog is of the stick: in the use against nature he had not his match" (1.1.14). This sodomite expires in the house of Florentine usurers who, like Ciapelletto himself, are referred to as "Lombards." Until the seventeenth century, the term "Lombard" was synonymous with "usurer," and as such it was often used in connection with Jews, as in Langland's reference in *Piers Plowman* to "Lumbardes of Lukes that lyven by lone as Jewes" (100.5.194). In 1376 an English act of parliament commanded that "All the Lombards who practice no profession than that of Moneychanger quit the land as soon as possible ... given that some among them ... have lately practiced in this land a very horrible vice which should not be named."[22]

Elizabethan writers on usury continue to identify usury with unnatural sexuality.[23] In 1598, Francis Meres encapsulated the connection neatly: "As Paederestie is unlawful, because it is against kinde: so usury and encrease by gold and silver is unlawful, because against nature; nature hath made them sterill and barren, and usurie makes them procreative."[24]

Although the modern world uses "sodomy" mainly to refer to particular sexual acts, the early modern period classed sex as sodomy whenever its end was pleasure rather than the proper *telos* of reproduction. Prostitution could thus readily fall into that category, and due to the element of financial profit, "bawdry" or pimping seemed an especially apt point of connection for usury and concupiscent sexuality. Jonson alludes to Aristotelian doctrine in his fifty-seventh epigram: "If, as their ends, their fruits were so the same / Bawdry and usury were one kind of game,"[25] and Miles Mosse cites Aristotle to the effect that "Usurers and Bawdes may well goe together."[26] Significantly for the action of the *Sonnets*, in which the speaker adopts the role of both usurer and bawd, Shakespeare seems particularly drawn to this metaphor. In *Timon of Athens* Apemantus decries "Poor rogues and usurer's men! Bawds between gold and want!" (2.2.6–2),[27] and in *Measure for Measure* the Clown makes a topical reference when he laments that "Twas never merry world since, of two usuries, the merriest [sexual] was put down, and the worser [financial] allow'd by order of law" (3.2.5–7).[28] The following exchange from *Twelfth Night* reveals the logic of the metaphor. The Clown has been given a coin:

> CLOWN: Would not a pair of these have bred, Sir?
> VIOLA: Yes, being kept together and put to use.
> CLOWN: I would play Lord Pandarus of Phrygia, Sir, to bring a Cressida to this Troilus. (3.1.54–8)

This economic metaphor guides the *Sonnets*' treatment of sexuality and informs the studiedly obscure emotional action described by the sequence. For the most part, the poems seem to endorse scholastic objections to sodomy as unproductive. And yet they also betray some of the strains that were beginning to wear at this tradition. The *Sonnets* often use the theme of usury to criticize conventional condemnations of nonreproductive sex and, at times, the poet comes close to endorsing a different kind of reproduction—one that can spring from traditionally barren activities such as money-lending and homoeroticism.[29]

II

The first 17 poems in Thorpe's sequence urge a young man to beget children. The major source for the theme, though not the imagery, seems to be Erasmus's, *Epistle to perswade a young gentleman to Mariage*, as reprinted in Thomas Wilson's *The Arte of Rhetorique* (1553). Erasmus's argument is solidly in the Thomistic tradition: reproduction, he emphasizes at length, is *natural*:

> For if to live well ... is to folowe the course of Nature, what thinge is so agreynge with Nature as Matrimonye? For there is nothing so naturall not onely unto mankinde, but also unto all other livinge creatures as it is to kepe their owne kinde from decaye, and through encrease of issue, to make the whole kinde immortall.[30]

It follows, for Erasmus, that any who choose not to take this course are unnatural and perverted: "Neither can I reporte for verye shame, into howe filthye offences they do often fall, that will not use that remedye whiche Nature hath graunted unto manne."[31]

This idea provides the conceptual framework within which the opening *Sonnets* conduct their meditations. But Shakespeare's imagery is his own: Unlike Erasmus he frequently uses financial terminology to proclaim the imperative that the youth reproduce. The first line of sonnet 1 summarizes the essential demand: "From fairest creatures we desire increase."[32] The word "increase" could mean both "reproduction" and "profit," and a prominent strand of imagery in the marriage sequence makes much of this ambiguity. The poet's essential argument is that the youth is squandering the metaphorical riches with which Nature has endowed him by failing to invest them profitably: He is a "tender churl [who] mak'st waste in niggarding" (12). Sonnet 2 reminds him that his "treasure" (6) will lose its "worth" (4) and render him "thriftless" (8) if it is not put out to "use" (9), thus producing interest in the form of a "fair child" (10). Sonnet 4 reproaches the youth's reluctance to breed in similar terms:

> Unthrifty loveliness, why dost thou spend
> Upon thyself thy beauty's legacy?
> Nature's bequest gives nothing, but doth lend,
> And being frank she lends to those are free (1–4)

The young man's beauty is again figured as an inheritance from Nature, in the form of a loan for which she will expect to be repaid with interest in the shape of offspring.[33] At present, however, he is being "unthrifty," squandering this legacy by spending it on himself. Booth uses the sexual implications of "spend" to suggest that the youth is being counseled against masturbation, a barren and therefore concupiscent sexual act.[34] This implication is made clearer in the lines that follow:

> Then, beauteous niggard, why dost thou abuse
> The bounteous largesse given thee to give?
> Profitless usurer, why dost thou use

So great a sum of sums, yet canst not live? (5–8)

As we saw in chapter three, to "abuse" something was to pervert it away from its Aristotelian *telos*, and the word was thus readily applicable to usury. Thus Nicholas Sander, arguing against the exaction of interest on fungibles, observes:

> ... when there is no use of a thing without the losse and putting away thereof, or when the thing is diminished in substance by the dayly using of yt: that is not properly *usus*, the use, but rather, as Cicero and Ulpian call yt, *Abusus*, the abuse, as yf we should saye in english, it is rather a wasting, than a using.[35]

The author of *Ususrie Araigned and Condemned* (1625) rests his case upon the distinction between the "ordained uses" of money and its "idle uses," or "abuses." He demands:

> Doe [usurers] not cherish Idlenesse in their Debtors, by lending to all idle uses? And doe they not maintayne themselves by Usurie in idlenesse; yea with the abuse of those Talents which God hath lent them for honest employment.... Policie hath so fashioned all Coyne, that it might bee fit for no use, but onely payment: And payment hath two currents, the ordained use, which is for private and publicke good; And the abuse in Usurie, which is for the Usurer's gayne alone.[36]

The image in line 7 of sonnet 4 is therefore in one sense unsurprising. The youth is called a "usurer" because he is not devoting the "largesse" (6) he has received from Nature to its teleologically correct end. Like a usurer, he violates nature. In another sense, however, the figure is confusing; we have just been informed that the youth was a borrower, not a lender; he was, in fact, criticized for his failure to be "free" in lending out the legacy he had borrowed from Nature. Here, it seems that he is indeed lending this "largesse" (he is called a "usurer"), but that he is doing so in a way that brings him no "profit" and by which he therefore cannot "live." The way in which the young man is presently "abusing" and "spending" his beauty, that is to say, will bring him no children and so prevent him from living in posterity. Once again, the usury imagery is employed so as to indicate that the youth is indulging in concupiscent practices. The unnatural nature of his activities is stressed in the sonnet's next quatrain:

> For having traffic with thyself alone,
> Thou of thyself thy sweet self dost deceive:

Then how when Nature calls thee to be gone,
What acceptable audit canst thou leave? (9-12)

Through his "traffic" with his "self," the youth cheats himself out of the reproduction of his "self," which would be a child (a similar assumption informs sonnet 3, in which he is chided for his "self-love to stop posterity" [8]). This "traffic" violates the demands of Nature, who will find his final "audit" unacceptable, as it fails to produce any interest on the loan she made him. The couplet urges the young man to take action to avoid this circumstance: "That unused beauty must be tombed with thee / That used, lives th'executor to be" (13-14). Only by "using" his beauty—by lending it out at interest—can the addressee produce a child who will live after him as his "executor." Whereas earlier the youth was a "profitless usurer" making no return on his investment, now he is urged to become profitable, to use his investment to produce offspring. The transition between the profitless and the profitable usurer is, therefore, identical to the transition between barren sodomy and fruitful reproductive intercourse.

This association of children with the interest earned by a usurer is an insistent theme of the early sonnets. Sonnet 9 warns that "beauty's waste hath in the world an end, / And kept unused the user so destroys it" (11-12), while sonnet 10 repeats the accusation that the youth is being "improvident" (2) and sonnet 13 reminds him that his beauty is merely held "in lease" (5). In sonnet 11, the youth is imagined as a coin, which nature intends should reproduce itself: "She carved thee for her seal, and meant thereby / Thou shouldst print more, nor let that copy die" (13-14). This choice of metaphor, of course, draws attention to a striking paradox. According to all traditional ethics, usury was not supposed to be reproductive. The false supposition that money could reproduce was precisely what was objectionable and unnatural about usury. In the context of the contemporary debate, the comparison of Nature to a usurer was startlingly paradoxical, as was the employment of usury as a rhetorical figure to encourage reproduction. The effect of surprise would have been enhanced when this argument was advanced as a corrective to unnatural, sodomitical desire.

It appears that the *Sonnets* subjected the teleological ethic, which declared sodomy and usury to be unnatural, to a sustained, wittily ironic, critical interrogation. The sequence alludes to the scholarly controversies surrounding these terms, using them as imaginative and tropological fuel to drive its narrative forward. In sonnet 6, the imperative for the youth to impregnate a woman is bluntly stated:

> Then let not winters ragged hand deface
> In thee thy summer ere thou be distilled:
> Make sweet some vial; treasure thou some place
> With beauty's treasure ere it be self-killed (1–4)

Once again, procreation is described in financial terms and presented as guaranteeing immortality through reproduction. But here the imagery is more explicitly sexual; the young man is urged to invest his "treasure" in "some vial" and thus avoid the barren fate of being "self-killed"—that is, both genetically extinguished and "killed" in the sexual sense, by himself.[37] The lines that follow employ the familiar trope to explore this conflict:

> That use is not forbidden usury
> Which happies those that pay the willing loan;
> That's for thyself to breed another thee,
> Or ten times happier be it ten for one (5–8)

The allusion here is to the Act of 1571, which legalized an interest rate of up to 10 percent, and to the justification commonly advanced that usury was legitimate as long as both parties in the transaction benefited. It might seem, then, that the speaker is taking sides with those who argued for a relaxation of the taboo on usury. By comparing his friends' biological offspring to the interest generated by usury, the speaker seems to endorse usury as a legitimate form of reproduction—to be claiming, with John Seldon, that "'Tis a vain thing to say, Money begats not Money, for that no doubt it does."[38]

However, such a reading neglects the great irony of the sequence, which is that, by urging his beloved friend to reproduce, the male speaker is necessarily urging him to transfer at least some of his affections to women. The speaker thus deprives himself of the youth's attentions, suggesting that heterosexual love is more fruitful and therefore, assuming Aristotelian teleology, more natural. But heterosexual procreation is consistently figured in terms of usury, which was generally agreed to be an *un*natural form of reproduction. The disreputable status of usury in Elizabethan England casts a disagreeable light on the tenor for which it is the vehicle. It seems, then, that rather than endorsing calls for the toleration of usury, the poet is deploying such arguments in a subtly ironic critique of the assumption that only reproductive sex is natural. If reproductive sex is usurious, as the *Sonnets* suggest, then according to traditional morality it is in fact *un*natural. If one responds that usury is actually *not* unnatural, then one has abandoned the teleology that also designates sodomy a sin against nature. Either way, the poet has subtly constructed a witty rhetorical vindication of homoerotic desire.

The question of what is natural is further troubled by the opening lines of sonnet 20:

> A woman's face with Nature's own hand painted
> Hast thou, the master-mistress of my passion;
> A woman's gentle heart, but not acquainted
> With shifting change, as is false women's fashion (1–4)

Face-painting was regularly castigated by Elizabethan pamphleteers on the grounds that it was unnatural, a human imposition upon the divine prerogative of creation. Attacks on cosmetics form a significant subgenre within Renaissance misogyny, and they serve to enhance the perception of women as "false," unreliable and deceptive. In these lines, the youth's face is "painted," but "with Nature's own hand." His beauty requires no cosmetics, it is not "false," and unlike women he is not "acquainted / With shifting change." To love such a creature is to love Nature's handiwork rather than humanity's; presumably, therefore, it is a "natural" form of love. But the suggestion that homoerotic love is being defended as natural is dissipated in lines 9–12:

> And for a woman wert thou first created,
> Till Nature as she wrought thee fell a-doting,
> And by addition me of thee defeated,
> By adding one thing to my purpose nothing.

Here it is Nature's "doting" on the youth that causes her to make him male. Being female herself, her natural affections could be directed only toward a man. Furthermore, this masculinization has "defeated" the speaker of his friend. His "purpose" would have been served if the young man had been endowed with "nothing"; since, however, he has "one thing," he is unavailable to the male poet. And yet no sooner has this conclusion been reached than it is in turn undermined by the couplet: "But since she pricked thee out for women's pleasure, / Mine be thy love, and thy love's use their treasure" (13–14). By the hand of Nature, the youth has been directed toward the love of women. This, one might therefore assume, would be the natural course for his love to take. But in a daring reversal, the speaker declares that the young man's love is "Mine," while assigning to women the "treasure" of "thy love's use."

We should recall here that in sonnet 6, the youth had been urged to loan his love to women, in return for interest in the form of children. The idea seems to be repeated here, and once again the unnatural reproduction that is usury is employed as an ironic figure for the natural reproduction that springs from heterosexual love. This time, however, the lines contain a fundamental ambiguity that subverts this interpretation. The word "use" can mean both the use of a sum loaned (this use being what the usurer sold), or the interest paid by the borrower for the use of the sum (this use being what the usurer earned). There is no way, in this poem, to tell which sense is intended. And yet the interpretation of these lines will be very different depending on which meaning one chooses. Either the female gender are borrowing the "use" of the lover, or they are loaning it. The speaker apparently believes the former: He plans to loan the youth's love to women and to earn interest on it (we recall here Shakespeare's frequent allusion in the plays to the conventional association of usury with pimping). I will argue, however, that we can trace a pattern in the sequence that strongly suggests that his machinations eventually go awry.[39]

III

In the opening sonnets, then, the speaker depicts himself as a usurer. How might such a dubious character justify his practices? The typical recourse of those who wanted to legitimize usury was to argue that the authoritative prohibitions were not to be taken literally but were intended as metaphors. In 1612, Roger Fenton noted that "The force of the Philosophers argument taken from the barrenesse of money, and the unnaturall brood of usury, being mingled with metaphors, if it be not rightly apprehended, is obscure and doubtful."[40] For Miles Mosse, Aristotle's statement that money is barren is merely a "Metaphore." The tropological status he imposes on Aristotle enables Mosse to argue that usury is a matter for the individual conscience, rather than for external law:

> And in this sence no doubt, that may truely be affirmed which I meete withall in the writings of many learned men, and which it seemeth they have all drawne from Aristotle's fountaine: namely that usurie is *contra legum natura*, contrarie to the lawe of nature. Not so much because it is against nature, for money to begette money, (in which sence one saide that usurie was *sodomia natura*, a kinde of sodomie in nature) but because it doth contrarie the verdict of the conscience, and so by consequent the lawe of nature, which ruleth in the same.[41]

A similar case was made regarding Deuteronomy's proscription of usury, which reads: "Unto a stranger thou mayest lend upon usury; but unto thy brother thou shalt not lend upon usury" (23:20). The traditional Christian interpretation was that, for the Jews, this commandment was to be taken in the literal sense. Because Christians believed that Jews were bound by the letter of the law, they thought that Deuteronomy forbade Jews to take interest from other Jews (their "brothers") but permitted them to take it from Gentiles (or "strangers").[42] As it applied to themselves, however, Christians believed that Deuteronomy, like all of the Old Testament, was to be interpreted in a figural, or "spiritual" sense. Because all men are, figurally speaking, "brothers" to a Christian (the reasoning went), this text prohibits Christians from taking interest from anyone.[43]

According to this logic, the speaker of the *Sonnets* takes a "Judaic" view of usury. He distinguishes between homosexual love (which, he frequently repeats, is directed toward a version of one's "self"), and heterosexual love, which is described as directed toward someone different and alien. Usury, he assumes, can legitimately be practiced in the latter case, and he imagines that he will act as a usurer, loaning out the youth's love to women and reaping interest in the form of genetic reproductions of his beloved. He also betrays a "Judaic" belief in the efficacy of the letter to grant eternal life, frequently announcing his intention to reproduce the youth through the epideisis of his verse. In sonnet 18, for instance, there is the confident assertion that "So long as men can breathe or eyes can see / So long lives this, and this gives life to thee" (13–14), and sonnet 19 is no less sanguine: "My love shall in my verse ever live young" (14). Sonnet 17 offers both consolations at once: "But were some child of yours alive that time, / You should live twice, in it and in my rhyme" (14), and this attempt to equate children, which only a woman can give the youth, with the verbal tribute that the poet can offer recurs in number 21: "O let me true in love but truly write, / And then believe me, my love is as fair/ As any mother's child" (9–11). However, the idea that the poet can reproduce his beloved in a manner that might rival natural reproduction is undermined as soon as it is formulated. In sonnet 24, the claim that the image is "true" is immediately contradicted by its location: "For through the painter must you see his skill, / To find where your true image pictur'd lies, / Which in my bosom's shop is hanging still" (5–7). This impulse to construct a living "image" of the beloved is vain and idolatrous, and the poet protests too much in sonnet 105: "Let not my love be call'd idolatry / Nor my beloved as an idol show" (1–2).

In many sonnets, the prospect of poetic immortality is unfavorably compared with genetic reproduction.[44] Sonnet 16 is frank in its opposition of linguistic reproduction to natural heterosexual procreation:

> But wherefore do not you a mightier way
> Make war upon this bloody tyrant Time,
> And fortify yourself in your decay
> With means more blessed than my barren rhyme? (1–4)

The poet's "rhyme" is "barren"; the "more blessed" means to generation is heterosexual union—the youth is reminded of the "maiden gardens" (6) who wish to "bear your living flowers / Much liker than your painted counterfeit" (7–8). The poet's "pupil pen" is inadequate to the task of procreation, and the youth is finally exhorted to "live drawn by your own sweet skill" (14). Similarly, sonnet 76 asks "Why is my verse so barren of new pride" (1), while in sonnet 83 the youth is said to "exceed / The barren tender of a poet's debt" (3–4). With this confession a subtle shift occurs in the speaker's position: He is no longer a creditor, as he had imagined himself in sonnet 20, but a debtor.

There are fairly clear parallels between this situation and the one described in the (presumably contemporaneous) *The Merchant of Venice*. For Shakespeare's contemporaries Venice was the archetypal mercantile city, and it was increasingly associated with capitalist financial power. By the end of the sixteenth century, due to a sharp rise in piracy, "Venetian financiers and merchants were less and less willing to accept the increasing risks of maritime ventures" and turned to capital investments of various forms instead,[45] a development that was signaled by the founding of the Banco di Rialto in 1587.[46] Shylock is a figure for usury as much as he is a stage Jew, and Shakespeare assumes that Judaism and usury share certain characteristics, including hardheartedness, legalism, literalism, and antisocial intentions. Shylock sophistically attempts to justify his usury by means of a spurious analogy with natural reproduction. He recounts the biblical story of how Jacob ensured that Laban's ewes would bear parti-colored lambs, which would be forfeit to Jacob. Antonio retorts that Shylock has drawn a false analogy between the natural reproduction of living things and the unnatural reproduction of dead money: "Was this inserted to make interest good? / Or is your gold and silver ewes and rams?" (1.3.86–7) Shylock's reply gloatingly concedes the point: "I cannot tell, I make it breed as fast" (1.3–88). Not understanding (or willfully denying) that money is barren, Shylock violates Aristotelian natural law. He also follows the supposedly Judaic, literalist exegesis of Deuteronomy, as Antonio reminds him:

> If thou wilt lend this money, lend it not
> As to thy friend, for when did friendship take
> A breed of barren metal of his friend?
> But lend it rather to thine enemy . . . (I, iii, 124–7)

Shylock confirms his legalism by his absurdly literalist interpretation of the bond contract in court. His concentration on the letter of the law blinds him to the spirit of grace, and he is led into what Marc Shell has identified as "verbal usury." As Shell explains:

> . . ."verbal usury" is an important technical term in the Jewish Talmud, the Christian church fathers, and in the Islamic Traditions. There it refers to the generation of an illegal—the church fathers say unnatural—supplement of verbal meaning by use of methods such as punning and flattering.[47]

Shell finds this concept exemplified in Shylock's disingenuous reasoning and his hairsplitting quibbles in court and elsewhere: "As the Jew uses moneys . . . to supplement principals, so he uses puns to exceed the proper meanings of words."[48]

The speaker of the *Sonnets* does his share of "punning and flattering" of course, and I think he is similarly portrayed as practicing "verbal usury," if by that term we understand with Shell "the generation of an . . . unnatural . . . supplement of verbal meaning."[49] We have seen how the poet imagines that the youth might be reproduced and immortalized by poetic epideisis, rather than by the begetting of children. Another way of putting this would be to say that he puts his faith in the letter, thus confusing artificial with natural reproduction. This is the reasoning of Shylock, who interprets the resemblance between the breeding of cattle and that of money in a literalistic fashion, concluding that what is in fact a purely analogical correspondence justifies the literal taking of interest.

There are further similarities between the situation of the poet and that of Shylock. The poet's determination to act as a usurer and loan his friend's love out for interest proves self-defeating. Sonnet 40 is the first to suggest that the transaction has not proceeded as the poet had anticipated:

> Take all my loves, my love, yea take them all:
> What hast thou then more than thou hadst before?

> No love, my love, that thou mayst true love call;
> All mine was thine, before thou hadst this more.
> Then if for my love thou my love receivest,
> I cannot blame thee for my love thou usest (1–6)

Stephen Booth is surely correct to find in the last line "an unpleasant suggestion of the poet's affection for the friend as capital put out at interest."[50] We recall here the ambiguity of the word "use" in the final line of sonnet 20: "Mine be thy love, and thy love's use their treasure." A similar ambivalence informs these lines: It is unclear whether the addressee is borrowing the use of the poet's love or loaning it out at usance. In sonnet 20 the question of who is the creditor and who is the debtor—that is, the question of to whom the principal belongs—is left unresolved. Here, however, the addressee is described as a "gentle thief" who has committed "robbery" (9). It now seems that a transfer of ownership has taken place, and that the scheme outlined in sonnet 20 has backfired. Sonnet 48 explicitly addresses the theme of miscalculation:

> How careful was I when I took my way,
> Each trifle under truest bars to thrust,
> That to my use it might unused stay
> From hands of falsehood, in sure wards of trust! (1–4)

But the poet's vigilance did not extend to his beloved ("Thee have I not locked up in any chest" [9]), and as a result he is "left a prey of every vulgar thief" (8). The addressee is not like the "unused" "trifle(s)" of which the poet has retained the "use"; on the contrary, he has been "used" and the poet has therefore lost the "use" of him.

It is, perhaps, reckless to claim of a sequence as profoundly ambivalent as the *Sonnets* that any definite conclusion is reached. But a resolution of sorts appears to take place in sonnet 134. To follow that poem's tortuous logic, it is necessary to quote it in full:

> So now I have confessed that he is thine,
> And I myself am mortgaged to thy will,
> Myself I'll forfeit, so that other mine
> Thou wilt restore to be my comfort still:
> But thou wilt not, nor will he not be free,
> For thou art covetous, and he is kind;
> He learned but surety-like to write for me
> Under that bond that him as fast doth bind.
> The statute of thy beauty thou wilt take,

> Thou usurer, that put'st forth all to use,
> And sue a friend came debtor for my sake,
> So him I lose through my unkind abuse.
> Him have I lost, thou hast both him and me;
> He pays the whole, and yet am I not free.

Let us recall again that in the couplet of sonnet 20 the speaker attempts to resolve his dilemma by retaining ownership of his friend's love while loaning it out to women in return for interest in the form of children. As we noted, however, the ambiguity of the word "use" allows for a different reading: that it is the female gender who are loaning the youth's love to the speaker. This latter interpretation is the situation assumed in sonnet 134, in which the train of thought and the context of the poem in the sequence indicate that its addressee is female. Whereas sonnet 20 declared "Mine be thy love, and thy love's use their treasure," in sonnet 134 "he is thine," and it is the woman who is the "usurer, that put'st forth all to use." Now the poet is the debtor, he has defaulted on the loan, and as a result is "mortgaged to thy will." He offers to forfeit himself to the woman, if he can thereby redeem and so retain possession of his friend.[51] But the idea is rejected because the other parties are unwilling; she, as a "usurer," being "covetous," and he being "kind."[52] The word "kind" means both "similar" and, preeminently in Shakespeare's lifetime, "natural." In 1612, for example, Fenton remarks of scholastic usury doctrine:

> Verily, though it bee no demonstration against every act of begetting money upon money by money; yet it sheweth this kind of increase to be very unkind, and to have but small resemblance to that naturall increase, which the God of nature hath established as most innocent among men.[53]

Shakespeare plays with this ambiguity in *The Merchant of Venice:*

> SHYLOCK: This is kind I offer.
> ANTONIO: This were kindness.
> SHYLOCK: This kindness will I show. (1.3.134–6)

Antonio is under the impression that the word "kind" here means "kin." By not taking monetary interest for the loan, Shylock will be treating Antonio "kindly"—as a "brother." But Shylock's grim vow gives it the sense of "according to kind," or "according to my nature." In this sonnet, the youth is "kind" to the speaker in the sense that he is male, and this "kindness" is emphasized by the constant references stressing their similarity—"my next self" (sonnet 133, line 6), or "that other mine" (sonnet 134, line 3). However, it is precisely because he is "kind" in this sense that the youth does not wish to leave the lady and is therefore also "kind" in the sense of "natural." By choosing heterosexual love, the young man is behaving according to "kind," as we are reminded when the poet blames his loss of his friend on "my unkind abuse" (12). It seems that sodomy and usury are both intended here: The reference is to the poet's intention to carry on a homoerotic relationship by acting in a usurious manner.

A further irony accrues when we learn that "He learned but surety-like to write for me / Under that bond that him as fast doth bind" (7–8), and that the lady is thus "sue[ing] a friend came debtor for my sake" (10). It seems that, in order to guarantee the poet's loan from the lady, the youth has undertaken to stand as surety for the repayment of the loan of himself. The cunning of this maneuver is that, even if the poet attempts to avoid repayment by defaulting on the loan, the principal will in any case be returned, because the principal is itself the guarantee. A forfeit of a guarantee, however, is not legally the same as the repayment of the principal, despite the fact that in this case the principal and the guarantee are identical. As a result, the defaulting poet remains "forfeit to thy will" even after he has forfeited his friend: "Him have I lost, thou hast both him and me; / He pays the whole, and yet am I not free" (13–14).

Shakespeare seems to have in mind here the antiusurious argument that fungibles cannot be lent, but only given away. Aquinas summarizes this case:

> ... there are certain things the use of which consists in their consumption: thus we consume wine when we use it for drink, and we consume wheat when we use it for food. Wherefore in suchlike things the use of the thing must not be reckoned apart from the thing itself, and whoever is granted the use of the thing is granted the thing itself; and for this reason, to lend things of this kind is to transfer the ownership.[54]

Money is a fungible, and therefore, according to the opponents of usury, it could not be loaned but only given away—to transfer its use was to transfer its ownership, as Shylock discovers. As the *Sonnets*' obsession with aging and mortality remind us, human beings are only too fungible. The poet is thus undone, ironically enough, by his very attempt to render his beloved immortal through genetic reproduction.

As Aquinas puts it, "to lend things of this kind is to transfer the ownership"; and so the poet finds that he has given his lover away when he had thought only to loan him.

The law has yet another hold on the poet. There is a notably punitive aspect to sonnets 133 and 134. It is as if the poet is being punished for his earlier determination to commit usury, and his misinterpretation of the nature of usury is being corrected. There are specific allusions here to Elizabethan legal and moral theory concerning usurers. Sixteenth-century legislation provided for the forfeiture by a convicted usurer of the sum lent.[55] The sixteenth-century translator of Aristotle's *Politics* claims that "There was an old lawe at Rome that forbad lending upon usury, upon paine, that the offender should forfait as much as the Usury amounted unto . . ."[56] This is also scholastic doctrine, as laid down by Aquinas: "he that paid usury has a certain claim on that property just as he has on the other goods of the usurer. Hence . . . it is commanded that the property be sold, and the price be restored, of course according to the amount taken in usury."[57]

Or, as the poet of the *Sonnets* puts it, "Him have I lost through my unkind abuse." Under the ironic restitution of Elizabethan law, it was the usurer who ended up paying the borrower, not the other way around. The borrower thus profited from the usurious transaction and became, in effect though not in law or intention, a "usurer." It seems to me that this is what happens in the *Sonnets*, where the Lady is ultimately revealed as the true "usurer." It is also, of course, what happens in *The Merchant of Venice*. Shylock interprets Deuteronomy literally and takes interest from "strangers." In court he is finally undone by his own literalism and forced to pay restitution. This is primarily financial, but as in the *Sonnets* a sexual element is introduced by the loss of his daughter to a Gentile, upon whom he is forced to bestow a portion of the reparation. Antonio suffers an analogous deprivation, losing Bassanio to Portia, and referring to himself as a "tainted whether of the flock" (4.1.114). The Merchant's forfeit parallels the Jew's, as the sodomite's sin parallels the usurer's. The poet of the *Sonnets* commits the sins of both Antonio and Shylock and suffers their penalty. However, this by no means precludes a sympathetic identification with the poet or the Jew. In the poems as in the play, the teleology that dictates that usury and sodomy are sins against nature is arraigned, searchingly examined, and—at times—bitingly criticized. The fact that the poet and the Jew ultimately fail in their usurious enterprises does not detract from the dramatic sympathy with which Shakespeare was perspicacious enough to endow their arguments.

CHAPTER FIVE

TYPOLOGY AND OBJECTIFICATION IN GEORGE HERBERT'S *The Temple*

> *It is a thing confirmed, that merchandicing is, as it were, the proper profession of the Nation of the Jews . . . wheresoever they go to dwell, there presently the Traficq begins to flourish.*
>
> —Menasseh ben Israel,
> To His Highnesse the Lord Protector *(1652)*[1]

> *. . . the Idolatry of some corrupt Christians, as they of the Romish faith, doth much keep [the Jews] back, who hate all kinds of Idolatry, though they them selves do in some sort adore and worship the Book of the Law.*
>
> —Thomas Calvert,
> The Blessed Jew of Morocco *(1648)*[2]

> *. . . a family of our nation was burnt, for confessing upon the wrack the truth of a certain accusation of a maid servant, who (provoked out of some disgust) said, that they had scourged, and whip't an image, which by the frequent lashes, issued forth a great deal of bloud, and crying with an out stretched voice, said unto them, why do you thus cruelly scourge me?*
>
> —Menasseh ben Israel, Vindiciae Judaerun *(1656)*[3]

I

It is a tribute to the innocent rationalism that shines through Menasseh ben Israel's powerful, poignant appeals for the readmission of the Jews into England that he evidently fails to grasp the nefarious intricacies of Christian antisemitism. The deplorable truth is that, for many Christians of the early modern period, the above quotation from Thomas Calvert provided an all-too-obvious connection between the two citations from ben Israel. "The Jews" were indeed "confirmed" as a figure for "Traficq" in the popular tropology of Renaissance Europe. They were also believed, by ignorant Christians, to idolize the letter of the law. It was thus an unfortunately simple matter to identify "the Jews" with every kind of idolatrous nominalism, whether this took the form of legalism, literalism, or financial value. In chapter two we saw how Luther accused Karlstadt of idolatry on the grounds of his obsessive iconoclasm; similarly, Judaic anti-idolatry was held to be covertly idolatrous in character, as ben Israel's story of Jews being burnt for scourging an image indicates. Our secular civilization is not always sufficiently cognizant of the extended afterlife enjoyed by such insidious constructions.

In the last chapter we saw how usury was associated in early modern England with carnal concupiscence and the transgression of natural teleology. In this chapter I will analyze the psychological effects of usury's opposite—redemption—as they are expressed in the poetics and theology of George Herbert. In a provocative essay published in 1966, Bernard Knieger drew attention to the striking pattern of financial imagery that runs through Herbert's *The Temple*. Although it is very conspicuous, this tropological tendency had gone largely unremarked by earlier critics, and the intriguing question that Knieger raises has also been neglected by subsequent ones:

> In the religious poetry of George Herbert we can observe the seemingly rather odd phenomenon of an otherworldly Christian using much worldly imagery in a nonpejorative sense . . . this religious, devotional poet often uses commercial imagery to express the very heart of his devotional experience. Why?[4]

Knieger essays an answer to his own question by invoking the conventional understanding of the crucifixion as payment of the debt incurred by sin. He suggests that "In a sense, God is for Herbert a gigantic accountant, whose accounting principle, however, is mercy rather than justice."[5] It might, however, be more precise to describe Herbert's God as an *anti*-accountant, who repeatedly tears up the balance sheets that record humanity's debt. Herbert's contemporaries evidently found it instructive to dwell on the antithesis between divine redemption and worldly usury. John Wing's *The Best Merchandize* (1622) is subtitled "a cleare discovery of the evident difference and admirable advantage betweene our traffike with God, for the true treasure; and with men, for temporall commodity," and his doggerel preface proceeds along predictable lines: "Noe desperate Debts, or Bankrupts in this trade, / God is the Credditour, Christ surety made."[6]

George Herbert's God is also consistently presented as the antithesis of usury. The speaker of "Faith" recalls that "I owed thousands and much more / I did beleeve that I did nothing owe, / And liv'd accordingly; my creditor / Beleeves so too, and lets me go" (13–16).[7] Typically, Herbert's speaker insists that he is indebted to God, and God responds by refusing to acknowledge the debt. In "Love Unknown," the narrator is amazed to find that "all my scores were by another paid, / Who took the debt upon him" (60–61). The human speaker in "Dialogue" laments the inadequacy of his sin-riddled soul to settle his account with God. His soul, he believes, is valueless; it is not "worth the having" (2). The divine voice replies by pointing out that souls are not evaluated by the criteria of human finance:

> What (childe) is the ballance thine,
> Thine the poise and measure?
> If I say, Thou shalt be mine;
> Finger not my treasure.
> What the gains in having thee
> Do amount to, onely he,
> Who for man was sold, can see;
> That transferr'd th'accounts to me. (9–16)

The economic sense of the word "redemption" is never far away from *The Temple*'s intricate study of the transcendence of justice by mercy, nor from Herbert's descriptions of how that process is manifested in the psyche of the individual believer. It is naturally most prominent in the poem entitled "Redemption," in which Christ is figured as the "rich Lord" (1), whose only action is instant accession to the petition of his "tenant": "[He] straight *your suit is granted* said, and died" (14). But this economic metaphor permeates *The Temple* as a whole, and in my opinion it ought to be regarded as the book's most crucial and revealing trope.

In the internal drama enacted by many of Herbert's poems, the speaker's repeated misunderstandings of the Christian principle of redemption cause him to lapse and relapse into a carnal and idolatrous mode of perception. In this, he is a representative type of humanity as a whole, as Herbert points out in "Ungratefulnesse":

> Lord, with what bountie and rare clemencie
> Hast thou redeem'd us from the grave!
> If thou hadst let us runne,
> Gladly had man ador'd the sunne,
> And thought his god most brave (1–6)

It is not particularly surprising that Herbert should associate salvation with the cancellation of debt: This figure is entirely conventional. Nor, as we saw in chapter four, is it unusual to find usury, the opposite of redemption, connected to idolatry. Herbert is singular, however, in the breadth and depth of the implications he deduces from these associations. *The Temple* examines the issue of financial value from every possible angle, elaborating its ramifications for ethics, epistemology, hermeneutics, aesthetics, and soteriology.

Perhaps, indeed, it is the versatility and ubiquity of Herbert's financial imagery that has obscured its importance in the eyes of modern critics. An economy, such as our own, that unreflectingly accepts the authenticity of exchange value does not tend to foster the habits of mind that can readily perceive the influence of capital operating in the spheres of semiotics or psychology. The fact is attested to by the very concept of an "economy," that is imagined as existing in a separate "sphere" from ideas or representation. But Herbert had no such concept. He did not think of "economic" matters in isolation from the question of the human soul's relation to its Creator, and he found it natural to express that relation in "economic" terms. The complex vicissitudes of this relationship preclude any rigid adherence to an economic dogma, and economics generally functions as the vehicle rather than the tenor of *The Temple*'s meditations. Thus, it would be simplistic to claim that Herbert is "against" exchange value. In *The Priest to the Temple,* for example, he compares a child's innocent preference for use value over exchange value to humanity's attachment to the visible and immediate world. The sensuous reality of use value thus stands for materialism, while the imperceptible nature of exchange value allows it to represent the invisible kingdom of heaven:

> Man would sit down at this world, God bids him sell it, and purchase a better: Just as a Father, who hath in his hand an apple, and a piece of Gold under it; the Child comes, and with pulling, gets the apple out of his Fathers hand: his Father bids him throw it away, and he will give him the gold for it, which the Child utterly refusing, eats it, and is troubled with wormes: So is the carnall and wilfull man with the worm of the grave in this world, and the worm of Conscience in the next.[8]

It is nevertheless true that when he considers money in literal rather than figurative terms, Herbert takes up a traditionally Aristotelian stance. This attitude is also found in *The Priest to the Temple*. In chapter 26, for instance, Herbert writes of wealth using the conventional concepts of "abuse" and "end": ". . . wealth is given to that end to supply our occasions. Now, if I do not give every thing its end, I abuse the Creature, I am false to my reason which should guide me, I offend the supreme Judge, in perverting that order which he hath set both to things, and to reason." This reasoning characterizes the didactic poems placed before the central section of *The Temple* and entitled "The Church Porch." In this opening section, the lengthy, moralistic "Perirrhanterium" proclaims the ethical superiority of use over exchange: ". . . Get to live; / Then live, and use it: els, it is not true / That thou hast gotten. Surely use alone / Makes money not a contemptible stone" (153–6). This assumption is so completely assimilated into Herbert's world view that its expression often seems trite: "What skills it, if a bag of stones or gold / About thy neck do drown thee? Raise thy head; / Take starres for money; starres not to be told / By any art, yet to be purchased" (169–72). The exchange value attached to gold is assumed here to be useless and illusory: The use value of gold is similar to that of any other stone. Human beings can "purchase" the stars, which metonymically represent the kingdom of heaven and therefore an authentically useful worth, but Herbert's point is to distinguish the figurative "money" with which heaven can be "purchased" from the literal, mundane money that represents worldly value. "Perirrhanterium" employs avarice as the paradigmatic instance of worldliness and suggests that it is a sin that involves a reversal of the natural relation of subject to object. Herbert cautions his reader "Lest gaining gain on thee" (164), and points out that "Wealth is the conjurer's devil; / Whom when he thinks he hath, the devil hath him"[9] (165–6). Toward the end of this introduction, Herbert introduces the crucial typological figure around which his entire work is structured: the transcendence of the external, literal, and objective temple of the Jews by the internal, figurative, and subjective "temple" of the Christian "heart": "Christ purg'd his temple; so must thou thy heart" (423). *The Temple*, he claims, will instruct the reader how to drive the figurative money-changers out of the figurative temple that is the human heart. This oscillation between the material temple and the spiritual "temple" of the heart is the primary technique through which Herbert considers the phenomenon that we might anachronistically term the "objectification of the subject."

"The Church Porch" accomplishes the requisite preliminaries to this process by recommending reforms in outward personal conduct, while the concluding poem, "The Church Militant," describes the historical and political manifestations of this internal struggle. The subject of the latter is the growth and spread of Christianity, envisaged as dogged at every turn by the pursuing specter of "sinne," which reveals itself in one form or another of idolatry. The most recent of these forms, according to Herbert, is financial:

> Ah, what a thing is man devoid of grace,
> Adoring garlick with an humble face,
> Begging his food of that which he may eat,
> Starving the while he worshippeth his meat!
> Who makes a root his god, how low is he,
> If God and man be sever'd infinitely!
> What wretchednesse can give him any room,
> Whose house is foul, while he adores his broom?
> None will beleeve this now, though money be
> In us the same transplanted foolerie. (111–120)

In this passage, Herbert explains how, like earlier forms of idol worship, the fetishization of money involves a topsy-turvy attitude to experience that mistakes the sign for the referent and the object for the subject. There is nothing remotely mystical about this. Herbert understands perfectly well that the baleful prominence of money is caused by the American gold that was pouring into Europe as he wrote. The idolatry that this influx of gold must inevitably produce will, Herbert accurately predicts, have a disastrous long-term effect on the health of European Christianity. The lines in which Herbert declares that "Religion stands tip-toe in our land / Readie to passe to the American strand" (235–6) have usually been read as an approving reference to the radical sectaries who were being forced into exile. Critics have puzzled over this reference, since it comes from a man who elsewhere appears to be a staunch conformist Anglican.[10] No one, so far as I know, has observed that in their context these lines cannot possibly refer to Englishmen. When Herbert declares "Then shall Religion to America flee," he imagines it spreading among the Indians, not among European immigrants. In the following lines, the reference to gold makes it clear that "We" refers to Europe as a whole, while "they" designates the native Americans rather than the puritan exiles:

> They have their times of Gospel, ev'n as we.
> My God, thou dost prepare for them a way
> By carrying first their gold from them away:
> For gold and grace did never yet agree:
> Religion alwaies sides with povertie.
> We think we rob them, but we think amisse:
> We are more poore, and they more rich by this.
> Thou wilt revenge their quarrell, making grace
> To pay our debts, and leave her ancient place
> To go to them, while that which now their nation
> But lends to us, shall be our desolation. (247–58)

It is generically appropriate that "The Church Porch" and "The Church Militant" make the political case against money fetishism, while the lyrics of "The Church" examine the corresponding impact of carnal temptation on the individual psyche. Avarice is, of course, only one avenue taken by such temptation. In the rest of this chapter we will see how Herbert imagines the connection between money fetishism and the myriad other manifestations of worldliness that he makes it his business to denounce.

II

Many of Herbert's poetic discussions of exchange value associate it with a confusion of subject and object.[11] Money, he repeatedly suggests, becomes an animate force to the same degree that human beings are reduced to mere things: The subjectification of the object and the objectification of the subject are parts of the same process. In "Providence," Herbert remarks how appropriate it is that God has placed precious metals within the earth—the same element of which the human body is made, and to which it must return. This design, Herbert insists, is providential:

> Thou hast hid metals: man may take them thence;
> But at his perill: when he digs the place,
> He makes a grave; as if the thing had sense,
> And threatend man, that he should fill the space. (81–4)

The attribution of a merely customary, human value to a natural object, such as takes place when gold is declared to be money, is in Herbert's view an act of fetishism: It is acting "as if the thing had sense." As such, it reverses the proper roles of subject and object, assigning agency to a mere metal and, by the same token, removing it from human beings. In "Avarice," he addresses money in the manner of an aristocrat to a court *parvenu:* "I know thy parentage is base and low: / Man found thee poore and dirtie in a mine" (3–4). The "great kingdome" (6) now possessed by money is no result of its natural qualities, and the financial power of gold is nothing more than externalized human power:

> Nay, thou hast got the face of man; for we
> Have with our stamp and seal transferr'd our right:
> Thou art the man, and man but drosse to thee.
> Man calleth thee his wealth, who made thee rich . . . (10–13)

In poems such as this, Herbert approaches a fully fledged understanding of alienation. The significance of this for his thought is so portentous that it is hard to fathom how many of his most distinguished critics have missed it. Helen Vendler, for example, dismisses "Avarice" out of hand: " . . . the motivation of the poem itself is entirely obscure. Why did Herbert feel moved to write 'Avarice'? And in sonnet form?. There is no breath of temptation in the poem, nothing to show that Herbert himself ever thought money powerful or attractive."[12] Of course this is true, but Vendler inexplicably fails to see the implications of Herbert's analysis of money as alienated human thought. She seems to assume that he is merely trotting out a trite denunciation of the lust for pelf. But it seems to me that Herbert's "economic" thought shares a common pattern and logic with his theology and his poetics, and that an awareness of this common element makes Herbert a richer and deeper poet than the pedantic preacher Vendler finds in "Avarice."

I said above that Herbert's God, or "Redeemer," is frequently defined in opposition to usury. This, regrettably, meant that he was defined in opposition to what Herbert understood as "Judaism." The identification of Judaism with usury is perhaps the most tragic instance in history of the practical application of tropological representation. Lacking any real experience of Jews, English people of the sixteenth and seventeenth centuries constructed an image of Judaism which they found theologically appropriate.[13] For example, Francis Bacon reports it as a common view "That usurers should have orange-tawney bonnets, because they do judaize."[14] Bacon does not say, as some of his continental contemporaries might have, that Jews *are* usurers; he says that Judaism is *like* usury. The perceived homology between Judaism and usury dictates that, even where the categories "Jew" and "usurer" are not *literally* coterminous, they are *figuratively* so. Thus in a Star Chamber case in 1605, the Lord Chancellor casually referred to usurers by the term "mercatores Juadizantes."[15] In *The Speculation of Usurie* (1596), Thomas Bell cites a passage from St. Bernard that illustrates this homological reasoning: "... if Jewes be wanting in any place, Christians that be usurers (a pitifull case) are found to surpasse them in Judaisme; if it be that we may terme them Christians, and not rather baptized Jewes."[16]

What is this figurative "Judaisme," in which Christian usurers "surpasse" literal Jews? As in Bacon's observation that usurers "judaize," the term must refer to some common element that was assumed to unite usury and Judaism. That element, in my opinion, is objectification. The people of Renaissance England thought of Judaism as a "carnal," or objectifying, religion, and it was this rather than any empirical evidence that made the connection of Judaism with usury seem plausible. Although they could not but admit the aniconic nature of Judaism, early modern Christians nevertheless found it appropriate to consider it an idolatrous religion, due to their expansive understanding of "idolatry." The Jews, it was claimed, made an idol out of the carnal law. They were therefore supposed to possess an entirely fleshly consciousness, which excluded them from the spiritual grace of the Gospel and which harmonized appropriately with their usurious business practices.

Like Shylock, Marlowe's Barabas simply equates his religion with his riches. Counting his treasures in *The Jew of Malta*'s opening scene, he unambiguously observes that "These are the Blessings promis'd to the Jewes, / And herein was old Abrams happinesse" (1.1.105–6).[17] Also like Shylock, Barabas is consistently connected to objectification,[18] as when he employs exchange value as a substitute or equivalent for his self: "I hope our credit in the Customehouse / Will serve as well as I were present there" (1.1.57–8). Barabas also anticipates Shylock by using literalist hermeneutics in order to exploit Christians, falsely assuring Mathias that his metaphorical conversation with Lodowick should in fact be taken according to the letter: "Tush man, we talk'd of Diamonds, not of Abigal!" (2.3.154). Most famously, he remarks on the paradox whereby immense financial value is held to be embodied in physically insignificant quantities of gold, in terms that parody the incarnation: "Infinite riches in a little roome" (37). The perception of value in gold is presented as an inverted travesty of the incarnation, which Marlowe evidently finds befitting in a race of "Christ-killers." Barabas and Shylock indicate how capitalism came to be associated with Judaism by that strain of antisemitism that has aptly been called "the socialism of fools." Even Karl

Marx, anything but a fool, consciously uses Judaism as a trope for exchange value:

> The Jew has emancipated himself in a Jewish manner, not only because he has acquired financial power, but also because, through him and also apart from him, *money* has become a world power and the practical Jewish spirit has become the practical spirit of the Christian nations. The Jews have become emancipated insofar as the Christians have become Jews.[19]

Marx means that the various financial practices that medieval Europe had condemned as "usury" and that it had, in theory though not in practice, restricted to the Jews, were now perfectly respectable procedures of capitalist business. This is the historical, or empirical, justification for Marx's figurative equation of Judaism with capitalism. But we can hear in his metaphor the distinct echo of an older, conceptual connection between them—a connection that is determined by the theological ancestry of the theory of exchange value. As we saw in the introduction, Marx claimed that capital was objectified labor power or, as he calls it in his early works, objectified "life-activity." These terms are often misunderstood and thought to refer to particular, concrete acts of labor. In fact, however, the concept of "labor power" is an abstraction from such individual acts of labor, and it can be identified with human subjective activity in general. As objectified labor power, then, capital is an alienated representation of human life itself. As Marx puts it in *On the Jewish Question:* "Money is the estranged essence of man's work and man's existence, and this alien essence dominates him, and he worships it."[20]

The earliest example of Christian *adversus Judaeos* polemic, Justin Martyr's *Dialogue with Trypho*, already contains the same elements of anti-Judaism that we find in Renaissance England. Justin quotes Jeremiah to show that the Jews' collective "heart is hardened" and claims that they "boast of . . . the flesh."[21] A direct consequence of this is their inability to see the "spiritual" significance of material things, even with regard to their own religion, about which Justin is eager to instruct them: "This is the symbolic meaning of unleavened bread, that you do not commit the old deeds of the bad leaven. You have understood everything in a carnal way . . ." (168–9). This emboldens Justin to claim the Jewish Scriptures for Christianity, "For we believe and obey them; whereas you, though you read them, do not grasp their spirit" (191). The rituals and prohibitions of the Old Testament law were imposed in accordance with the Israelites' tendency to idolatry; a tendency that, Justin boasts, Christians have left behind:

> You still continued to practice idolatry—in the times of Elias, when God was enumerating those who had not bowed the knee to Baal, He could count only seven thousand. And in Isaias He scolds you for having sacrificed your children to idols. But we Christians, because we refuse to offer sacrifice to those whom we formerly worshipped, suffer the most severe punishments, and even rejoice in enduring the death penalty, because we believe that one day God will raise us up again through Christ, and will make us free for ever from corruption, pain and death. And we are positive that the ordinances imposed upon you on account of your people's hardness of heart are in no way conducive to acts of justice and piety. (217–8)

For an example of how deeply this reasoning underlay the English Renaissance conception of Judaism, we need look no farther than Shylock. His opening lines announce his location within this Christian hermeneutic economy. On first laying eyes on Antonio, he remarks, "How like a fawning publican he looks!" (1.3.41). The allusion is to the parable of the pharisee and the publican, which is the main text in which Jesus differentiates between the dispensation of works, represented by the public religious observance of the pharisee, and the dispensation of faith, represented by the sinning yet sincerely penitent publican. Shylock is thus immediately associated with the letter of the law, and he solidifies this association through his absurd and pedantic literalism during the trial scene. The fact that he literally wishes to exact a pound of flesh connects him to carnality and shows his readiness to draw an equation between human life and a financial sum. But what marks him most specifically as an alien is his practice of usury, which Shakespeare is careful to distinguish from ordinary avarice. Usury, we are told in the play's many echoes of contemporary economic pamphlets, is immoral because it is "a breed of barren metal" (3.3.134). It makes money reproduce as if it were a natural, living thing. But not only is money not alive, it is the objectified representation of life: In a sense, it is the reverse of life. Shylock's breeding of money bespeaks a fatal reversal of subject and object: He treats dead things as though they were alive, and as a consequence he is driven to seek the death of people who actually are alive. The Biblical text referred to here is "the letter killeth, but the spirit giveth life," especially as expounded by Augustine: "the teaching of law without the life-giving spirit is 'the letter that killeth.'"[22]

Shylock can often seem sympathetic to modern readers, because we admire his passionate claim to equality before the law. For a sixteenth- or seventeenth-century audience, however, this claim would merely have provided further evidence of his legalistic carnality. Despite the fact that, as a Jew, he is *essentially* different from the Christians, Shylock asserts the right to be considered *equivalent* to them in the eyes of the law. This insistence on what the play's original audience would certainly have perceived as a false equivalence is presented as an imposition of *nomos* onto *phusis,* akin to the imposition of customary, quantitative exchange value onto natural, qualitative use value. Perhaps a less canonical example will serve to illustrate the axiomatic nature of these homologies for our period. In "The Bride's Ornament," from *Divine and Moral Speculations* (1654), Robert Aylett writes:

> As in each Market Town and common Mart,
> There is of Weights and Measures but one size,
> And Standard, which true right to all doth part,
> And Weight and Measure justly doth comprise;
> Ev'n so in this Worlds Market men devise
> One Law to meate out ev'ry Man his due,
> And by that Law the Judges ought assise
> All their Decrees and Judgements just and trew,
> And not in stead of Laws to broach Opinions new.
> (271–279)[23]

Exchange value, the value of the "Mart," is a common denominator that makes distinct essences equivalent, and in "this Worlds Market" the law functions in precisely the same manner with regard to men. Aylett's sentiments seem quite republican here. But the lines that follow draw a cautionary connection among this mode of equivalence, legalistic literalism and carnal sensuality:

> But as in Man we soul and body finde,
> So Laws consist of Letter and true Sense;
> And as the body place gives to the minde,
> So the Laws Letter with Obedience,
> To the true Sense and Soul of Law consents.
> Who Letter of the Law seek to maintain,
> And leave her minde and meanings excellence,
> Are like them that their bodies good to gain,
> Both Soul and Body hazard to eternall pain. (280–288)

The psychological tendency Aylett describes in the last four lines—a stubborn refusal to move beyond the letter, the sign, the body—was termed "carnality" in the Renaissance and is known to modern philosophy as "objectification." In the Renaissance, and in some circles for quite a long time afterward, carnality was closely intertwined with what was understood to be "Judaism." The fleshly dispensation of the Jews was connected simultaneously with the fetishization of money as capital and with the letter of the law and literalism in its interpretation. It is not difficult to trace the logic through which this connection is sustained: For money to reproduce as capital, it must be conceived of as valuable *in itself*. It must not be thought of as a sign or token, which merely represents commodities in order to facilitate their exchange. It must not simply stand for something beyond itself; it must be viewed as an end in itself—its value must be imagined as inherent rather than referential. The correlative of this in the sphere of hermeneutics is a rigid, materialistic literalism, a refusal to look beyond the letter of the signifier which was often referred to as an antiteleological "abuse"—hence the facility with which John Weemse declares that "the word of God is still the word of God, although [the Jews] abuse it to a wrong end."[24] As Barbara Lewalski explains, "the 'meer letter,' or 'the carnal sense,' is frequently equated with the 'sense of the Jews' now wholly abrogated by Christ."[25] Hence Shylock's inflexible adherence to his bond, and hence, in the view of Christian typologists, the inability of the Jews to perceive that the literal, historical events of the Old Testament were the material signs designating the new, spiritual dispensation instituted by the incarnation and sacrifice of Christ.[26]

The problem lies in the human tendency to fetishize signs, which is really to forget that they are signs at all. Idolatry, in such descriptions as the following from Calvin, is the adoration of the empty signifier:

> Let us remember, therefore, that [Paul] is here treating of ceremonies not taken in their true and native signification, but when wrested to a false and vicious interpretation, not of the legitimate use, but of the superstitious abuse of them. What wonder, then, if ceremonies, when separated from Christ, are devoid of all virtue? All signs become null when the thing signified is taken away.[27]

A Platonizing strain entered very early into Christian hermeneutics and encouraged its adherents, the foremost among whom was Origen, to portray the Old Testament types as "fleshly" signs which received their "spiritual" referents in the life of Christ.[28] Christian typology thus evolves into a kind of historicized Platonism, where a succession of spiritual significances is revealed lurking behind precedent material shadows, not by means of Socratic syllogisms or Plotinian contemplation but in the course of the chronological unfolding of human history.

The lack of sophistication displayed by George Herbert with regard to Judaism is thus the effect of historical rather than personal causes. It is nevertheless hard for a modern reader to see certain poems in *The Temple* as anything but anti-Judaic.[29] This no doubt explains why several of Herbert's most important poems are barely mentioned in many eminent studies of his work. Stanley Fish notes the lack of critical attention given to "The Jews" in particular, pointing out that "Martz, Summers, Stein and Vendler do not even list it in their indexes."[30] Neither do Lewalski, Singleton, Sherwood, Clarke, Hodgkins, Lull, or Veith, while Strier[31] and Todd[32] mention it only once, in passing. The importance of typology to *The Temple* is impossible to ignore, but critics have understandably been reluctant to follow through the implications of this emphasis. Harold Toliver puts it delicately when he observes that Herbert "stakes his reading, both of Scripture and of the lyric persona in it, on the Pauline movement from Old to New Testaments, which is a movement from cultural specificity to Hellenic abstraction.... that movement sets Herbert apart from the Hebraicism of some of his contemporaries..."[33] Herbert's thought is deeply teleological, and *The Temple* consists of a systematic, repeated "cancellation of lesser meanings—regional, perhaps more precise, certainly more anecdotal—on behalf of greater, logocentric ones."[34] The "lesser meanings" that Herbert is constantly concerned to obviate and transcend are the "carnal" elements of life and consciousness, and he perceives and utilizes Judaism as a synecdoche for those elements.

Herbert's anti-Judaism is thus not an embarrassing foible or aberration: It is absolutely fundamental to his theology and his art. The imagery he associates with Judaism in "The Jews" is identical to that employed by Shakespeare and Marlowe: barrenness, death, usury, legalism and literalism are its leading characteristics:

> Poore nation, whose sweet sap, and juice
> Our cyens have purloin'd, and left you drie:
> Whose streams we got by the Apostles sluice,
> And use in baptisme, while ye pine and die:
> Who by not keeping once, became a debtor;
> And now by keeping lose the letter (1–6)

This sort of thing would be of little interest if Herbert were seriously essaying a diagnosis of Judaism, but of course his real concern is with the implications of the relationship between the old and the new dispensations for the interior condition of the Christian psyche. He explains this in "Self-condemnation":

> Thou who condemnest Jewish hate,
> For choosing Barabbas a murderer
> Befor the Lord of Glorie;
> Look back upon thine own estate,
> Call home thine eye (that busie wanderer)
> That choice may be thy storie (1–6)

This is entirely conventional typology: The story of the Jewish nation is the story of the Christian individual in figurative form. But Herbert puts a particular emphasis on this relationship. We experience a kind of interior Judaism, he claims, when we feel attracted to the things of this world and the pleasures of the flesh. To love material things is to love mortality; it is to choose death over life. This is a "Jewish choice," because it is the fulfillment of the choice prefigured in the Jews' preference of Barabas to Jesus:

> He that doth love, and love amisse
> The worlds delights before true Christian joy,
> Hath made a Jewish choice:
> The world an ancient murderer is . . . (7–10)

In the third stanza the poem's biblical model shifts from Barabas to Judas, and also from the thanatropic attachment to mortality that characterizes all worldliness to the paradigmatic epitome of worldliness that is financial value. This mode of value, Herbert notes, is not merely unethical; it is ontologically "false":

> He that hath made a sorrie wedding
> Between his soul and gold, and hath preferr'd
> False gain before the true,
> Hath done what he condemnes in reading:
> For he hath sold for money his deare Lord,
> And is a Judas-Jew. (13–18)

Herbert uses the word "Jew" here in much the same way as Marx uses it in the passage cited above from *On the Jewish Question:* as a conceptually appropriate trope for exchange value. To be a "Jew" is to prefer the "false gain" of "money" above the "true" gain available only to the "soul." The hermeneutic habit that made Judaism seem appropriate for this purpose is typological, as Herbert indicates in "The Bunch of Grapes":

> For as the Jews of old by Gods command
> Travell'd, and saw no town;
> So now each Christian hath his journeys spann'd:
> Their storie pennes and sets us down.
> A single deed is small renown.
> Gods works are wide, and let in future times;
> His ancient justice overflows our crimes. (8–14)

There is a revealing difference in critical opinion concerning these lines. Rosemund Tuve believes that they show how "Herbert is seriously interested in the idea that his case too is covered, taken count of, in an eternally true series of events that preceded him in time; in other words he reads history and biblical story as one great web of metaphor."[35] The poem's psychology works by locating the experience of the individual subject within an overarching, objective context, and it thus escapes "the mere conveyance of a particular individual's emotion at a given time, that thin subject with which modern readers have to be content."[36] For Richard Strier, in contrast, "the whole point of this line in context is to provide a historical and religious *validation* of Herbert's concern with his own experience.... The implications of this stanza are exactly the opposite of those demanded by Tuve's antimodernist polemic."[37] In fact, however, Tuve and Strier seem to be arguing past each other. For Herbert, the effect of typology is precisely to transcend and render obsolete the opposition between subject and object.[38] To interpret one's experience in typological form is to institute a system of mediation between the subjective psyche of the individual and the objective process of history. "The Bunch of Grapes" explicitly recommends just such a mode of interpretation:

> Then have we too our guardian fires and clouds;
> Our Scripture-dew drops fast:
> We have our sands and serpents, tents and shrowds;
> Alas! our murmurings come not last. (15–18)

A typological hermeneutic involves a rigorously symbolic reading of the empirical. The Christian must learn to see "sands and serpents, tents and shrowds" within the mundane phenomena of everyday experience. Alone among Christian hermeneutic procedures, typology insists that not only the *signs* of the Bible but also their *referents* must be interpreted symbolically. Christian typology is an instrument for extending the realm of signification from text to world; it is a way of understanding the world as a text. As the *Catholic Encyclopedia* explains, "The text is the sign conveying the literal sense, but the literal sense is the sign expressing the typical." In the words of Augustine's *City of God*, typology is "an eloquence of things, not of words."[39] And as Herbert puts it in "The H. Scriptures II":

> Such are thy secrets, which my life makes good,
> And comments on thee: for in ev'ry thing
> Thy words do finde me out, and parallels bring,
> And in another make me understood. (9–12)

Accordingly, Hebert demands that we take the sensual world to be a series of signs that point toward imperceptible referents.[40] We should beware, however, of an over-literalist interpretation, such as the speaker lapses into in lines 19–21 of "The Bunch of Grapes": "But where's the cluster? Where's the taste / Of mine inheritance? Lord, if I must borrow, /Let me as well take up their joy, as sorrow." At this stage in the poem, he imagines that there must be a strictly legalistic, one-to-one correspondence between his experience and that of the Israelites. He assumed that he is "borrow[ing]" from them and that the typological relation is in the nature of a bill of credit. As a result of this assumption, he feels cheated when he does not find a precise correspondence in his own experience for the cluster of grapes picked by Moses' scouts at Eschol (Numbers 13:23). In the final stanza, however, the speaker comes to understand that such legalistic haggling is inappropriate, and this insight is achieved when he attains an accurate typological interpretation of the poem's central image. Rather than scanning his own experience for some comfort or blessing that might correspond to the Israelites' grapes, he realizes that the cluster is to be regarded as a different kind of sign. It is, he realizes, a type of Christ, and participation in Christ removes the need for the worldly signs that merely prefigure him:

> But can he want the grape, who hath the wine?
> I have their fruit and more.
> Blessed be God, who prosper'd Noahs vine,
> And made it bring forth grapes good store.
> But much more him I must adore,
> Who of the Laws sowre juice sweet wine did make,
> Ev'n God himself being pressed for my sake. (22–28)

The new dispensation is to the old as wine is to grapes: It is its "fruit," its purpose and final cause. The grapes remain in the wine, but the wine is more than the grapes: It is the *telos* of the grapes, and the grapes prefigure the wine *in potentia*. The Old Testament God "who prosper'd Noah's vine" is to be reverenced, but his ultimate and true revelation has the effect of transcending the worldly images that represent him, and this entails the recognition by human beings of the symbolic nature of experience. To continue to pay attention to the grapes rather than the wine would be idolatry—it would be to "rest in Nature, not the God of Nature" ("The Pulley," 14)—and this is the kind of idolatry of which the Jews are convicted by virtue of their persistent attention to the literal level of the Old Testament narrative.

III

The Temple announces the centrality of typology to its project in the very title, which alludes to the scriptural trope of the human heart as the temple of the Holy Spirit. This was an especially attractive figure for Protestants because of its facility for expressing the internalization of faith. The external, objective temple of the Old Testament is transcended by the internal, subjective "temple" of the New, just as the external trappings of Catholicism are brushed aside by the interior faith of the Protestant believer. Furthermore, the image of the temple lays a particularly heavy stress on the internalization of religion, because even within the Old Testament we read of the contrast between the literal, physical temple of Solomon and its ideal prototype within the mind of David. Solomon's temple was magnificent, being largely constructed from gold (1 Kings 6:21–22). But Solomon himself acknowledges the fact that God can never literally dwell in matter: "Behold, the heaven and heaven of heavens cannot contain thee; how much less this house that I have builded?" (1 Kings 8:27) From Herbert's Protestant perspective, God dwells on earth only within the human heart, as is testified by his incarnation in human form. The incarnation is prefigured in the *idea* of the temple, which took shape in David's heart and of which the Lord specifically approves (1 Kings 8:17–18, 2 Chron. 6:7–9). Solomon's literal temple, on the other hand, soon proves susceptible to defilement by idolatry, despite God's warning (1 Kings 9:6–7).

With the New Testament's internalization of the temple, the objective, literal idols with which Solomon polluted the house of the Lord also become subjective and figurative, as in 2 Corinthians 16:

"what agreement hath the temple of God with idols? For ye are the temple of the living God . . ." In numerous scriptural texts, the transcendence of the temple by the heart is associated with the transcendence of Jewish law by Christian faith. Such, for instance, was the Christian interpretation of Jeremiah 31:33: "After those days, saith the LORD, I will put my law in their inward parts, and write it in their hearts; and will be their God, and they shall be my people." As elaborated in the Pauline epistles, such prophecies bespoke the fact that justification is by faith alone:

> For when the Gentiles, which have not the law, do by nature the things contained in he law, these, having not the law, are a law unto themselves. Which shew the work of the law written in their hearts . . . (Romans 2:14–15)
> Forasmuch as ye are manifestly declared to be the epistle of Christ ministered by us, written not with ink, but with the Spirit of the living God; not in tables of stone, but in fleshy tables of the heart . . . (2 Corinthians 3:3)[41]

The process of expelling the subjective idols from the figurative temple is constantly hampered by the tendency of the heart to become "hard." The main biblical allusion here is to Pharoah, and the bondage of Israel in Egypt, which is typologically associated by Christians with subservience to the law of the old dispensation. Hardness of heart is mollified through the influence of the Spirit, as in Ezekiel 36:26: "A new heart also will I give you, and a new spirit will I put within you: and I will take away the stony heart out of your flesh." As Calvin notes, this is a process that can work both ways, so that "When his spirit is taken away, our hearts harden into stones."[42] The concept of the "heart" is clearly central to Herbert's devotion—Walton reports that the text for Herbert's first sermon was "keep thy heart with all diligence"[43]—and the incessant reverberation between the hard and the spiritual heart is the predominant theme of *The Temple*.

Herbert describes his struggle for salvation as an unceasing battle against the process of objectification, which turns the human heart into a stone, an insensate thing. The opening poem of "The Church," "The Altar," inaugurates the complex analysis of this metaphor: "A broken altar, Lord, thy servant rears, / Made of a heart, and cemented with tears" (1–2).[44] The visible altar that we can see on the page—in the shape made by the poem's lines—is manifestly not "broken" but whole. The reader's attention is thus drawn to the fact that the "broken altar" referred to must be internal and subjective.[45] This is confirmed by the following lines: "Whose parts are as thy hand did frame; / No workman's tool hath touched the same" (3–4). Herbert refers here to Exodus 20:25: "And if thou wilt make me an altar of stone, thou shalt not build it of hewn stone: for if thou lift up thy tool upon it, thou hast polluted it."[46] This text is readily amenable to the Protestant prohibition of "works righteousness," and in the context of *The Temple* the allusion indicates that the poems will be authentic to the degree that they exhibit the author's "heart" in unmediated fashion, scorning to obscure God's handiwork by the prideful ostentation of poetic wit. We find the same association of the "heart" with sincerity, and its opposition to "wit," in *The Priest to the Temple*:

> the character of his Sermon is Holiness; he is not witty, or learned, or eloquent, but Holy. . . . dipping, and seasoning all our words and sentences in our hearts, before they come into our mouths, truly affecting, and cordially expressing all that we say; so that the auditors may plainly perceive that every word is hart-deep.

There is no suggestion, either here or in the poetry, of any suspicion of "words" as such. Instead, there is an insistence that words must be "hart-deep": They must, as we might put it, "come from" the heart. Herbert makes a case for an aesthetics of correspondence between subjective thoughts and their objective manifestations in words. As he writes in "A True Hymn," "The finenesse which a hymne or psalme affords, / Is when the soul unto the lines accords" (9–10). This, I think, is what Herbert means when he says that "no workman's tool hath touched" his poetic altar: His poems aspire to represent his heart in externalized but unmediated form.[47]

Due to the centrality of the image of the heart in Catholic devotion, Herbert's choice of this figure as the main focus of his meditation has a controversial aspect.[48] *The Temple* is an attempt to rethink this image in Protestant terms by interiorizing and spiritualizing it. In Catholic meditation, concentration on the literal, physical heart of Mary or Jesus is an important and necessary stage in the mental quest for the love and compassion of which the material heart is a symbol. For example, Richard Crawshaw's "The Flaming Heart" indicates that the pity evoked by contemplation of St. Theresa's physical wound transforms her heart from a literal, passive object into an active, metaphorical subject: "Love's passives are his activ'st part, / The wounded is the wounding heart" (73–4). In Herbert, by contrast, the physical heart is purely metaphorical. On those occasions when it becomes active, as in the lengthy "Love Unknown" or in "The H. Scriptures I," where Herbert enjoins God to "Let my heart / Suck ev'ry letter" (1–2), the sole purpose is its own mortification. The heart, in Herbert, is vivified precisely to the degree that it is "spiritualized," and this process involves the simultaneous (and homologous) flight from literalism and from the flesh. He occasionally even evinces some distrust of the physical manifestation of the heart, as in "Giddinesse": "Surely if each one saw anothers heart, / There would be no commerce, / No sale or bargain passe . . ." (21–3). (We may note in passing Herbert's automatic assumption that commercial exchange is based upon deceit, so that it would be impossible if our "hearts" were visible.) In "Sepulchre," the rocky tomb in which Jesus' body was interred is presented as tropologically apposite, because his death occurred as a result of his compatriots' hardheartedness: "Where our hard hearts have took up stones to braine thee, / And missing this, most falsly did arraigne thee; / Onely these stones in quiet entertain thee" (13–15). The biblical reference once again links hardness of heart with Judaism; it is to John 10:31, "Then the Jews took up stones again to stone him." The familiar cluster of associations is invoked, with "the Jews" once again standing for every kind of objectification:

> And as of old the Law by heav'nly art
> Was writ in stone; so thou, which also art
> The letter of the word, find'st no fit heart
>   To hold thee. (17–20)

A two-fold process of spiritualization seems to be taking place here. First, there is the transformation of the external, Judaic law of *torah* and *nomos* into an internal law, said by Paul to belong to the gentiles and written "in the heart." Second, there is a hardening of the heart itself, which renders the interior law just as ineffective for salvation as that of the old dispensation and prevents Christ from dwelling within us. This is what I have called the "interior Judaism," which Herbert exhorts his readers to resist. The same line of thought informs "Nature":

> O smooth my rugged heart, and there
> Engrave thy rev'rend Law and fear;
> Or make a new one, since the old
>   Is saplesse grown,
>   And a much fitter stone
> To hide my dust, then thee to hold. (13–18)

The pivotal word "Or" above signals the speaker's recognition that Christian "works righteousness" is merely Judaic legalism writ large. The transition from the law written in stone to the law written in the heart is here called fruitless and "saplesse," because the figurative heart has itself become a figurative stone. The point, which is the point of *The Temple* as a whole, is that we should adopt toward our "heart" the same attitude as Christianity adopts toward Judaism, since the objective relationship between the law and gospel is reenacted on the subjective level within each individual soul.

IV

Herbert's insistence on the interpenetration of subject and object is diametrically opposed to Baconian epistemology. The first principle of empiricism is that the objective world is external to the subjective observer. *The Temple* espouses instead a belief in the correspondence between the subjective and objective dimensions. As Tuve notes, *The Temple* is animated by "Not only acceptance of universal meaningfulness but systematic correspondences between meanings..."[49] Harold Toliver has pointed to "Herbert's evident distrust of Baconian science,"[50] finding a wary ambivalence in the official letter of thanks that Herbert, in his capacity as University Orator, addressed to Bacon following his gift of the *Instauration Magna:* "God grant that the same advances which thou hast made in the sphere of nature, thou mayest also make in that of grace."[51] In contrast to Bacon, Herbert is always concerned to seek after final causes, and Toliver rightly summarizes the project of *The Temple* as a "quest for a teleological fable."[52]

In "The Pearl," Herbert pursues this quest by applying his characteristic cancellation of human modes of evaluation to Baconian science. The poem's epigraph from Matthew 13 indicates that this poem's theme is to be the transcendence of earthly by heavenly value: "45. Again, the kingdom of heaven is like unto a merchant man, seeking goodly pearls; 46. Who, when he had found one pearl of great price, went and sold all he had, and bought it." The opening stanza addresses itself to "the wayes of learning" (1), which are associated with the tendency to exceed or violently distort the natural world. Herbert claims familiarity with "What reason hath from nature borrowed, / Or of it self, a good huswife, spunne / In laws and policie" (3–5). The kind of reason Herbert discusses here either "borrow[s]" its insights from nature or spins the second nature of *nomos* out of its own entrails. Correspondingly, it can either approach nature in a friendly, harmonious fashion, or it can bring an inquisitorial hostility to its investigations, so that Herbert's speaker is knowledgeable concerning both "What willing nature speaks" and "what forc'd by fire" (6).

The knowledge attainable through science, however, is reduced to insignificance by the stanza's last line, "Yet I love thee" (10), and the following stanzas repeat this pattern with regard to ambitious "honour" (11) and sensual "pleasure" (21) respectively. What is important for us is the fact that Herbert classes Baconian empiricism among such archetypally carnal temptations as ambition and sensuality. In fact, empiricism is for Herbert a *species* of carnality. The Baconian scientist holds, as his most basic methodological principle, that any subjective feeling or "bias" he may bring to his observation of the world must be eliminated from his practice. The difference between an alchemist and a chemist, like that between an astrologer and an astronomer, is that the latter does not look for correspondences between his subjective condition and the objective world that he studies. He perceives that world as a wholly external, alien thing, a *donnee*. He thus robs the world of its subjective or, as Herbert says, its "spiritual" element. This is the same error committed by sensuality and ambition. With regard to the latter, for example, Herbert mentions his experience of "How many drammes of spirit there must be / To sell my life unto my friends or foes" (18–19). The exchange of spirit for worldly place and advantage is here described as a market transaction, and the psychological effect of this deal is shown in this poem to consist in objectification.

"The Pearl" offers a guide to resistance against all forms of carnal temptation. The poem's final stanza announces that the speaker's knowledge of science, honor, and pleasure have merely served to confirm him in his estimation of their value relative to God:

> I know all these, and have them in my hand:
> Therefore not sealed, but with open eyes
> I flie to thee, and fully understand
> Both the main sale, and the commodities;
> And at what rate and price I have thy love (31–35)

The speaker proudly asserts his discernment in matters of value, his ability to identify and reject mere "commodities." The conclusion he draws from this knowledge is that God is to be approached *vertically*, by climbing out of the world on the heavenly "silk twist" (38), which recalls both Jacob's ladder and the Homeric image of the "golden chain," as used by William Perkins and countless other writers of the English Renaissance.[53] The speaker's mode of evaluation has taught him to aspire to heaven by rejecting the world, rather than by rooting around among empirical phenomena as Bacon recommended:

> Yet through the labyrinths, not my groveling wit,
> But thy silk twist let down from heav'n to me,
> Doth both conduct and teach me, how by it
> To climbe to thee. (37–40)

"The Agonie" opens with a similar dismissal of empirical investigation in favor of teleological theology:

> Philosophers have measur'd mountains,
> Fathom'd the depths of seas, of states, and kings,
> Walk'd with a staffe to heav'n, and traced fountains:
> But there are two vast, spacious things,
> The which to measure it doth more behove:
> Yet few there are that sound them; Sinne and Love. (1–6)

"Vanitie I" repeats the point. In that poem's final stanza, empirical science is criticized for its failure to recognize the subjective, spiritual significance implanted in such objective natural phenomena as "showres and frosts" (25), and its entire enterprise is consequently implicated in the ultimate objectification, which prefers the mortal world before eternal life:

> What hath not man sought out and found,
> But his deare God? Who yet his glorious law
> Embosomes in us, mellowing the ground
> With showres and frosts, with love & aw,
> So that we need not say, Where's this command?
> Poore man, thou searchest round
> To finde out death, but missest life at hand. (22–28)

This poem's previous stanzas have personified Baconian science in the figures of the "subtil Chymick" (15) who "strip[s] the creature naked" (16); the "nimble Diver" (8) who seeks a literal rather than figurative "dearely-earned pearl" (10); and the "fleet Astronomer" (1) who "Surveys" the heavens "as if he had designed / To make a purchase there" (4–5). Vendler finds in this poem a "fearful repudiation . . . of intellectual enquiry."[54] However, Herbert is not attacking intellectual enquiry as such, but merely empiricism. He evidently feels that such an approach produces a dead, empty (we might say "reified") vision of the universe, which denudes it of its creator. Viewed in such a way, the things of creation appear in a similar light as the commodities laid out in a shop window, on which the scientist gazes "as if he had designed / To make a purchase" (4–5).

Describing the vain temptations of worldly things as if they were exhibited for sale is a favorite technique of Herbert's. In "Vertue," for instance, we can clearly see the deflating, unmasking effect of this figure: "Sweet spring, full of sweet dayes and roses, / A box where sweets compacted lie" (9–10). The pun on the last word is hardly necessary. The reader will have grasped the point by virtue of the difference between the natural appearance of spring as it is described in line 9, and line 10's comparison of spring to an artificially packaged, or "compacted," "box" of "sweets," which has been designed to tempt and allure. The satirical impact of an undifferentiated catalogue of commodities is often seen as an innovation of Alexander Pope, who used such lists as "Puff, powders, patches, Bibles, billet-doux"[55] to demonstrate the vapidity of his victims. Pope's point in this line from "The Rape of the Lock" is that Belinda cannot distinguish between the objects he enumerates; to her, articles of quite different essential natures have become equivalent. John Bunyan anticipates this technique in his portrayal of "Vanity Fair": "at this Fair are all such Merchandize sold, as Houses, Lands, Trades, Places, Honours, Preferments, Titles, Countreys, Kingdoms, Lusts, Pleasures, and Delights of all sorts, as Whores, Bauds, Wives, Husbands, Children . . ."[56] Fifty years before Bunyan, however, Herbert was using the same method to satirize worldliness, as in "Dotage":

> False glozing pleasure, casks of happinesse,
> Foolish night-fires, women's and children's wishes,
> Chases in Arras, guilded empitnesse,
> Shadows well mounted, dreams in a career,
> Embroider'd lyes, nothing between two dishes;
> These are the pleasures here. (1–6)

As Singleton perceptively observes regarding these lines: "It is as if the eye were moving over the surface of a courtly world at random, noting here a tapestry, there some dishes, and intermixing these objects indifferently with thoughts and feelings and fancies."[57] The same device is used in "The Quidditie": "My God, a verse is not a crown, / No point of honour or gay suit, / No hawk, or banquet, or renown, / Nor a good sword, nor yet a lute . . ." (1–4). There is an anticipation here of what Frederic Jameson, referring to the postmodern art of Andy Warhol, has termed the "new depthlessness."[58] Warhol's paintings of tins of baked beans lay bare the process of commodification by presenting its objects removed from their contexts; Herbert's undifferentiated lists of sublunary pleasures imply that a similarly distorted sense of value pertains among the fashionable courtiers of his society.

It is this kind of superficial imagery against which Herbert protests in the "Jordan" poems. It is now pretty generally accepted that Herbert does not, paradoxically and hypocritically, denounce poetic representation per se. Rather, his ire is directed against what he considers *bad* poetry—the "winding stair" and "painted chair" that disguise the "course-spunne lines" criticized in "Jordan (I)." One of the sonnets not included in *The Temple* more nearly approaches a renunciation of metaphors as such:

> Each cloud distills thy praise, and doth forbid
> Poets to turn it to another use.
> Roses and Lillies speak thee; and to make
> A pair of Cheeks of them, is thy abuse. (4–7)

But in *The Temple* itself, Herbert's position is more subtle. In "Jordan (I)," for instance, the "friend"'s advice is not to avoid figuration per se but, like a canny customer, to shun vain expenditure on the overpriced things of this world: "There is in Love a sweetness readie penn'd / Copie out only that and save expense" (13–14). The most incisive critics of Herbert have noticed that the "Jordan" poems are cautions against interior idolatry. In them, Tuve finds Herbert "concerned with the idolatry of substituting the shadows of beauty, truth and love for their essential forms, but the idolatry he here detects is detected in himself rather than in others . . ."[59] Guernsey agrees, asking:

> what does the speaker reject in poems which critics have called iconoclastic? Does he not critique the "idolatrous" assumption that God could be present in textual reality. . . . I think just the opposite is true. . . . The idol was not the artefact; the idol was the too self conscious self cut off from God in the production of the artefact. (110–11)[60]

While I agree with Tuve and Guernsey, contra Fish, that Herbert does not seek to annihilate the self but to purge its interior idols, I differ with them concerning the nature of those idols. Herbert's psychological idols are neither Tuve's Platonic shadows nor Guernsey's "too self-conscious self." He indicates their nature clearly enough in "The Church Porch": "Christ purg'd his temple; so must thou thy heart" (423). We must, that is to say, expel from our "heart" the psychological, typological equivalents of the money-changers driven from the temple by Jesus. "Jordan (II)" goes into further detail concerning the kind of idolatry Herbert eschews:

> When first my lines of heav'nly joyes made mention,
> Such was their lustre, they did so excell,
> That I sought out quaint words and trim invention;
> My thoughts began to burnish, sprout, and swell,
> Curling with metaphors a plain intention,
> Decking the sense, as if it were to sell. (1–6)

This is, plainly enough, a protest against the commodification of language. The difficulty facing a modern reader is not in recognizing this fact but in understanding the concept. How could language be commodified; what does Herbert mean by "Decking the sense, as if it were to sell"? It is the same difficulty we face when Shakespeare informs us: "That love is merchandiz'd whose rich esteeming / The owner's tongue doth publish every where."[61] The only possible modern translation of "merchandiz'd" is "commodified," and yet we are not immediately familiar with the notion of commodified love, so that Shakespeare's precise meaning, like Herbert's, is elusive. One possibility is that in "Jordan (II)," Herbert is condemning poetry that is literally composed in order to be sold, much like the antitheatricalists we studied in chapter three. I think, however, that our preceding investigations will allow us to put forward a more plausible suggestion. What Herbert intends by this phrase is the *fetishization of the signifier*. When selling or buying—when exchanging—one's attention is distracted away from use value and directed towards exchange value. Exchange value is no part of *phusis,* it is part of *nomos*. It is not a natural essence, it is a customary sign. This sign, as Herbert very often points out, has a strong, empirically observable tendency to float free of its referents. It tends, in other words, to invite idolatry. Money, for Herbert, is this idolized signifier ("None will believe this now, though money be / In us the same transplanted foolery"). In that case, "Decking the sense, as if it were to sell" would involve not the simple use of images and metaphors (the phrase itself is metaphorical) but their fetishistic adoration. It would involve a fascination with the letter and a neglect of the spirit. It would lead to a quasi-Warholian focus on the surface appearance of things and an idolatrous triumph of custom over nature. In fact, if we want to know what Herbert intends by "Decking the sense, as if it were to sell," we could do worse than to look around us.

Chapter Six

Alchemical and Financial Value in the Poetry of John Donne

> ... *in this sign all men can find salvation.*
>
> —*Goethe,* Faust II *(6081–82)*[1]

> *The great lord has the alchemy perfectly.*
>
> —*Marco Polo, on Kubla Khan's printing of paper money*[2]

I

In one of his *Sacramental Meditations,* Edward Taylor uses a financial conceit to consider the perennial Calvinist question of how a believer can be certain of election: "Am I thy Gold? Or Purse, Lord, for thy Wealth; / Whether in mine, or mint refinde for thee?" (1–2).[3] Either of these alternatives would be acceptable to Taylor, but this should not prevent us from noticing the difference between them. The speaker is either "gold" from a "mine," or "wealth" from a "mint." The former metaphor suggests a natural, authentic substance, the latter implies a customary, artificial value. The speaker goes on to indicate that he does not feel pure enough to be authentic "gold," and he asks God to "count me o're thyselfe, / Lest gold washt face, and brass in Heart I bee" (3–4). Of course, counting gold will not show whether or not it is counterfeit. Rather, counting gold will compute the amount of financial value it represents. As the second stanza reveals, the poem is a plea to be judged by the criteria of monetary value and not by that of metallurgic purity:

> Am I new minted by thy Stamp indeed?
> Mine Eyes are dim; I cannot clearly see.
> Be thou my Spectacles that I may read
> Thine Image, and Inscription stampt on mee.
> If thy bright Image do upon me stand
> I am a Golden Angell in thy hand. (7–12)

Brought to the touchstone for trial, all human beings must be found lacking in purity. But even if the speaker should prove base metal beneath his gilded appearance, he understands that his value is not derived from himself but from his sovereign's "Image, and Inscription stampt on me." His metaphorical specie content is irrelevant; the seal of the sovereign is sufficient to authenticate him as legal tender, so that he becomes "a Golden Angell" (the pun, of course, is on the gold coins—often of dubious purity—which were known as "angels"). Just as base or impure metals are miraculously given value by the "Stamp" or "Image" of the sovereign, so fallen humanity can be recognized as "new minted" by virtue of bearing the image of God. Taylor's conceit on "Angell" is one instance of his heavy borrowing from Donne, in this case from "The Bracelet," which will be discussed at length below. But Taylor conspicuously lacks Donne's ironic awareness that the comparison of the soul to financial value implies ethical danger. His hope in this poem is that, lacking the inherent qualities that would give him intrinsic worth, he can have an external value imputed to him by heavenly authority so that, as he ingenuously puts it, "I shall be thy Money" (17).

Taylor is in grave danger here of falling into the archetypal Calvinist error of taking the appearance of sanctification for the reality. It is an error described by Donne in "A Litany," in which he warns lest "plenty, God's image and seal / Makes us idolatrous, / And love it, not him whom it should reveal" (185–6).[4] Like Taylor, Donne frequently thinks of his relationship to God in financial terms. Unlike his imitator, however, Donne conceives of monetary value as inauthentic and illusory. Indeed, it is precisely the loss of authenticity, exemplified by the imposition of exchange value on use value, and by the more general displacement of *phusis* by *nomos,* which provokes the epistemological and emotional crises that play such predominant roles in the intellectual dramas of Donne's verse.

Donne frequently chooses to describe these crises in the language of alchemy. As was mentioned in chapter five, alchemy is a form of science that predates the Baconian alienation of subject and object. The alchemist did not, as the modern chemist does, conceive of the materials he studied as wholly alien to his subjective perceptions of them. Rather, alchemy assumed a unity of subject and object, so that the condition of the practitioner's soul and the course of his experiments were indissolubly linked. Alchemy presupposes that the subject/object dichotomy is false, and alchemists thought of the chemical reactions they observed as spiritualizations of matter and materializations of spirit. Alchemical theory, logic, and imagery thus provided excellent vehicles for consideration of the shifts and developments in the relation of subject and object that took place during this period.[5] Over the course of the seventeenth century, a tension developed between the Aristotelian precepts of alchemy and the Baconian method of the new science. This tension was usually imperceptible to contemporaries, and it is often discernible within the work of single individuals, such as Newton and Boyle, as much as in differences between competing scholars or schools of thought. It is nonetheless significant for that, however. In this chapter, I will show how this tension operates in the poetry of John Donne and delineate its influence on his ideas about linguistic and financial representation.[6]

In his recent study of Goethe's *Faust,* Hans-Christophe Binswanger comments that "the modern economy is a continuation of alchemy by other means."[7] In *Faust,* the Emperor is delighted to find that the paper certificates that Mephistopheles has introduced into circulation are accepted for money by his people as readily as if they were pure gold. Goethe presents this process as a kind of perverted alchemical magic. He has understood, comments Binswanger, that "It is not vital to alchemy's aim, in the sense of increasing wealth, that lead be actually transmuted into gold. It will suffice if a substance of no value is transformed into one of value: paper, for example, into money."[8] In *The Coiners of Language,* Jean-Joseph Goux claims that Mallarme's "Magic" evinces a similar insight. Binswanger and Goux both argue that the perspicuity of their preferred author enabled him to presage the nature of the postmodern economy with uncanny accuracy. An exchange-based economy, they note, creates value out of nothing, as alchemy once tried to do. As Goux puts it:

> To make gold, not from the lead in some obscure crucible of concoctions, calcinations, solutions, and coagulations, but in the surplus value of industry, trade, and financial speculation: in our present-day

economy, the philosophers' stone has become the prosaic money in the ledgers of capital.⁹

In this chapter, I will argue that the recognition that capitalism is a form of perverted alchemy precedes either Mallarme or Goethe. It can be clearly discerned in much of the English literature of the seventeenth century, in which the contrast between the Aristotelian philosophy of genuine alchemy and the mundane sorcery by which money is made to reproduce was regularly adduced as evidence for the turpitude and absurdity of exchange value. As late as 1645, the alchemist Eyraeneus Philalethes Cosmopolita called money "that prop of the antichristian Beast" and predicted that in a few years, it would be "dashed in pieces" by alchemy.[10] John Donne, in particular, sees profound significance in the fate of alchemy, but his interest in the subject is far from indicating eccentricity. Rather, it suggests the degree to which Donne's thought is immersed in and responsive to the predominant intellectual currents of his age.

It is, perhaps, the most familiar cliche of twentieth-century literary criticism to say that this tension between Aristotelian and Baconian epistemologies informs the literary style of the "metaphysical poets." For T. S. Eliot, Donne and Marvell formed an heroic rearguard, defending the organic, integrated universe against the materialist and positivist forces of dissociation. The genius of Donne, claims Eliot, lay not so much in his ability to resist the objectifying tendencies of his age as in his awareness of those tendencies and his ability to give them formal expression in his verse. Eliot famously refers to "the sensuous interest of Donne in his own thoughts as objects," and argues that "this interest naturally led him to expression by conceits."[11] E. M. W. Tillyard saw the metaphysical compulsion to yoke the heterogeneous as a reaction against the disintegration of the system of correspondences. Tillyard finds that, over the course of the sixteenth century, such "equivalences shaded off into resemblances.... It was through their retention of the main points and their flexibility in interpreting the details that the Elizabethans were able to use these great correspondences in their attempt to tame a bursting and pullulating world."[12] Hence, for instance, the metaphysical conceit, which derives its power from its firm belief in an actual as well as a figurative connection between vehicle and tenor. The poet's "wit" was conceived of as observing and expressing these correspondences rather than as inventing them. As Marjorie Hope Nicolson puts it: "Our ancestors thought that what we call 'analogy' was *truth,* inscribed by God in the nature of things."[13]

It is of course true that, as Jonathan Dollimore and many others have pointed out,[14] scholars like Eliot, Tillyard, and Nicolson ignore the subaltern elements of society and universalize the ideas of the dominant classes. They also concentrate on literary texts to the exclusion of wider political or economic concerns. But is this necessarily a barrier to the understanding of politics or economics? As we saw in the introduction, the postmodern environment seems increasingly happy to consider political, economic, and linguistic modes of representation as not only connected but homologous. That is to say, it is beginning to look as if the *formal* structure of representation has a distinct history of development that overrides the specificity of the spheres in which it is manifested. It may also be that the people of the sixteenth and early seventeenth centuries took this unity for granted, and that the modern belief in the separability of such "spheres" as economics, politics, and linguistics is itself good evidence for the Eliotian dissociation of sensibility. My working assumption here will be that Donne, like many other writers of his age, found in the ancient art of alchemy a discourse through which he could simultaneously consider developments in the area we call "economic" and conflicts in the fields we refer to as "psychology" and "religion."

It may seem incongruous to us that the vogue for alchemy flourished alongside the burgeoning of positivist science, but it did not necessarily seem so to the people of the seventeenth century. They did not always perceive the contradictions that we find between these systems of thought, and individuals who were interested in one also tended to be interested in the other.[15] Isaac Newton's alchemical activity is the most famous example of this, but only because it was one of the latest. However, the contradictions between Aristotelian and Baconian epistemologies are no less real for the fact that the people of the Renaissance were often unaware of them. Alchemy (which stands in relation to chemistry as astrology does to astronomy) conceives of the material world as connected to the world of ideas through an intricate system of "correspondences," which were revealed to human beings as analogical resemblances among the various levels of creation. This system of thought argued for a fundamental harmony between subject and object: The human being, it contended, was a microcosm of creation. George Herbert expresses the idea succinctly in "Man":

> Man is all symmetrie,
> Full of proportions, one limbe to another,
> And all to all the world besides:

Each part may call the farthest, brother:
And head with foot hath private amitie,
And both with moons and tides. (13–18)[16]

The objective universe and our subjective experience of that universe were created in a relation of *correspondence* with one another. Although that correspondence has been obscured since the Fall, it remains perceptible in the system of analogies and resemblances that careful observers notice between the subjective mind and external creation, as the next stanza of Herbert's poem suggests. It begins by noting that a disharmonious, predatory relationship now exists between "man" and the universe, and the reference to astronomy connects this development to the new philosophy: "Nothing hath got so farre, / But Man hath caught and kept it, as his prey. / His eyes dismount the highest starre" (19–21). And yet the lines immediately following reassert the unity of microcosm and macrocosm without any acknowledgment of the contradiction: "He is in little all the sphere. / Herbs gladly cure our flesh; because that they / Finde their acquaintance there." (22–24).

It seems, then, that the mutual exclusivity of empirical science and the universe of correspondences was not immediately apparent to many Renaissance thinkers, and this despite the fact that Bacon had clearly declared it in the *Novum Organon*. It is precisely the perception of a systematic correspondence between subject and object to which Bacon objects:

> It is incredible what a number of idols have been introduced into philosophy by the reduction of natural operations to a correspondence with human actions, that is, by imagining that nature acts as man does.... The human understanding is of its own nature prone to suppose the existence of more order and regularity in the world than it finds. And though there be many things in nature which are singular and unmatched, yet it devises for them conjugates and parallels and relatives which do not exist.[17]

By this definition, the paradigmatic Baconian "idol" was alchemy. As is well known, Bacon valued alchemy only for its practical successes in adding to our instrumental knowledge of physical matter. Its ultimate end and purpose he regarded as at best a distraction from pragmatic investigation:

> Nor can it be denied that the alchymists have made several discoveries, and presented mankind with useful inventions. But we may well apply

to them the fable of the old man, who bequeathed to his sons some gold buried in his garden, pretending not to know the exact spot, whereupon they worked diligently in digging the vineyard, and though they found no gold, the vintage was rendered more abundant by their labour.[18]

But such skepticism did not deter some of the best minds of the sixteenth and seventeenth centuries from diverting a huge amount of their time and energies into alchemical investigations. What was the source of alchemy's persistent appeal? The founding document of Western alchemy is the *Emerald Table,* attributed to Hermes Trismegistus. It opens with the basic proposition: "That which is beneath is like that which is above: & that which is above, is like that which is beneath, to work the miracles of one thing. And as all things have proceeded from one, by the mediation of one, so all things have sprung from this one thing by adaptation."[19] Here we have the seminal form of the system of correspondences. The disjunctions between earth and heaven, spirit and matter, subject and object, are declared to be illusory. These apparent polarities are, in reality, subsumed within an overriding totality. Consequently, sublunary phenomena and superlunary noumena correspond to each other, and this correspondence is manifest in the chain of analogical resemblances that can, with effort, be discerned within the visible universe. This attitude assumes that the world is a system of signs in which the diligent observer can detect the presence of an ulterior reality. The most famous alchemist of the Renaissance, Paracelsus, says of the ideal realm that: "Hereto also do refer the vertues and Operations of all creatures, and their use, they being stamped or markt with their arcanums, signs, characters and figures . . ."[20]

Clearly, this approach to the world has profound implications for poetics. In fact, the perception and demonstration of hitherto unperceived analogies between different elements of creation has frequently been advanced as the very definition of poetry. Aristotle's *Poetics* argues that, with regard to poetic composition, "the greatest thing by far is to have a command of metaphor. This alone cannot be imparted by another; it is the mark of genius, for to make good metaphors implies an eye for resemblances."[21] Whereas a modern reader might imagine the poet as inventing these resemblances and imposing them upon objects that are actually different and distinct, for Aristotle these resemblances are real, and poetic genius consists in the ability not to invent but to recognize them. Since they viewed subjectively perceived correspondences among different levels of phenomena as the discovery of truth, alchemists, like poets, felt free to use symbols with a purely subjective significance. The connotations of a particular symbol in the alchemist's mind were a perfectly legitimate part of their art, for they viewed the subjective and the objective meanings of symbols as interpenetrative. Such a semiotics is anathema to empiricism. John Locke describes such "*Inconstancy*" as a "great abuse of Words," for "Words being intended for signs of my *Ideas*, to make them known to others not by any natural signification but by a voluntary imposition, 'tis plain cheat and abuse when I make them stand sometimes for one thing and sometimes for another." It is, he says, as if a man at the market were to sell "several Things under the same Name." Locke attacks above all the confusion of language and world made "by those who look upon *Essences* and *Species* as real established Things in Nature."[22] The Aristotelian and the Baconian views of the world, then, have divergent attitudes toward representation, and this difference logically extends to representation in both financial and linguistic forms.

The function of money is figurative: It is a common denominator that expresses the figurative (as opposed to the literal or material) value of things. As a figurative medium, money is used to create resemblances between things; it allows us to conceive of a figurative equivalence between objects that are essentially distinct. As Rice Vaughan explains in *Of Coins and Coinage* (pub. 1675):

> Thus did Money grow inseparably necessary to all Exchange, to make the things exchanged equal in value, for that all exchange is either by the actual or intellectual valuation of Money; that is to say, Either the thing is exchanged for Money, or if it be exchanged for another thing, the measure of that exchange is how much Money either of the things exchanged is conceived to be worth; and Practice hath found out that in values, which the Geometricians have found out in quantities, that two lines which are equal to a third line, are equal to one another: So is money a third line, by which all things are made equal in value, and therefore it is not ill compared to the Materia Prima, because, though it serves actually to no use almost, it serves potentially to all uses.[23]

Vaughan's reference here to the alchemical concept of the *prima materia* (the chaotic substance out of which, according to Plato's *Timaeus*, the demiurge molded the universe) is intriguing but misleading. His preceding argument notes that money consists in quantity rather than quality. This is what gives it the ability to render essentially distinct qualities equivalent. Certainly the *prima materia* plays a similar role: It is the common element out of which the other four have been formed and into which, in the alchemical tradition, they can once again be reduced in the flasks of the laboratory. However, alchemy does not think of the *prima materia* as an abstract quantitative medium of equivalence but as a literal, physical, and qualitative object. The alchemical notion of value, by extension, is profoundly qualitative—more so, even, than that of the "bullionist" political economists. For a bullionist like Vaughan, financial value is identified with the material body of gold. For an alchemist, however, the value of gold is not financial at all but moral and ontological. The very concept of an autonomous financial mode of evaluation is alien and contradictory to the alchemical world view. Despite this, alchemy paradoxically provided a discursive field in which, during our period, the concept of autonomous financial value was able to take root and flower. Let us now observe some concrete examples of that process.

II

The cornerstone of alchemy is the theory of correspondence between the microcosm and the macrocosm. Donne's *Satire V* offers a typical endorsement of this theory: "If all things be in all, /As I think, since all, which were, are, and shall / Be, be made of the same elements: / Each thing, each thing implies or represents. / Then man is a world..." (9–13).[24] In the seventeenth century, the concept of the microcosm was associated with the alchemy of Paracelsus, with whose reworking of Aristotle's theory of the elements Donne is evidently familiar. It was increasingly objected, however, that Paracelsian science relied on the empirically untenable equation of tropological resemblance with ontological unity. In other words, it translated analogy into homology. Bacon remarked that "the ancient opinion that man was *miscrocosmus,* an abstract or model of the world, hath been fantastically strained by Paracelsus and the alchemists...,"[25] and Daniel Sennert noted in 1619 that "the Analogie of the great and little World is extended too large by the Chymists, because they make not an Analogie, but an identity, or the same thing."[26] The seventeenth-century scientist Kepler anticipates Doctor Johnson on Donne when he complains of the sixteenth-century alchemist Fludd's assumption that "what is below is like that which is above.... But in order to make this analogy fit all cases he often has to drag in his comparisons by the hair."[27] The problems with Paracelsus's "Microcosmical Dreams," wrote Van Helmont in 1662, arise "by literally, and not metaphorically understanding them, which sense or meaning doth always banish it self from the History of natural things."[28]

As these increasingly numerous and cogent criticisms suggest, it was impossible for alchemy to long survive the collapse of the analogical universe. Alchemy is the practical attempt to realize the spiritual essence, or *telos,* of matter. It assumes that the objective existence of a thing is only a representation of its ideal form. The alchemist sought to rectify this situation, breaking down and reconstituting imperfect matter in such a way as to bring it to the perfection of its natural end. Following Aristotle, alchemists believed that all matter consisted of the four elements of earth, air, fire, and water, mixed in various proportions, and that imbalances between the elements were the causes of sickness, decay and mortality (as Donne puts it in "The Good Morrow," "Whatever dies was not mixt equally" [19]). They tried to dissolve metals into the undifferentiated *prima materia,* from which substance they hoped to extract the *quinta essentia,* the fifth element, tincture, elixir, or "philosopher's stone," by means of which they held it possible to reconstitute the elements in perfectly harmonious proportion and so bring fallen matter to spiritual perfection.[29]

The philosopher's stone, then, was the conduit between spirit and matter, "a corporeal spirit and a spiritual body," as Isaac Newton put it.[30] In the alchemist's flasks, solid matter evaporated into airy nothingness and reappeared as liquid, which could in turn be congealed again into solidity. The alchemist believed himself to be operating on the border between material appearance and spiritual essence, and his aim was to win control of that border. The attempt to manufacture gold was, of course, subsidiary to that end. In the alchemical system of hierarchies, gold was conceived of as the highest form and *telos* of metal. The fact that it neither rusts nor decays led to the assumption that, of all created matter, gold must contain the most perfect mixture of the four elements. The transmutation of base metals into gold would therefore indicate the presence of the elixir, and this alone explains the centrality of gold-making to the alchemical endeavor.

The moral distinction between gold's intrinsic qualities and its function as the abstract medium of exchange remained undiminished throughout the seventeenth century. Writing in 1685, William Clark denounces the malign influence of gold in the contemporary world ("This is the Standard, which doth regulate / The actions of men; and sets a Rate / On every Head; this puts a Valuation / On every Kingdom, State and Corporation.... For gold, for Gold, all's bartered now") immediately before qualifying his attack by discussing its intrinsic "virtues":

> Yet that I may give this same Gold its due,
> As't has its Vices, for its Virtues too
> Are Eminent, which Artists do relate,
> Who of the state of Minerals do treate.
> 'Tis prov'd by these, then in their Operations,
> (Which surely are the best of Demonstrations)
> That gold is such a Mettal, as the fire,
> (In which all other Minerals expire,
> At least much of their Weight and Substance lose
> In every trial) though from Bellows nose,
> Suppli'd with constant aid; yet after all
> Can not subdue this solid Mineral;
> Or make it quit the very smallest grain,
> Of Weight, which in its Ore it did contain.[31] (189–202)

Clark still finds it plausible to argue that the natural, material properties of gold bespeak a "virtue" that is to be distinguished from, and preferred to, the metal's financial significance, and in lines like these we can faintly make out the glimmering, dying embers of the alchemist's furnace. Any attempt to use alchemy to enrich oneself was diametrically opposed to the spirit of the entire project. Even to conceive of gold as containing a financial or quantitative value, as opposed to an essential or qualitative "virtue," is to reveal a world view in direct and irreconcilable contradiction to alchemical ontology. The true alchemist valued gold for its natural, elemental properties and not for the financial value that human beings had arbitrarily imposed upon it. Gold being the *telos* of all metals, alchemists held that all metals were developing, at an infinitesimally slow rate, into gold, which was believed to grow in the earth, like plants, through the warming agency of the sun. The alchemist merely tried to speed this natural process along by the introduction of human "art"; he had nothing to do with the supernatural substitution of nominal for natural value that is involved in the making of money.

However, the distinction between the spiritually oriented, idealistic adept who sought to assist nature in her operations and the materialistic "puffer" or "sooty empirick" who attempted to pervert natural processes for financial gain was not always obvious to the outsider, as we can tell by the prevalence of didactic satire on this subject. In English literature of the late middle ages, the figure of the fraudulent alchemist is frequently used as a metonym for the vanity of worldliness and covetousness in general. False alchemy, which perverted a philosophy the purpose of which was to spiritualize matter into a means for material enrichment, provided an excellent synecdoche to express the inverted priorities involved in materialism. In fact, false alchemy does not seem to have been thoroughly distinguished from usury, which, as we saw in chapter four, also violated the natural *telos* of money, by making it "breed" and "multiply." The term "multiplication" is often applied to alchemy as well as to usury. In the *Confessio Amantis,* John Gower writes of "Philosophres" how "with gret diligence / Thei founden thilke experience, / Which cleped is Alconomie, / Wherof the Selver multeplie / Thei made and ek the gold also."[32] Thomas Norton's *Ordinall of Alchemy* (1477) is more overtly critical: "And ver they rayle with perjury; / Saying how they can Multiplie / Gold and Silver, and in such wise / With promise thei please the Covetise."[33] A statute of Henry IV refers interchangeably to usury and alchemy: "It is ordained and stablished, That none from henceforth shall use to multiply Gold or Silver, nor use the craft of Multiplication."[34]

Whereas sincere practitioners of the art worked in alliance with nature, the covetous "puffers" and their "multiplication" were portrayed as struggling against her. Alexander Barclay's *Ecologues* (1515) inveighs against such men "wening by pollicy / Nature to alter, and coyne to multiply,"[35] while Reginald Scot's *Discoverie of Witchcraft* (1584) includes "the craft of Alcumistrie, otherwise called Multiplication."[36] The best-known example of this tradition is Chaucer's *Canon's Yeoman's Tale,* in which "multiplying" is blamed for all the economic ills of the land:

> Considereth, sires, how that, in ech staat,
> Bitwixe men and gold ther is debaat
> So ferforth that unnethes is ther noon.
> This multiplying blent so many oon
> That in good feith I trowe that it bee
> The cause grettest of swich scarsetee. (835–40)

False alchemy is not merely a distortion of true alchemy: It is its antithesis. Every true alchemist would have agreed that the "multiplying" of gold was destructive if pursued as an end in itself. Thus, for example, Elias Ashmole included the *Canon's Yeoman's Tale* in his *Theatrum Chemicum Britannicum* (1652) on the assumption that, by exposing the tricks of the charlatans, it advanced the true alchemical project. Ashmole gives the conventional advice to aspiring adepts:

> Let me tell them they may become *happier* and expect a *Blessing* in what they seeke . . . if they can study this *Science* and not pursue it for Transmutation of Metals sake only . . . [for] certainly the lucre of that

will fix a *Curse* upon their *Endeavors,* and plunge them headlong into an unfathom'd depth of *Misfortune*.[37]

To seek to multiply gold was to conceive of it as a quantity rather than as a quality. It was to envisage it as financial value rather than as the most spiritually perfect *telos* of metals. It bespoke a confusion of the Aristotelian category of *nomos,* or custom (to which sphere money belonged) with that of *phusis,* or nature (whose metallurgic masterpiece was gold). So egregiously did this error militate against the most basic tenets of true alchemy that it could actually be used as a negative definition of the art itself. Alchemy, in short, was everything that "multiplication" was not.[38] *The Hermetic Museum,* a collection of alchemical writings originally published in 1628, contains this typical declaration by Nicarus: "Our gold and silver are not the gold and silver of the vulgar. We call gold the water which rises into the air when exposed to fire. Verily, this gold is not the gold of the vulgar."[39] The "gold" spoken of here is symbolic, as opposed to literal, and this distinction between the alchemists' gold and "the gold of the vulgar" is constantly stressed in alchemical writings of the Renaissance. To a true alchemist, the idea that gold was the physical embodiment of monetary value seemed fetishistic. The real significance of gold was spiritual, and its physical properties were merely signs pointing the way to that significance. The same was true of the other materials on which the alchemist worked, and practitioners of the art carefully refer to "our" sulphur or "our" mercury to distinguish their symbolic interpretation of those substances from the naive positivism of "the vulgar." These latter happily accepted the distinction, and expressions such as "the philosophers' mercury," and "the philosophers' stone" entered into common parlance.[40]

By the end of the sixteenth century, the "multiplication" of financial value was an unavoidable fact of economic life.[41] Early political economists still felt compelled to assert a natural correspondence between objects and their values, but they could only do so by diluting the concept of correspondence, straining the analogies between subject and object after the fashion of the metaphysical conceit. This passage from Gerard de Malynes's *The Maintenance of Free Trade* (1622) is symptomatic: "For as the Elements are joyned by Symbolization, the Ayre to the Fire by warmness; the Water to the Ayre, by Moisture; the Earth to the Water, by coldness: So is exchange joyned to monyes, and monyes to commodities, by their proper qualities and effects."[42] Malynes obviously feels it necessary to argue that the mysteries of financial exchange are determined by the natural or "proper qualities" of things such as money and commodities—things that most of his contemporaries suspected of having no natural existence whatsoever. Like the alchemists, he uses Aristotle's theory of the elements, but the kind of value he deduces from his analogy was increasingly seen as incompatible with alchemy's teleological assumptions. As Stanton J. Linden notes,[43] the development of market economics coincided a with dramatic increase in the number of published works about alchemy and also with a new seriousness that surrounded the subject. As L. C. Knights long ago pointed out:

> ... many of the features of popular and dramatic satire in this period that are often spoken of as unrelated "curiosities of the age," were in fact significant aspects of a single movement, a movement that has resulted today in the complete dominance of money in an acquisitive society. Satires on alchemy, for example . . . had an obvious relation to the gold fever that was liable to sweep the population at any moment . . . [44]

The topical opening speech of Ben Jonson's *Mercury Vindicated from the Alchemists at Court* confirms Knights's thesis. It declares that the claims of nature are in the process of being displaced by the human inventions of "art":

> Soft, subtile fire, thou soul of art,
> Now do thy part
> On weaker Nature, that through age is lamed.
> Take but thy time, now she is old,
> And the sun her friend grown cold,
> She will no more in strife with thee be named.
> Look but how few confess her now
> In cheek or brow!
> From every head, almost, how she is frighted!
> The very age abhors her so
> That it learnes to speak and go
> As if by art alone it could be righted.[45]

Jonson announces here the victory of *nomos* over *phusis*, which involves the triumph of exchange value over use value. The satirical portrayal of alchemy in Jonson's masque depicts the struggle of art against nature by means of a competition between a natural and an artificial conception of value. Part of the alchemical process was the attempt to "fix" volatile mercury in order that it might be combined with sulphur to produce the stone. In Jonson's masque this endeavor is represented as an effort by Vulcan to capture Mercury. The latter figure is portrayed as the source of a value that is impossible to pin down: "I am their crude and their sublimate, their precipitous and their unctuous, their male and their female, sometimes their hermaphrodite; what they list to style me. . . . I am their bill of credit still that passes for their victuals and house-room." Mercury can "pass for" anything; he resembles a floating signifier in linguistics or a bill of exchange in economics. He represents a kind of value that is ultimately financial, and this is why Jonson employs him to convey the displacement of nature by art in the enterprise of the "puffers." With his usual nod to the antitheatricalists, Jonson's address to the reader in *The Alchemist* links the art of the "puffer" to the art of the playwright as a similar violation of nature:

> . . . beware at what hands thou receiv'st thy commodity; for thou wert never more fair i' the way to be cozened than in this age in poetry, especially in plays: wherin now the concupiscence of dances and antic so reigneth, as to run away from Nature and be afraid of her is the only point of art that tickles the spectators.[46]

The fundamental irony of *The Alchemist* is established in the first scene, when Subtle uses the idealist language of alchemy to describe the worldly advancement that Face has achieved through his help. He demands whether he has not:

> Sublimed thee and exalted thee and fixed thee
> I' the third region, called our state of grace?
> Wrought thee to spirit, to quintessence, with pains
> Would twice have won me the philosophers' work?
> (1.1.68–71)

The joke, in the case of every character, is their misunderstanding or perversion of the true purpose of alchemy. This perversion is contrasted with real alchemy by being consistently characterized as unnatural. Face calls Subtle a "smoky persecutor of nature" (1.4.100), while Subtle comments that Sir Epicure Mammon will "make / Nature ashamed" (1.4.25–6) with his alchemical lust to "turn the age to gold" (1.4.29). What Mammon has in mind, we understand, is a far cry from the "golden age" of Plato and Virgil, which the true alchemists sometimes thought they might restore. Mammon thinks of gold as financial value, not as the spiritual perfection of elemental matter. He is perfectly well aware that this opinion is at odds with the tenets of true alchemy, but he rationalizes this variance on the grounds that his relation to the project is not on the level of production but of exchange. Consequently, he declares, the necessity for any correspondence between the subjective condition of the alchemist and the objective success of the operation is removed. The great chain of being that unites spirit and matter, microcosm and macrocosm, is broken. In the following exchange, the sceptic Don Surly is shocked by Mammon's unrestrained sensuality, and points out that one who aspires to have the stone

> ... must be *homo frugi,*
> A pious, holy, and religious man,
> One free from mortal sin, a very virgin.
> MAMMON: That makes it, sir, he is so. But I buy it.
> My venture brings it me. (2.3.97–101)

Throughout his satire, however, Jonson treats the philosophical assumptions of true alchemy with respect, and his mockery of the greedy gulls is the sharper for this respect. Mammon is interested in the art for the wrong reasons, and Subtle is a fraudulent exponent, but in the following conversation they both reveal their creator's accurate grasp of alchemy's Aristotelian teleology. Subtle asks Surly if he believes that chickens are hatched from eggs:

> SURLY: If I should?
> SUBTLE: Why, I think that the greater miracle.
> No egg, but differs from a chicken more,
> Than metals in themselves.
> SURLY: That cannot be.
> The egg's ordained by nature to that end,
> And is a chicken *in potentia.*
> SUBTLE: The same we say of lead and other metals,
> Which would be gold if they had time.
> MAMMON: And that our art doth further.
> SUBTLE: Aye, for 'twere absurd
> To think that nature in the earth bred gold
> Perfect, i'th' instant. Something went before.
> There must be remoter matter. (2.3.129–39)

A serious debate is taking place here in which Subtle advances the viewpoint of natural teleology against Surly's skeptical empiricism. Jonson's sympathies are with the latter, but he does not mock Subtle's philosophy as he does his greed. This debate runs through a great deal of seventeenth-century literature, albeit expressed in an obsolete vocabulary, and thus often undiscerned by modern critics. Lyndy Abraham's recent book *Marvell and Alchemy* has shown how alchemical images and concepts inform the writing of this period to an extent unimaginable to those unfamiliar with its technical terminology. In what follows, I shall try to show how John Donne's poetry manipulates such figures to reflect the passing of the Aristotelian world view of which alchemy was a vital theoretical manifestation.[47]

III

Donne generally uses alchemical imagery to espouse a conventional Christian teleology, as in the "Epitaph on Himself": "Parents make us earth, and souls dignify / Us to be glass; here to grow gold we lie" (13–14). He asserts here an analogical, and also an actual, resemblance between gradations of material substance and those of human nature. Our "earth[ly]" body is produced by physical procreation, while the possession of a soul makes us into "glass," which, alluding to 1 Corinthians 13:12, suggests a semitransparent conduit between earth and heaven. The last phrase indicates that our purpose on earth is to allow God to cultivate us to perfection, as metals are aided in their development toward the condition of gold by the beneficent heat of the sun. This was a conventional image, enlisted by countless Renaissance divines, such as Richard Sibbes: "For the grace of God is a blessed Alcumist; where it touches it makes good and religious."[48] Herbert uses the same metaphor with negligent familiarity in "Easter" ("as his death calcined thee to dust, / His life may make thee gold, and much more just" [5–6]) and in "To all Saints and Angels" he describes Mary as "the holy mine, whence came the gold, / The great restorative for all decay" (6–7). He gives the metaphor more careful consideration in "The Elixir":

> All may of thee partake:
>   Nothing can be so mean,
> Which with his tincture (for thy sake)
>   Will not grow bright and clean.
>
> A servant with this clause
>   Makes drudgerie divine:
> Who sweeps a room, as for thy laws,
>   Makes that and th' action fine.
>
> This is the famous stone
>   That turneth all to gold:
> For that which God doth touch and own
>   Cannot for lesse be told (13–24).[49]

Divine grace is here compared to the philosopher's stone. Its effect is to transform the nature of human existence, and it does this by directing our attention to our proper *telos*. The alchemists' "tincture" brings base metals to their natural *telos* in gold, just as grace directs human actions to their proper end in God and thus "Makes drudgerie divine" and "turneth all to gold."[50] Obviously, "gold" is not intended literally here. When Herbert and Donne say that God makes human beings into "gold," they refer to the "philosophers' gold"—the symbolic (but nonetheless real) significance of gold as the perfect form of matter. This significance renders gold analogous (and thus homologous) to the perfected soul, which is the highest form and *telos* of a human being. Donne follows a similar line of reasoning in his "Letter to the Lady Carey, and Mistress Essex Rich, from Amiens." Human virtue on earth, writes Donne, can only ever be a step on the path to perfection: "We'are thus parcel-gilt; to gold we'are grown, / When virtue is our soul's complexion" (31–2). By a logical extension of this alchemical metaphor, Christ is often figured as the stone, or "tincture," by means of which the human soul can be brought to perfection, as in "Resurrection, Imperfect": "He was all gold when he lay down, but rose / All tincture, and doth not alone dispose / Leaden and iron wills to good, but is / Of power to make even sinful flesh like his" (13–16).

In his flattery of patrons, Donne's alchemical imagery seems to reflect an easy confidence in a consistent philosophy. In "To the Countess of Huntingdon," he remarks on virtue's special effect on the Countess. Referring to virtue and addressing the Countess, Donne claims "She gilded us: but you are gold, and she; / Us she informed, but transubstantiates you; / Soft dispositions which ductile be, / Elixir-like, she makes not clean, but new" (25–8). In "To E. of D. with Six Holy Sonnets," Donne's anonymous patron receives a similar compliment when he or she is said to act "As fire these drossy rhymes to purify, / Or, as elixir, to change them to gold; / You are that alchemist which always had / Wit, whose one spark could make good things of bad" (11–14). "Wit," as Donne describes it here, is the ability to recognize and express the correspondences between the different levels of creation, which unite earth to heaven, and thus to "make good things of bad."

However, the very fact that "wit" is necessary to establish such correspondences indicates that they are not immediately visible but have to be laboriously sought out. In several poems, Donne uses alchemy in a less confident manner, to depict the growing strains wearing at the integrated universe of correspondences. Alchemy becomes a synecdoche for the entire scholastic world picture, which is presented as threatened by encroaching skepticism. "Who would not laugh at me," asks Donne in "The Broken Heart," alluding to the empirically implausible claims of alchemy, "if I should say / I saw a flask of powder burn a day?" (7–8). In "The Cross," "multiplication" is invoked as an exemplary instance of what happens when a good means is perverted to a bad end: "But, as oft alchemists do coiners prove, / So may a self-despising, get self-love" (37–8), When, in "Love's Alchemy," Donne adopts the persona of a cynical anti-Platonist to argue that spiritual love is an illusion, he finds an instructive analogue for this idea in the figure of the alchemist whose spiritual quest is diverted to material purposes:

> And as no chemic yet th'elixir got,
> But glorifies his pregnant pot,
> If by the way to him befall
> Some odiferous thing, or medicinal,
> So, lovers dream a rich and long delight,
> But get a winter–seeming summer's night. (7–12)

"Love's Growth" describes a similar crisis in Platonic love. The speaker is alarmed to find that his love is increasing, since this means that it must inhabit the sublunary realm of change that is ethically inferior to the ideal sphere in which he had previously assumed it resided: "I scarce believe my love to be so pure / As I had thought it was, / Because it doth endure / Vicissitude, and season" (1–4). He explores this problem in alchemical terms. Love, he decides, must be "no quintessence / But mixed of all stuffs" (8–9); it is an earthly phenomenon and, as such, "elemented" (13). However, the second stanza finds consolation in the idea that change is not bad if it involves continual "additions" (22), and the poem ends by expressing this notion through a financial image: "As princes do in times of action get / New taxes, and remit them not in peace, / No winter shall abate the spring's increase" (26–8). The speaker's conception of love has undergone a metamorphosis within this poem. Love is no longer a Platonic Idea and thus eternal and immutable like the alchemist's quintessence. Rather, the speaker comes to understand, love is like money, and therefore susceptible to unceasing multiplication, or "increase."

This is the same logic that was to discredit the essentialist view whereby gold was valued for its intrinsic qualities rather than as a representation of financial value. Donne acknowledges the obsolescence of this view in "Love's Progress":

> I, when I value gold, may think upon
> The ductileness, the application,
> The wholesomeness, the ingenuity,
> From rust, from soil, from fire ever free,
> But if I love it, 'tis because 'tis made
> By our new nature, use, the soul of trade. (11–16)

"Use" in the last line means "custom," Aristotle's "second nature," which is also, in the form of exchange value, "the soul of trade." Donne's comparison of money to a "soul" is archly ironic, and a similar tension between metaphysical and commercial notions of value provides the complicated conceit that informs his most minute poetic examination of value, "The Bracelet." The speaker of this poem has lost his mistress's gold chain, and she has demanded that he give twelve gold coins, called "angels" after the image stamped on them, to be melted down so that a replacement can be made. He begins by denying that his sorrow is caused by any analogical resemblance between the bracelet and the woman. He believes, in fact, that to attribute any real significance to such resemblances is foolish and old-fashioned: "Not that in colour it was like thy hair . . . / Nor for that silly old morality / That as those links are tied, our love should be" (1, 5–6). Instead, we are told with cynical ambiguity, what he regrets is "the bitter cost" (8).

The rest of the poem uses the commonplace pun on the word "angels" to play on the various senses in which this "cost" can be understood. These coins, we gather, are pure and unalloyed gold. Metaphorically speaking, then, they are unfallen, "righteous angels, which as yet / No leaven of vile solder did admit" (9–10). However, the literal and the metaphorical readings of these "angels" are contradictory: the former makes them financial (they are literally coins) while the latter sees them as metaphysical (they represent angels, both in the sense that they are stamped with the image of an angel and in the sense that they stand for angels in the poet's conceit). The reader is forced to choose between these two senses of the term, since they lead to opposed interpretations of the speaker's argument. If, for example, the reference to "Angels, which heaven commanded to provide / All things to me, and be my faithful guide" (13–14) is read figuratively, as referring to the heavenly angels that the coins represent, then the sentiment is conventionally pious. If, on the other hand, they are read literally, as referring to the monetary value of the coins themselves, the speaker is making a blasphemous joke. In similar fashion, the "purity" of the "angels" means that they do not deserve to be "damned" and burned in the fire like Lucifer, while the "purity" of the coins means that they are too "good" to be melted down to make a bracelet. Their destruction would be of no concern, we are told, if they were French crowns, which are clipped (as Donne puts it, "circumcised most Jewishly" [28]), or Spanish pistolets

> Which, negligently left unrounded, look
> Like many-angled figures in the book
> Of some great conjurer, that would enforce
> Nature, as these do justice, from her course (33–36)

The "conjurer's" attempt to pervert the course of nature is likened to the flood of Spanish gold from the Americas, which transformed the European economy and the states of nations. In Herbert, and sometimes in Donne, the figurative "philosophers' gold" is used as a corrective contrast to this malignant influence of gold-as-money. But in this poem, the speaker singles out the "philosophers' gold" for special criticism. The "conjurer" in the above lines is a perverter of nature, not her assistant. A little later, the poet announces that he would not care about losing his angels if they were made of the philosophers' gold:

> Or were it such gold as that wherewithal
> Almighty chemics from each mineral
> Having by subtle fire a soul out-pulled,
> Are dirtily and desperately gulled:
> I would not spit to quench the fire they were in,
> For, they are guilty of much heinous sin. (43–8)

The "chemics" are not accused of fraudulence here but of foolishness; it is they themselves who are "gulled." The point is that the kind of gold they seek is of no financial value, and so the cynical speaker feels that they are fools to pursue it. Their ability to extract the "soul" of matter is conceded, however—they are truly able to separate form from substance—and this idea lies behind the scholastic debate in which the speaker now engages his mistress. She consoles his loss with the observation that the material body of the angels will survive: "Thou say'st (alas) the gold doth still remain, / Though it be changed, and put into a chain" (69–70). This materialist approach, as the speaker wittily points out, would deprive the gold of its soul, in the Aristotelian sense that the soul is the form of the body: "For form gives being, and their form is gone" (76).

The poem continues to argue by analogy in its concluding malediction. The finder of the lost bracelet is informed that "Gold being the heaviest metal amongst all / May my most heavy curse upon you fall" (93–4), and the closing lines employ the alchemical properties of gold to humorous effect:

> But I forgive; repent thee honest man:
> Gold is restorative, restore it then.
> But if from it thou be'st loth to depart,
> Because 'tis cordial, would 'twere at thy heart. (111–4)

Here, Donne mocks the health-giving properties attributed to gold by alchemy as if their falsity were self-evident. It would seem rash, however, to attribute this opinion to Donne himself. Rather, he appears to be using the speaker's anti-Platonism to reflect the persona's cynical and opportunistic character.

Certainly, Donne's most extended philosophical poems, the "Anniversaries," invest alchemy with the utmost *gravitas*. It has often been said that these two long poems discuss the terminal crisis of "the Elizabethan world-picture." They mourn the integrated universe at length, and its loss is reflected in the decline of such arts as alchemy and astrology:

> The art is lost, and correspondence too.
> For heaven gives little, and the earth takes less,
> And man least knows their trade, and purposes.
> If this commerce 'twist heaven and earth were not
> Embarred, and all this traffic quite forgot,
> She, for whose loss we have lamented thus,
> Would work more fully and powerfully on us. (396–402)

If poems like "The Bracelet" use this change as the occasion for punning jests, the "Anniversaries" represent it as a cosmic tragedy. The once-animate universe is now "dead, yea putrified, since she / Thy'intrinsic balm and thy preservative, / Can never be renewed, thou never live" (56–8). In alchemy, "putrefaction" was a necessary preliminary to the revivification of matter in a higher form, and the "balm" was the substance that promoted natural healing and restoration in all created matter. The death of the world is thus envisaged as a negative alchemy, much as in the "Nocturnal upon St. Lucy's Day," which consists of a dense series of allusions to the stage in the alchemical process, known as the *nigredo*, in which the distinct elements are broken down and degraded into the *prima materia*. Through this imagery, the speaker's personal depression is made to correspond, in microcosmic fashion, to the death of the universe. In "The Anatomy of the World," Donne remarks on the physical inferiority of his contemporaries to the men described in the Bible:

> But this were light, did our less volume hold
> All the old text; or had we changed to gold
> Their silver; or disposed into less glass
> Spirits of virtue, which then scattered was.
> But 'tis not so . . . (147–51)

History has not followed the alchemical, teleological pattern of progress toward spiritual perfection, and the death of Elizabeth Drury, we are asked to believe, explains this fact.[51] The question of exactly what Drury represents in these poems has been much belabored. Donne famously told Ben Jonson that she was "the Idea of a woman," while William Empson incredulously remarked that "The only way to make the poem sensible is to accept Elizabeth Drury as the Logos."[52] Most often, though, the poem compares her to the alchemical elixir, or tincture, which had once held out the hope that human beings might find a way to redeem fallen matter. As such, Elizabeth Drury was a kind of anti-Eve:

> She in whom virtue was so much refined,
> That for allay unto so pure a mind
> She took the weaker sex, she that could drive
> The poisoning tincture, and the stain of Eve,
> Out of her thoughts, and deeds; and purify
> All, by a true religious alchemy (177–82)

As Lyndy Abraham has shown, Maria Fairfax plays a similar alchemical role in Marvell's "Upon Appleton House." Unlike Marvell, however, Donne describes the world's death, which follows upon Drury's, in monetary images. Elizabeth, he repeatedly emphasizes, was the source of a kind of value vastly superior to the financial: "that rich Indy which doth gold inter, / Is but as single money, coined from her" (233–4), "For air, and fire but thick gross bodies were, / And liveliest stones but drowsy, and pale to her" (367–8). Due to her death, a cosmic devaluation has taken place, which is analogous to the dilution of gold carried out in the alchemist's flasks: "As gold falls sick being stung with mercury, / All the world's parts of such complexion be" (345–6). Donne stops short of likening the dead girl to Christ, but her redemptive power is impressive nonetheless, "Who though she could not transubstantiate / All states to gold, yet gilded every state" (417–8).

The second "Anniversary," "The Progress of the Soul," drives home the point. Elizabeth Drury's worth is again defined by way of contrast with financial value, and Donne expresses this by mentioning gold in an obviously figurative context, as when he writes that "in all she did / Some figure of the Golden Times was hid" (69–70). The dead girl is represented as the Idea of the Good, from which all authentic value on earth is derived. But with characteristic irony, Donne describes this Platonic process of emanation through a financial trope. Elizabeth Drury is "she whose rich beauty lent / Mintage to others' beauties, for they went / But for so much as they were like to her" (223–5), and "She coined, in this, that her impressions gave / To all our actions all the worth they have" (369–70). The metaphor seems strangely incongruous. How can the emanation of material phenomena from ideal forms be analogous to the derivation of financial value from the authority of the mint? In fact, it is through this ironic disjunction between the ethical status of vehicle and tenor that Donne expresses the process of deterioration which is the theme of the "Anniversaries." The world that Donne observes and about which he writes, like the world evoked by Marvell in that other alchemical epic, "Upon Appleton House," is "not what once it was."[53] It looks less like a world emanated from eternal Ideas, to which sublunary phenomena naturally correspond, and more like a world created artificially, out of man-made, customary modes of representation. The following lines encapsulate this development, using the replacement of "precious gold" by "copper coins" as the tropological epitome of such idolatry:

> But as the heathen make them several gods,
> Of all God's benefits, and all his rods,
> (For as the wine, and corn, and onions are
> God unto them, so agues are, and war)
> And as by changing that whole precious gold
> To such small copper coins, they lost the old,
> And lost their only God, who ever must
> Be sought alone, and not in such a thrust (425–32)

The fetishistic adoration of material things is an epistemological error of the same order and kind as the recognition of value in money. Elizabeth Drury's own mode of perception is the antithesis of, and the antidote to, such idolatry. She was one

> Who with God's presence was acquainted so,
> (Hearing, and speaking to him) as to know
> His face in any natural stone, or tree,
> Better than when in images they be (451–5)

The difference between Elizabeth's hermeneutic and that of the "heathens" is subtle but fundamental. She reads God's presence in the "Book of Creatures," recognizing that the phenomenal world is a collection of signs designating noumenal referents. The idolatrous heathens, by contrast, assume that material things actually *are* divine. This is precisely the same distinction as that between the alchemical approach to gold as an expression of metaphysical perfection and the fetishistic view of gold as the incarnation of financial value. Donne indicates as much in his closing benediction to the dead girl: "nor wouldst thou be content, / To take this, for my second year's true rent, / Did this coin bear any other stamp, than his, / That gave thee power to do, me, to say this" (519–22). These lines compare the words of the poem to a "coin" which derives its value from the fact that it bears God's "stamp," and they provide a resolutely optimistic ending to an extremely pessimistic poem. They cannot, however, erase the impression left by the repeated refrain "she, she is dead" that the mode of value represented by Elizabeth Drury has forever passed away from the world, any more than they can alleviate the despair Donne expresses about the consequences of its demise.

Chapter Seven

The Politics of Character in Milton's Divorce Tracts

> *Idolatrie is the greatest sinne, because it dissolves the marriage betwixt Christ and his Church: This idolatry is spirituall adultery; for the which the Lord repudiates his Church.*
>
> —John Weemse
> A Treatise of the Foure Degenerate Sonnes *(1636)*[1]

> *Nunquam privatum esse sapientum*
>
> —Cicero

I

Up to this point we have been emphasizing the ways in which writers of the English Renaissance used Aristotelian metaphysics as a weapon in the rearguard action against modernity. But any notion that these writers were being "conservative" springs from the assumption, which we discussed in the introduction, that the historical success of capitalism means that it was, in this period, a "progressive" force. It should be clear by now that it certainly did not appear as such to the people of the seventeenth century, nor was Aristotle widely considered "conservative" until after the Restoration. In this chapter we will look at Milton's use of Aristotelian politics for avant-garde, revolutionary purposes. Milton does not write about commodity fetishism, or even about economics, but his whole career shows an obsession with idolatry, in the widest sense of the term. Rather than return to the well-documented treatments of this concept in *Eikonoklastes* or the scene of Eve's temptation in *Paradise Lost*, however, it may be more interesting to study Milton's theory of idolatry at a microcosmic level. Under the immense personal and emotional strain of the divorce controversy, Milton was impelled to construct a theory of idolatry as false consciousness, which he later imported, substantially unchanged, into his mature opinions on politics and religion. That theory rests upon the belief that idolatry results from ignorance of natural teleology. As Milton puts it in *Tetrachordon*, "the prime ends of mariage, are the whole strength and validity therof, without which matrimony is like an Idol, nothing in the world."[2]

There has recently been a great deal of debate over the relative influence on Milton's politics of two discordant revolutionary ideologies: classical republicanism and radical Protestant theology.[3] In the mid-seventeenth century, the search for intellectual precedents and rationalizations of the English revolution brought these two traditions into an uneasy alliance, and Milton, like many other revolutionary apologists, drew on both of them. Of course, the two schools of thought are not necessarily incompatible. J. G. A. Pocock notes one point of connection between them:

> The context in which men attain their final end—or recover their *prima forma*, though this concept might not have been antinomian enough for the radical saints of the New Model—is that of apocalypse; the "end" of Aristotelian teleology is still united with the eschatological "end" of prophetic time.[4]

The Aristotelian "end" of man is the good, defined as "an activity of soul in accordance with virtue,"[5] and the belief that one can or has fulfilled that end is certainly amenable to Protestant antinomianism. Furthermore, as Sharon Achinstein points out, Milton's "conception of virtue . . . melds the religious notion of conscience with a classical sense of civic duty."[6] On the other hand, there are significant differences between the classical and the Christian notions of "virtue" and the "good," which dictate that, as Nigel Smith puts it: "Classical republicanism, properly conceived, would in many ways be in conflict with the millenarian, chiliastic and perfectionist Protestantism of the sects."[7] The problem faced by Milton, as a Protestant Republican, is that the definition of the "good" offered by millennial sanctification and that attainable through Aristotelian virtue are in many ways mutually exclusive and contradictory. They have been characterized as such ever since Augustine's *City of God* asserted that pagan ethics are incompatible with true, Christian virtue.[8] Millenialism relies on faith; civic humanist virtue relies on works. Antinomianism abolishes the law; republicanism institutes the rule of law. The saints are sanctified by grace; the virtuous are distinguished by their own strength of character. Radical Protestant freedom is negative and private—it is the ability to speak and worship according to the dictates of conscience; civic humanist liberty is positive and public—it is the ability to participate fully in the government of the *res publica*. While daunting, however, these contradictions are not quite insuperable. I believe that Milton finds a common denominator in the accounts given by these two traditions of psychological objectification and that the agreement of Roman and Christian morality on this point leads him to make the tendency to objectification (or rather the ability to resist that tendency) the central issue of his mature political theory.

The intellectual sources of seventeenth-century republicanism, like those of revolutionary Protestantism, are various. A full account of influences on the former would have to include the book of Judges, as well as Cato and Cicero, Petrarch and Machiavelli. The radical religions of the English civil war incorporated yet more diverse traditions, from the Gnostics and Manichees to the Lollards and Anabaptists. However, brevity demands that we isolate here those precursors whose influence seems most seminal. Broadly speaking, the political ideas of the classical republicans and their descendants, the Renaissance civic humanists, were based upon Aristotle's *Politics* and *Nicomachean Ethics*, while the intellectual sources of radical Protestantism are found in Paul's epistles, especially as expounded by Martin Luther. Under the pressure of the divorce controversy, Milton achieves an intellectual breakthrough that dominates his later politics and theology. He comes to the realization that Aristotle and Paul share one fundamental tenet: They argue that interior and exterior slavery are of the same nature and therefore concomitant and inseparable. Furthermore, Aristotle and Paul both claim that exterior and interior slavery consist in "carnality," the subjection of the spirit to the flesh. This identification of carnality with servility becomes a constant strain that runs throughout Milton's career and provides the consistent element in his apparently vacillating theories of politics and religion.

II

Although this argument recurs at every stage of Milton's career, it was first hammered into shape during the divorce controversy of 1643–45. The divorce tracts offer a exhaustive ethical analysis of the individual character, and the issue of character is obviously central to Milton's politics. Throughout the many vicissitudes in his political opinions, he holds consistently to one basic proposition: A nation should be governed by its "best" citizens. This conviction overrides any commitment to particular forms of government. Milton is not even opposed to monarchy per se, but only to the rule of the ethically inadequate. As he puts it in the first *Defence of the English People*, "Monarchy has indeed been praised by many famous men, provided that the sole ruler is the best of men and fully deserving of the crown, otherwise monarchy sinks rapidly into the worst tyranny" (4.1:427).[9] By extension, a sinful populace is incapable of exercising sovereignty over itself. Just as a tyrant transforms free subjects into slaves, so a slavish mentality on the part of the population must inevitably bring about tyranny in the ruler. In 1654, Milton warned:

> my fellow countrymen, your own character is a mighty factor in the acquisition or retention of liberty. Unless your liberty is such as can neither be won or lost by arms, but is of that kind alone which, sprung from piety, justice, temperance, in short true virtue . . . there will not be lacking one who will surely wrench [it] from you (4.2:680).[10]

And in *Paradise Lost*, the Archangel Michael divulges the political consequences of man's failure to attain such virtue:

> Therefore since hee permits
> Within himself unworthy Powers to reign
> Over free reason, God in Judgment just
> Subjects him from without to violent Lords;
> Who oft as undeservedly enthrall
> His outward freedom. (12:90–95)[11]

In fact, Milton bases his politics on his theory of character. Monarchy becomes unacceptable—it turns into tyranny—only if the personal character of the king is degenerate. "If I inveigh against tyrants," Milton demands, "what is that to kings? . . . As much as a good man differs from a bad, so much do I maintain that a king differs from a tyrant" (4.2:561). This emphasis on personality even renders Milton ready to countenance formal political tyranny in certain circumstances. Of Julius Caesar he comments: "If indeed I had wished any tyrant spared it would have been he, for although he forcibly established his rule in the republic yet he did perhaps best deserve to rule" (4.1:449). This is an remarkable confession for a Renaissance republican to make. Milton signals here that he is not a Brutus but a Cicero, whose Phillipics attack the character rather than the politics of his opponents. The personal abuse that fills Milton's polemic is not gratuitous but rests upon deep-seated assumptions about the connection of the personal to the political sphere. He is convinced that the personal peccadilloes of opponents such as Salmasius and More are the direct consequences of their royalism. Similarly, his encomia exalt the personal qualities rather than the statecraft of his heroes. The famous paean to Cromwell as subjugator of his own "vain hopes, fears, desires" culminates in a succinct expression of Milton's political doctrine: "there is nothing in human society more pleasing to God, or more agreeable to reason, nothing in the state more just, nothing more expedient, than the rule of the man most fit to rule" (4.1:671–2).

Obviously, then, the question becomes: How do we know who is "most fit to rule"? In the divorce tracts, Milton approaches the issue through a judicious blend of Aristotle's description of "natural slavery" with Paul's conception of the "fleshly" mind,[12] and he lays heavy stress upon their association of servility with all kinds of carnality. A carnal consciousness is a token of natural slavery, while a spiritual cast of mind reveals one naturally independent and competent in self-rule, and the respective characteristics Milton assigns to carnality and spirituality in the divorce tracts eventually come to inform his view of state politics. Let us begin by considering the influence of Aristotle on Milton's theory of subjective politics. In *Of Reformation* Milton urges the reader to "looke what the grounds, and causes are of single happiness to one man, the same shall ye find them to a whole state, as Aristotle both in his ethicks and politicks, from the principles of reason layes down" (1:572). As Milton notes, Aristotle's *Politics* and *Nicomachean Ethics* draw causal analogies between private and public affairs.[13] The *Politics* distinguishes three kinds of authority, and each one is given both a subjective and an objective dimension. Firstly, there is the kind of authority exercised by a ruler over his subjects. Aristotle compares this kind of authority to the rule of a father over his children (1259b1),[14] and also to the rule of intellect over appetite (1254b1). Secondly, there is the authority of a husband over his wife, which is said to be "political" (1259b1) and which is compared to the dominance of reason over passion. Finally, there is the authority of a master over a slave, which is analogous to the rule of the soul over the body (1252b1). This kind of authority is correctly and appropriately tyrannical: "Tyrannical too is the rule of master over slaves; for it is the advantage of the master that is brought about in it."[15]

Aristotle's most pressing concern is to establish that this latter type of rule is different in kind from the other two, and he attacks those who miss the distinction. The Barbarians, for example, equate the power of husbands over wives with that of masters over slaves: Aristotle tells us that this is because Barbarians are slaves by nature (and, therefore presumably, incapable of conceiving of any other kind of authority) (1252b1). Similarly, in the *Ethics,* we are informed that, whereas naturally "the association of a father with his sons bears the form of monarchy . . . among the Persians the rule of the father is tyrannical; they use their sons as slaves" (1160b1, 24–29).[16] In Aristotle's view, the confusion of the master/slave relationship with other modes of authority is the very definition of political tyranny, and this became a commonplace of Protestant Republican theory. The United Provinces's Declaration of Independence (1581) justified their revolt on these grounds:

> God did not create the people slaves to their prince, to obey his commands, whether right or wrong, but rather the prince for the sake of the subjects (without which he could be no prince), to govern them according to equity, to love and support them as a father his children or a shepherd his flock. . . . And when he does not behave thus, but, on the contrary, oppresses them, seeking opportunities to infringe their ancient customs and privileges, exacting from them slavish compliance, then he is no longer a prince, but a tyrant, and the subjects are to consider him in no other view.[17]

How does Aristotle distinguish the master/slave relation from the others? First, the slave differs from a child, a free subject, or a woman in that the purpose of his life is to serve the ends of another. He has an "alterior" existence that is alien to him, being his master's and not his own. It follows that the slave does not enjoy an independent being but is a "part of" his master: "one who does not belong to himself by nature, but is another's, though a human being, is by nature a slave" (1254a1). Furthermore, there are people (primarily Barbarians) who "naturally" serve ends that are not proper to themselves, and so these people are "natural" slaves, and it is good and just that they are enslaved. Second, Aristotle identifies servility with the body. The "most slavish" forms of labor are "those in which the body is most used" (1258bl). Slaves are described as purely sensual beings, "wholly lacking the deliberative element" (1260al,12). Aquinas's gloss brings home the equation of direction towards an alterior *telos* with the absence of the rational capacity: "the rational creature, since it is of itself (de se), is not ordered to another [creature] as to an end, e.g., a man to a man."[18] The *Ethics* elaborates further, claiming that slaves are capable of enjoying "bodily pleasures" but not true happiness, since they are incapable of "virtuous activity." Aristotle evidently intends a conceptual as well as a figural valence by his comparison of the master/slave relation to that of the mind to the body: "that which can forsee with the mind is the naturally ruling and naturally mastering element, while that which can do these things with the body is the naturally ruled and slave" *(Politics,* 1252bl).

The two definitive characteristics of "natural slavery" in Aristotle, then, are alterity and carnality. The process of reasoning that links these two qualities appears to run as follows: A slave is one who naturally serves an end that is not his own. Virtuous activity is the pursuit of one's own proper end, therefore the slave cannot be virtuous. The proper end of a human being is the good life, which is a life of the intellect, of "contemplation" (1177a15). However, a slave does not pursue this end, but instead fulfills purely physical functions and enjoys merely sensual pleasures. The analogy to the relationship between mind and body is precise: The function of the body is to serve the mind in physical matters, freeing it to fulfill the *telos* of the whole human being. For Aristotle, slavery is an objectified condition:

> For where there is nothing common to ruler and ruled, there is not friendship either, since there is not justice; e.g., between craftsman and tool, soul and body, master and slave; the latter in each case is benefitted by that which uses it, but there is no friendship nor justice towards lifeless things. But neither is there friendship towards a horse or ox, nor to a slave qua slave. For there is nothing common to the two parties; the slave is a living tool and the tool a lifeless slave.[19]

The kind of authority exercised by a master over a slave is homologous to that exercised by the mind over the body. This kind of authority is sharply differentiated from that of the intellectual and rational elements of the mind over the appetitive and passionate. These are divisions *within* the mind, rather than between the mind and something wholly alterior to it. They are therefore likened to the rule of a husband over a wife, a father over his children, and a ruler over his subjects, since these modes of authority are exercised over free people who fulfill their own ends rather than those of another.

Aristotle's desire to separate the master/slave relation from other forms of rule springs from the dire political consequences of confusing them. In the *Nicomachean Ethics* we are told that kingship is perverted into tyranny when the king pursues his own ends to the exclusion of those of his subjects:

> The deviation from monarchy is tyranny; for both are forms of one-man rule, but there is the greatest difference between them; the tyrant looks to his own advantage, the king to that of his subjects. For a man is not a king unless he is sufficient to himself and excels his subjects in all good things; and such a man needs nothing further; therefore he will not look to his own interests but to those of his subjects; for a king who is not like that would be a mere titular king. Now tyranny is the very contrary of this; the tyrant pursues his own good.[20]

The subjects of such a king, following the logic of the *Politics*, would be transformed into slaves, serving the ends of their ruler rather than their own. Equally, a king degenerates into a tyrant when the legitimacy by which he rules is de facto, or carnal, rather than based on his superior intellectual and moral virtue. As Aquinas comments: "in human government disorder results from a man being set in authority, not on account of his excelling intelligence, but because he has usurped the government by bodily force, or has been appointed to rule through motives of sensual affection..."[21] In Milton's work, this Aristotelian concept of natural slavery mediates between subjective and objective politics. For Milton, a natural slave is one whose body rules his mind: Such a person pursues pleasures of the sense rather than those of the intellect and thus fails to attain the end proper to human beings. This signals his slavish disposition, since to be a slave is to serve an end that is not proper to oneself but alterior, and thus incites (and even deserves) subjection to tyrannous authority. Milton's argument for divorce, like his later argument for the right to depose a tyrant, is based upon Aristotle's teleology. In *The Doctrine and Discipline of Divorce* he offers a conventional Aristotelian anatomy of marriage:

> ... the material cause of matrimony is man and woman; the Author and efficient, God and their consent, the internal Form and the soul of this relation, is conjugal love arising from a mutual fitnes to the final causes of wedlock, help and society in Religion, Civil and Domestic conversation, which includes as an inferior end the fulfilling of natural desire, and specifical increase (2:608)

The primary end of marriage, writes Milton following Aristotle's stress on "contemplation," is spiritual "conversation," as opposed to corporeal congress. He alleges biblical testimony for this opinion: "God in the first ordinance of marriage, taught us to what end he did it, in words expresly implying the apt and cheerfull conversation of man with woman . . . not mentioning the purpose of generation till afterwards, as being but a secondary end in dignity" (2:235). Where such conversation is impossible, the marriage is void by definition, since "All Ordinances are establisht in thir end" (2:623) and "no cov'nant whatsoever obliges against the main end both of it self, and of the parties cov'nanting" (2:245). The Anglicans, according to Milton, reveal their carnality through their belief that the proper end of marriage is procreation, which leads them to allow divorce on grounds of adultery or nonconsummation, but not of psychological incompatibility: "he who affirms adultery to be the highest breach, affirms the bed to be the highest end of mariage, which is in truth a grosse and borish opinion" (2:269). As we might expect, Milton equates this carnal violation of natural teleology with idolatry: "to injoyn the indissoluble keeping of marriage found unfit against the good of man both soul and body, as hath been evidenc't, is to make an Idol of marriage" (2:276).

This carnality explains why the established church exalts the civil power of the monarch to spiritual preeminence. It also clearly indicates that the prelates are incapable of conceiving of any other power relationship than that between master and slave. As we have seen, the imposition of the master/slave relation onto that of ruler and subject is Aristotle's definition of tyranny, and Milton believes that carnally minded people must always think in terms of tyranny and slavery.[22] As he asks in *Tetrachordon*, "What is this, besides tyranny, but to turn nature upside down, to make both religion, and the minde of man wait upon the slavish errands of the body . . ." (2:599). To subordinate the spirit to the flesh is to make the mind "a servant of its own vassall" (2:598). Like Aristotle, Milton extrapolates a theory of subjective politics from the master/slave relation, explaining the reactionary views of those whose minds are distorted by "a double tyrannie, of Custom from without, and blind affections within" as follows: "being slaves within doors, no wonder that they strive so much to have the public State conformably govern'd to the inward vitious rule, by which they govern themselves" (3:90). Milton's politics depend upon this sense of internal servitude, the idea that people cannot be free politically while they remain "slaves within doors," serving an improper, because carnal, *telos*. Thus far, then, his thinking is in accordance with the basic tenets of classical republicanism.

For a mind trained in Christian theology, however, the concept of natural slavery would also evoke the Pauline contrast between the bondage of the law and the freedom of grace—the dichotomy upon which Protestant antinomianism would construct its argument. The enslavement of the Israelites in Egypt and Babylon, and their liberations from these servitudes, provide Paul with the typological figures through which he conveys the relationship of the old to the new covenant. The key text here is John 8:

> 34. . . . Verily, verily, I say unto you, Whosoever committeth sin is the servant of sin.
> 35. And the servant abideth not in the house forever: but the Son abideth ever.
> 36. If the Son therefore shall make ye free, ye shall be free indeed.[23]

As in Aristotle, a sharp distinction is drawn here between the authority of a master over a servant and that of a father over a son. The former is analogous to the condition of mankind subjected to sin and therefore in need of the coercive law of Moses, while the latter is appropriate for redeemed mankind, whose liberation from the flesh frees them from external compulsion. In Galatians 4, Paul applies his typological hermeneutics to the story from Genesis:

> 22. For it is written, that Abraham had two sons, the one by a bondmaid, the other by a free-woman.
> 23. But he who was of the bondwoman was born after the flesh: but he of the freewoman was by promise.
> 24. Which things are an allegory, for these are the two covenants . . .
> . . . .
> 29. But as then he that was born after the flesh persecuted him that was born after the Spirit, even so it is now.
> 30. Nevertheless what saith the scripture? Cast out the bondwoman and her son: for the son of the bondwoman shall not be heir with the son of the freewoman.
> 31. So then, brethren, we are not children of the bondwoman, but of the free.

Paul's typology thus firmly associates the old, fleshly dispensation with slavery and the new, spiritual dispensation with freedom, and Milton frequently endorses this association, for example in the *Christian Doc-*

trine: "Constraint and slavery are as inseparable from the law as liberty is from the gospel" (6:535). In *Tetrachordon,* he invokes Paul's epistle to the Ephesians to show that Genesis's reference to man and woman becoming "one flesh" should not be taken literally, as the canon law assumes: "there was never a more spiritual mystery then this Gospel taught us under the terms of body and flesh; yet nothing less intended then that wee should stick there" (2:606). In the Pauline tradition, Milton reminds us, "one flesh" means "one minde, as well as one body" (2:610). Paul depicts the tyranny of the flesh over the spirit as simultaneously subjective (the internal dominance of carnal desire) and objective (the external "oppression" of the seed of Sarah by the seed of Hagar). In Protestant exegesis of Paul, this position constantly teeters on the brink of antinomianism. In his *Commentary on Galatians,* Martin Luther deduces his doctrine of justification by faith alone from this Pauline division between the flesh and the spirit. Luther identifies works with the flesh and faith with the spirit: "the flesh or old man must be coupled with the law and works: the spirit or new man must be joined with the promise of God and his mercy."[24] This opposition between the carnally minded and the spiritually minded could be taken to imply that the elect were subject to no law, and during the English revolution this implication was often invoked to advocate the millennial rule of the saints on earth.

This reminds us that their many similarities should not lead us to believe that the fusion of Aristotle and Paul was a straightforward matter. In particular, the ways in which they state the opposition between slavery and freedom have widely divergent political implications. The neo-Pauline distinction between the elect and the reprobate could be extrapolated to justify not only the chiliastic rule of the saints but also an antinomian view of law and personal morality. Against this there is the Aristotelian rule of virtue, as exemplified in the Roman republic and revived by the civic humanists of Renaissance Italy. The traditional view of Milton is that he leaned toward the former but was prevented by class or temperament from drawing the logical political conclusions from his theological antinomianism.[25] This approach has recently been challenged by Skinner, Norbrook, and others, who present Milton as an anglicizer of Italian republicanism, albeit one whose humanism is tainted by apocalyptic overtones. In the rest of this chapter, we return to the relatively neglected terrain of Milton's divorce pamphlets in an attempt to understand his negotiation between these influences at a formative stage of his political career.

III

The divorce tracts transpose the central question raised by the revolution—How do we know who is "best fit to rule"?—onto the domestic sphere. Like the later treatises on government, they are concerned above all with the question of how to differentiate between "good" people and the rest, and their main argument is that the distinguishing characteristic of the "good" is the possession of a spiritual and free, rather than a fleshly and servile, consciousness. Throughout the controversy, Milton is concerned that his readers should not make the mistake of thinking the issue merely private. He goes out of his way to emphasize the wider political implications of his subject. *The Doctrine and Discipline* announces that "no effect of tyranny can sit more heavily on the Common-wealth, then this houshold unhappiness on the family. And farewell all hope of true Reformation in the state, while such an evil as this lies undiscern'd or unregarded in the house" (2:229–30). A man trapped in such a marriage will be "dead to the Common-wealth" (2:632), because "as a whole people is in proportion to an ill government, so is one man to an ill marriage" (2:229).

In these works, Milton carefully constructs an anatomy of the "servile" mind, which he attributes simultaneously to his polemical opponents and to the hypothetical "unfit consort" in an unhappy marriage. It is an amalgam of sensuality, literalism, legalism, and idolatry—mental tendencies that are united through their orientation toward the flesh as opposed to the spirit.[26] Milton repeatedly claims that such tendencies are "slavish" and that their possessors are natural slaves, guided by "abject and servil principles" (2:223). When a virtuous man[27] finds himself wedded to such a partner, the absolute disparity between the spouses' psychological status automatically confers the right to divorce. It has been suggested that the divorce tracts lack a coherent argument and that this causes Milton to lapse into mere personal abuse. In fact, however, throughout Milton's career, such seemingly personal remarks are intended to emphasize the sensuality, thus the servility, and so the reactionary politics of antagonists like Salmasius, More, and the "Serving-man" of *Colasterion*.

Milton notes that the established church's canon law allows divorce for physical adultery while forbidding it for psychological incompatibility, or "spiritual adultery." It thus assumes that the end of marriage is physical reproduction rather than spiritual "conversation." This position, according to Milton, privileges the flesh over the spirit and so reverses the Aristotelian and Pauline ethical hierarchies. The church's servile attitude in the face of monarchical tyranny is therefore of a piece with, and a logical consequence of, its approach to divorce. The prelatical doctrine involves a literalist or, in Pauline terminology, a "fleshly" reading of Christ's permission to divorce in case of "fornication," a word it understands in a narrowly physical sense. The preference for the literal over the figurative, or "spiritual," significance thus neatly coincides with the inability to perceive a spiritual valence to the notion of adultery. It also reveals the established church's legalism, as the prelates interpret the Gospel as more rigid and constricting than the law itself.

Milton's contemporaries interpreted his uncompromising assertion of the spirit over the letter as antinomianism. *The Doctrine and Discipline* was read as an argument for "divorce at pleasure," and thus as rationalizing and encouraging sexual "license." Its author was assumed to be one who believed God's elect were free, not just from the civil and ceremonial law of the Mosaic dispensation but also from the moral law, and indeed from law in general.[28] As his accusers proclaimed, Milton's pronounced emphasis on the spirit over the letter does indeed draw upon antinomian typology. But he is extremely careful to distinguish his position from that of the sectaries. In fact, he points out that the issue of divorce is actually in all of Scripture the *least* amenable to an antinomian interpretation. The antinomian appeal is always from the bondage of the law to the freedom of the gospel. On the matter of divorce however, and only on that matter, the gospel is more restrictive, more confining, than the law. Deuteronomy 24:1 allows the Israelites to put away a wife for any "uncleanness" they may find in her, by which, according to Milton "is refer'd to the mind, as well as to the body" (2:244). But when the Pharisees tempt Jesus by asking his opinion of this doctrine, he answers:

> ... Moses because of the hardness of your hearts suffered you to put away your wives: but from the beginning it was not so.
> And I say unto you, Whosoever shall put away his wife, except it be for fornication, and shall marry another, committeth adultery ...
> (Matt.19:8–9)

So uniquely, and from an antinomian perspective incomprehensibly, Christ seems to lay down the law, restricting human freedom more severely than does the law itself. Milton resolves this paradox by criticizing the Pharisees' interpretation of the law. They read the "uncleanness" of the mind to mean any fault in the woman: "This law the Pharisees depraving, extended to any slight contentious cause whatsoever" (2:326). In fact, however, a careful reader will see that the text is far from endorsing fancy or whim: "That wee may not esteem this law to be a meer authorizing of license, as the Pharisees took it, Moses adds the reason, for some uncleanness found" (2:620). Milton claims that "uncleanness" refers to an absolute, objective difference between the partners. In *De Doctrina,* he stresses that Deuteronomy only applies "if the cause is a real one, not a mere fiction" (6:374). Because the pharisees do not understand "uncleanness" in this way, but read it as a legal sanction for license, they assume that Deuteronomy allows them divorce at pleasure. This legalistic libertinism is the "hardness of your hearts" by which Christ explains the Deuteronomic law—Deuteronomy will seem to license divorce at pleasure only to those who are "hard-hearted," or under the law, and who will thus consider themselves bound to commit license when a literalist interpretation of the law demands it. In the case of divorce, then, legalism is seen to result in antinomianism.[29]

The apparent contradiction whereby the Gospel seems stricter than the law is thus resolved when it is understood that law and license are mutually determining. Licentiousness is not the opposite of legalism but its flip side and inseparable accomplice (an insight paralleled in *Areopagitica,* where "licensed" publication is the opposite of true liberty). License, in fact, presupposes the existence of external constraint, from which the beneficiary of license is temporarily excused, whereas true liberty recognizes no such exterior compulsion.[30] Antinomianism, then, is not freedom from the law but another form of servitude to it. In fact, the law actually brings license into being. Thus Milton remarks of one who would forbid divorce that "'tis he that commits all the whordom and adulterie, which himselfe adjudges" (3:334). To insist on the letter of the law with regard to divorce will lead to the perversion of the law away from its proper *telos:* "the first good consequence of such a relaxe will bee the justifying of Papal stews, joyn'd with a toleration of epidemick whordom. Justice must revolt from the end of her authority, and become the patron of that wherof she was created the punisher" (2:305). The automatic assumption that the "stews" would be "Papal" indicates the deeply ingrained habit of thought by which Protestant English people connected Popery with commodification and sensuality. Milton shows far greater indulgence to the Protestant sects, asking whether it is not likely that Anabaptism, Familism, and antinomianism "proceed not partly, if not chiefly, from the restraint of some lawfull liberty, which ought to be giv'n men, and is deny'd them" (2:326), and claiming that if the divorce law is relaxed, many will be "regain'd from obscure and giddy sects" and "dissolute and brutish license" (2:270). The pharisaical and antinomian readings coincide: If the Old Testament really advocates divorce at pleasure, then Moses must be classed "among the Anabaptists; as one who to a holy nation . . . gave laws breaking the bonds of marriage to inordinate lust" (2:269). The matter of divorce is of central importance because the exegetical labor it compels lays bare this secret complicity.

In sonnet 12, the Pharisees' error is repeated by Milton's Presbyterian enemies, whose legalism makes them the real antinomians. They

> bawl for freedom in their senseless mood,
> And still revolt when truth would set them free.
> License they mean when they cry liberty;
> For who loves that, must first be wise and good. (9–12)

The Presbyterians assume that Milton argues for "license" because, like the Pharisees, they believe that Deuteronomy's "uncleanness" means any subjective fault in the woman. Milton, in contrast, is arguing for "liberty" to divorce when there is an absolute, objective, irreconcilable difference between the partners. The fact that his opponents miss this distinction is testimony to their own slavish characters and thus neatly confirms Milton's belief in such objective mental incompatibilities between the "wise and good" and the rest of humanity. To interpret the law as license betrays a slavish hermeneutic because it involves a misconception of the law's *telos*: "it is destructive to the end of Law, and blasphemous to the honour of the lawgiver licencing, so is it as pernicious to the person licenc't" (2:290). Only a good man will be able to employ a spiritual hermeneutics that will lead him past the narrowly literal interpretation of Scripture; only a good man will be able to recognize the existence of absolute differences between good and bad people (the kind of difference that alone justifies a divorce); only a good man will thus be able to distinguish liberty from license; therefore only a good man can be free from the law. In private as in public life, only a good man is fit to rule.

IV

Milton was naturally infuriated by the charge of libertinism. In fairness, however, it is easy to see how the subtleties of his position eluded his audience. He does, after all, argue for divorce on the grounds of psychological incompatibility. How, his opponents demanded, can this be distinguished from simple divorce at pleasure? The author of the *Answer* to *The Doctrine and Discipline* remarks on

> the inconveniencies that would follow if divorce were suffered, for this disagreement of disposition and unfitnesse of minde, as for example, it would be an occasion to the corrupt heart of man without any just cause at all, meerely for to satisfie his lust, to pretend causes of divorce where there is none; and to make quarrels and live discontentedly with his Wife, to the end he might have a pretence for to put her away: who sees not, how many thousands of lustfull and libidinous men would be parting from their Wives every week and marrying others . . . [31]

Milton's opponents, in other words, denied that there could be an objective criterion of subjective incompatibility. Was not any such criterion merely a threadbare disguise for purely personal desire and antinomian "license"?

The Aristotelian response is teleological. Milton points out that "no ordinance human or from heav'n can binde against the good of man; so that to keep them strictly against that end, is all one with to breake them" (2:588). The Pauline response is typological.[32] In Matthew 19, Christ forbids divorce except for "fornication." Milton's adversaries interpret this literally. But Milton says that it must be interpreted figuratively, to include spiritual as well as fleshly infidelity. To allow divorce for the sins of the flesh but not for spiritual differences is to reveal a carnal consciousness that in turn bespeaks a slavish mentality. This "canonicall tyranny" (2:238) makes marriage itself into a "tyrannesse" (2:277), who condemns people to "the ignoblest, and the lowest slavery that a human shape can be put to" (2:626). Her victims must bear a "servil yoke" (2:599), and "grind in the mill of a servile and undelighted copulation" (3:258) with a "spiritles mate" (2:251) who is herself figured as an amalgam of idolatry and carnality—"an image of earth and fleam" (3:254)—and so suffer the dreadful fate of becoming "a living soule bound to a dead corps" (2:326).

Milton assumes that literalism is itself a form of fleshliness and therefore of servility. He had already connected literalism, servility, legalism, and idolatry in *Of Reformation:*

Hence men came to scan the Scriptures, by the Letter, and in the Covenant of our Redemption, magnifi'd the external signs more then the quickning power of the Spirit, and yet looking on them through their own guiltinesse with a Servile feare, and finding as little comfort, or rather terror from them againe, they knew not how to hide their Slavish approach to Gods behests by them not understood, not worthily receav'd, but by cloaking their Servile crouching to all Religious Presentments, sometimes lawfull, sometimes Idolatrous, under the name of humility. (1:522)

In *The Doctrine and Discipline* Milton inveighs against "alphabeticall [i.e., literalist] servility" (2:280) and "that letter-bound servility of the Canon Doctors" (2:338) that must issue in "literal [i.e., both literalist and literal] bondage" (2:715). In contrast, Christ's oblique, figurative way of speaking is connected to mastery and sovereignty: Jesus speaks "like a maister, scattering the heavenly grain of his doctrin like pearle heer and there, which requires a skilfull and laborious gatherer" (2:338). His opponents' reading techniques thus reveal their inadequacy to understand the meaning of liberty—a recurrent motif in all of Milton's pamphlets is the rhetorical division of his audience into those fit to understand his message and those so sunk in the flesh as to be insensible.[33] The author of the *Answer*, for instance, admits his mystification at Milton's claim that true marriage is spiritual rather than fleshly:

> we desire the next time you write, to tell us the meaning of this fit conversing soule. We have heard that Angels converse with one another as they are Spirits; but for Husbands and Wives . . . we know no conversing with one another, but what is by words or actions. (32)

This materialism, for Milton, is self-refuting, for it displays the Answerer's unmitigated sensuality and therefore his natural servility. In response, *Colasterion* again divides his audience into two:

> All persons of gentle breeding (I say gentle, though the Barrow grunt at the word) I know will apprehend and bee satisfy'd in what I spake, how unpleasing and discontenting the society of the body must needs be between those whose mindes cannot bee sociable. But what should a man say more to a snout in this pickle, what language can be low and degenerat anough? (2:747)

The Answerer's literalist prose clearly reveals him to be "som mechanic" (2:725), and Milton is delighted to discover that he really is, in life as in art, "an actual Serving-man" (2:726). It is entirely natural, then, that he believes that only physical adultery justifies divorce. The Answerer (his identity is sadly lost to history) is incapable of understanding the intolerable nature of spiritual differences but insists upon "the wrongfull suffering of all those sad breaches and abuses in Mariage to a remediless thraldom" (2:728). This is because he has a "fleshly" consciousness that blinds him to "the gentlest ends of mariage." His carnality leads him into a literalist reading of Scripture, and this indicates his slavish disposition, which makes him eager to submit to the tyranny of canon law:

> how should hee, a Servingman by nature and by function . . . ever come to know, or feel within himself, what the meaning is of gentle? . . . Yet altogether without art sure hee is not; for who could have devis'd to give us more briefly a better description of his own Servility? (2:741)

The personal abuse of the theological and political tracts retains this rigorous thematic unity, focusing clearly on the slavish nature of the opponents. In Milton's first *Defence,* for example, Salmasius is addressed thus: "You knight of the lash, concealer of slavery's blemishes, eternal shame even to your own land, you are so foul a procurer and hireling pimp of slavery that even the lowest slaves on any auction block should hate and despise you" (4:461).

Milton thus refers us back to the politics of the personality. To be good is to be free; to be sinful is to be a slave. All Moses allows, he says in *The Doctrine and Discipline,* is that "if any good and peaceable man should discover some helples disagreement or dislike of mind or body . . . he might dismiss her" (2:306). What differentiates the righteous divorce for "helples disagreement" from licentious divorce for "any slight contentious cause" is simply the character of the man who divorces: "God intended not license heer to every humor, but to such remediles greevances as might move a good, and honest and faithfull man then to divorce" (2:621). The distinguishing factor does not lie in the nature of the offense for which one may divorce, which may include "any notable disobedience, or intractable cariage of the wife to the husband" and even "the love of earthly things, or worldly pleasures" (2:672). It is purely a matter of character. Thus for a bad, servile man, the Mosaic dispensation will indeed mean license:

> Now that many licentious and hard-hearted men took hold of this Law to cloak their bad purposes, is nothing strange to beleeve. And these were they, not for whom Moses made the Law, God forbid, but whose

> hardnes of heart taking ill advantage by this law he held it better to suffer . . . rather then good men should loose their just and lawfull priviledge of remedy . . . (2:307)

As Milton argues in *Areopagitica,* even if many people are corrupted by exposure to indecent material, "God sure esteems the growth and compleating of one vertuous person, more than the restraint of ten vitious" (2:528). All should be free to read, just as all should be free to divorce; many will abuse this liberty and turn it into license, but the good man will use this temptation as material to further augment his virtue.

Just as Milton's conviction that the "good" should exercise political sovereignty transcends any attachment to particular forms of government, so his conception of what makes a man "good" (the cultivation of a spiritual rather than a fleshly consciousness) overrides his loyalty to any particular body of theology. As we have seen, he is quite prepared to borrow the charismatic vocabulary of the antinomians, even though he is fundamentally opposed to their basic precepts. In similar fashion, he is not afraid to draw upon the humanist psychology of civic republicanism, despite the difficulties of assimilating it into the Protestant millenialism that he also invokes. He feels confident in attempting this feat because his reading of civic republicanism stresses the idea that carnality is natural slavery—the same idea that appeals to him in radical Protestantism. At the beginning of *The Doctrine and Discipline,* Milton predicts that his case will meet with

> two severall oppositions: the one from those who having sworn themselves to long custom and the letter of the text, will not out of the road: the other from those whose grosse and vulgar apprehensions conceit but low of matrimonial purposes, and in the work of male and female think they have all. (2:240)

As the argument develops, however, it becomes clear that these two oppositions (literalism and sensuality) are not "severall" at all. Rather, they are two aspects of the single mental tendency to carnality, the objectification of what is properly spiritual.

V

Let us now return to the dramatic expansion undergone in the divorce tracts by the concept of "idolatry." We can clearly see that, for

Milton, a departure from *telos* produces idolatry. In the capacious concept of idolatry, Milton's blend of Aristotle's teleology with Paul's aniconicity becomes utterly seamless: "the prime ends of mariage, are the whole strength and validity therof, without which matrimony is like an Idol, nothing in the world" (2:628–9). Scripture frequently connects religious and sexual infidelity, as in the cases of the idolatrous wives of Solomon and Samson, and the Wisdom of Solomon's proclamation that "the idea of making idols was the beginning of fornication" (14:12). As we have seen, Milton is determined that physical adultery should not be the sole grounds for divorce. He therefore announces his intention of "drawing a parallel argument from the ground of divorcing an Idolatresse" (2:260). Milton considers "whether Idolatry or Adultery be the greatest violation of marriage" and concludes, on Aristotelian grounds, that it must be the former, since "Idolatry smites directly against the prime end [of marriage]" (2:269).[34] In *Tetrachordon*'s commentary on I Corinthians, Paul's association of monotheism with monogamy provides verification that "adultery" is to be understood as spiritual and figurative, not physical and literal: "if the husband must bee as Christ to the Wife, then must the wife bee as the Church to her husband. If ther bee a perpetual contrariety of minde in the Church toward Christ, Christ himselfe threat'ns to divorce such a spouse, and hath oft don it" (2:732).

According to Milton's gloss, Paul's declaration that a Christian is "not under bondage" when married to an idolator sanctions divorce, for "to have idolatries and superstitions ever before his eyes . . . must needs by bondage to a christian" (2:688). Furthermore, the Protestant Reformation and the English Revolution, according to Milton, are divorces, whereby a contract is abrogated in case of idolatry. In *The Doctrine and Discipline* he maintains that "a right beleever ought to divorce an idolatrous heretick" (2:264–5), lest she "pervert him to superstition by her enticing sorcery" (2:260). Idolatry is the iconographic equivalent of hermeneutical literalism, and opposition to idolatry is expressed through a vocabulary of grace and spirit that has strong antinomian overtones. A literalist interpretation of Christ's prohibition of divorce is idolatrous, in precisely the same way that a literalist reading of his instructions at the Last Supper produces the doctrine of transubstantiation—the paradigmatic instance of idolatry for Protestants. Taken literally, Jesus' words on divorce "are as much against plain equity, and the mercy of religion, as those words of *Take, eat, this is my body*, elementally understood, are against nature and sense"

(2:325). It follows that the Anglican view of marriage is idolatrous in the precise, theological sense of the term: "Mariage [is] the Papists Sacrament, and unfit mariage the Protestants Idoll" (2:275).

But Milton is not content with the literal sense of idolatry.[35] For those who have ears to hear, Paul's concept of bondage will encompass any kind of carnal consciousness: "the Apostle is evident anough, *we are not under bondage,* trusting that he is writing to those who are not ignorant what bondage is . . ." (2:690). Milton uses Paul's typology to argue that the Old Testament prohibitions of literal idolatry must be interpreted by Christians in "spiritual" terms: "although the firmer legall pollution be now don off, yet there is a spirituall contagion in Idolatry as much to be shun'd . . ." (2:262). We should recall here that Christ allows for divorce only in case of "fornication." Having interpreted "fornication" in its figurative biblical sense of "idolatry" in *The Doctrine and Discipline,* Milton extends the figure much further in *Tetrachordon.* "Fornication," we now find,

> signifies the apparent alienation of mind not to idolatry (which may seem to answer the act of adultery) but farre on this side, to any point of will worship, though to the true God; some times it notes the love of earthly things, or worldly pleasures though in a right beleever, some times the least suspicion of unwitting idolatry (2:672).[36]

"Fornication" is no longer simply idolatry, which stands in relation to monotheism as adultery does to monogamy. Now it designates the entire orientation of "fleshly" consciousness, conceived as an "alienation of mind" that renders its adherents utterly unfit for the society of the "good." Such a mind automatically converts the phenomena of the material world into idols, and it is thus unsurprising that, in Milton's clinching argument, "the prostrate worshippers of custom" (2:439) will lose sight of the proper end of marriage and fetishize the institution itself, so that marriage becomes "worship like some Indian deity" (2:277).

It thus seems clear that Milton's distinction between servile and independent ways of thinking depends upon the extended valence he gives to the notion of carnality, through which concept he reconciles the contradictions between classical and Christian influences on his thought. In Aristotelian terms the opposition is between the free and the servile, in Pauline terms it is between the spiritual and the fleshly.

The latter terms of these polarities indicate a state of mind in which spirit is systematically reduced to matter and the subject to an object. For Milton the servile and the fleshly are coterminous, as are the free and the spiritual to which they stand in opposition. His opponents were confused by his insistence that this distinction is "natural," or objective, despite the fact that it is simultaneously "spiritual," or subjective. They failed to grasp that Milton's purpose was precisely to transcend the polarity between subject and object by demonstrating the inseparable fusion between the person and the *polis*. And perhaps the current interest in "identity politics," with its conviction that "the personal is political," indicates that his project still retains some pertinence.

Chapter Eight

Thomas Traherne:

A Critique of Political Economy

> *In English writers of the seventeenth-century we still often find the word "worth" used for use-value and "value" for exchange-value. This is quite in accordance with the spirit of a language that likes to use a Teutonic word for the actual thing, and a Romance word for its reflection.*
>
> —Karl Marx, *Capital*[1]

I

After the Restoration, the explicit discourse of anti-idolatry gradually fades out of economic debates. Despite this, my final two chapters will suggest that the theological and philosophical logic that established the homology between idolatry and commodity fetishism remained embedded in people's minds, and that this homology was to prove an influential ancestor of subsequent criticisms of the market economy. The science of political economy became respectable quite suddenly in the years immediately following the Restoration. In chapter one we examined the pioneering work in the field carried out earlier in the seventeenth century by writers such as Mun, Malynes, and Misseldon, but these merchants were well outside the mainstream of contemporary thought. Before 1660 there were few specialists in what we call "economics," and most people who did write about economic affairs approached them from an essentially *ethical* perspective. Their aim was to evaluate economic behavior according to the standards of the classical and biblical traditions. As we saw in chapter four, for example, the practical utility of usury was besides the point: The debate was waged between those who held that money-lending was always in direct contravention of Deuteronomy and Aristotle, and those who claimed that these texts winked at the practice under certain conditions. For Restoration political economists such as Petty, Barbon, and Locke, in contrast, the central questions at issue were fundamentally *instrumental*. They sought to discover which economic policies would most efficiently enrich the nation, and they aimed at developing a science of "political arithmatick" that would enable them to calculate these policies with precision.

It is not necessary to be a materialist or a determinist to observe that the early political economists spoke for the mercantile interest. Their discipline was, in essence, the theoretical study of trade, with particular emphasis on the possibilities and means for improving the profits that could be made from trading. From this perspective, ancient ethical strictures against the everyday practices of the marketplace quickly came to appear as anachronistic impediments. A market economy depends upon people's capacity to conceive of objects as commodities. The population must be convinced that the value of objects is determined not by their inherent qualities but by their exchangeability on the market. The aim of political economy was to rationalize, justify, and explain this "exchange value," and it is possible to trace, in the economic tracts of the seventeenth century, the incremental progress of reasoning by which it achieved this aim. Rice Vaughan's *Discourse of Coins and Coinage,* for instance, represents an intermediate stage in this process:

> Use and Delight, or the opinion of them, are the true causes why all things have a Value and Price set upon them, but the Proportion of that value and price is wholly governed by Rarity and Abundance: And therefore the Proportion of value between Gold and Silver must needs differ in several Times and Places, according to the scarcity or abundance of those Mettals.[2]

Vaughan draws several confusing distinctions here: between "Use" and "Delight"; between both of these and "the opinion of them"; between "Value" and "Price"; and between both of these and their "Proportion." The confusion arises from the fact that he is attempting to give a post facto theoretical rationale for an established empirical situation. Vaughan can clearly see from experience that the value of gold and silver is not inherent but relational; from this he concludes that there must exist a form of value that is distinct from the use to which an object can be put. There must be, in other words, a mode of value that is determined by "opinion" and by "Rarity and Abundance"; that is to say, by the market and by the law of supply and demand.

The biggest stumbling block faced by the new science was the fact that, as we have seen, exchange value had traditionally been conceived of as ethically dubious and ontologically illusory.[3] In order to circumvent this problem, political economy transformed the terms of the debate. It was impossible to participate in the discourse of political economy without accepting the a priori legitimacy of the market, interest, and exchange value. Political economists observed that these phenomena indisputably enjoyed a prosperous empirical existence and assumed that any serious analysis would have to come to terms with them, rather than merely dismissing them on ethical grounds. With the rapid development of political economy after the Restoration, it became ineffective and unconvincing to attack the market simply by citing traditional authority, and those sections of society that had an interest in opposing it by other means were not yet intellectually coherent enough to mount an effective critique on the unfamiliar discursive terrain of "economics." This is not to say, however, that critical thought about the market was altogether impossible. This chapter examines one isolated and idiosyncratic attempt to question the most basic assumptions of political economy. The work of Thomas Traherne does not engage the political economists in empirical terms, but it essays a critique of exchange value that diagnoses the dire spiritual consequences of so radical a departure from the classical and biblical traditions.

The fact that Traherne is participating in a debate about economics has not, to my knowledge, been remarked on before. Although Christopher Hill makes a case for Traherne's "communism of the imagination,"[4] he does not move beyond the poet's frequent declarations that the things of this world ought to be shared in common to an analysis of the understanding of value that leads Traherne to this conclusion. This is not to suggest that critics have failed to notice Traherne's obvious obsession with the issue of value, but they have generally framed the question in exclusively Christian or Neoplatonic terms. They have therefore missed what I regard as Traherne's deliberate intervention in the contemporary economic conversation. For instance, in the *Centuries of Meditation* Traherne recalls:

> ... thus I thought within my self: GOD being, as we generaly believ, infinit in Goodness, it is most Consonant and Agreeable with His nature, that the Best Things should be most Common, for nothing is more Naturall to infinit Goodness, then to make the Best Things most frequent; and only Things Worthless, Scarce. Then I began to Enquire what Things were most Common: Air, Light, Heaven and Earth, Water, the Sun, Trees, Men and Women, Cities Temples &c. These I found Common and Obvious to all: Rubies Pearls Diamonds Gold and Silver, these I found scarce, and to the most Denied. Then began I to consider and compare the value of them, which I measured by their Serviceableness, and by the Excellencies which would be found in them, should they be taken away. And in Conclusion I saw clearly, that there was a Real Valuableness in all the Common things; in the Scarce, a feigned.[5]

Addressing Traherne's concepts of "real" and "feigned" value as delineated in passages such as this, Graham Dowell concentrates on the distinction between private property and "common things." He cites Genesis 1.31 ("God saw all he had made, and indeed it was very good"), and observes that "It is his delight in 'common things' that makes Traherne a truly incarnational writer."[6] Dowell is of course correct, but his comment does not illuminate the grounds for the distinction that Traherne draws between "real" and "feigned" modes of evaluation. The key to Traherne's thought, it seems to me, does not lie in any facile, proto-Rousseauian "communism of the imagination," but rather in his sophisticated (though by the 1670s somewhat old-fashioned) Aristotelian differentiation between use value and exchange value.

This critical blindness with regard to Traherne is understandable, because he is concerned with denouncing the psychological effects of the market rather than with studying its material operations. Furthermore, it is itself a testimony to the historical triumph of political economy that any root-and-branch attack on the market per se can seem eccentric from today's perspective. The consequence has been that critics have missed the economic dimension of Traherne's thought, usually preferring to approach him as part of the English Neoplatonist school, to point out his refutations of Calvinism, or to remark on his striking anticipations of Romanticism. The connections between Traherne and the Cambridge Platonists were first pointed out by T. O. Beachcroft, who found a shared "Interplay between reason and faith" in his work.[7] However, while such an interplay certainly characterizes the thought of Platonists like Cudworth, Whichcote, and More, it is hard to see much evidence for the conventional senses of either pre-Enlightenment "reason" or post-Protestant "faith" in Traherne's corpus. Carol L. Marks concludes that Traherne is too unique a thinker to be categorized in this way: "We may, then, speak best of affinities with, rather than debts to, the Cambridge Platonists: the portrait of Traherne's mind shows an eclectic intellect and—more important in shaping Traherne's persistent individuality—original, highly personal feelings."[8] Elsewhere, Marks further qualifies Traherne's Platonism, observing that "For all his Platonism [Traherne] avoided the spirit-matter duality."[9] This, however, begs the question of how anyone who eschews that particular duality can legitimately be called a "Platonist" at all. It should become clear from my argument that I view Traherne as an Aristotelian, whose concern is not with the spirit-matter duality but with two opposing ways of evaluating the material world.

Rosalie L. Colie argues that Traherne's optimistic moral schema prefigures the Romantics and "runs counter to the general trend of seventeenth-century ethics, where man knows good by knowing evil and measures his salvation against his awareness of damnation."[10] It seems to me, however, that Traherne is greatly concerned with the nature of evil—he simply does not express this concern in the conventional vocabulary of sin and damnation but instead employs the terms and concepts of political economy. Donald R. Dickson claims that "As a Christian Neoplatonist, Traherne viewed the corporeal world as a less perfect (because material) manifestation of the pure intelligibility of God's mind."[11] But this ignores Traherne's frequent claims that the problem lies with human perception and not at all with matter itself, which he repeatedly describes as holy and sacred. Barbara Lewalski goes too far in the other direction when she writes that "For Traherne, the divine truth shining through God's creatures and God's words renders them so glorious that they need only to be displayed and seen."[12] The problem raised by Traherne, surely, is precisely that God's glory *cannot* be seen by customary perception. Marjorie Hope Nicolson has summed up the history of Traherne's critical reception as follows:

> Mystic as he was, he seemed to the critics who discovered his poetry in the nineteenth century to have lived apart from his time in a timeless universe, as remote from the discoveries of his age as his own works remained for more than two hundred years. [However] We know now that Traherne was deeply affected by the discoveries of the new science and the implications of the new philosophy.[13]

However, over 40 years after those words were published, there is still no critical study that analyzes Traherne's relationship with that most influential of the "new sciences," political economy. Of course, it would be foolish to deny the existence of other, competing tendencies within Traherne's work. His affinities with the Cambridge Platonists, his anti-Calvinism, and his anticipation of the Romantics are particularly clear, for example, in his numerous celebrations of the purity of the infant soul. However, Traherne differs radically from the Cambridge men in his attitude toward matter. Whereas Whichcote and Cudworth denigrate the phenomena of the sensual world, which they view as ontologically inferior to ideal forms, Traherne consistently exalts the dignity, and even the divinity, of material things. The problem, as Traherne presents it, is emphatically not with matter per se; it is rather with a systematically mistaken tendency of human perception. To employ his own vocabulary, human beings fail to "value" or "esteem" the things around them properly, and they are consequently unable to "enjoy" or to "possess" them. Traherne identifies this erroneous and alienated mode of perception as the epistemological effect of the market economy, and his general philosophical conclusions follow from his economic premises. The oft-remarked singularity of his thought stems from its unique historical location: It is a critique of political economy that postdates the era when such a critique could be mounted using purely religious criteria, but that antedates the time when it could be advanced on materialist grounds.

II

Traherne's surviving work was composed over a period of only five years (1668–73), and it shows a striking unanimity of theme and vocabulary. In poetry and prose alike, he repeats certain key words—"Worth," "Value," "Use," "Prize," "Esteem," "Possess," "Enjoy"—in incantatory patterns, forcing the reader's attention closely on their various significances in the mode of ancient meditative techniques.[14] Similarly, he rehearses the same fundamental argument in several different forms, attempting to inculcate its truth through sustained contemplation of the basic idea. His stated purpose is to distance the reader from habitual and customary ways of looking at the world and to reawaken a childlike sense of "Wonder," which, as he endlessly laments, has become obscured. Many critics have argued or assumed that Traherne views this false consciousness as part of the eternal human condition—as a result of the Fall, for example, or of the myopic materialism that afflicts the denizens of Plato's cave. But I would suggest that Traherne in fact identifies a very local and specific cause of what he calls, in the poem of the same name, "Misapprehension":

> Men are not wise in their Tru Interest,
> Nor in the Worth of what they long possest:
> They know no more what is their Own
> Than they the Valu of't have known. (2:118.1–4)

His aim, as he tells the reader in the *Centuries of Meditation,* is to rectify this situation, thus "making you Possessor of the Whole World" (2:4). This would amount to a psychological revolution, which Traherne explicitly contrasts with the recently defeated eschatological praxis that characterized the Rule of the Saints: "I will not by the Nois of Bloody Wars, and the Dethroning of Kings, advance you to Glory: but by the Gentle Ways of Peace and Lov" (1:4). We should not, however, allow Traherne's advocacy of peaceful means to distract us from the fact that his end remains the chiliastic advancement of humanity to "Glory." Our imposition of a false mode of value on creation is, according to Traherne, a sin against the divinely ordained *telos* of humanity; consequently, to correct this erroneous evaluation is to achieve mankind's proper *telos*. Traherne often elides the distinction between *telos* and *eschaton* in a manner recalling Milton's syncretizing of Aristotelian and antinomian notions of the "end," which we studied in chapter seven:

> Can you be Holy without Accomplishing the End for which you are Created? Can you be Divine unless you be Holy? Can you Accomplish the End for which you were Created, unless you be Righteous? Can you then be Righteous, unless you be Just in rendering to Things their Due Esteem? All Things were made to be yours. And you were made to Prize them according to their value: which is your Office and Duty, the end for which you were Created, and the Means whereby you Enjoy. The End for which you were Created is that by Prizing all that God hath don, you may Enjoy your self and Him in Blessedness. (1:7)

This "holy" teleology is contrasted, throughout Traherne's work, with the abandonment of *telos,* which is the necessary philosophical prerequisite of a money economy: "men get one Hundred Pound a year that they may get another; and having two covet Eight, and there is no End of all their Labor; becaus the Desire of their Soul is insatiable" (1:12). The meaning here is not that desire is insatiable or bad per se, but that the prevalent form taken by desire in contemporary society is mistaken. The mode of desire that Traherne denigrates as unnatural is known to us as *consumerism:*

> Socrates was wont to say, *They are most Happy and neerest the Gods that needed Nothing.* And coming once up into the Exchange at Athens, where they that Traded Asked Him, What will you Buy; what do you lack? After he had Gravely Walkt up into the Middle, spreading forth his Hands and turning about, *Good Gods,* saith he, *who would hav thought there were so many Things in the World which I do not want!* And so left the Place under the Reproach of Nature. (1:20)

The starting point of Traherne's moral investigation into economic matters is the Aristotelian distinction between nature and custom. In the *Magna Moralia,* Aristotle notes that "the reason why custom is held to be so strong is that it turns things into nature."[15] Traherne focuses in on this notion of a manmade, "second" nature. In *Christian Ethics,* he remarks on the tenacity of habit: "by long Custome it turns into a second Nature, and becomes at last as Necessary as Life it self."[16] In the poems and the *Centuries,* the notion of custom acquires a larger ethical dimension than it attains in Aristotle. Again and again, Traherne repeats that this artificial nature is ontologically inauthentic and morally corrupting, and he argues that the individual's gradual acclimatization to this "second nature," rather than any universal effects of the Fall, is the true source of mankind's alienation from God.

Traherne thus strongly rejects the concept of original sin. In the *Centuries,* the innocent perception of childhood is often contrasted with the erroneous viewpoint of the adult world, and Traherne exhorts his reader to rebel against the latter in the name of the former:

> Your Enjoyment of the World is never right, till you so Esteem it, that evry thing in it, is more your Treasure, then a Kings Exchequer full of Gold and Silver.... I remember the Time, when the Dust of the Streets were as precious as Gold to my Infant Eys, and now they are more precious to the Ey of Reason. (1:13–14)

Traherne asserts his conviction that the way in which adults experience the world is thoroughly, systematically, mistaken and corrupt. His position seems to be that, while children are free from the taint of Adam's sin, each of us experiences an individual fall from grace in the course of adapting to the demands of the adult world. He is convinced, as he says in the *Centuries,* that "our misery proceedeth ten thousand times more from the outward Bondage of Opinion and

Custom, then from any inward corruption or Deprevation of Nature" (1:115). The primary effect of this fall into adulthood, as Traherne describes it, is the imposition of a false or artificial mode of perception, which obscures the true, natural, and divinely ordained creation:

> To Contemn the World, and to Enjoy the World, are Things contrary to each other. How then can we contemn the World which we are Born to Enjoy? Truly there are two Worlds. One was made by God, the other by Men. . . . As Nothing is more Easy then to Think, so nothing is more Difficult then to Think Well. The Easiness of Thinking we received from God, the Difficulty of thinking Well, proceedeth from our selvs. . . . So that an Evil Habit, and Custom hav made it Difficult to think well, not Nature. For by Nature, nothing is so Difficult as to Think amiss. (1:5)

This is a polarity that structures all of Traherne's thought. There are two worlds, or rather, two ways of looking at the world. One is natural, God-given, and ethically benign; the other is artificial, man-made, and ethically malign. The first is characteristic of children, but the process of growing into adulthood involves a transition to the second, inferior world. Through a rigorous program of "meditation," however, it may be possible to defamiliarize the postlapsarian illusions of adulthood and re-experience the "wonder" that surrounds everyday phenomena in infancy. As Traherne famously puts it, "I must becom a Child again" (2:18.60).

There are two obvious ancient sources for Traherne's moral argument here. First, there is the biblical injunction against idolizing anything of human origin. Second, there is Aristotle's distinction between natural use value and conventional exchange value,[17] and his consequent insistence that "money has not a natural but a conventional existence."[18] In biblical and classical times, however, mercantile interests were far from the position of economic and ideological prominence that they had attained in Restoration England. Traherne can see more clearly than Aristotle the consequences of market psychology in the society that surrounds him, and he rails against its fetishistic "devised wants" (1:17) and illusory riches:

> The Riches of Darkness are those which Men hav made, during their Ignorance of God Almightie's Treasures. . . . For having refused those which God made, and taken to themselvs Treasures of their own, they invented scarce and Rare, Insufficient, Hard to be Gotten, litle, movable and useless Treasures. Yet as violently Persue them as if they were

> the most Necessary and Excellent Things in the whole World. And tho they are all Mad, yet having made a Combination they seem Wise; and it is a hard matter to persuade them either to Truth or Reason. (1:16–17)

For Traherne as for Aristotle, to view an object in terms of its exchange value is to pervert it away from its natural end—to view it as something that by nature it is not. In logical contrast, use value is natural and beneficial, as Traherne writes in *Christian Ethics*, "the Relation between the Use and Excellency of things is so near and intimate, that as nothing Useless can be at all excellent, so is every Excellence in every Being founded in its usefulness" (38–39).

This opposition between a true, intrinsic, or "proper" use value and a false, or imaginary, exchange value was still accepted by the earliest political economists. Indeed, a large portion of seventeenth-century economic discussion centered around the paradox whereby exchange value could simultaneously be ontologically illusory and yet empirically real. In chapter one we observed the progress of this debate, from the certainty of the earliest participants that exchange value is "feigned," through a series of increasingly confident attempts to place it on an equal footing with use value. Thus, Bernardo Davanzati's *Discourse Upon Coins* (1588) clearly equates financial value with Aristotle's "second nature," and points out what is evidently for the author an axiomatic connection with idolatry:

> Now, Gold and Silver contribute very little in their own nature to our Lives, for which all Earthly Things seem to have been created. Yet Men, as if they would make Nature asham'd of this, have agreed to make those Metals of equal value to all other things, to make 'em the Price and Measure of all, and Instruments of changing and exchanging whatever can be found good in this World. . . . This is likewise the Reason why many have made 'em their Gods, seeing 'em perform almost impossibilities.[19]

Francis Bacon is also representative of this view when he declares that financial value is "feigned" because it refers to no practical, or "real," use:

> Of great riches there is no real use, except it be in the distribution; the rest is but conceit; so saith Salomon, Where much is, there are many to consume it; and what hath the owner but the sight of it with his eyes? The personal fruition in any man cannot reach to feel great riches: there is a custody of them; or a power of dole and donative of

them, or a fame of them, but no solid use to the owner. Do you not see what feigned prices are set upon little stones and rarities?[20]

Writing in 1622, Edward Misselden still accepts Aristotle's categories: "The matter of Trade, is either Naturall or Artificial. The Natural matter of Commerce is Merchandize: which Merchants from the end of Trade have stiled Commodities. The Artificiall matter of Commerce is Money..."[21] However, the idea that financial value was "artificiall" proved problematic for later political economists because of the Aristotelian assumption that what was artificial was less "real" than what was natural. The most basic aim of mature political economy was to establish that exchange value was by no means artificial or illusory; that it was, on the contrary, at least as real and substantial as the supposedly natural, inherent qualities that make up an object's use value. In the early seventeenth century, economists clung stubbornly to the notion that money's true value was actually use value and not exchange value at all, since value somehow resided in the inherent, material properties of gold and silver. But by the end of the century, thinkers were forced to reevaluate this issue, because coins of equal denomination (and therefore equal value) now contained vastly different amounts of gold and silver. In *A Treatise of Taxes* (1662), William Petty takes a conservative, "bullionist" approach to the issue, differentiating between money's "natural" or "intrinsick" and its "artificial" or "extrinsic" value,[22] while in *Quantulumcunque* (1682), he was still arguing that

> Money made of Gold and Silver is the best Rule of Commerce, and must therefore be equal [i.e., in the amount of specie it contains], or else it is no Rule; and consequently no Money, and but bare Metal which was Money before it was worn and abused into Inequality.[23]

By the time of the "Financial Revolution" of the 1690s,[24] however, Petty found that this view was becoming untenable. In his *Political Anatomy of Ireland* (1691), he admits that money is, by its very nature, pure exchange value. The notion that financial value is inherent in the material bodies of the precious metals was coming to seem superstitious and obsolete, and Petty now understands that gold is simply a commodity the value of which fluctuates with the market like any other:

> Money is understood to be the uniform Measure and Rule for the Value of all Commodities. But whether in that sence there be any Money, or such Rule in the World, I know not... tho most are perswaded that

Gold and Silver Money is such. For.... The proportion of value between pure Gold and fine Silver, alters as the Earth and Industry of Men produce more of one than of the other.... Gold is but a Commodity very like Money.[25]

We can see in the mutation of Petty's opinion the obsolescence of the bullionist conception of money. For the first time in modern European history, people were being forced to confront and rationalize the fact that financial value was a purely artificial product of the imagination. Traherne shows the influence of this process when he remarks on "Gold and Silver being the very Refuse of Nature, and the Worst Things in Gods Kingdom. Howbeit truly Good in their Proper Places" (1:146). By reading these sentences in the light of the contemporary economic debate, we can see that his meaning is that gold and silver are good per se, with regard to their use value, in the natural form of metals in which God created them. Use value, as Aristotle says, is intrinsic or "proper to the thing," and this is what Traherne means when he says that precious metals are "truly Good in their Proper Places." As exchange value, however, fraught with the fetishistic baggage of human invention, they are not merely evil but the very "Worst Things in Gods Kingdom." In fact, exchange value is not of God's kingdom at all: It is not natural, not created by God, and yet—as Traherne sees clearly enough—it is rapidly acquiring a tyrannical power over human perception of the created world.

Many of Traherne's more worldly contemporaries preferred to come to terms with this situation rather than join him in his passionate but impotent protests. For example, Nicholas Barbon's *A Discourse of Trade* (1690) attempts a bold redefinition of the category of use value. He asserts that "The Value of all Wares arises from their Use; Things of no Use, have no Value."[26] However, Barbon then makes it clear that he understands "use" in a far wider sense than his predecessors:

> The Uses of Things, are to supply the Wants and Necessities of Man: There are Two General Wants that Mankind is born with; the Wants of the Body, and the Wants of the Mind; To supply these two Necessities, all things under the Sun become useful, and therefore have a Value.[27]

Barbon is obviously concerned with establishing exchange value as real value, even though it is evidently of no immediate, material use. Consequently, he expands the category "useful" to include those things that satisfy "the Wants of the Mind." These, he claims, are "infinite"—they can include "every thing that is rare, can gratifie [man's] Senses, adorn his Bodie, and promote the Ease, Pleasure, and Pomp of Life."[28] But Barbon's argument is that these desires are by no means artificial but are "as natural to the Soul, as Hunger to the Body."[29] From this, he is able to deduce that the market value of things is actually the *correct* value, despite the fact that (as he is quite willing to admit) it is purely the product of the human imagination:

> There is no fixt Price or Value of any thing for the Wares of Trades. . . . the Use of most things being to supply the Wants of the Mind, and not the Necessitys of the Body; and those Wants, most of them proceeding from imagination, the Mind Changeth; the things grow out of Use, and so lose their Value.[30]

Barbon's is, in fact, the earliest fully fledged theory of market value. His position is that value is a matter of supply and demand, and he can thus proceed to the discovery that even the value of precious metals and stones is humanly imposed rather than intrinsic. Of gold and silver he remarks that

> It is only the Scarcity that keeps up the Value, and not any Intrinsick Vertue or Quality in the Metals; For if the Vertue were to be considered, the Affrican that gives Gold for Knives, and Things made of Iron, would have the Odds in the Exchange; Iron being a much more Useful metal, than either Gold or Silver. . . . Nothing in it self hath a certain Value; One thing is as much worth as another: And it is time, and place, that give a difference to the Value of all things.[31]

This is the death knell of Aristotelian natural teleology. Henceforth the Western world will regard value as relational rather than as essential, and exchange value will displace use value as the criterion of an object's true worth. John Locke's *Considerations of the Consequences of the Lowering of Interest* (1691) succinctly explains that the true value of precious metals is not qualitative but quantitative: It does not lie in their natural qualities but in their function as the pure form of exchange value:

> For Mankind, having consented to put an imaginary Value upon Gold and Silver by reason of the Durablenes, Scarcity, and not being very liable to be Counterfeited, have made them by general consent the common Pledges, whereby Men are assured, in Exchange for them to receive equally valuable things to those they parted with for any quantity of those Metals. By which means it comes to pass, that the Intrinsick Value regarded in these Metals made the common Barter, is nothing but the quantity which Men give or receive of

them. . . . The intrinsick Value of Silver and Gold used in Commerce is nothing but their quantity.[32]

In the case of gold and silver, exchange value completely displaces use value, so that the use value of these metals actually *is* their exchange value. In this sense, gold is the paradigmatic instance of exchange value, and this, I think, is the reasoning behind Traherne's constant use of gold as a synecdoche for exchange value as a whole. The aim of Locke, Barbon, and Petty is to demonstrate that "imaginary," nonmaterial exchange value is just as legitimate and "real" as use value. The market, they assert, has an equal, or even greater, claim to be the determinant of legitimate value as does the use to which an object can be put. As Joyce Oldham Appleby has noted, this argument launches Western society on its voyage toward free-floating capital and the autonomy of representation: "The removal of key links in production and consumption from the range of tactile experience promoted the creation of symbolic representations. Price, rate, and credit began to stand in place of the bargain, the payment, the contract they represented."[33]

Of course, the Western tradition which stretches from Aristotle to Bacon had always acknowledged the empirical existence of exchange value, but it had been unanimous in describing that value as artificial, therefore as unreal, and consequently as an ethically reprehensible phenomenon the power of which should be severely restricted by both individual morality and national law. As late as 1666, Edward Ford could attack the Dutch for having advanced "their little country (not so big, not fruitful as one English County) from Poor Distressed States, to be Hogans-Mogans, and all by a real cheat, for no considerate man can believe that they have so much Money in their Banks, as they give out bills for."[34] The political economists campaigned for the removal of such restrictive attitudes. They claimed that the law of supply and demand *really* determines the *true* value of things, asserting with Hobbes that "The value of all things contracted for, is measured by the Appetite of the Contractors: and therefore the just value, is that which they be contented to give."[35] It is against this claim that Thomas Traherne takes up arms in his oeuvre.

III

In several passages, Traherne distinguishes between the "Real Valuableness" of natural objects and the "feigned" value of commodities. The existence of this "feigned" exchange value is, for Traherne, the most pressing problem besetting the human race, and he frequently emphasizes its difference from natural use, as in "The Apostasy": "A juicy herb, or spire of grass, / In useful virtue, native green, / An emerald doth surpass; / Hath in't more value, tho less seen" (2:95.4–7). Since it is an idolatrous fetishization of the products of human imagination, "feigned" value actively obscures the "real" value that the beneficent deity has provided in the natural world. Traherne laments the fact that we do not appreciate such things as the sun, air, earth, or sea, and declares that "could we always be Sensible of their Use and Value; we should be always Delighted with their Wealth and Glory" (1:6). We are being asked here to distinguish between "use" and "value," in the sense that the words are used by writers like Locke and Barbon, with the former term referring to the inherent, practical qualities of the object and the latter to its market price.

In confirmation of the point made by Marx in the epigraph of this chapter, Traherne generally uses "worth" to refer to use value, and "value" to mean exchange value, which is determined by the market: "... Worthless and Useless go together. [But] A Piece of Gold cannot be Valued, unless we Know how it relates to Clothes, to Wine, to Victuals, to the Esteem of Men, and to the Owner" (1:143). The tendency of Traherne's contemporaries was to elide this distinction, and they increasingly failed to differentiate between the intrinsically useful, essential "worth" of objects and the financial "value" they represented. In protest, Traherne urges his readers to attempt to view the world from a higher perspective, which involves an accurate estimation of what is valuable: "our Thoughts are then like his when we hav such Conceptions of all objects as God hath, and Prize all Things according to their value. For God doth Prize all Things rightly" (1:7). At present, however, Traherne sees no sign of this happening. On the contrary, "[men] invent Ways to make them selvs Miserable in the Presence of Riches. They Study a thousand New fangled Treasures, which God never made: and then Griev and Repine that they be not Happy. They Dote on their own Works, and Neglect Gods" (1:16).

Although he does not use the word, and although he is in many ways a post-Christian thinker, it seems from such passages that Traherne still considers exchange value to be idolatry, the worship of "the works of men's hands." In keeping with the mode of thought we are tracing, he connects this fetishism with ignorance of final causes. In "The Vision" he encourages his reader to look beneath the empirical manifestations of divine beneficence and to discern their *telos*, thus recognizing that we are not to adore the "fountain" but the "spring" of which it is the visible sign:

> To see the fountain is a blessed thing.
> It is to see the King
> Of Glory face to face; but yet the end,
> The glorious wondrous end, is more;
> And yet the fountain there we comprehend,
> The spring we there adore
> For in the end the fountain best is shown,
> As by effects the cause is known. (2:28.41–48)

In "The Anticipation," Traherne explains that the empirical world (symbolized by the "fountain") is simply the sensible manifestation of *telos,* and must be regarded as such if idolatry is to be avoided: "Before / The world, we do adore / This glorious end: because all benefit / From it proceeds. Both are the very same. / The end and fountain differ but in name" (2:160.32–36). The *Centuries of Meditation* purport to provide the reader with the intellectual equipment to eschew fetishism. Traherne's hope is that his audience will experience a revelation similar to his own, when

> I evidently saw, that the Way to becom Rich and Blessed, was not by heaping Accidental and Devised Riches to make ourselvs great in the vulgar maner, but to approach more near, and to see more Clearly with the Ey of our understanding, the Beauties and Glories of the whole world: and to hav communion with the Deity in the Riches of GOD and Nature. (1:149)

He is even more clear and succinct in the poetry. Traherne's verse is filled with proto-Blakean celebrations of infantile bliss and purity. Part of the sense of wonder that suffuses his writing springs from his rapt fascination with childish innocence, which flies in the face of centuries of Christian orthodoxy. In the poem called "Innocence," he makes it clear that he views his own childhood as a prelapsarian condition: "I was an Adam there, / A little Adam in a sphere" (2:18.52). He asks how this could be: "Whether it be that Nature is so pure, / And Custom only vicious" (2:18.37–38), and in "Nature" he concludes "That Custom is a Second Nature, we / Most Plainly find by Natures Purity" (2:60.1–2). The point is further emphasized in "Right Apprehension": "How wise was I / In Infancy! / I saw then in the clearest Light; / But corrupt Custom is a second Night" (2:123.5–8).

For our purposes, the important point to note is that Traherne equates this fall into customary "second nature" with the child's developing ability to recognize financial value. The postlapsarian consciousness is characterized by its reprehensible tendency to perceive a financial significance, an exchange value, in the objective world, which obscures its God-given, natural qualities. His poems stress this point at length. In "Eden" Traherne recalls his innocent infant perceptions thus: "Only what Adam in his first Estate, / Did I behold; / Hard Silver and Drie Gold / As yet lay under Ground" (2:14.29–32), and in "Right Apprehension" he addresses his younger self:

> Ah! Happy Infant! Wealthy Heir!
> How blessed did the Hev'n and Earth appear
> Before thou knew'st there was a thing
> Call'd Gold! Barren of Good; of Ill the Spring
> Beyond Compare! (2:126.81–85)

Infancy, we are told in "Eden," is blind to the value of "Vain Costly Toys" (2:12.23), and the young child finds the natural phenomena around him vastly more valuable. In "The Salutation," the earth and sky seem like "New Burnisht Joys! / Which yellow Gold and Pearl excell!" (2:4.19–20). In "Wonder" Traherne again recalls his youthful incapacity to distinguish financial value from natural value. All of the ordinary phenomena of experience seem, to the infant's eye, to be quite as valuable as the gems that have been assigned monetary preeminence by custom: "The Streets were pavd with Golden Stones.... Rich Diamond and Pearl and Gold / In evry Place was seen" (2:33.41–42).

"Right Apprehension" begins by noting that the common opinion of the mass of mankind recognizes only an illusory form of value: "Giv but to things their tru Esteem, / And those which now so vile and worthless seem / Will so much fill and pleas the Mind, / That we shall there the only Riches find" (2:123.1–4). The problem preventing us from recognizing "tru Esteem" is the fact that "We're sold / For worthless gold" (13–14). Gold is "worthless" because it is *useless,* and Traherne insists that use value is the only *real* value. He explains this by means of an extended comparison between gold, the source of artificial exchange value, and the fruitful earth, which functions as a synecdoche for natural use value. Traherne observes that "A Globe of Earth is better far / Than if it were a Globe of Gold (25–26), and goes on to expand:

> A Globe of Gold must Barren be,
> Untill'd and Useless: We should neither see

> Trees, Flowers, Grass, or Corn
> Such a Metalline Massy Globe adorn:
> As Splendor blinds,
> So Hardness binds;
> No Fruitfulness it can produce;
> A Golden World can't be of any Use. (41–48)

The point is repeated in the *Centuries,* where Traherne laments the folly of his contemporaries, who

> rejoyce in a Piece of Gold more then in the Sun: and get a few little Glittering Stones and call them Jewels. And admire them becaus they be Resplendent like the stars, and Transparent like the Air, and Pellucid like the sea. But the stars them selvs which are ten thousand Times more usefull Great and Glorious, they Disregard. (1:17)

The only true value, for Traherne, is use value, which is true because it has been created by God. The recognition of exchange value is therefore idolatrous and blasphemous, and also inexplicably illogical, since God has clearly indicated the sources of true value to us by making them the necessities of life:

> It was His Wisdom made you Need the Sun. It was His Goodness made you need the sea. Be sensible of what you need, or Enjoy neither. Consider how much you need them. For thence they Derive their Value. . . . Would you not give all the Gold and Silver in the Indies for such a Treasure? (1:23)

As we have seen, however, during the period in which Traherne was composing these words thinkers like Petty, Barbon, and Locke were developing the intellectual rationalizations of exchange value, which laid the foundations of the science of economics. This theoretical enterprise was itself a rather belated response to a situation that had long enjoyed a de facto legitimacy. By the 1670s, most educated people had grown accustomed to the predominance of exchange value. There is a sense of fighting for a lost cause (and more than a touch of pique) in some of Traherne's indignant protests:

> Were all the Earth filthy Mires, or Devouring Quicksands; firm Land would be an unspeakable Treasure. Wee it all Beaten Gold it would be of no value. It is a Treasure therefore of far Greater valu to a noble Spirit, then if the Globe of the Earth were all Gold. A Noble Spirit being only that which can Survey it all, and Comprehend its Uses. (1:62)

Traherne understood that such "noble spirits" were becoming rare indeed. In his poetry as in his prose, he argues that financial value has dire spiritual consequences for those who are deceived by it. In "Right Apprehension," he employs the scriptural trope of the barren fig tree to characterize such people as "fruitless," that is, useless in a spiritual sense because of their inability to grasp the value of "The Useful Earth [which] they count vile Dirst and Dross" (2:125.52). Just as the Psalmist described idolaters as resembling the idols they adore, so Traherne's miser resembles his gold:

> But being, like his loved Gold,
> Stiff, barren, hard impenetrable; tho told
> He should be otherwise: He is
> Uncapable of any hev'nly Bliss.
> His Gold and he
> Do well agree;
> For he's a formal Hypocrite,
> Like *that* Unfruitful, yet on th' outside bright.
> (2:125–6.73–80)

In the *Centuries* Traherne often draws attention to the supreme usefulness of the sun, and his aim in doing so is to teach his readers to "abhor the Madness of those who esteem a Purs of Gold more then it" (1:60). The flourishing consumer society of Restoration London appeared to him as a massive collective error of evaluation, and Traherne compares this modern form of idolatry unfavorably with the "noble spirits" of the reputedly idolatrous Indians:

> ... verily there is no Salvage Nation under the Cope of Heaven, that is more absurdly Barbarous than the Christian World. They that go Naked and Drink Water and liv upon Roots are like Adam, or Angels in Comparison of us. But they indeed that call Beads and Glass Buttons Jewels, and Dress them selvs with feather, and buy pieces of Brass and broken hafts of Knives of our Merchant are som what like us. But We Pass them in Barbarous Opinions, and Monstrous Apprehensions ... (1:117–118)

The innocence of the savage is the same as the innocence of the child, and this innocence consists in the inability to recognize the fetishistic value of a commodity, which inevitably displaces the real, natural value of the useful world. Traherne is in no doubt that the stakes in the struggle against commodity fetishism are high indeed:

> You would not think how these Barbarous Inventions spoyle your Knowledg. They put Grubs and Worms in Mens Heads: that are Enemies

to all Pure and True Apprehensions, and eat out all thir Happines. They make it impossible for them, in whom they reign, to believ there is any Excellency in the Works of GOD, or to taste any Sweetness in the Nobility of Nature, or to Prize any Common, tho never so Great a Blessing. They alienat men from the Life of GOD, and at last make them to live without GOD in the World. To liv the Life of GOD is to live to all the Works of GOD, and to enjoy them in His Image, from which they are Wholy Diverted that follow fashions. Their fancies are corrupted with other Gingles. (1:118)

In the *Centuries*, Traherne undertakes an intricate examination of exactly what is involved in the falling away from childlike purity, and it is here that his critique of exchange value is most detailed. He recalls that in his childhood he was blind to the fetishistic appeal of commodities:

It was a Difficult matter to persuade me that the Tinsild Ware upon a Hobby hors was a fine thing. They did impose upon me, and Obtrude their Gifts that made me believ a Ribban or a Feather Curious. I could not see where the Curiousness or fineness: And to Teach me that a Purs of Gold was of any valu seemed impossible, the Art by which it becomes so, and the reasons for which it is accounted so were so Deep and Hidden to my Inexperience.... Natural Things are Glorious, and to know them Glorious: But to call things preternatural Natural, Monstrous. Yet all they do it, who esteem Gold Silver Houses Lands Clothes &c. The Riches of Nature, which are indeed the Riches of Invention. Nature Knows no such Riches, but Art and Error makes them. (1:116)[36]

Childhood perception is characterized by an inability to recognize exchange value. The idea of money, the notion that things can have a value that is separate and distinct from their intrinsic, immediate usefulness, is foreign to children. Furthermore, the recognition of financial value constitutes a lapse away from innocence and a fall into corruption, because it involves the replacement of nature by custom, the "second nature" that is a merely human invention. Traherne goes on to recall how, as he grew older

I began among my Play fellows to prize a Drum, a fine Coat, a Peny, a Gilded Book &c. Who before never Dreamd of any such Wealth.... So that the Strange Riches of Mans Invention quite overcame the Riches of Nature. Being learned more laboriously and in the second Place. (1:116–117)

The urgent tone implies that he sees the seduction of children by means of exchange value as a pressing, topical concern. Traherne's declared purpose in setting down his thoughts in writing is to describe the subtle techniques of corruption by which the works of God are obscured in our perceptions by the idols of commodity fetishism:

> By this let Nurses, and those Parents that desire Holy Children learn to make them Possessors of Heaven and Earth betimes, to remove silly Objects from before them, to Magnify nothing but what is Great indeed, and to talk of God to them and of His Works and Ways before they can either Speak or go. For Nothing is so Easy as to teach the Truth becaus the Nature of the Thing confirms the Doctrine. As when we say the Sun is Glorious, A Man is a Beautifull Creature, Soveraign over Beasts and Fowls and Fishes, The Stars Minister unto us, The World was made for you, &c. But to say This House is yours, and these Lands are another Mans and this Bauble is a Jewel and this Gugaw a fine Thing, this Rattle makes Musick &c. Is deadly Barbarous and uncouth to a little Child; and makes him suspect all you say, becaus the Nature of the Thing contradicts your Words. Yet doth that Blot out all Noble and Divine Ideas, Dissettle his foundation, render him uncertain in all Things, and Divide him from GOD. To teach him those Objects are little vanities, and that tho GOD made them, by the Ministry of Man, yet Better and more Glorious Things are more to be Esteemed, is Natural and Easy. (1:117)

It is here, of course, that Traherne most nearly approaches Rousseau and the Romantics. In fact, one might make a strong case (albeit one that lies beyond the scope of the present study) that the Aristotelian critique of the market is the forgotten rational basis behind Romanticism's idealization of innocent children, noble savages and rural peasants, for these otherwise disparate groups share in common an inability to understand the concept of monetary value. R. H. Tawney's famous declaration that "the last of the Schoolmen was Karl Marx"[37] is provocative but ultimately unsatisfying: Marxist socialism is too steeped in the milieu of Enlightenment rationalism to bear close comparison to the tradition of Aristotelian teleology. In this chapter I have tried to suggest that, in the field of economics at least, Tawney's epithet might more accurately be applied to Thomas Traherne.

Chapter Nine

John Bunyan's One-Dimensional Man

> *I do not by any means depict the capitalist and the landowner in rosy colours. But individuals are dealt with here only in so far as they are the personifications of economic categories, the bearers of particular class-relations and interests. My standpoint . . . can less than any other make the individual responsible for relations whose creature he remains, socially speaking, however much he may subjectively raise himself above them.*
>
> —Karl Marx, preface to the first edition of Capital

I

In the figure of "Mr. Badman," John Bunyan presents us with the nightmare vision depicted in Psalm 135: an animate idol whose objectified status is demonstrated by his blithe confidence in his autonomous subjectivity. In this chapter, I argue that Bunyan employs the emergent generic characteristics of the novel in order to satirize and deflate that confidence. Several critics have recently drawn suggestive analogies between the birth of the novel and the first stirrings of financial capital. Colin Nicholson finds that, in the eighteenth century, "developing strategies of finance and commerce infiltrate rival assumptions and effects into literary structures of argument and response,"[1] while Walter Benn Michaels observes that early prose fiction is "structured by an economy in which excess is seen to generate the power of both capitalism and the novel."² Marc Shell argues that, with the rise of the novel, "the new forms of metaphorization or exchanges of meaning that accompanied the new forms of economic symbolization and production were changing the meaning of meaning itself,"³ and James Thompson claims that "In eighteenth-century England, both political economy and the novel grow out of concerns with value and variables,"⁴ due to "a semiological crisis in the concept of value"⁵ which came to a head in the recoinage debate of the 1680s and 90s. Michael McKeon argues that the novel is the product of a "reification"⁶ of consciousness that took place alongside the rise to dominance of the market economy: "The fetishization of the commodity under capitalism transforms it from a social relation into a mysterious social thing. In an analogous fashion, we might say, the result of the fetishization of Protestant allegory is that mysterious yet familiar thing, the novel."⁷ In her ground breaking study of Daniel Defoe, Sandra Sherman focuses on the effect that the new money economy of the early eighteenth century had on literary representations of the self, arguing that "the *irrationality* of the market, infiltrated into discourse, subjects the self to chronic contingency."⁸ Sherman claims that Defoe's work is the first to reflect this process:

> To the (considerable) degree that *The Complete English Tradesman* systematically portrays mental as a consequence of mercantile processes, it is unprecedented. Its insight is that the mind is formed by economic formations. While this is a post-Marxist commonplace, the virtual absence of such discourse before Defoe is a measure of the text's significance.⁹

It seems to me that Sherman is unnecessarily uncompromising in her claims for Defoe's originality. I would argue that there is an earlier analysis of what she calls "the psyche of the Tradesman" that is presented in an even more germinal form of the novel. I have in mind John Bunyan's *The Life and Death of Mr. Badman,* and I hope to show that Bunyan's abandonment of his previous, allegorical mode in favor of a semirealist, protonovelistic form is intimately involved with his denunciation of the economic practices of market society. The central character of Badman himself is Bunyan's comment on the reification of subjectivity that takes place under market conditions, and the subtle, transitional blend of allegory and realism with which Badman is presented provides the formal means by which Bunyan delineates the psychological effects of large-scale commodity exchange.

Bunyan is generally thought of as an allegorist rather than a novelist, and his preferred mode of allegory is personification, or *prosopopeia*.[10] This device allows the writer to manipulate the degree to which the behavior of the allegorical figure corresponds to the abstract quality of which it is a representation. As Joan Webber has noted, the preface to Bunyan's spiritual autobiography, *Grace Abounding to the Chief of Sinners*, "goes very far toward making allegories of himself and his congregation."[11] In the proem to the first part of his *The Pilgrim's Progress* Bunyan informs us that his allegory emerged unexpectedly, as if of its own volition, during the composition of a different, more realistic text:

> ... I writing of the Way
> And Race of Saints in this our Gospel-Day,
> Fell suddenly into an Allegory
> About their Journey, and the way to Glory [12]

The allegorical perspective forces itself upon Bunyan, intruding into his attempt to give a realistic account of the world. He simply cannot help perceiving the operations of abstract concepts in the affairs of the empirical world. As Thomas Luxon notes:

> Life in "this world" is unavoidably reinstated as an allegory of true life, so Bunyan's much-celebrated "realism" literally *is* allegory. Thus, the only escape from this "carnal," and therefore utterly allegorical, existence is to be newly born into that other world, the one that is never quite present, always yet to come.[13]

Using the example of Talkative, Luxon shows how *The Pilgrim's Progress*'s false pilgrims are "reified personifications of the true pilgrims' stubborn attachment to worldly things and worldly thinking."[14] The "progress" made by Christian is in one sense his successive unmasking of such seemingly autonomous individuals as mere incarnate abstractions. Luxon reminds us of Calvin's description of the human mind as "a perpetual forge of idols" and shows how Bunyan follows Calvin in assuming that the tendency to fetishize aspects of our spiritual experience is an ineradicable element of postlapsarian human nature. In Calvinist epistemology, therefore, the distinguishing characteristic of a Christian is not that he can avoid this idolatrous perspective but that he is *conscious* that his perspective is idolatrous.

This consciousness is difficult for Christian to maintain because, in keeping with their proto-novelistic status, the bad characters of *The*

Pilgrim's Progress frequently assert their independence from the abstract quality the name of which they bear. Unlike the figures of allegory, the actions of a character in a realistic novel are not predetermined by the dictates of genre. In fact, it is this individuality of his characters, the fact that they seem to break free from the determining power of their allegorical referents, that has attracted generations of modern readers to Bunyan. Coleridge sums up this appeal concisely when he exempts *The Pilgrim's Progress* from his condemnation of allegory as an arid "translation of abstract notions into a picture language which is itself nothing but an abstraction from objects of the senses." Bunyan's realism, in Coleridge's view, liberates him from this prison-house of abstraction:

> . . . that admirable allegory, the first part of the Pilgrim's Progress, which delights everyone, the interest is so great that spite of all the writer's attempts to force the allegoric purpose on the Reader's mind by his strange names—Old Stupidity of the Tower of honesty, &c., &c.,— his piety was baffled by his Genius, the Bunyan of Parnassus had the better of Bunyan of the Conventicle—and . . . we go on with his characters as real persons, who had been nicknamed by their neighbours.[15]

But Coleridge does not notice that his belief that Bunyan's figures are freely acting individuals chimes with the self-image of several distinctly dubious characters. The avaricious "By-Ends" protests, upon being correctly identified by Christian, that "This is not my name, but indeed it is a nickname that is given to me by some that cannot abide me"(99–100).[16] (The very name "By-Ends" suggests a departure from Aristotelian teleology; the term was used in the seventeenth-century to mean the pursuit of selfish ends instead of the good). In reply, Christian insists that By-Ends' allegorical title is identical with his essential nature: "I fear this name belongs to you more properly than you are willing we should think it doth" (100). As in the case of Badman, the irony here arises from the fact that By-Ends's illusions about his own identity are themselves evidence of his absolute predetermination by his allegorical essence. As he puts it: "The worst that ever I did to give them occasion to give me this name, was, that I had always the luck to jump in my Judgement with the present way of the times, whatever it was, and my chance was to get thereby" (100). In the context of Restoration England, this indicates that By-Ends is a Latitudinarian, who feels that it is legitimate to adapt his religious practice to the demands of the secular government. He assuages his conscience with the pretence that his trimming springs from spontaneous changes in his free "Judgement," but Christian knows that his opinions are actually predetermined by his pursuit of self-interest. Thus, when the pilgrims pass by the Silver Mine at Lucre Hill, Christian accurately predicts that By-Ends will fall into it, "for his principles lead him that way" (107). By-Ends operates under the delusion that he is an autonomous agent, and the joke springs from the reader's recognition that this delusion is itself evidence of his absolutely predetermined behavior.

This exchange is one of several in which the bad characters assert their autonomous individuality only to be corrected by a virtuous figure who equates them with an allegorical abstraction. Bunyan again deploys this device to comic effect in *The Holy War*. In one of that work's trial scenes, a character who has been "indicted by the name of False-Peace" responds: "I acknowledge that my name is Mr. Peace, but that my name is Falsepeace I utterly deny . . . my name is not Falsepeace but Peace. Wherefore, I cannot plead to this indictment, forasmuch as my name is not inserted therein."[17] It is, of course, allegorically entirely predictable that a character named "Falsepeace" should falsely claim to be called Peace. Like By-Ends and Badman, Falsepeace unwittingly reveals his allegorical status in the very act of denying it. Bunyan revels in this kind of humor and displays his comic genius to best effect in this context. For example, "Mr. Searchtruth" is called as a witness against Falsepeace and treats the court to a lengthy reminiscence:

> I was his playfellow, only I was somewhat older than he; and when his mother did use to call him home from his play, she used to say Falsepeace, Falsepeace, come home quick, or I'll fetch you. Yea, I knew him when he sucked; and though I was then but little, yet I can remember that when his mother did use to sit at the door with him, or did play with him in her arms, she would call him twenty times together, My little Falsepeace, my pretty Falsepeace, and O my sweet rogue Falsepeace; and again, O my little bird Falsepeace; and how do I love my child. (311)

Stanley Fish has pointed out that Christian's conversion coincides with his beginning to view the world as an allegory. The characters who fail to notice this, but instead take an empirical, materialist view of reality, are presented as morally inferior: "The source of danger and of potential error is to be located in the world as it usually appears, and, more precisely, in the perpetual habits that yield and create it."[18] Before his conversion, Christian is referred to only as a "man in rags" who inhabits a realistic environment along with his family and neighbors. Only after his conversion and embarkation on the "pilgrimage" do he and his fellow creatures take on the dimensions of allegory, so that the "neighbors" who run after him to attempt to dissuade him from his journey acquire the names "Obstinate" and "Pliable." From the perspective of the elect, Bunyan suggests, the fallen world appears to be populated by objectified, one-dimensional figures whose behavior is predetermined by a providence beyond their ken, and this is how things appear to Christian after his conversion. Caroline Van Dyke provides another example, noting that, although critics have complained that the figure of "Help," who rescues Christian from the Slough of Despond, is a facile use of allegory: "Bunyan's point is precisely that Christian here escapes from a disabling experience into an allegorical understanding of it in terms of Christian doctrine."[19]

Just as Christian's redeemed perspective turns the world into an allegory for him in the first part of *The Pilgrim's Progress,* in part two the party's progressive sanctification as they approach the Heavenly City is signaled by their incremental casting off of their abstract allegorical identities. One character declares that "Not Honesty, in the abstract, but Old Honest is my name" (247). Another is informed that "Mercy is thy name, by Mercy shall thou be sustained" (288); thus the individual is distinguished from the abstraction. Just before crossing the River of Death, Feeble-mind completes the process: "As for my feeble mind, that I will leave behind me, for that I will have no need of that in the place wither I go. . . . I desire that you, Mr. Valiant, would bury it in a dunghill" (307–8). The entry into heaven is also the moment of freedom from abstraction, as Feeble-mind escapes from his allegorical prison. This escape, however, is achieved only through an understanding of the origin and nature of the prison.

It is precisely such an understanding that Mr. Badman lacks, and it is in *The Life and Death of Mr. Badman* that Bunyan's manipulation of the figural status of his characters in order to comment on their moral qualities is most pronounced. In this work, Bunyan abandons Christian's redeemed perspective, which recognizes the fallen world as an objectified allegory, and instead adopts the viewpoint of an abstract personification who is unaware of his own status. As with By-Ends and Falsepeace, Mr. Badman's belief that he is a free agent comically reveals the inflexible necessity that actually determines his behavior. It may be rather surprising to recall that *Mr. Badman* was intended to be a companion volume to the first part of *The Pilgrim's Progress.* There are so many differences of form, style, and subject matter that it is hard to conceive of the two works as forming a pair. Nevertheless, Bunyan's preface to *Badman*'s first edition makes it clear that he perceives a parallel relationship between the two works:

> As I was considering with myself, what I had written concerning the *Progress* of the *Pilgrim* from this World to Glory; and how it had been acceptable to many in this Nation: It came again into my head to write, as then, of him that was going to Heaven, so now, of the Life and Death of the Ungodly, and of their travel from this world to *Hell*. The which in this I have done, and have put it, as thou seest, under the Name and Title of *Mr. Badman:* a Name very proper for such a subject . . . [20]

Bunyan seems to view Mr. Badman and Christian, the hero of *The Pilgrim's Progress,* as forming a symbiotic relationship. Just as the earlier work explored the nature of the regenerate soul, so now Bunyan extends his allegorical rendering of Calvinist psychology by offering his readers an abstract personification of reprobation.

Of course, there are plenty of reprobate figures in *The Pilgrim's Progress,* but they are externalized: Christian and the reader experience them as alien entities, rather than as elements within their own minds.[21] The figural mode of *Mr. Badman* is very different. In this work, the title character is the only allegorical figure, and the temptations and distractions he encounters are conceived of as internal to his psyche. Bunyan deploys these formal differences in order to suggest that the reprobate and the just perceive the world in radically different ways. Christian's elect status is indicated by the fact that he conceives of the world as peopled by walking abstractions, whereas Badman's reprobation is conveyed through his delusion that he is no abstraction but an independent, autonomous agent.[22]

The world Badman inhabits is portrayed as realistic, indeed topical. Neither Mr. Badman nor his neighbors show any awareness that theirs is an allegorical landscape, and it is left to the narrator, Wiseman, to explain this to his pupil, Attentive. The latter evinces some confusion on this point, incredulously protesting at one stage "but do you think Mr. Badman would have been so base?" and requiring repeated reminders as to the essential, definitive nature of Badman's badness. Bunyan inserts numerous anecdotes from real life to drive home his allegorical lessons, and he apparently intends a local denunciation of Restoration England as well as a general description of the unregenerate soul.[23] In the preface he claims that "*England* shakes and totters already, by reason of the burden that *Mr. Badman* and his friends have wickedly laid upon it," and explains his decision to publish on the grounds that "wickedness like a flood is like to drown our English world" (7). When Attentive enters he is bewailing "the badness of the times," and Wiseman responds that "bad they will be, until men are better: for they are bad men that make bad times" (13). Bunyan gives Badman himself many naturalistic personal features, indicating that his nonallegorical neighbors and relations regard him as a perfectly ordinary individual, having him speak in a lively, colloquial vernacular, and even reporting that he is "tall, and fair" (66). If *Mr. Badman* has a claim to be the first English novel, then its protagonist, with his life's progress through an historically and geographically realistic environment, deserves to be recognized as one of the earliest examples of a novelistic character.[24] Bunyan even anticipates novelistic convention with his prefatory assurance that the story is *literally* true: "Yea, I think I may truly say that to the best of my remembrance, all the things that here I discourse of, I mean as to matter of fact, have been acted upon the stage of this world, even many times before mine eyes" (1).

But what makes *Badman* such a pivotal work is the fact that, as well as being a quasirealistic individual, Mr. Badman is simultaneously a walking allegorical abstraction. Bunyan is equally insistent on this point and repeatedly reminds the reader of the absolutely determining power of Badman's figural status. At one stage Wiseman asks: "But what need I thus talk of the particular actions, or rather prodigious sins of Mr. Badman, when his whole Life and all his actions, went as it were to the making up one massie body of sin?" (126–7). It often seems that "Mr. Badman" is nothing more than a theologically precise personification of the Calvinist concept of predestined reprobation. Wiseman stresses that despite the good influence of his parents, Badman's earliest behavior "manifested him to be notoriously infected by original corruption" (17). We are constantly told that Badman's badness is intrinsic, that it is his essence, and that his actions are completely predetermined by the definitive quality of badness, so that his behavior is the outward manifestation of the abstract quality for which he is an allegorical figure: "they be not bad deeds that make a bad man, but he is already a bad man that doth bad deeds" (89).

Bunyan expresses this predestined evil at the level of allegorical form, through the comically exact correspondence between vehicle and tenor. Mr. Badman acts badly because, unbeknown to himself, he is a character in an allegory who personifies the abstract quality of badness. Thus it is noted that "Badman had all advantages to be good, but continued Badman still" (40), that "this beginning was bad; but what shall I say? 'Twas like Mr. Badman himself" (69), and that, while he had the resources to settle honestly with his creditors, "had he done so, he had not done like himself, like Mr. *Badman;* had he, I say, dealt like an honest man, he had then gone out of Mr. *Badman's* road" (89–90). Badman's will is thus in a double bondage: At the theological level he acts badly because he is predestined to reprobation, and on the formal level he acts badly because he is an allegorical personification of badness.[25]

The contradiction between Badman's protonovelistic individual traits and his unwavering adherence to his allegorical role thus echoes the paradox whereby Badman's badness is both essential to his nature and historically specific to Restoration England. Although he is said to represent reprobate humanity in abstract and general form, Badman's actual transgressions are remarkably specific. They center closely around the topical economic issues of Restoration England, particularly the growing prominence of the market economy and the burgeoning power of finance. In fact, Mr. Badman appears to enjoy a dual allegorical significance—he is a hybrid personification. He is certainly a figure for unregenerate human nature, but he is also an embodiment of the market economy, driven along his path of sin and reprobation by his relentless pursuit of economic self-interest.[26]

Badman earns his living as an unspecified, and thus generic, kind of shopkeeper, whose occupation Bunyan summarizes as "making the Shekel great." Fully a third of the book is devoted to cataloguing Badman's nefarious business practices, which include not only overt deceit, such as fraudulent bankruptcy or the use of false weights and measures, but also aspects of market behavior that were becoming acceptable even in Bunyan's time. Mr. Badman is repeatedly said to practice "extortion," which is here defined simply as the canny exploitation of market forces. Wiseman remarks that

> Mr. Badman also had this art; could he get a man at advantage, that is, if his chapman durst not go from him, or if the commodity he wanted could not for the present be conveniently had elsewhere, then let him look to himself, he would surely make his purse-strings crack; he would exact upon him without any pity or conscience. (108)

This, the characters agree, is "extortion," which "is most commonly committed by men of trade, who without all conscience, when they have the advantage, will make a prey of their neighbour" (108). A long discussion follows noting the contemporary prevalence of this sin. Those guilty of it are

> ... above all your hucksters, that buy up the poor man's victuals by wholesale, and sell it to him again for unreasonable gains, by retail, and as we call it by piecemeal; they are got into a way, after a stinging rate, to play their game upon such by extortion: I mean such who buy up butter, cheese, eggs, bacon, &c. by wholesale, and sell it again, as they call it, by pennyworths, two pennyworths, a halfpennyworth, or the like, to the poor, all the week after the market is past. (109)

In fact, *Mr. Badman* is a polemical intervention in the contemporary debate about economic morality. In that debate, the traditional standards of the moral economy derived from Aristotle's *Politics* and from Deuteronomy were being incrementally displaced by rationalizations of large scale trade and capital investment.[27] Bunyan takes up a firmly conservative stance, defending the scholastic standard of the "just price" and the "good conscience" that enables traders to adhere to it. These concepts depend upon the Aristotelian claims that the worth of objects is essential and that it is a violation of natural morality to manipulate the value of things in order to exploit the market. Attentive points out to Wiseman that "you seem to import that it is not lawful for a man to make the best of his own." His mentor gladly concedes the point:

> If by making the best, you mean to sell for as much as by hook or by crook he can get for his commodity; then I say it is not lawful. And if I should say the contrary, I should justify Mr. Badman and all the rest of that gang; but that I shall never do, for the word of God condemns them. (110)

It is immoral to replace inherent value with the market price. To attempt to maximize one's profit in exchange is to take advantage either of one's neighbors' "ignorance," "necessity," or "fondness" for one's commodity. It is precisely this tendency of market participants to seek their own advantage that is represented in the figure of Mr. Badman:

> WISEMAN: ... a man ... should not always sell too dear nor buy as cheap as he can, but should use good conscience to God and charity to his neighbour in both.
> ATTENTIVE: But were some men here to hear you, I believe they would laugh you to scorn.
> WISEMAN: I question that not at all, for so Mr. Badman used to do when any man told him of his faults ...

The pursuit of self-interest in exchange transactions is both unacceptably selfish in itself ("He that sells his commodity as dear, or for as much money as he can, seeks himself and himself only" [112]), and also inevitably involves the trader in many other sins:

> If it be lawful for me to sell my commodity . . . as dear as I can, then there can be no sin in my trading, how unreasonably soever I manage my calling, whether by lying, swearing, cursing, cheating, for all this is but to sell my commodity as dear as I can. But that there is sin in these is evident, therefore I may not sell my commodity always as dear as I can. (113)[28]

And in fact Bunyan is careful to connect even those of Badman's sins that are not obviously economic in nature to his status as a trader. The earliest of his vices to manifest itself, we are told, was lying. Attentive wonders why people tell lies, and the first motive given by both Wiseman and the marginal note is economic: "you shall have some that will lye it over and over, and that for a penny profit" (19). Similarly, the motive for swearing is "frequently to get gain thereby" (29), and Wiseman advises that "no buyer should lay out one farthing with him that is a common swearer in his calling" (29). Furthermore, this mode of economic malpractice is highly contagious, so that "if a master be unconscionable in his dealing, and trades with lying words; or if bad commodities be avouched to be good, or if he seeks after unreasonable gain, or the like, his servant sees it, and it is enough to undo him" (4).

Bunyan's Aristotelian-scholastic view of economic morality had been hammered into the minds of ordinary Englishmen by generations of preachers and pamphleteers. For instance, in Arthur Dent's *The Plaine Man's Pathway to Heaven* (1601), a copy of which Bunyan received as part of his wife's dowry, the wise Theologus remarks that

> It is too true, that lying and dissembling are most rife, and over-common amongst all sorts of men; but especially it both overflows and superabounds in shopkeepers and [their] servants. For both these make a trade and occupation of it. *They can do no other but lie.* It cleaveth to them as the nail to the boot.[29]

Dent's "honest man" Philargus concurs, demanding "what is their life (if customers come in apace) but swearing, lying, dissembling and deceiving. They will lie as fast, as a Dog will trot"(155). The market economy, with its inducements to pride, luxury, avarice, and venality, is identified in Bunyan, as in Dent, as an important cause of sin, and sin becomes second nature to those involved in economic exchange.[30]

It seems that we are being offered another, more historically specific, explanation for Badman's badness than his status as the embodiment of unregenerate human nature: He is also the personification of market forces. Perhaps the best way to describe him is as a symbol of the action of unregenerate human nature when left exposed to the free play of the market, undefended by biblical or classical strictures concerning fairness in trade. "What think you of Mr. Badman now?" asks Wiseman, after detailing the antihero's relentless pursuit of "his own advantage." "Think!" replies Attentive, "Why I can think no other but that he was a man left to himself" (100). Unconfined by traditional morality, egocentric and individualistic, ruthlessly competitive in the pursuit of his self-interest, Mr. Badman stands simultaneously for the sinful nature of the human race as a whole and for that nature as it appears when it is allowed to express itself without restraint, as in the burgeoning market economy of Restoration England. Mr. Badman, in fact, represents the entrance onto the literary stage of Hobbesian man.

II

The assumption that the pursuit of self-interest is a natural, and thus ineradicable, element of the human character is central to the Hobbesian view of the world, and especially to the science of political economy to which that world view gave rise in Restoration England. Hobbes's belief in universal selfishness, his opinion that "of all Voluntary Acts, the Object is to every man his own Good,"[31] leads him to conclude that the free market is the most natural means of determining value. He scorns those traditionalist commentators who argue "As if it were Injustice to sell dearer than we buy; or to give more to a man than he merits. The value of all things contracted for, is measured by the Appetite of the Contractors: and therefore the just value, is that which they be contented to give."[32] For Hobbes, the "just price" is the market price, whereas for Bunyan it is a value inherent in the object itself, so that any attempt to sell or buy for other than an object's intrinsic worth is "extortion." If this is so, a Hobbesian would retort, then all men are extortioners by nature. In fact, the inevitability of market participants' pursuit of self-interest provided the early political economists with the single constant factor they needed in order to construct a rational science out of the apparently random fluctuations of large-scale trading economies. It could be argued that the Calvinist notion of total depravity had already abandoned the world of "works" to irremediable carnality. However, Calvinism regards our fallen state as an immoral condition to be struggled against through the incessant quest for faith, whereas political economy blithely accepts it as the unavoidable, amoral engine of economic activity.

In the retailer, self-interest takes the form of attempting to maximize profit; in the consumer it takes the form of attempting to satisfy desires at the lowest possible cost. Early rationalizations of the market assumed that people will not repress or attempt to quell their self-interest but that they will always pursue it to the best of their abilities. Joyce Oldham Appleby has shown how this embryonic political economy retained the influence of the Calvinist doctrine of total depravity, being founded on the assumption that, in the marketplace, people will always and inevitably behave in a selfish manner:

> As a social activity, economics offered only once source of predictability: a consistent pattern of human behavior. . . . if, in certain areas, observers found a behavior so consistent as to be predictable, that social area would lend itself to scientific investigation. Thus, the conception of human nature embedded in discussions of economic behavior became crucial to the adoption of the scientific mode of analysis. All the theorizing about economic life that imputed lawfulness to market relations rested upon the inevitable desire of the market participants to seek their profit while reaching a bargain.[33]

In order to become the object of a rational science, human activity must be abstracted—individual actions must be quantified in statistical form. The theoretical tool that William Petty, the founder of bourgeois economics, sought to provide for the science he called "political arithmatick" was the ability to consider human activity in the *abstract:* He attempts to find ways in which "an Equation may be made between drudging Labour, and Favour, Acquaintance, Interest, Friends, Eloquence, Reputation, Power, Authority, &c."[34] These qualitative attributes of human behavior must, in Petty's view, be translated into quantifiable terms. This technique of abstraction is an indispensable prerequisite for political economy, which seeks to conjure out of the millions of particular, individual exchanges an abstract "market" defined by regularities that can then become the object of scientific investigation.[35] Since the "market" is actually made up of many local instances of human activity, it can only come into conceptual existence through a deliberate mental act of abstraction. And since each of these individual acts of exchange are supposed to share the common characteristic that in them each participant is seeking his own advantage, this presupposition of universal selfishness became the very foundation of political economy. It seems to me that the abstract figure of total depravity that is Bunyan's "Mr. Badman" represents a grotesque, parodic rendering of precisely this objectified and abstracted conception of human nature.[36]

The burgeoning science of political economy thus assumed that what Christian ethics called sin and depravity was the natural condition of properly functioning economic man. In the works of the early political economists, we find impulses and lusts which must be condemned as sinful from a Christian viewpoint celebrated for their economic benefits. As Nicholas Barbon remarks in *A Discourse of Trade* (1690):

> The Wants of the Mind are infinite, Man naturally Aspires, and as his Mind is elevated, his Senses grow more refined, and more capable of Delight; his Desires are inlarged, and his Wants increase with his Wishes, which is for every thing that is rare, can gratifie his Senses, adorn his Body, and promote the Ease, Pleasure, and Pomp of Life.[37]

In his *Discourses Upon Trade* (1691), Sir Dudley North makes a more explicit connection between sinful behavior and material prosperity:

> The main spur to Trade, or rather to Industry and Ingenuity, is the exorbitant Appetites of Men. . . . The Glutton works hard to purchase Delicacies, wherewith to gorge himself; the Gamester, for Money to venture at Play; the Miser, to hoard; and so others. Now in their pursuit of those Appetites, other Men less exorbitant are benefitted . . .[38]

It is not only that the market exploits mankind's sinful nature: North also argues that, to the extent that they participate in the market, human beings will inevitably pursue their private interest at the expense of others. Indeed, he practically identifies the free market with the untrammeled pursuit of self-interest:

> For whenever Men consult for the Publick Good, as for the advancement of Trade, wherein all are concerned, they usually esteem the immediate Interest of their own to be the common Measure of Good and Evil. And there are many, who to gain a little in their own Trades, care not how much others suffer; and each Man strives, that all others must be forc'd, in their dealings, to act subserviently for his Profit, but under the covert of the Publick.[39]

If we look forward 30 years, we can see how the ethical questions raised by Petty, Barbon, and North reach fruition in the happy assertion of Bernard Mandeville that private vices are public benefits. In *The Fable of the Bees* (1723), Mandeville takes mischievous pleasure in pointing out the hypocrisy of participants in the market who claim to be acting out of altruism, pointing out that many of them "would be starved in half a year's time if pride and luxury were at once to be banished from the nation."[40] Envy, avarice, gluttony, pride, lust—all of these, according to Mandeville, are absolutely necessary for the prosperous flourishing of a market economy. Moreover, it is both inevitable and natural that, in such an economy, human beings will act in a selfish manner and pursue their own self-interest at the expense of others.

This sense of the absolute predetermination of human actions was conceived of by contemporaries as a form of objectification: thus William Law (1724) railed against Mandeville: "you describe yourself as a *Machine*."[41] But in fact Mandeville merely follows the Calvinist notion of total depravity to its logical conclusion. If "it is impossible that man, mere fallen man, should act with any other view but to please himself,"[42] then the moralistic strictures of the clergy against avarice and ambition must be futile and hypocritical. As a result, Mandeville concludes that moral virtue is not intrinsic, but relational: "things are only good and evil in reference to something else, and according to the light and position they are placed in."[43] This declaration is at root a transference to the sphere of personal morality of the economic contention, expressed in such works as John Asgill's *Several Assertions Proved* (1696) that "all Value is by comparison"[44] and Barbon's *Discourse Concerning Coining the New Money Lighter* (1696) that "things have no Value in themselves; it is opinion and fashion brings them into use, and gives them a value."[45]

The Life and Death of Mr. Badman is at once a satirical protest against this emergent capitalist morality and a minute analysis of its psychological effects. Bunyan uses the determining power of the abstract quality of badness over the individual who personifies it as a way of reflecting on the contention that the relentless pursuit of self-interest is part of human nature. Badman must always act badly, partly because he is a predestined reprobate but more specifically and emphatically because he must always try "to make the best of his own." Bunyan expresses this through his deployment of figural devices, reminding the reader that Badman will inevitably act badly because he is an allegorical personification of essential badness. The irony, however, is that Badman himself is utterly committed to a relativist understanding of value and morality. He remains blissfully ignorant as to the true nature of his own condition. In fact, he experiences himself as entirely autonomous and self-determining. He fancies himself a mercurial, transgressive, amorphous character who is able to exchange one identity for another according to the dictates of circumstance:

> And, to pursue his ends the better, he began now to study to please all men, and to suit himself to any company; he could now be as they, say as they, that is, if he listed; and then he would list, when he perceived that by so doing he might either make them his customers or creditors for his commodities.... He would oftentimes please himself with the thought of what he could do in this matter, saying within himself, I can be religious and irreligious, I can be anything or nothing; I can swear, and speak against swearing; I can lie, and speak against lying; I can drink, wench, be unclean, and defraud, and not be troubled for it. Now I enjoy my self, and am master of my own ways, and not they of me. (83–84)[46]

Of course, the humor lies in the fact that the reader has already been shown how completely Badman's "ways" are predetermined by his intrinsic identity. He acts as he does because of what he *is:* an allegorical personification of badness. His illusions of chimerical independence are thus clearly revealed as ideological obfuscations necessitated by the pursuit of "his ends." Badman believes that his identity is defined by the opinion in which he is held by others, and Bunyan repeatedly informs us that the community at large views Badman benignly. But the reader knows him to be determined, at both the allegorical and the naturalistic levels, by the essential quality of badness, and we are thus able to recognize his fantasies of autonomy as false consciousness. Bunyan shows us, in other words, that Badman's appearance, his "value," systematically contradicts his inherent "worth."

III

Bunyan's figural technique in *Badman* parallels the process of commodification, by means of which essential differences are displaced by the leveling equivalence of exchange value. As Barbon noted in 1696, "one sort of Wares are as good as another, if the Values be equal. An hundred pounds worth of Lead or Iron, is as good as an hundred pounds worth of Silver or Gold."[47] Once again, it was left to the cynical forthrightness of Mandeville to reveal the ethical implications of this economic doctrine. In his *Enquiry into the Origin of Honour* (1732), Mandeville announces the transfiguration of the classical notion of "virtue"—a quality that is intrinsic to an individual—into the modern concept of "honour"—an attribute bestowed by public opinion. The desire for honour springs from "self-liking," by which Mandeville intends the pride that he assumes everyone feels when contemplating their own character. The suggestion, not advanced without a certain satisfaction, is "that we are Idols to our Selves, and that Honour is diametrically opposite to Christianity."[48]

Although no critic has, to my knowledge, remarked upon it, Mandeville's phrasing may contain a deliberate allusion to *The Pilgrim's Progress:* Christian's claim in Vanity Fair "That Christianity and the Customs of our Town of Vanity were Diametrically opposite, and could not be reconciled" (93). As Christopher Hill has remarked, Vanity Fair represents simultaneously the market and the idolatrous consciousness associated with such an economy.[49] Certainly in speeches like the one quoted above, Mr. Badman makes an idol of his "self," and in Bunyan's address to the reader he compares his portrait of Badman to the "images" of the deceased that are sometimes displayed at funerals. In *The Holy War,* Lucifer also connect the market with the dissembling manipulation of identity: "You know Mansoul is a market town; and a town that delights in commerce; what therefore if some of our Diabolonians shall feign themselves far countrymen, and shall go out and bring to the market of Mansoul some of our wares to sell . . ." (245). The implication is that the social mobility and theatrical shifts in identity that a market economy facilitates are in reality masks, fantasies which disguise the deeper predetermination of the character of market participants.

Through his satire of such characters, Bunyan depicts the process whereby Aristotelian essentialism was elbowed aside by the symbolic, shifting, chimerical identities produced by exchange value. *Mr. Badman* is his most extended comment upon this process. In the following exchange Attentive points it out to Wiseman with uncharacteristic acuity:

> WISEMAN: He that useth not good conscience to God, and charity to his neighbour, in buying and selling, dwells next door to an Infidel, and is near of kin to Mr. Badman.
> ATTENTIVE: Well, but what will you say to this question? You know that there is no settled price set by God upon any commodity that is bought and sold under the sun; but all things that we buy and sell, do ebb and flow, as to price,

> like the tide. How then shall a man of tender conscience do, neither to wrong the seller, buyer, nor himself, in buying and selling of commodities?
>
> WISEMAN: This question is thought to be frivolous by all that are of Mr. Badman's way; 'tis also difficult in it self: yet I will endeavour to shape you an answer ... (115)

As it turns out, however, Wiseman can only fall back upon the scholastic "good conscience" and recommend "much moderation in dealing." The inadequacy of his response pays reluctant testimony to the degree to which the market's dominance had already made it impractical and unrealistic to insist on a traditional essentialist ethics in economic practice.[50]

For Bunyan was well aware that the value of things was henceforth to be fixed by the market, and he acknowledged the profound implications of this fact for traditional ethics. With the collapse of the idea that an object's worth is inherent, the entire edifice of Aristotelian essentialism begins to totter and the commodity form displaces *telos*. Hobbes's dictum, quoted above, that "of all Voluntary Acts, the Object is to every man his own Good," is a materialist, quantified version of Aristotelian teleology. In Aristotle, of course, the *telos* of man is the Good, which is conceived of as an ideal essence to be striven toward. For Hobbes, the goal of any man's free actions is "his own Good" in the narrowly economic, quantifiable sense. Thus were the foundations laid of the anti-essentialist conception of the subject that has finally triumphed along with market capitalism in the postmodern era. With capitalist social mobility, human identity becomes fluid and relational; with the rise of usury and credit the opinion of others comes to define personal worth; with the growth of mercantile wealth and power, disguise, theatricality, and shape-shifting become predominant themes in literature. With the birth of Mr. Badman, Western society embarks on its long journey towards the hyper-real.

Notes

* Cited from M. H. Abrams, ed., *The Norton Anthology of English Literature* (New York: Norton, 1993), 2:1297.

Introduction

1. Unless otherwise specified, Biblical quotations are from the King James version.
2. Thomas Taylor, *To the People at and about Stafford* (London, 1679), 7.
3. Oswald Spengler, *The Decline of the West*, trans. Charles Francis Atkinson (Oxford: Oxford University Press, 1991), 398.
4. Lucy Hutchinson, *Memoirs of the Life of Colonel John Hutchinson*, edited by N. H. Keeble (London: J. M. Dent, 1995), 51.
5. Ibid., 26.
6. "Since she whom I lov'd," lines 5–6. Quoted from John Donne, *The Complete English Poems*, edited by C. A. Patrides (London: J. M. Dent, 1985).
7. "The Pulley," 13–14, *The English Poems of George Herbert*, edited by C.A. Patrides (London: J. M. Dent, 1974), 167. Gregory of Nazianzus describes idolatry as a "transferral to the creature of the honour due the creator." As Aquinas explains, "the term *idolatry* was used to signify any worship of a creature, even without the use of images." Cited in Alain Besançon, *The Forbidden Image: An Intellectual History of Iconoclasm* (Chicago: University of Chicago Press, 2000), 66.
8. David Hawkes, *Ideology* (New York: Routledge, 1996).
9. For Milton's favorable opinion of usury, see *The Doctrine and Discipline of Divorce*, in *Complete Prose Works of John Milton*, edited by Ernest Sirluck (New Haven, CT: Yale University Press, 1959), 2:322.
10. James Holstun, *Ehud's Dagger: Class Struggle in the English Revolution* (New York: Verso, 2000). Holstun conclusively establishes the importance of class consciousness to the religious and political discourses of the era, and his barbs against revisionist historians and new historicist literary critics who ignore the category of class are timely and appropriate. But Holstun's conception of the class struggle appears to depart

from the conventional, materialist Marxist understanding of the term and to imply a more nuanced interpretation of "class" conflict. He writes:

> In this book, I will argue that the English Revolution was a class struggle. By that, I don't mean the quasi-natural collision of a declining gentry, or the aristocracy, or the feudal countryside with a rising gentry, or the bourgeoisie, or a proto-capitalist London. Rather, I mean the struggle among various groups that were endeavoring to maintain or transform the relations of production (87–88).

Whereas a member of one social class would have been immediately distinguishable from a member of another, it is surely very likely, even inevitable, that the same individual would oscillate, both objectively and subjectively, between actions and opinions that tended to "maintain" and those that tended to "transform" relations of production.

11. Cited in Christopher Hill, *Antichrist in Seventeenth-Century England* (New York: Verso, 1990), 116–117.
12. See Maurice Dobb, *Studies in the Development of Capitalism* (London: G. Routledge and K. Paul, 1946), 55–56.
13. R. H. Tawney, *Religion and the Rise of Capitalism* (Gloucester, MA.: P. Smith, 1962), ix.
14. Tawney, *Religion,* 315–317.
15. Christopher Hill, *The English Revolution, 1640* (London: Lawrence and Wishart, 1941), 9. Elsewhere, Hill confidently declares that "most historians would agree that there is some connection between the Puritan and the *bourgeois* virtues," *The Century of Revolution, 1603–1714* (New York: Norton, 1961), 63, emphasis in the original.
16. Cited in Gertrude Himmelfarb, *The New History and the Old* (Cambridge, Mass.: Belknap Press of Harvard University, 1987), 79–80.
17. Christopher Hill, *Intellectual Origins of the English Revolution* (Oxford: Clarendon Press, 1965), 89–90.
18. "Bacon gave a co-operative programme and sense of purpose to merchants, artisans, and philosophers, each of whom hitherto had seen only in part. This was his first great achievement." Hill, *Intellectual Origins,* 87.
19. Ibid., 95.
20. A similar assumption regarding historical progress lurks behind Eric Hobsbawm's claim that the crisis of the seventeenth century resulted from "the failure to surmount certain general obstacles which still stood in the way of the full development of capitalism." ("The Crisis of the Seventeenth Century," in *Crisis in Europe 1560–1660,* edited by Trevor Aston [London: Routledge and Kegan Paul, 1965] 5–58,

29). Regardless of how just or rational the seventeenth-century case against capitalism might have been, it is always difficult to sympathize with "obstacles" to "development."
21. As Immanuel Wallerstein puts it:

> The Marxist embrace of an evolutionary model of progress has been an enormous trap, which socialists have begun to suspect only recently.... It is simply not true that capitalism as a historical system has represented progress over the various previous historical systems that it destroyed or transformed. (*Historical Capitalism* [London: Verso, 1983], 98.)

22. Cited in Harvey J. Kaye, *The British Marxist Historians: An Introductory Analysis* (New York: St. Martin's Press, 1995), 39.
23. Christopher Hill, "Marxism and History," *Science and Society* 3 (spring 1948): 53.
24. Perry Anderson, *Lineages of the Absolutist State* (London: N. L. B., 1974), 42.
25. See Robert Brenner, *Merchants and Revolution: Commercial Change, Political Conflict and London's Overseas Traders, 1550–1653* (Cambridge: Cambridge University Press, 1993).
26. Anderson, *Lineages*, 17.
27. Ibid., 142.
28. See also Immanuel Wallerstein, *The Modern World-System* (New York: Academic Press, 1974), 1:159–160.
29. See Ernest Mandel's introduction to Karl Marx, *Capital: A Critique of Political Economy*, trans. Ben Fowkes (London: Penguin Books, 1976), 42.
30. Marx, *Capital*, 129.
31. Ibid., 135.
32. Karl Marx, *The Economic and Philosophical Manuscripts of 1844*, trans. Martin Milligan, edited by Dirk J. Struik (New York: International Publishers, 1964), 111–112.
33. Karl Marx, *Capital* vol. 3, trans. Ernest Untermann (Chicago: C. H. Kerr and Company, 1909), 812.
34. Marx, *Capital*, 247.
35. Paul Sweezy, ed., *The Transition from Feudalism to Capitalism* (London: Verso, 1976), 49.
36. Immanuel Wallerstein, *The Capitalist World-Economy* (Cambridge: Cambridge University Press, 1979), 5. Wallerstein's thesis is challenged by Robert Brenner in his "Agrarian Class Structure and Economic Development in Pre-Industrial Europe," *Past & Present*, 70 (February 1976): 30–75.
37. Ellen Meiskins Wood, *The Pristine Culture of Capitalism: A Historical Essay on Old Regimes and Modern States* (New York: Verso, 1991), 98–99. See also Grant McCracken's analysis of the origins of

consumer culture in sixteenth-century London, in *Culture and Consumption* (Bloomington: Indiana University Press, 1988) 11–16.
38. In *Political Economy and the Rise of Capitalism* (Berkeley: University of California Press, 1988), David McNally hints at a possible explanation for Anderson's reluctance to acknowledge the existence of early modern capitalism. McNally convincingly argues that English capitalism is originally not an urban but an agrarian phenomenon, having as its essential prerequisites the expropriation of the peasantry and the refashioning of "farming as an economic activity based upon the production of agricultural commodities for profit on the market" (xii).
39. Neal Wood, *Foundations of Political Economy: Some Early Tudor Views on State and Society* (Berkeley: University of California Press, 1994), 1.
40. Wallerstein, *Historical Capitalism,* 42. Elsewhere in the same work, Wallerstein declares: "My own view is that the genesis of this historical system is located in late-fifteenth-century Europe, that the system expanded in space over time to cover the entire globe by the late nineteenth century, and that it still today covers the entire globe" (19).
41. The seminal theoretical studies of this convergence include Jean Baudrillard, *For a Critique of the Political Economy of the Sign* (New York: Telos Press, 1981); Frederic Jameson, *Postmodernism: or, The Cultural Logic of Late Capitalism* (Durham: University of North Carolina Press, 1991); and Jean-Francois Lyotard, *Libidinal Economy,* trans. Iain Hamilton Grant (Bloomington: Indiana University Press, 1993). For examples of economists who participate in the new economic criticism, see Warren J. Samuels, ed., *Economics as Discourse: An Analysis of the Language of Economists* (Boston: Kluwer Academic, 1990); and A. Klamer, D. N. McClosky and R. M. Solow, eds., *The Consequences of Economic Rhetoric* (Cambridge: Cambridge University Press, 1988).
42. Mark Osteen and Martha Woodmansee, "Taking Account of the New Economic Criticism: An Historical Introduction," in *The New Economic Criticism: Studies at the Intersection of Literature and Economics,* edited by Martha Woodmansee and Mark Osteen (New York: Routledge, 1999), 3. In addition to the centrally important works of Marc Shell and Jean-Joseph Goux, Woodmansee and Osteen mention several seminal influences on the new economic criticism, including: Ferruccio Rossi-Landi, *Linguistics and Economics* (The Hague: Mouton, 1975); Kurt Heinzelman, *The Economics of the Imagination* (Amherst: University of Massachusetts Press, 1980); Donald N. McClosky, *The Rhetoric of Economics* (Madison: University of Wisconsin Press, 1985); Walter Benn Michaels, *The Gold Standard and the Logic of Naturalism* (Berkeley: University of California Press, 1987).

43. Osteen and Woodmansee, "Taking Account," 4.
44. Gregory P. LaBlanc, "Economics and Literary History: An Economist's Perspective," *New Literary History* 31:2 (spring 2000): 355–377.
45. Osteen and Woodmansee, "Taking Account," 408.
46. Hence Pierre Bourdieu's protest: "The charge of economism which is often brought against me consists of treating the homology between the economic field . . . and the fields of cultural production . . . as an identity, pure and simple . . ." *In Other Words: Essays Towards a Reflexive Sociology,* trans. Matthew Adamson (Stanford, CA: Stanford University Press, 1990), 111.
47. Deirdre McClosky, *Knowledge and Persuasion in Economics* (Cambridge: Cambridge University Press, 1994), 336. See also Jack Amariglio, "Economics as a Postmodern Discourse," in W. J. Samuels (ed.), *Economics as Discourse: An Analysis of the Language of Economists* (Boston: Kluwer Academic, 1990), 15–46; and Robert M. Solow, "Comments from Inside Economics," in *The Consequences of Economic Rhetoric,* 31–37.
48. Osteen and Woodmansee, "Taking Account," 381.
49. See especially Lawrence Birken, *Consuming Desire: Sexual Science and the Emergence of a Culture of Abundance 1871–1914* (Ithaca: Cornell University Press, 1988).
50. Marc Shell, *Money, Language and Thought: Literary and Philosophical Economics from the Medieval to the Modern Era* (Baltimore: Johns Hopkins University Press, 1993), 180. See also Marc Shell, *Art and Money* (Chicago: University of Chicago Press, 1995).
51. Shell, *Money, Language and Thought,* 43.
52. Jean-Joseph Goux: *Symbolic Economies: After Marx and Freud,* trans. Jennifer Curtiss Gage (Ithaca: Cornell University Press, 1990), 18. For an interesting application of economic concepts to literary criticism, see June Howard, *Form and History in American Literary Naturalism* (Chapel Hill: University of North Carolina Press, 1985). For an equally interesting application of literary critical concepts to economics, see Willie Henderson, *Economics as Literature* (London: Routledge, 1995).
53. Jean-Joseph Goux, *The Coiners of Language,* trans. Jennifer Curtiss Gage (Norman: University of Oklahoma Press, 1994), 19, emphasis in the original. See Mohamed Zayani, *Reading the Symptom: Frank Norris, Theodore Dreiser and the Dynamics of Capitalism* (New York: Peter Lang, 1999), for what might be described as a marriage between Goux and Slavoj Zizek. One important difference between the work of thinkers such as Goux and Zizek and my approach here is their introduction of psychoanalytical concepts into their studies of the relations between financial and linguistic semantics. As Goux puts it, recalling the genesis of his project in the introduction to *Symbolic*

Economies: "what had previously been analyzed separately as phallocentrism (Freud, Lacan), as logocentrism (Derrida), and as the rule of exchange by the monetary medium (Marx), it was now possible to conceive as part of a unified process" (4). While not questioning the importance of Freud and Lacan to the study of representation in the twenty-first century, I have found so little correspondence between their theoretical frame of reference and that of the writers analyzed here as to convince me that to apply their theories in this study would risk anachronism. The spiritual effects of early modern political economy were discussed and understood by those who experienced them in a theological rather than a psychoanalytical vocabulary, and I have tried to study these writers in their own terms.

54. Goux, *Coiners of Language,* 65, emphases in original.
55. Ibid., 17.
56. Ibid.
57. Ibid., 18.
58. Ibid.
59. Ibid., 129.
60. Ibid.
61. Ibid., 77.
62. Cited in Shell, *Money, Language and Thought,* 84n1.
63. Ibid., 191.
64. Edmund Spenser, *The Faerie Queene,* ed. J. C. Smith and E. de Selincourt (Oxford: Clarendon Press, 1926), 2.7.39.1–5.
65. Ben Jonson, *Volpone,* ed. Philip Brockbank (New York: Norton, 1992), 1.1.1–3, 11–13, 22–23.
66. William Clark, *The grand Tryal: or, Poetical Exercitations upon the book of Job* (1685), part 3, chap. 28, retrieved from Chadwick-Healey's *Literature on Line,* available 5/1/01: http://lion.chadwick.com/home.cgi?source=config2.cfg.

CHAPTER 1

1. Immanuel Wallerstein, *Historical Capitalism* (London: Verso, 1983), 40–41.
2. Aristotle, *On the Generation of Animals,* trans. A. Platt, 1.715a3–7, in *The Complete Works of Aristotle,* edited by Jonathan Barnes (Princeton: Princeton University Press, 1984) 1: 1111.
3. Aristotle, *Metaphysics,* ed. and trans. W. D. Ross, 994b9–10 (Oxford: Clarendon Press, 1924) 2:1571.
4. Aristotle, *Nicomachean Ethics,* trans. W. D. Ross, revised by J. O. Urmson, 1.7.1097a17–18 in Barnes, *Complete Works* 2:1734.
5. Aristotle, *Magna Moralia,* trans. St. G. Stock, 1.1.1182a34–35 in Barnes, *Complete Works* 2:1869.

6. Aristotle, *Nicomachean Ethics,* trans. J. E. C. Welldon (Buffalo, NY: Prometheus Books, 1987), 1.7. p.24. I cite Welldon's translation here because I prefer "virtue" to "excellence" (e.g., at 1098a1 p.17 and 1102a1, p.6), which is used by the revised Oxford translation. "Virtue" is the English term generally employed by writers in the sixteenth and seventeenth centuries.
7. See especially Thomas Aquinas, *Summa Contra Gentiles* chapters 2–63, in *Basic Writings of Saint Thomas Aquinas* 2 vols., ed. Anton C. Pegis (New York: Random House, 1945), 2:5–113).
8. Charles G. Hebermann et al, eds., *The Catholic Encyclopedia,* vol.8 (New York: Appleton, 1907).
9. See Aristotle, *Magna Moralia* 1182b12–15, where Aristotle differentiates between the Idea of the Good, and the immanent good.
10. For a detailed study of the complex religious reaction to Baconian empiricism, see John Dillenberger, *Protestant Thought and Natural Science* (Westport, CT: Greenwood Publishing Group, 1977).
11. See Aristotle, *Nicomachean Ethics* trans. W. D. Ross:

    Money, then, acting as a measure, makes goods commensurate and equates them. . . . Now in truth it is impossible that things differing so much should become commensurate, but with reference to demand they may become sufficiently so. There must, then, be a unit, and that fixed by agreement [i.e., custom] (for which reason it is called money); for it is this that makes all things commensurate, since all things are measured by money. (5.5.1133b1, 15–22)

12. Aristotle, *Politics,* trans. Carnes Lord (Chicago: University of Chicago Press, 1984), 1257a1, 7–10, p.46. Subsequent references are from this edition.
13. As Heraclitus had already seen: "All things are an equal exchange for fire and fire for all things, as goods are for gold and gold for goods." See "Heraclitus and the Money Form" in Marc Shell, *The Economy of Literature* (Baltimore: Johns Hopkins University Press, 1978), 49–62, 2n3.
14. Aristotle, *Nicomachean Ethics,* trans. J. E. C. Welldon, 5.8. p.161. Aristotle's theory of money was axiomatic in the West until the late seventeenth century. See J. T. Noonan, *The Scholastic Analysis of Usury* (Cambridge, MA: Harvard University Press, 1957); Arnaud Berthold, *Aristote et l'argent* (Paris: F. Maspero, 1981); Odd Langholm, *Wealth and Money in the Aristotelian Tradition* (Bergen: Universitetforlagen, 1983) and his *The Aristotelian Analysis of Usury* (Bergen: Universitetforlagen, 1984).
15. Gratian gives this argument a Christian inflection:

    Whosoever buys a thing, not that he may sell it whole and unchanged, but that it may be a material for fashioning something, he is no merchant. But the man who buys it in order that he may gain by selling it again unchanged and as he bought it, that man is of the buyers and sellers who are cast forth from God's temple. (Cit. R. H. Tawney, *Religion and the Rise of Capitalism* (Gloucester, MA: P. Smith, 1962), 35.

By the mid-seventeenth century, the English mercantilists were regularly making this distinction without any invidious ethical comparisons. In *The Merchant's Mappe of Commerce* (London, 1638), Lewes Roberts distinguishes three kinds of "merchandizing: "The first is goods for goods, and this is termed bartering. The second is goods for money, and this is termed bargaining, and the third is money for money, and this is properly amongst Merchants, (in these days termed) exchanging" (12). See also the *Nicomachean Ethics:* "The life of money-making is one undertaken under compulsion, and wealth is evidently not the good we are seeking; for it is merely useful for the sake of something else" (1096a1). *The Complete Works of Aristotle,* ed. Jonathan Barnes (Princeton: Princeton University Press, 1984), 2:1732.

16. Aristotle, *Politics,* 1258bl, 49–50.
17. Commentary on Aristotle's *Politiques,* trans. from Greek into French by Loys Le Roy and from French into English by I. D. (London, 1598), 46, 48.
18. See Robert Brenner, *Merchants and Revolution: Commercial Change, Political Conflict and London's Overseas Traders,* 1550–1653 (Cambridge: Cambridge University Press, 1993).
19. Ulrich Langer has pointed to a "profound dependence on forms of late scholastic thought" in the humanist "new learning" of the Renaissance (*Divine and Poetics Freedom in the Renaissance: Nominalist Theology and Literature in France and Italy* [Princeton: Princeton University Press, 1990], 12).
20. Cited in Christopher Hill, *Antichrist in Seventeenth-Century England* (New York: Verso, 1990), 29.
21. *The Works of Francis Bacon* (7 vols. popular edition), ed. James Spedding, R. L. Ellis and D. D. Heath (London, 1857–59), 1:168. Unless otherwise specified, subsequent in-text references to Bacon are from this edition.
22. See also Walter Raleigh's relegation of the divinity to practical irrelevance in his *History of the World* when he inquires after historical causality: "To say that God was pleased to have it so, were a true but an idle answer (for His secret will is the cause of all things).... Wherefore we may boldly look into the second causes." Cited in Christopher Hill, *Intellectual Origins of the English Revolution* (Oxford: Clarendon Press, 1965), 181. In the same work, Hill cites less sanguine views of the abandonment of *telos,* such as Robert Gray's *An Alarum to England* (1609): "amongst us at this day, if any

strange accidents do happen, either in the air, or in the earth, or in the waters, . . . we refer them to some material cause or other, being unwilling (as it were) to acknowledge God to have a hand in this," and Thomas Hall's *Histrio-Mastix* (1654), which attacks the "presumption, if not impiety, in taking men off from [God], the first, to ascribe all or too much to Nature and second causes" (182).

23. Bacon's theory of the idols alludes to the Homeric usage of *eidolon* as "phantom." This notion provides a hinge between the theological concept of a false god and the secular concept of a false idea. For example, compare William Perkins's remark that "A thing fained in the mind by imagination is an idoll" (*A Warning Against the Idolatrie of the Last Times,* cit. James R. Siemon, *Shakespearean Iconoclasm,* [Berkeley: University of California Press, 1985], 45) with Hobbes's *Leviathan:*

> Before our Saviour preached, it was the generall Religion of the Gentiles, to worship for Gods, those Appearances that remain in the Brain from the impression of external Bodies upon the organs of their Senses, which are commonly called *Ideas, Idols, Phantasms, Conceits,* as being Representations of those externall Bodies, which cause them, and have nothing in them of reality, no more than the things which seem to stand before us in a Dream. (*Leviathan* ed. C. B. MacPherson [London: Penguin Books, 1985], 665).

24. See Ann Kibbey, *The Interpretation of Material Shapes in Puritanism* (Cambridge: Cambridge University Press, 1986), 47.
25. Francis Bacon, "Of the True Greatness of the Kingdom of Britain," 7:39–40.
26. Francis Bacon, "Of Usury," in *Francis Bacon,* ed. Brian Vickers (Oxford: Oxford University Press, 1996), 422.
27. Isaac Gervaise, *The System or Theory of the Trade of the World* (1720), retrieved from *McMaster University Archive for the History of Economic Thought,* available 5/1/01: http://www.socsci.mcmaster.ca/~econ/ugcm/3113/.
28. For fascinating recent studies that analyze the progressive recognition of value in the commodity form at the level of everyday life, and particularly its implications for aesthetics, see Simon Schama, *The Embarrassment of Riches: An Interpretation of Dutch Culture in the Golden Age* (New York: Alfred A. Knopf, 1987), and Lisa Jardine, *Worldly Goods: A New History of the Renaissance* (New York: Doubleday, 1996).
29. The American Indians recognized the Spaniards' attitude to gold as animist, as Marx reminds us: "The savages of Cuba regarded gold as a fetish of the Spaniards. They celebrated a feast in its honour, sang in a circle around it and then threw it into the sea." *Rheinische*

Zeitung no. 298, 10/25/1842. See also Montaigne's comparison of the Aztec's use of gold as a material from which to manufacture useful or beautiful objects with the Spaniards' melting down of these objects in order to mint gold coins (*The Essays of Montaigne*, trans. George B. Ives [Cambridge, MA: Harvard University Press, 1925], 4:94).

30. Nicholas Barbon, *A Discourse of Trade* (1690; reprint Baltimore: Johns Hopkins Press, 1905), 18.
31. Kristof Glamann, "The Changing Patterns of Trade," in *The Cambridge Economic History of Europe*, ed. E. E. Rich and C. H. Wilson (Cambridge: Cambridge University Press, 1977), 5:265.
32. Perry Anderson, *Lineages of the Absolutist State* (London: N. L. B., 1974), 22.
33. Immanuel Wallerstein, *The Modern World-System* (New York: Academic Press, 1974), 1:39–41.
34. Glyn Davies, *A History of Money from Ancient Times to the Present Day* (Cardiff: University of Wales Press, 1994), 187.
35. See Constantine G. Caffentzis, *Clipped Coins, Abused Words and Civil Government: John Locke's Philosophy of Money* (New York: Autonomedia, 1989).
36. R. H. Tawney and Eileen Power (eds.), *Tudor Economic Documents* (London: Longmans, 1924)2:176–203; Neal Wood, *Foundations of Political Economy: Some Early Tudor Views on State and Society* (Berkeley: University of California Press, 1994), 15.
37. David McNally, *Political Economy and the Rise of Capitalism: A Reinterpretation* (Berkeley: University of California Press, 1988), 5. Conrad Russell suggests a 500 percent increase in the price of "cheaper commodities" over the sixteenth century, in *The Crisis of Parliaments: English History 1509–1660* (Oxford: Oxford University Press, 1971), 6.
38. Tawney, *Religion and the Rise of Capitalism*, 137.
39. "Between 1542 and 1547 English silver about 400,000 pounds was reminted into coins worth 526,000 pounds." (McNally, *Political Economy,* 27)
40. See Davies, *A History of Money,* 230.
41. Hermann van der Wee: "Monetary, Credit and Banking Systems," in *The Cambridge Economic History of Europe* 5:290.
42. Thomas Violet, *Mysteries and Secrets of Trade and Mint-affairs* (London, 1653), 4.
43. See Davies, *A History of Money,* 232.
44. Ibid., 279.
45. James Grant discusses this concept in a postmodern context in *Money of the Mind* (New York: Farrar Straus Giroux, 1992).
46. See C. H. Wilson, "Trade, Society and the State," in *The Cambridge Economic History of Europe* 4:487–576.

47. David McNally notes the vagueness of the term "mercantilism," but suggests that it may serve as a "convenient shorthand" for texts that discussed "questions of a mercantile nature" (*Political Economy*, 23). Essentially, the word designates an area of interest as much as it does a theoretical school. See Eli F. Heckscher, *Mercantilism*, trans. Mendel Shapiro (London: G. Allen and Unwin, 1934); D. C. Coleman, ed., *Revisions in Mercantilism* (London: Metheun, 1969); Robert Ashton, *City and the Court, 1603–1643* (Cambridge: Cambridge University Press, 1979); George O'Brien, *An Essay on Medieval Economic Teaching* (London: Longmans, Green and Co., 1920); Paul Sweezy et al. (eds.), *The Transition from Feudalism to Capitalism* (London: Verso, 1976); Eric Hobsbawm, "The Seventeenth Century in the Development of Capitalism," *Science and Society* 24 (1960).
48. Violet, *Mysteries*, 39.
49. Edward Misselden, *Free Trade, or The Meanes to Make Trade Flourish* (1622, reprint New York: Da Capo Press, 1970), 20–1. Andrea Finkelstein has recently argued that the earliest political economists took a more dubious view of trade than has usually been recognized: "the [seventeenth] century's major 'economic' writers were as ambivalent about market values and their power to transform society as were their contemporaries in religion, politics, and natural philosophy, and for the same reason: they were afraid that there was something inherently chaotic in a market society." (*Harmony and Balance: An Intellectual History of Seventeenth-century Economic Thought* [Ann Arbor: University of Michigan Press, 2000], 2.
50. Ibid., 6–7.
51. Gerard de Malynes, *The Maintenance of Free Trade* (1622), retrieved from *McMaster University Archive for the History of Economic Thought*, available 5/1/01: http://www.socsci.mcmaster.ca/~econ/ugcm/3113/malynes/malynes.txt. Unless otherwise specified, reference to de Malynes will be from this source.
52. Rice Vaughan, *Of Coins and Coinage* (1675), retrieved from *McMaster University Archive for the History of Economic Thought*, available 5/1/01: http://www.socsci.mcmaster.ca/~econ/ugcm/3113/vaughan/coin.
53. Thomas Mun, *England's Treasure by Foreign Trade*, in *Masterworks of Economics*, edited by Leonard Dalton Abbot (Garden City, NJ: Doubleday, 1946), 21.
54. Ibid., 21.
55. Ibid., 22.
56. Ibid., 23.
57. Cited in Karl Marx, *Capital* vol.1, trans. Ben Fowkes (London: Penguin Books, 1976), 226n36.

58. Sir Dudley North, *Discourses upon Trade* (1691, reprint Baltimore: Johns Hopkins Press, 1907), 14.
59. Ibid., 24.
60. John Locke, *Some Considerations of the Consequences of the Lowering of Interest* (1691), retrieved from McMaster University Archive for the History of Economic Thought, available 5/1/01: http://socserv2.socsci.mcmaster.ca:80/~econ/ugcm/3113/locke/consid.txt.
61. Mun, *England's Treasure*, 16.
62. Adam Smith, *An Inquiry into the Nature and Causes of the Wealth of Nations* (New York: Random House, 1994), 321.
63. David Hume "Of Interest" (1752), in *Writings on Economics*, ed. Eugene Rotwein (Edinburgh: Nelson, 1955), 48.
64. John Law, *Money and Trade Considered* (1705), retrieved from McMaster University Archive for the History of Economic Thought, available 5/1/01: http://www.socsci.mcmaster.ca/~econ/ugcm/3113/law/mon.txt.

CHAPTER 2

1. John Calvin, *Institutes of the Christian Religion*, trans. Henry Beveridge (London: J. Clarke, 1949), 2:32.
2. Karl Marx and Friedrich Engels, *Collected Works* (New York: International Publishers, 1975), 3:290. Unless otherwise specified, references to Marx will be to this edition.
3. Karl Marx, *Introduction to a Critique of Political Economy* (1857), 5:314.
4. Karl Marx, *Capital*, trans. David Fernbach (New York: Vintage Books, 1982), 3:727.
5. Ludwig Feuerbach, *The Essence of Christianity*, trans. George Eliot (New York: Harper, 1957), 13.
6. Karl Marx, *Capital*, trans. Ben Fowkes (London: Penguin Books, 1975), 1:165. Twenty-five years earlier Marx had identified alienated labor with religious idolatry in more sanguine terms:

   ... the criticism of religion is the prerequisite of all criticism.... Man, who has found only the reflection of himself in the fantastic reality of heaven, where he sought a superman, will no longer feel disposed to find the mere appearance of himself, the non-man ["Unmensch"], where he seeks and must seek his true reality. (*Critique of Hegel's Philosophy of Right*, trans. Annette Jolin and Joseph O'Malley [Cambridge: Cambridge University Press, 1970], 54.)

7. Jacques Derrida, *Specters of Marx: the State of the Debt, the Work of Mourning, and the New International*, trans. Peggy Kamuf (New York: Routledge, 1994), 45.

8. Jean Baudrillard, *Simulations*, trans. Paul Foss, Paul Patton and Philip Beitchman (New York: Semiotext(e), 1983), 8.
9. Studies of the literary implications of Reformation iconoclasm include James R. Sieman, *Shakespearean Iconoclasm* (Berkeley: University of California Press, 1985); Patrick Collinson, *From Iconoclasm to Iconophobia: the Cultural Impact of the Second English Reformation* (Reading, University of Reading Press, 1986); Phillipe Desan, *L'Imaginaire Economique de la Renaissance* (Mont-de-Marsan, 1993); Carlos Eire, *War Against the Idols: the Reformation of Worship from Erasmus to Calvin* (Cambridge: Cambridge University Press, 1986); Ernest B. Gilman, *Iconoclasm and Poetry in the English Reformation* (Chicago: University of Chicago Press, 1986), and Kenneth Gross, *Spenserian Poetics: Idolatry, Iconoclasm and Magic* (Ithaca: Cornell University Press, 1985). For an approach oriented toward the visual arts, see John Dillenberger, *Images and Relics: Theological Perceptions and Visual Images in Sixteenth-Century Europe* (Oxford: Oxford University Press, 1999).
10. *The Wisdom of Solomon*, commentary by Ernest G. Clarke (Cambridge: Cambridge University Press, 1973), 90.
11. Augustine, *Commentary on the Psalms*. See also Clement of Alexandria, *Exhortation to the Heathen* 4.61–2: "While you bestow the greatest pains that the image may be fashioned with the most exquisite beauty possible, you exercise no care to guard against your becoming like images for stupidity" (cit. Pelikan, 55–7).
12. Calvin, *Institutes* 2:93. We can perceive the persistent influence of this Psalm throughout this period, for example in Thomas Cooper's *Wilie Beguile ye, or the Worldling's Gaine* (London, 1621). Cooper repeats the conventional equation of account of idolatry and commodity fetishism, before pointing out that this epistemological error stamps its impression on the "worldlings" own subjectivity: "Doe they not in distrust of Gods providence, usually make Idols of these things, and so are given up to make Idols of themselves? . . . As they use their goods as Babies, onely to gaze and play withall, so they make babies and sots of themselves, fit onely to be gazed at . . . (25–26).
13. John Wheeler, *A Treatise of Commerce* (London, 1601), 6–7.
14. Thus Martin Luther remind his readers that "flesh, according to St. Paul . . . means everything that is born from the flesh, i.e., the entire self, body and soul, including our reason and all our senses." *Preface to Romans*, in *Selections from his Writings*, ed. John Dillenberger (New York: Doubleday, 1958), 25.
15. Augustine, "Of the Spirit and the Letter," 6.4.12–15, in *Later Works*, trans. John Burnaby (Philadelphia: Westminster Press, 1955), 198.
16. Tertullian, *De Idololatria*, trans. J. H. Waszink and J. C. M. van Winden (New York: E. J. Brill, 1987), 25.

17. Thomas Aquinas, *Summa Theologica*, trans. Fathers of the English Dominican Province (London: R. T. Washbourne, 1918), 94.2.2. See also the Wisdom of Solomon 14:27: "the worship of idols not to be named is the beginning and cause and end of every evil."
18. Calvin, *Institutes,* 2:97.
19. Arminius, "Disputation 23: On Idolatry," in *Writings,* trans. James Nichols (Grand Rapids, MI: Baker Book House, 1956), 1:603.
20. Richard Bernard, *The Isle of Man* (London, 1627), 201, sig. K5.
21. Ibid., 185.
22. Nicholas Bacon (1509–79), "Agaynste Covetousnes," from *The Recreations of His Age* (London, 1619), retrieved from Chadwick-Healey's *Literature On Line,* available 5/1/01 http://lion.chadwick.com/home.cgi?source=config2.cfg.
23. This distinction is also found in Zwingli's distinction between the "Gott," or icon, and the "Abgott," or idol, which he describes as "inner gods" (cit. Gilman, *Iconoclasm,* 41).
24. Plato, *Timaeus* 52c, cited in Moshe Barasch, *Icon: Studies in the History of an Idea* (New York: New York University Press, 1992), 27–8.
25. Hence Jesus' statement "He that hath seen me hath seen the Father," John 14:9.
26. Alain Besancon, *The Forbidden Image: An Intellectual History of Iconoclasm,* trans. Jane Marie Todd (Chicago: University of Chicago Press, 2000), 14.
27. Augustine, *The City of God against the Pagans,* trans. William M. Green (Cambridge, MA: Harvard University Press, 1963), 2:355–6. See also Barasch, *Icon,* 29.
28. See Jaroslav Pelikan, *Imago Dei: The Byzantine Apologia for Icons* (Princeton: Princeton University Press, 1990), 27–8. See also Besancon, *Forbidden Image,* 109–146, and Leslie Brubaker, "The Sacred Image," in *The Sacred Image East and West,* edited by Robert Ousterhout and Leslie Brubaker (Chicago: University of Chicago Press, 1995), 1–24.
29. John Julius Norwich, *Byzantium: the Apogee* (New York: Alfred A. Knopf, 1992), 53. For an account of the prevalence of such superstition in medieval Europe, see especially Keith Thomas, *Religion and the Decline of Magic* (New York: Simon and Schuster, 1975). The extent of popular belief in the miraculous power of images on the eve of the Reformation leads Carlos Eire to conclude that "The images, in short, had come alive." (*War Against the Idols,* 21).
30. See Jaroslav Pelikan, *The Spirit of Eastern Christendom, 600–700* (Chicago: University of Chicago Press, 1974).
31. Daniel J. Sahas, ed., *Icon and Logos: Sources in Eighth-Century Iconoclasm* (Toronto: University of Toronto Press, 1986), 106. Unless otherwise specified, in-text sources from the Byzantine controversy are from this edition.

32. Cited in Barasch, *Icons*, 144–5.
33. Johannes Eck, "On Not Removing Images," in *A Reformation Debate: Karlstadt, Emser and Eck on Sacred Images*, trans. Bryan D. Mangrum and Giuseppe Scavizzi (Toronto: Victoria University, 1991), 101.
34. The implication is that idolaters fall prey to a generalized fetishization of matter—really, a kind of pantheism in which the material world is equated with the second person of the trinity. This charge against idolatry is commonplace during the Renaissance.
35. The thought of the Counter-Reformation, however, was more influenced by Aquinas's Platonic claim that the images deserve the same honor as the prototype (*Summae Theologia* 3.25.1–4).
36. Cited in Barasch, *Icon*, 269.
37. Cited in Besancon, *Forbidden Image*, 130–131.
38. Theodore the Studite, *On the Holy Icons*, 3.C2, cit. Barasch, *Icon*, 275.
39. Ibid., 276.
40. Ibid.
41. The most extensive analysis of this phenomenon is S. R. F. Price, *Rituals and Power: The Roman Imperial Cult in Asia Minor* (Cambridge: Cambridge University Press, 1984).
42. Athanasius, *Orations against the Arians*, 3.5, cited in Pelikan, *Imago Dei*, 38. See also Gregory of Nazianzus: "The emperor must have adoration, whereby his dignity is increased: and not only that 'adoratio' which he receives in person, but also the 'adoratio' that he receives in his statues and pictures, so that the veneration paid to him may be without boundary or limit." (Cited in Romilly James Heald Jenkins, *Byzantium: The Imperial Centuries, A.D. 610–1071* [London: Weidenfeld and Nicolson, 1966], 77–8).
43. Marc Shell, *Money, Languae and Thought* (Berkeley: University of California Press, 1982), 180n4. The Roman concept of emperor-worship would provide plentiful ammunition for Protestant Republicans in the seventeenth century, who adduced against it texts such as the following from the Wisdom of Solomon:

> Then the ungodly custom, grown strong with time, was kept as a law, and at the command of monarchs graven images were worshiped.
>
> When men could not honor monarchs in their presence, since they lived at a distance, they imagined their appearance far away, and made a visible image of the king whom they honored, so that by their zeal they might flatter the absent one as though present.
>
> Then the ambition of the craftsman impelled even those who did not know the king to intensify their worship.

For he, perhaps wishing to please his ruler, skillfully forced the likeness to take more beautiful form.

And the multitude, attracted by the charm of his work, now regarded as an object of worship the one whom shortly before they had honored as a man.

And this became a hidden trap for mankind, because men, in bondage to misfortune or to royal authority, bestowed on objects of stone or wood the name that ought not to be shared (14:16–21).

44. See David Hawkes, *Ideology* (New York: Routledge, 1996), 26–30.
45. Earl of Rochester, "On Rome's Pardons," in *Complete Poems and Plays*, ed. Paddy Lyons (London: J. M. Dent, 1993), 43, lines 1–4. There is some dispute as to the authorship of this poem, but it does not seem surprising to find Rochester repeating Protestant cliches for derisive effect.
46. Alexander Cooke, *Worke, More Worke, and a little More Worke for a Masse Priest* (London, 1630), 75.
47. Martin Luther, *An Appeal to the Ruling Class of German Nationality*, in Dillenberger (ed.), *Selections*, 429–30. Unless otherwise specified, subsequent quotations from Luther will be from this edition. As R. H. Tawney notes, "The Papacy was, in a sense, the greatest financial institution of the middle ages." *Religion and the Rise of Capitalism* (Gloucester, MA: P. Smith, 1962), 29.
48. Luther's most extended analyses of the secular market are the sermons published as "Of Trade and Usury." His conclusion is in agreement with the scholastic tradition: "How can there be anything good then in trade? How can it be without sin when such injustice [the profit motive] is the chief maxim and the rule of the whole business?" In *On Moral Business: Classical and Contemporary Resourses for Ethics in Economic Life*, ed. Max Stackhouse, Dennis P. McCann, Shirley J. Roels, and Preston N. Williams (Grand Rapids, MI: William B. Eerdmans Publishing, 1995), 175.
49. See Richard Friedenthal, *Luther: His Life and Times*, trans. John Nowell (London: Weidenfeld & Nicolson, 1970), 134.
50. In Luther's view, the basic error of the Mass is the pattern for all liturgical folly: "In every sacrament, the merely outward sign is incomparably less important than the thing symbolized. . . . [however] this monstrous state of affairs arose at the time when, contrary to Christian love, we began, in our folly, to pursue worldly wealth. God showed it by that terrible sign, namely, that we preferred the outer signs rather than the things themselves" (261–262).
51. Thus, for example, the Catholic church concluded that the moral condition of the priest has no effect on the efficacy of his acts: "That is what has happened to the mass; it has been transformed, by the teaching of godless men, into a good work. They themselves call it an *opus operatum*. . . . From that starting point they have gone on to

the last folly of asserting that, because the mass avails by virtue of its *opus operatum*, it is no less beneficial to others even if it be hurtful to a celebrant priest who is a wicked man. That is the foundation of sand on which they base their 'applications,' 'participations,' sodlaities, anniversaries, and an infinite number of other profitable, money-making schemes of that kind" (282).
52. Hugh Hilarie, "The Resurrection of the Masse," retrieved from Chadwick-Healey's *Literature On Line*, available 5/1/01: http://lion.chadwick.com/home.cgi?source=config2.cfg.
53. See George H. Williams, *The Radical Reformation* (Philadelphia: Westminster Press, 1962), 41.
54. Andreas Karlstadt, *On the Removal of Images*, in Mangrum and Scavizzi, *A Reformation Debate*, 25.
55. Ibid., 23.
56. Ibid., 26.
57. Martin Luther, "Against the Heavenly Prophets in the Matter of Images and Sacraments" part 1, trans. Bernhard Erling, in *Selected Writings*, ed. Theodore G. Tappert (Philadelphia: Westminster Press, 1967), 162. Ulrich Zwingli, although himself an extreme iconoclast, elaborates a sophisticated distinction between these internal idols in the heart ("die abgotten") and their externalized manifestation as icons ("dem gotzen"). See Eire, *War Against the Idols*, 84.
58. Hieronymus Emser, "That One Should Not Remove Images," in Mangrum and Scavizzi, *A Reformation Debate*, 58.
59. Karlstadt, *On the Removal of Images*, 36.
60. Calvin, *Institutes*, 2:560.
61. Ibid., 2:594.
62. John Calvin, Letter to Martin Bucer, Jan. 12, 1538, in *Selections From His Writings*, edited by John Dillenberger (Oxford: Oxford University Press, 1975), 47.
63. Calvin, *Institutes*, 2:569.
64. Ibid., 2:555.
65. Ibid., 2:552.
66. Ibid., 2:573.
67. Gregory Scott, "Against the Sacrifice of the Masse" (1574), retrieved from Chadwick-Healey's *Literature On Line*, available 5/1/01: http:lion.chadwick.com/home.cgi?source=config2.cfg.

Chapter 3

1. Alain Besancon, *The Forbidden Image: An Intellectual History of Iconoclasm*, trans. Jean Marie Todd (Chicago: University of Chicago Press, 2000), 382.
2. John Northbrooke, *A Treatise Wherein Dicing, Dauncing, Vaine Plaies or Enterludes... ar reproov'd* (London, 1577?), 23–4.

3. Stephen Gosson, *The Ephemerides of Philo . . . And a Short Apologie of the Schoole of Abuse* (London, 1579), 83.
4. Thomas Nashe, *The Anatomie of Absurditie* (London, 1589), Bii.
5. Thomas Heywood, *An Apology for Actors* (London, 1612), F2–3.
6. Francis Rous, *The Diseases of the Time* (London, 1622), 306.
7. Prefatory verse to Heywood's *Apology for Actors*, A.
8. Thomas Lodge, *A Reply to Stephen Gosson's Schoole of Abuse* (1580?), in *The Complete Works of Thomas Lodge*, edited by Edmund Gosse (Glasgow: Hunterian Club, 1883; New York: Johnson Reprint Corporation, 1963), 1:41.
9. The word was regularly used in this sense. See, for example, Henry Denham on hoarding farmers: "they use themselves in so shamefully abusing the good gifts of God, enhauncing the price of Corne of meere covetousnesse to enryche theym selves . . . ," *The Pitiful Estate of this Time Present* (London, 1564), Bii.
10. Puttenham, *English Poesie* (1589), 190.
11. Aristotle's *Politiques,* translated from Greek into French by Loys Le Roy and from French into English by I. D (London, 1598), 46.
12. Ibid., 48.
13. Cited in E. K. Chambers, *The Elizabethan Stage* (Oxford: Clarendon Press, 1923), 4:276.
14. Northbrooke, *A Treatise*, C3, 29.
15. Anthony Munday, *A Second and Third Blast of Retrait from Plaies and Theaters* (London, 1580), 109.
16. *Th'overthrow of Stage-Plays, by the way of a controversie betwixt D. Gager and D Rainolds* (1599), 4, A3.
17. Dudley Fenner, *A Short an Profitable Treatise* (Middleburgh, 1587), A5.
18. William Prynne, *Histrio-Mastix* (London, 1633), 323.
19. Henry Chettle, *Kind-harts Dreame* (London, 1592), C3.
20. William Rankins, *A Mirror of Monsters* (London, 1587), 3. Objections to the commodification of the theater continued to be raised through the eighteenth century, most notably by Rousseau. Adam Smith indicates that the arguments of Gosson and Prynne are by no means dead when he remarks that:

> There are some very agreeable and beautiful talents of which the possession commands a certain sort of admiration; but of which the exercise *for the sake of gain* is considered, whether from reason or prejudice, as a sort of public prostitution. (*The Wealth of Nations* edited by Edwinn Cannan [New York: The Modern Library], 123, emphasis added).

21. Elizabethan and Jacobean Londoners frequently remarked on the commercialization of their environment. An anonymous pamphlet from the mid-sixteenth century reported: "And now from the Tower

to Westminster along, every street is full of [luxuries], and their shops glister and shine of glasses, painted cruses, gay daggers, etc., that is able to make any temperate man to gaze on them and to buy somewhat, though it serve no purpose necessary" (cited in L. Knights, *Drama and Society in the Age of Jonson* [London: Chatto & Windus, 1962]). John Cooke's *Epigrams served out in 52 several Dishes* (London, 1604) personified this phenomenon:

> There's an out-landish man now newly landed,
> With rare inventions, rich conceited tires;
> From Court unto the Citty he is bandied,
> To shew his wares which suddainely inspires
> The inconstant fancie of the foolish buyers,
> The price is great, therefore the wares the better,
> Halfe on't downe paid, halfe on't remaine his debtor
> And this superfluous waste expence in spending,
> Makes Courtiers ever borrowing, never lending.

22. The influence of commodification on aesthetics in the Renaissance has been applied to the sphere of the visual arts by Richard Goldthwaite in *Wealth and the Demand for Art in Italy, 1300–1600* (Baltimore: Johns Hopkins University Press, 1993).
23. Thomas Dekker, *The Gull's Horn-Book,* in *The Non-Dramatic Works of Thomas Dekker,* edited by Alexander B. Grosart (1885, reprint New York: Russell and Russell, 1963), 2:246.
24. Stephen Gosson: *Playes Confuted in Five Actions* (London, 1582), B. See Arthur Kinney, *Markets of Bawdrie: The Dramatic Criticism of Stephen Gosson* (Salzburg: Institut fur Englische Sprache und Literatur, 1974).
25. Gosson, *Playes Confuted,* G6.
26. Jean-Christophe Agnew, *Worlds Apart: the Market and the Theater in Anglo-American Thought, 1550–1750* (Cambridge: Cambridge University Press, 1986); Douglas Bruster, *Drama and the Market in the Age of Shakespeare* (Cambridge: Cambridge University Press, 1992), and Jean E. Howard, *The Stage and Social Struggle in Early Modern England* (London: Routledge, 1994). For a salutary qualification of these critics, see Scott Cutler Shershaw, "Idols of the Marketplace: Rethinking the Economic Determinism of Renaissance Drama," *Renaissance Drama* n.s. 26 (1995). See also F. J. Fisher, "The Development of London as a Center of Conspicuous Consumption in the Sixteenth and Seventeenth Centuries" in *London and the English Economy, 1500–1700* (London: Hambledon Press, 1990); Karen Newman, "City Talk: Women and Commodification in Jonson's Epicene," *ELH* 56, no.3 (autumn, 1989): 503–518; and Christopher Pye, "The Theater, the Market, and the Subject of History," *ELH* 61, no.3 (autumn, 1994): 501–522. A wider-ranging, comprehensive overview of the

entire antitheatrical tradition is presented by Jonas Barish in *The Antitheatrical Prejudice* (Berkeley: University of California Press, 1981).
27. Agnew, *Worlds Apart*, 10.
28. Howard, *The Stage and Social Struggle*, 23.
29. On the connection of "abuse" with idolatry, see John Phillips, *The Reformation of Images* (Berkeley: University of California Press, 1973), 89–91, 114–117; Michael O'Connor, "The Idolatrous Eye: Iconoclasm, Antitheatricalism and the Image of the Elizabethan Theater," *ELH* 52, no.2 (summer, 1985): 279–310; Carlos Eire, *War Against the Idols* (Cambridge: Cambridge University Press, 1986), and Ernest B. Gilman, *Iconoclasm and Poetry in the English Reformation* (Chicago: University of Chicago Press, 1986).
30. John Stockwood, 25.
31. Rous, *Diseases*, 299.
32. John Donne, *Sermons*, ed. George R. Potter and Evelyn M. Simpson (Berkeley, University of California Press 1953–62), 7:432. A century earlier, we find the antitheatrical case anticipated precisely by Hieronymus Emser, in a pamphlet against Luther. When he declares that "there is nothing on earth so good that evil cannot pervert or misuse," Emser intends by the term any manifestation of worldliness. Defending Erasmus against charges of iconoclasm, for instance, Emser claims "he does not condemn in general the lighting of candles or other outward ceremonies, but only the abuse of over reliance on these external things, in favour of which the inward, spiritual things, which concern us more, are omitted..." (Cited in "That One Should Not Remove Images," in *A Reformation Debate: Karlstadt, Emser, and Eck on Sacred Images*, trans. Bryan D. Mangrum and Giuseppe Scavizzi (Toronto: Victoria University, 1991), 74, 76.
33. John Weemse, *A Treatise of the Four Degenerate Sonnes* (London, 1636), 226.
34. Henry Clark, *A Rod Discover'd, found, & set forth to Whip the Idolaters* (London, 1659), 23.
35. The anonymous author of *Usurie Araigned and Condemned* (London, 1625) proposes to inform his readers "What is the politicke use of Coyne. What private and publicke good it doth, being rightly used. What private and publicke wrongs, being abused in Usurie" (A3). A similar usage occurs in John Toland's translation of Bernardo Davanzati's *Discourse Upon Coins,* originally written in 1588 (London, 1694, retrieved from *McMaster University Archive for the History of Economic Thought,* available 5/1/00: http:www.socsci.mcmaster.ca/~econ/ugcm/3113/davanzati/coins). Davanzati refutes those who claim that "Money was a very ill Invention" because of the abstract, nonmaterial, fetishistic nature of financial value. He claims that the opponents of money believe that the desire for money is worse than the desire for other possessions "because so much of those could not

be laid up and preserv'd, as there may be treasur'd of this." In response, Davanzati notes that " ... every thing has two Handles, and may be well or ill taken and us'd; as Reason, Physick and Law are often abus'd to the Destruction of Mankind; but are they for this prohibited in the Common-wealth?" (16).

36. Augustine, *Christian Doctrine,* trans. D. W. Robertson Jr. (New York: Liberal Arts Press, 1958), 1.3.
37. Ibid., 1.4.
38. Thomas Cooper, *Wilie Beguile ye, or the Worldling's Gaine* (London, 1621), 26.
39. *The Book of Common Prayer,* ed. W. M. Campion and W. J. Beamont (New York, 1872), 24.
40. *The Massacre of Money* (1602), 239–53, retrieved from Chadwick-Healey's *Literature On Line,* available 5/1/01: http://lion.chadwick.com/home.cgi?source=config.cfg.
41. Prynne, for example, cites Tertullian 29 times in his (admittedly vast) *Histrio-Mastix.* The other major source for Renaissance antitheatricalism was Augustine's *City of God,* books 1–3, which blame the Romans' doting on the theater for the collapse of the empire. Cicero protests against paying money to players in *On Duties,* trans. Hubert M. Poteat (Chicago: University of Chicago Press, 1950), 519.
42. Tertullian, *De Idololatria,* trans. J. H. Waszink and J. C. M. van Winden (New York: E. J. Brill, 1987), 23, 25.
43. Tertullian, *De Spectaculis,* trans. Rudolph Arbesmann, in *Disciplinary, Moral and Aesthetic Works* (New York: Fathers of the Church, 1959), 59.
44. Tertullian, *De Spectaculis,* 50.
45. Tertullian, *De Culta Feminam,* in Arbesmann, 123–126.
46. As Tertullian goes on to explain:

   ... it is clear that all these profane pleasures of worldly spectacles ... and even idolatry itself, derive their material from the creatures of God. But that is no reason why a Christian should devote himself to the madness of the circus or the cruelties of the arena or the foulness of the theater, just because God created horses, panthers and the human voice; any more than he can commit idolatry with impunity because the incense and the wine and the fire which feeds on them; and the animals which are the victims, are Gods workmanship, since even the material thing which is adored is God's creature (Ibid., 127)

   In his *Sermons,* Augustine repeats Tertullian's point that "it is a great error, a great madness, to transfer to things which men use in an evil way the evil of the one who misuses them," cited in *Patrology,* ed. Johannes Quasten, trans. Angelo di Bernadino (Westminster, MD:

Newman Press, 1950), 4:417. The argument entered Protestant discourse via Luther's dispute with the arch-iconoclast Karlstadt, which we discussed in chapter two. Luther claims that there is no need to remove images, which are good in themselves; the real task is to remove the idols "in the heart" which lead to their abuse: "Against the Heavenly Prophets in the Matter of Images and Sacraments," part 1, trans. Bernhard Erling, in *Selected Writings,* edited by Theodore G. Tappert (Philadelphia: Fortress Press, 1967), 160–175. Calvin takes a similar view of idolatry in the *Institutes,* bk.1, ch.11.

47. Tertullian, *De Idololatria,* 25.
48. Northbrooke, *A Treatise,* 25.
49. Gosson, *Playes Confuted,* 84.
50. John Howson, *A Sermon Preached at St. Paul's Crosse* (London, 1597), 17–18. The word "abuse" was often employed in economic thought to designate the fetishistic pursuit of money as an end in itself. Thus the author of *The Use and Abuses of Money* (1651) closely follows Aristotle:

    [Money] had not its Original, as all other Creatures, immediately by Creation, but by Invention. . . . That Money or Coin is *summum bonum* is so far from my opinion, that I rather think a covetous desire thereof is *summum malum*. And yet that Money or Coin is absolutely requisite, and necessary, may appear for the reasons before given, which render the universal goodness of it. And yet there is nothing so good but it may be abused, which rule holds good, if we speak of money, when dayly experience makes it manifest, that nothing is more abused than it. (3, 5)

    See also Augustine: "greed is not a defect in the gold that is desired but in the man who loves it perversely . . . ," *City of God,* trans. Gerald G. Walsh, Demetrius B. Zema, Grace Monahan and Daniel J. Honan (New York: Fathers of the Church, 1950), 255.
51. See also Aristotle's attacks on the sophists for selling their skills on the market in *De Sophisticus Elenchis* 165a23 and 171b28, and Socrates' denigration of the rhapsodes on the grounds that they sell their arts for money and therefore pervert them away from the pursuit of truth, in Plato's *Ion,* in *Collected Dialogues,* edited by Edith Hamilton and Huntington Cairnes (Princeton: Princeton University Press, 1961), 221.
52. Prynne, *Histrio-Mastix,* 112.
53. Anthony Munday et al, *A Second and Third Blast of Retrait from Plaies and Theaters* (London, 1580; New York: Johnson Reprint Corp., 1972), 66, 89.
54. Rous, *Diseases,* 308–9.
55. Augustine, *On Christian Doctrine,* 9.

56. Bartholomew Traheron, *A Warning to England to Repente* (London, 1558), 18.
57. Gosson, *Playes Confuted*, E6.
58. Prynne, *Histrio-Mastix*, 1935.
59. Ibid., 113–4.
60. Ibid., 1035.
61. See Kenneth Gross's account of the rapid extension undergone by the term "idolatry" during the sixteenth and seventeenth centuries:

    While, for Plato, representations fall short because they are subject to the flux of time and opinion, the historicizing emphasis of the Bible suggests that it is the very delusive stillness and fixity of the idolatrous image or word which betray both the flux of human imagination and divine revelation. . . . From this argument follows the extension of iconoclasm to attacks on ritual, legalism, syncretistic mythology, false prophecy—and finally to the crucial identification of idolatry with false forms of reading and writing.

    Spenserian Poetics and Idolatry, Iconoclasm and Magic (Ithaca: Cornell University Press, 1985), 30.
62. Laura Levine, in *Men in Women's Clothing* (Cambridge: Cambridge University Press, 1994), shows how Shakespeare and Jonson address the arguments raised by such polemicists as Gosson and Stubbes. For Levine, these anxieties are centered on gender and sexuality. However, many of the plays performed in the public theaters also interrogate the emerging money economy with which they were accused of complicity. For example, in the induction to *Bartholomew Fair*, Ben Jonson wryly notes the commercial theater's confounding of aesthetic quality with market success:

    It is further agreed that every person here shall have his or their free-will of censure, to like or dislike at their own charge, the author having departed with this right: it shall be lawful for any man to judge his six pen'orth, his twelve pen'orth, so to his eighteen pence, two shillings, half a crown, to the value of his place . . .

    In *Three Comedies* edited by Michael Jamieson (London: Penguin Books, 1985) 333, lines 77–82.
63. See Jonas Barish, "Jonson and the Loathed Stage" in *A Celebration of Ben Jonson* edited by William Blisset, Julian Patrick and R. W. Van Fossen (Toronto: University of Toronto Press, 1973), and John Gordon Sweeney, *Jonson and the Psychology of Public Theater* (Princeton: Princeton University Press, 1985).
64. Philip J. Finkelpearl argues persuasively that its heavy debts to archaic forms such as the morality drama and the estates satire prove that

Histrio-Mastix was not performed on the commercial stage. Rather, he claims, it was written for festivities at the Inns of Court. See Finkelpearl, "John Marston's *Histrio-Mastix* as an Inns of Court Play: a Hypothesis," *Huntington Library Quarterly* 29 (1966), 223–34.

65. For an extended discussion of the significance of "superfluity" to the antitheaticalists, see Sandra Clark, *The Elizabethan Pamphleteers* (Rutherford, NJ: Farleigh Dickinson University Press, 1983).
66. Munday et al, *A Second and Third Blast*, 75–6.
67. Karl Marx and Freidrich Engels, *Collected Works* (New York: International Publishers, 1975). Marx cites the passage from *Timon* in *Capital* 28:100, *The German Ideology* 5:230–31, *Notes towards a Critique of Political Economy* 29:451–452, and *Economic and Philosophical Manuscripts* 3:323–324. The connection between Marx's notion of commodity fetishism and older theories of idolatry has been brilliantly illustrated by W. J. T. Mitchell, in *Iconology: Image, Text, Ideology* (Chicago: University of Chicago Press, 1986), 160–208, and Shakespeare's description of psychological and social objectification is detailed in Hugh Grady, *Shakespeare's Universal Wolf: Postmodern Studies in Early Modern Reification* (Oxford: Oxford University Press, 1996).
68. Marx and Engels, *Collected Works*, 3:324.
69. See Guy Debord's Tertullianesque *Society of the Spectacle* (Detroit: Red and Black, 1970): "This is the principle of commodity fetishism; the domination of society by 'intangible as well as tangible things' which reaches its absolute fulfillment in the spectacle, where the tangible world is replaced by a selection of images which exist above it, and which at the same time are recognized as the tangible *par excellence*." (no.36)

Chapter 4

1. Ezra Pound, *Cantos* (New York: New Directions, 1986), 250.
2. *Usurie Araigned and Condemned* (London, 1625), 14, 25.
3. Michel Foucault, *The History of Sexuality*, vol.1, trans. Robert Hurley (New York: Penguin Books, 1978), 5–6.
4. See for example Immanuel Wallerstein's reference to "the steady rise of an ascetic sexual morality from the sixteenth to the eighteenth centuries and all that it imposed on family structures to make them adapt to a capitalist world." *The Modern World-System* vol. 2 (New York: Academic Press, 1980), 26.
5. Foucault, *History*, 37.
6. Ibid., 12.
7. In 1601, Gerard de Malynes lays the blame for the worrying growth in social mobility at usury's door: "But let this monster be destroyed,

and every man will return unto his quietness, and live within his bounds and calling, using such trade as he ought to do." *St. George for England* (1610), cit. L. C. Knights, *Drama and Society in the Age of Jonson* (London: Chatto & Windus, 1937), 140.
8. Park Honan, *Shakespeare: A Life* (Oxford: Oxford University Press, 1998), 37.
9. The most comprehensive treatment of this debate is Norman Jones, *God and the Moneylenders: Usury and Law in Early Modern England* (Oxford: Oxford University Press, 1989). See also R. H. Tawney and Eileen Power, eds., *Tudor Economic Documents* (New York: Longmans, Green and Co., 1951), 2:133–75; 3:305–404.
10. Neal Wood, *Foundations of Political Economy: Some Early Tudor Views on State and Society* (Berkeley: University of California Press, 1994), 19.
11. Hugh Hilarie, *The Resurrection of the Masse* (1554), retrieved from Chadwick-Healey's *Literature On Line*, available 5/1/01: http://lion.chadwick.com/home.cgi?source=config2.cfg.
12. Bartholomew Traheron, *A Warning to England to Repent* (1558), 12.
13. John Weemse, *A Traetise of the Foure Degenerate Sonnes* (London, 1636), 202. Weemse also opines that "Idolatrie is . . . a viler sin then the sin of Sodome. . . . It is a sin like unto beastialitie, when a man lyes with a beast" (245).
14. John Bale, *Comedy Concernynge Thre Lawes,* ed. Peter Happe (Cambridge: D. S. Brewer, 1985), 525.
15. Thomas Bancroft, "216. Money, a fruitfull commodity," from *Two bookes of epigrammes and epitaphs* (1639), retrieved from Chadwick-Healey's *Literature On Line*, available 5/1/01: http://lion.chadwick.com/home.cgi?source=config2.cfg.
16. In similar fashion, as R. H. Tawney reminds us, "The typical usurer was apt, indeed, to outrage not one, but all, of the decencies of social intercourse." (*Religion and the Rise of Capitalism* [Gloucester, MA: P. Smith, 1962], 161). Recent studies also emphasize the inclusivity of the term "sodomy" during the Renaissance. In *Sodometries: Renaissance Texts, Modern Sexualities* (Stanford: Stanford University Press, 1992), Jonathan Goldberg proposes that sodomy is "a relational term, a measure whose geometry we do not know, whose (a)symmetries we are to explore" (xv). Alan Bray notes that in the Renaissance sodomy "was also a political and a religious crime," in *Queering the Renaissance,* ed. Jonathan Goldberg (Durham: Duke University Press, 1994), 41, and Gregory Bredbeck sees the word as "defining the unacceptable," in *Sodomy and Interpretation* (Ithaca: Cornell University Press, 1991), 10. Stephen Orgel goes so far as to say that "Charges of sodomy always occur in relation to other kinds of subversion; the activity has no independent existence in the Renaissance mind . . . ," "Nobody's Perfect: or Why Did the English

Stage Take Boys for Women," *Displacing Homophobia: Gay Male Perspectives in Literature and Culture,* ed. Ronald R. Butters, John M. Clum and Michael Moon (Durham: Duke University Press, 1989), 20. See also Michael Rocke, *Forbidden Friendships: Homosexuality and Male Culture in Renaissance Florence* (New York: Oxford University Press, 1996), and Will Fisher: "Queer Money," *ELH* 66, no.1 (1999), 1–23.
17. Thomas Aquinas, *On the Sentences* 4.33.1.3, cit. John T. Noonan, *Contraception: A History of its Treatment by the Catholic Theologians and Canonists* (Cambridge, MA: Belknap Press of Harvard University Press, 1966), 236–7.
18. A relic of this struggle is the word "bugger," long a popular term for "sodomite," which derives from "Bulgar" and originally referred to the Bogomil heretics of south-eastern Europe. Up to the Renaissance, the term designated a wider range of perversion than the sexual. Derrick Sherman Bailey remarks on "the extent to which *bougre* and *herite* were actually identified in medieval thought," *Homosexuality and the Western Christian Tradition* (Hamden, CT: Archon Books, 1975), 136; while David E. Greenberg tells how "interest-takers were sometimes called *bougres* that is, heretics. Probably because the urban patriciate engaged in both practices, and because heretics were already believed to favor sodomy, usury and sodomy also became linked in the popular mind . . . ," *The Construction of Homosexuality* (Chicago: University of Chicago Press, 1988), 295. See also Bailey, *Homosexuality*, 141.
19. Cit. Noonan, *Contraception*, 54.
20. Cit. Bailey, *Homosexuality*, 25.
21. Dante, *Inferno*, 11.46–51. Mark Mussa (Bloomington: Indiana University Press, 1971), 90 translates these lines as follows:

> One can use violence against the deity
> by heartfelt disbelief or by cursing Him,
> or by despising Nature and God's bounty;
> therefore the smallest round stamps with its seal
> both Sodom and Cahors . . .

Cahors was a French town notorious for, and therefore synonymous with, usury.
22. Cit. Jonathan Goldberg ed., *Reclaiming Sodom* (New York: Routledge, 1994), 46. The *OED* notes a dialect usage of "lomber" meaning "to idle," and cites a reference from 1678: "sick o'th' Lombard feaver, or of the idles." The painter Sodoma was a native of Lombardy.
23. For example Nicholas Sander describes usury thus, after Aristotle and Plutarch:

> Now those thinges which are begotten, are lyke to them by which they are begotten. In usurie, mony bringeth forth

mony: wherefore that kind of gayning is specially against nature.... The usurers do also mocke at those rules of nature, whiche affirme, that of nothing, nothing can be begotten. But yet emong them, usurie is begotten of that, which is not, nor never was. *A Briefe Treatise of Usurie* (London, 1568), 51.

Henry Smith gives the argument Biblical corroboration:

When God had finished his creation, he said unto man, and unto beasts, and unto fishes, Increase and multiplie, but he never said unto money, increase and multiplie, because it is a dead thing which hath no seede, and therefore is not fit to ingender. Therefoe he which saith to his money, increase and multiply, beggetteth a monstrous birth, like Anah, which devised a creature which God had not created before. *The Examination of Usurie* (London, 1591), 15.

24. Francis Meres, *Palladis Tamia* (London, 1598). 322.
25. Ben Jonson, *Epigrams and the Forest*, ed. Richard Dutton (Manchester: Fyfield, 1984), 46.
26. *The Araignment and Conviction of Usury* (London, 1595), 8.
27. Unless otherwise specified, quotations from Shakespeare's plays are from G. Blakemore Evans ed., *The Riverside Shakespeare* (Boston: Houghton Mifflin, 1974). See Michael Chorost, "Biological Finance in Shakespeare's *Timon of Athens*," *English Literary Renaissance* 21 (1991): 349–370.
28. See E. Pearlman, "Shakespeare, Freud, and the Two Usuries," *English Literary Renaissance* 2 (1972): 217–236.
29. Lars Engle perceives a similar tendency when he remarks on the *Sonnets*' "anti-essentialist or anti-Platonic analysis of value," (Chicago: University of Chicago Press, 1993), 24. However, Engle is not concerned with usury and sodomy but with the poems' approach to subjectivity.
30. Erasmus, *An Epistle*, in Thomas Wilson, *The Arte of Rhetorique* (1553; reprint New York: Da Capo Press, 1969), 26.
31. Ibid., 28
32. Quotations from the *Sonnets* are from Stephen Booth, ed., *Shakespeare's Sonnets* (New Haven: Yale University Press, 1977).
33. The sentiment is echoed by the Duke in *Measure for Measure:*

    ... Nature never lends
    The smallest scruple of her excellence
    But, like an unthrifty goddess, she determines
    Herself the glory of a creditor,
    Both thanks and use. (3.2.37–41)

34. Booth, *Shakespeare's Sonnets*, 142–3.
35. Nicholas Sander, *A Briefe Tratise*, 54.

36. *Usurie Araigned and Condemned* (1625), 25–26.
37. There may also be a homoerotic valence to the word "self." Thorpe's edition prints "thyself" as two words, and the speaker of the *Sonnets* habitually refers to his lover as his "self," as in sonnet 62, "Sin of self-love possesseth all mine eye." It was, of course, a Renaissance commonplace to follow Cicero in declaring of a lover that "even another hym self shal his frende bee to hym," *The Booke of Freendship*, trans. John Harryngton (London, 1562), 12.
38. Cit. L. C. Knights, *Drama and Society*, 110. This is the interpretation favored by John B. Mishco, who aims to "demonstrate that the first seventeen sonnets of the sequence radically denounce traditional condemnations of usury." Mishco concedes that the *Sonnets* frequently seem disparaging of usury, and that in *The Merchant of Venice*, Shakespeare appears to offer an orthodox denunciation of money-lending. He is therefore led to conclude that "Shakespeare's economic thinking is itself contradictory" ("'That Use Is Not Forbidden Usury': Shakespeare's Procreation Sonnets and the Problem of Usury," in *Subjects on the World's Stage: Essays on British Literature of the Middle Ages and the Renaissance*, edited by David G. Allen and Robert A. White [London: Associated University Presses, 1995], 266). However, Mishco takes no account of the sodomy theme, which significantly complicates his reading of the *Sonnets*. I argue that this apparent contradiction disappears if we keep in mind the close association—or rather the *homology*—of usury with sodomy in the sixteenth-century mind.
39. Peter C. Herman has recently pointed to the procreation sequence's provocative employment of usury imagery, and he also draws attention to the homology between usury and homoeroticism ("What's the Use? Or, The Problematic of Economy in Shakespeare's Procreation Sonnets," in *Shakespeare's Sonnets: Critical Essays*, edited by James Schiffer [New York: Garland Publishers, 1999] 263–283). Herman perceptively notes the first 20 sonnets' "mercantilizing of sexuality" (268), but his essay only discusses the opening 20 poems in Thorpe's sequence and does not consider the ways in which the usury metaphor is developed in the later sonnets. His conclusion that "the homoerotic relationship between the speaker and the addressee gradually replaces the economic relationship" (276) holds good for the procreation sequence but, as we shall see, the usury theme reemerges in the later sonnets, to disrupt and destroy homoeroticism, replacing it with an economy of heterosexual reproduction. The process to which Herman rightly points in the opening sonnets is thus reversed in the sequence as a whole.
40. Roger Fenton, *A Treatise of Usurie* (London, 1612), 65.

41. *The Araignment and Conviction of Usury*, 110.
42. This is the logic which, from the Christian perspective, renders Shylock's plea for equality before the law contradictory and hypocritical. It also provides the rationale for the states' persecution of Barabas in Marlowe's *The Jew of Malta:*

    BARABAS: Are strangers with your tribute to be tax'd?
    2. KNIGHT: Have strangers leave with us to get their wealth? Then let them with us contribute.
    BARABAS: How, equally?
    Governer: No, Jew, like infidels. (1.2.59–63)

43. As Aquinas puts it:

    The Jews were forbidden to take usury from their brethren, i.e., from other Jews. By this we are given to understand that to take usury from any man is simply evil, because we ought to treat every man as our neighbor and brother, especially in the state of the Gospel, whereto all are called.

    Cit. Benjamin Nelson, *The Idea of Usury: from Tribal Brotherhood to Universal Otherhood* (Princeton: Princeton University Press, 1949), 14. Sander expressed it thus in Shakespeare's lifetime: "The carnall Jewes had certain infidels to their enemies: whom as they might kil, so might they oppresse hem with usurie. But now seing everie man is both our neighbor, and our brother: we may not take usurie of any man at al" (*A Briefe Treatise,* 7). See Martin D. Yaffe, *Shylock and the Jewish Question* (Baltimore: Johns Hopkins University Press, 1997). See also Odd Langholm, *The Aristotelian Analysis of Usury* (Bergen: Universitetsforlaget, 1984), 18 - 19. By the seventeenth century, however, Christian moralists were often prepared to relax this prohibition. Writing on the way to Massachusetts in 1630, John Winthrop equates "justice" with "Commerce," and he differentiates both from "mercy":

    Quest. What rule must wee observe in lending?
       Ans. Thou must observe whether thy brother hath present or probable or possible means of repaying thee, if there be none of those, thou must give him according to his necessity, rather then lend him as he requires; if he hath present means of repaying thee, thou art to look at him not as an act of mercy, but by way of Commerce, wherein thou arte to walk by the rule of justice; but if his means of repaying thee be only probable or possible, then is hee an object of thy mercy, thou must lend him, though there be danger of losing it, Deut. 15. 7. If any of thy brethren be poore &c., thou shalt lend him sufficient. (*A Modell of Christian Charity,* 1630).

44. See T. S. Eliot's remark regarding Donne's "The Extasie": "the 'begetting' of 'pictures' is a figure which violates nature" (*The Varieties of*

Metaphysical Poetry: the Clark Lectures at Trinity College, Cambridge, 1926, and the Turnball Lectures at the Johns Hopkins University, 1933, ed. Ronald Schuchard (London: Faber and Faber, 1993), 110). See also Thomas M. Greene's observation that the *Sonnets*' claims for the power of linguistic over sexual reproduction "tend to appear in the couplets . . . [which] tend to lack the energy of the negative vision in the twelve lines that precede them. The final affirmation in its flaccidity tends to refute itself . . ." ("Pitiful Thrivers: Failed Husbandry in the *Sonnets*," in *Shakespeare and the Question of Theory*, edited by Patricia Parker and Geoffrey Hartman [New York: Metheun, 1985], 234). For an extended discussion of Shakespeare's treatment of idolatry in *A Winter's Tale* see Julia Reinhard Lupton, *Afterlives of the Saints: Hagiography, Typology and Renaissance Literature* (Stanford: Stanford University Press, 1996).

45. *The Cambridge Economic History of Europe*, edited by J. H. Clapham and Eileen Power (Cambridge: Cambridge University Press, 1941), 4:450, 4:490–1.
46. Glyn Davies, *A History of Money: From Ancient Times to the Present Day* (Cardiff: University of Wales Press), 233.
47. Marc Shell, "The Wether and the Ewe: Verbal Usury in *The Merchant of Venice*," *The Kenyon Review* 1, no.4, (fall 1979), 65–92.
48. Ibid., 67.
49. Joel Fineman concurs, arguing that

    in his sonnets Shakespeare substitutes for this ideal and idealizing characterization of visionary language . . . a different account that characterizes language as something corruptingly linguistic rather than something ideally specular, as something duplicitously verbal as opposed to something singly visible.

    Shakespeare's Perjur'd Eye: The Invention of Poetic Subjectivity in the Sonnets (Berkeley: University of California Press, 1986), 15.
50. Booth, *Shakespeare's Sonnets*, 200.
51. A similar request has been made, and rejected, on logical grounds, in the preceding sonnet (133):

    Prison my heart in thy steel bosom's ward,
    But then my friend's heart let my poor heart bail;
    Whoe'er keeps me, let my heart be his guard,
    Thou canst not then use rigor in my jail.
    And yet thou wilt; for I, being pent in thee,
    Perforce am thine, and all that is in me. (9–14)

    Clearly, the poet cannot gain possession of the youth by giving himself up to the lady, because if she owns him she necessarily also owns all that he owns and would therefore still own the youth.

52. See also *Timon of Athens:* "Is not thy kindness subtle, covetous, / If not a usuring kindness, and as rich men deal gifts, / Expecting in return twenty for one?" (2.2.60–2)
53. Fenton, *A Treatise of Usurie*, 95.
54. Thomas Aquinas, *Summa Theologica*, trans. Fathers of the English Dominican Province, (Westminster, MD: Christian Classics, 1981) 2:330–1.
55. See Tawney and Power (eds.), *Tudor Economic Documents*, 2:142–3.
56. *Aristotle's Politiques*, trans. from Greek into French by Loys Le Roy, and from French into English by I. D. (London, 1598), 51.
57. Aquinas, *Summa Theologica*, 339. John T. Noonan argues that the rationale behind this was that usury was a sin against nature, rather than against charity. It violated natural justice, and "A sin against justice entailed the obligation of reparation of the damage or restitution of the loss, as condition for absolution; a sin against charity required simply internal sorrow for forgiveness." *The Scholastic Analysis of Usury* (Cambridge, MA: Harvard University Press, 1957), 30.

Chapter 5

1. Menasseh ben Israel, *To His Highnesse the Lord Protector* (London, 1652), 1–2.
2. Thomas Calvert, *The Blessed Jew of Marocco, or A Blackmoor made White* (London, 1648), 45–46.
3. Menasseh ben Israel, *Vindicae Judeaorum* (London, 1656), 11.
4. Bernard Knieger, "The Purchase-Sale: Patterns of Business Imagery in the Poetry of George Herbert," *SEL* 6 (1966): 109–24, quotation from 111.
5. Ibid., 113.
6. John Wing, *The Best Merchandize* (Flushing, 1622).
7. C. A. Patrides, ed., *The English Poems of George Herbert* (London: J. M. Dent, 1974). Subsequent in-text references to Herbert's poetry are from this edition.
8. George Herbert, *The Country Parson, The Temple*, ed. John N. Wall Jr. (New York: Paulist Press, 1989), 98.
9. The "conjurer" in question is presumably an alchemist.
10. There is, of course, considerable debate as to the precise nature of Herbert's theology. For Barbara Lewalski, the speaker of *The Temple* is "a Calvinist in theology" (*Protestant Poetics and the Sixteenth-century Religious Lyric* [Princeton: Princeton University Press, 1979], 286), while for Richard Strier he is a traditional Lutheran (*Love Known: Theology and Experience in George Herbert's Poetry* [Chicago: University of Chicago Press, 1983]). Rosemund Tuve, *A Reading of George Herbert* (Chicago: University of Chicago Press, 1952) and Louis Martz, *The*

Poetry of Meditation: A Study of English Literature of the Seventeenth Century (New Haven: Yale University Press, 1954) put greater stress on the heritage of his thought in Catholic scholasticism. The view of Herbert as the epitome of conventional Anglicanism was established for modern criticism by Jospeh Summers, in *George Herbert, His Religion and Art*, (Cambridge, MA: Harvard University Press, 1954). Gene Edward Veith refers to the "wars of religion" that dominate Herbert criticism, between "roundheads" such as Lewalski and Strier and "cavaliers" such as Tuve and Martz. (*Reformation Spirituality: The Religion of George Herbert* (Lewisburg, PA: Bucknell University Press, 1985). See also Christopher Hodgkins, *Authority, Church and Society in George Herbert: Return to the Middle Way* (Columbia: University of Missouri Press, 1993), 10. On Herbert's theology in general, see A. D. Nuttall, *Overheard by God: Fiction and Prayer in Herbert, Milton, Dante and St. John* (New York: Routledge, 1980); Heather A. R. Asals, *Equivocal Predication: George Herbert's Way to God* (Toronto: University of Toronto Press, 1981); Camille Wells Slights, *The Casuistical Tradition in Shakespeare, Donne, Herbert and Milton* (Princeton: Princeton University Press, 1981), and Stanley Stewart, *George Herbert* (Boston: Twayne Publishers, 1986).

11. To emphasize, I am not arguing that Herbert believes that exchange value *causes* this reversal. Rather, exchange value is one manifestation of it. The reversal of the subject/object relation takes place in many different contexts in *The Temple*, as several critics have pointed out. For example, Veith finds in *The Temple* "the subjective correlative ... to objective Protestant doctrine" (*Reformation Spirituality*, 24), while John N. Wall notes that "One of the chief modes of transformation Herbert employs is the speaker's move from the role of lover to that of beloved ..." (*Transformations of the Word: Spenser, Herbert, Vaughan* [Athens: University of Georgia Press, 1988], 196).

12. Helen Vendler, *The Poetry of George Herbert* (Cambridge, MA: Harvard University Press, 1975), 180–1.

13. See Harold Fisch, *Jerusalem and Albion: The Hebraic Factor in Seventeenth-century Literature* (London: Routledge & K. Paul, 1964); Barbara K. Lewalski, "Biblical Allusion and Allegory in *The Merchant of Venice*, in *Twentieth-Century Interpretations of The Merchant of Venice*, edited by Sylvan Barnet (Englewood Cliffs, NJ: Prentice Hall 1970); Edgar Rosenberg, *From Shylock to Svengali: Jewish Stereotypes in English Fiction* (Stanford: Stanford University Press, 1960); Michael Walzer, *Exodus and Revolution* (New York: Basic Books, 1985) and James Shapiro, *Shakespeare and the Jews* (New York: Columbia University Press, 1996). For an excellent analysis of the connections between typology and iconoclasm in the Renaissance as a whole, see Julia Reinhard Lupton, *Afterlives of the Saint: Hagiography, Typology and Renaissance Literature* (Stanford: Stanford University Press, 1996), 156–60.

14. Francis Bacon, "Of Usury," in *Francis Bacon,* ed. Brian Vickers (Oxford: Oxford University Press, 1996), 421.
15. Cited in Norman Jones, *God and the Moneylenders: Usury and Law in Early Modern England* (Oxford: B. Blackwell, 1989), 170.
16. Thomas Bell, *The Speculation of Usurie* (London, 1596), sig.C.
17. Quotations from Marlowe are from E. D. Pendry, ed., *Complete Poems and Plays* (London: J. M. Dent, 1976).
18. The young Marx connects Shylock with objectification in the *Rheinische Zeitung* no. 307, 11/3/1842. Marx quotes *The Merchant of Venice* (4.1.302–313) in order to compare Shylock's equation of a financial sum to a pound of flesh with the Rhenish landowners' commutation of timber thieves' legal fines into unpaid labor: "We have, however, reached a point where the forest owner, in exchange for his piece of wood, receives what was once a human being." Retrieved from http://csf.colorado.edu/psn/marx/Archive/1842-RZ/1842-Wood/index.html#p5. Available 5/1/01.
19. Jean-Joseph Goux comments acutely on this passage:

    What has gone unobserved by those who are surprised by the anti-Judaism of... Karl Marx is that if the critique of money entails by association the critique of Jews, it is nevertheless a perfectly Judaic gesture. In denouncing the fetishism of money, Marx repeats a pattern quite comparable to the critique of idolatry that comprises the religious orientation of Judaism. Moses' iconoclastic furor, which smashes the graven images imagined by pagans to represent or even embody their gods, is continued in the Marxian critique of fetishism.

    (*Symbolic Economies: after Marx and Freud,* trans. Jennifer Curtiss Gage [Ithaca: Cornell University Press, 1990], 159–60). See also Julius Carlebach, *Karl Marx and the Radical Critique of Judaism* (London: Routledge and Kegan Paul, 1978).
20. Karl Marx, "On the Jewish Question," in *Collected Works of Karl Marx and Frederick Engels* (New York: International Publishers, 1975), 3:172.
21. Justin Martyr, *Saint Justin Martyr,* trans. Thomas B. Falls (New York: Christian Heritage, 1948), 165–6. Unless otherwise specified, subsequent references to Justin Martyr will be to this edition.
22. Augustine, *On the Spirit and the Letter,* chapter 20, ed. W. J. Sparrow (New York: Macmillan, 1925). For Augustine's influence on Herbert, see William H. Pahlka, *Saint Augustine's Meter and George Herbert's Will,* (Kent OH: Kent State University Press, 1987).
23. Robert Aylett, *Divine and Moral Speculations* (1654), retrieved from Chadwick-Healey's *Literature On Line,* available 5/1/01: http://lion.chadwick.com/home.cgi?source=config2.cfg

24. John Weemse, *A Treatise of the Foure Degenerate Sonnes* (London, 1636), 341.
25. Lewalski, *Protestant Poetics*, 114.
26. Ibid., 114. The definitive twentieth-century study of typology in literature is Erich Auerbach's "Figura," in *Scenes from the Drama of European Literature* (New York: Meridian Books, 1959), 11–76. See also Barbara Lewalski, "Typology and Poetry: A Consideration of Herbert, Vaughan and Marvell," in *Illustrious Evidence: Approaches to English Literature of the Early Seventeenth Century* edited by Earl Miner (Berkeley: University of California Press, 1975); Earl Miner, ed., *Literary Uses of Typology from the Late Middle Ages to the Present*, Princeton: Princeton University Press, 1977); J. S. Preus, *From Shadow to Promise: Old Testament Interpretation from Augustine to the Young Luther* (Cambridge, MA: Harvard University Press, 1969); Sacvan Bercovitch, ed., *Typology and Early American Literature* (Amherst: University of Massachusetts Press, 1972), and Paul J. Korshin, *Typologies in England, 1650–1820* (Princeton: Princeton University Press, 1982).
27. John Calvin, *Institutes of the Christian Religion* 2 vols., ed. John T. McNeill, trans. Ford Lewis Battles (Philadelphia: Westminster Press, 1960) vol.1 bk. 4 ch. 14, sect. 25, p.1301.
28. So great was Origen's revulsion from the "flesh" that he cut off his own penis.
29. I use this term rather than "anti-semitic" because Herbert's hostility is not directed against the Jews as a people but against their religion. I recognize, however, that in many contexts this distinction becomes over-nice.
30. Stanley Fish, *The Living Temple: George Herbert and Catechizing* (Berkeley: University of California Press, 1978), 140–1.
31. Strier, *Love Known*, 221.
32. Richard Todd, *The Opacity of Signs: Acts of Interpretation in George Herbert's The Temple* (Columbia, MO: University of Missouri Press, 1986), 55.
33. Harold Toliver, *George Herbert's Christian Narrative* (University Park, PA: Pennsylvania State University Press, 1993), 20.
34. Ibid., 49.
35. Rosemund Tuve, *A Reading of George Herbert* (London: Faber and Faber, 1952), 117.
36. Ibid.
37. Strier, *Love Known*, 156. See also Strier's "Ironic Humanism in *The Temple*," in *'Too Rich to Clothe the Sunne': Essays on George Herbert*, edited by Claude Summers and Ted-Larry Pebworth (Pittsburgh: University of Pittsburgh Press, 1980), 34–39.
38. As Barbara Leah Harman notes, revising Barbara Lewalski's opinion that *The Temple* enacts successive interiorizations of theological issues:

Typology does not "personalize theology"; it theologizes the personal, and makes unavailable the very notion of a "radically personal" account. In Herbert's typological poems persons do not appropriate and rewrite Scripture: Scripture appropriates and rewrites them.... the competition between personal and scriptural stories is eliminated and ... their unity is stressed in its place.
Costly Monuments: Representations of the Self in George Herbert's Poetry, (Cambridge MA: Harvard University Press, 1982), 189. Chana Bloch comments that, with regard to Herbert, "we must finally put aside the distinction between public and private.... What we may call the 'biblical mode' encompasses these oppositions: Herbert learned from the Bible to write poems at once public and private ..."
Spelling the Word: George Herbert and the Bible (Berkeley: University of California Press, 1985), 199. See also Julia Carolyn Guernsey, *The Pulse of Praise: Form as Second Self in the Poetry of George Herbert,* Newark: University of Delaware Press, 1999).

39. Augustine, *City of God,* trans. Gerald G. Walsh, Demetrius B. Zema, Grace Monahan and Daniel J. Honan, (New York: Fathers of the Church, 1950), 41.
40. As Rosemund Tuve puts it
  ... [Herbert] reads the spirit in the letter. Not *into* but *in;* he writes in symbols because he thus sees the world, both outside and inside himself; he sees it as a web of significances not as a collection on phenomena which we may either endow with significance or leave unendowed. He writes not of events or facts, but of meanings and values, and he uncovers rather than creates these meanings. (*A Reading,*103–4)
  More recently, Richard Todd envisages *The Temple* as repeatedly rejecting the surface appearances of empirical phenomena: "Herbert is frequently confronted with experience that at first sight appears meaningless. He must learn to interpret it as having 'significance': it comes to be seen as a divine sign or 'visible word.'" *The Opacity of Signs,* 46.
41. For a brilliant account of Paul's typology, see Alan F. Segal, *Paul the Convert: The Apostolate and Apostasy of Saul the Pharisee* (New Haven: Yale University Press, 1990).
42. Calvin, *Institutes* 2.3.9.
43. Izaac Walton, *The Lives of Dr. John Donne, Sir Henry Wotton, Mr. Richard Hooker, Mr. George Herbert and Dr. Robert Sanderson* (London, 1866), 281. See also Susanne Woods, "The Unhewn Stones of Herbert's Verse," *George Herbert Journal* 4 (1981).
44. See Psalms 52:17: "The sacrifices of God are a broken spirit: a broken and a contrite heart. O God, thou wilt not despise."
45. This despite the fact that, as Guernsey notes, "The Altar" pointedly distinguishes between the speaker's "heart" and his

self, becoming "the locus of a subjective consciousness somewhat separate from the I-speaker's" (*Pulse of Praise,* 49). Terry G. Sherwood also notes that, in this poem, the heart is simultaneously altar and sacrifice. It thus represents a unity of subject and object that transcends the merely objective sacrificial animals of the Old Testament. (*Herbert's Prayerful Art* [Toronto: University of Toronto Press, 1989], 17). See also Vendler, *Poetry,* 61–3.
46. See also Deuteronomy 27:5: "And there shalt thou build an altar unto the Lord thy God, an altar of stones: thou shalt not lift up any iron tool upon them."
47. Stanley Fish disagrees, claiming that "the temple of Herbert's title is the 'spirituall Temple' that is built up by catechisms to be the dwelling-place of God. Others have identified that place with something the poems image or present: I will argue that it is something they would create, not on the page or in space, but in the heart of the reader" (*The Living Temple,* 54).
48. See Albert C. Labriola, "Herbert, Crashaw and the *Scholas Cordis* Tradition," *George Herbert Journal* 2 (1978): 13–23. See also Todd, *Opacity of Signs,* 115.
49. Tuve, *A Reading,* 104.
50. Toliver, *George Herbert,* 4.
51. Cited in Toliver, *George Herbert,* 22.
52. Ibid., 38.
53. Homer, *Iliad,* 8.19. See Arthur Lovejoy, *The Great Chain of Being* (Cambridge, MA: Harvard University Press, 1936). See also Genesis 28:12.
54. Vendler, *Poetry,* 182.
55. Alexander Pope, "The Rape of the Lock," 138.
56. John Bunyan, *The Pilgrim's Progress,* ed. N. H. Keeble (Oxford: Oxford University Press, 1984), 73. Bunyan goes on to qualify this undifferentiated catalogue: "But as in other fairs, some one Commodity is as the chief of all the fair, so the Ware of Rome and her Merchandize is greatly promoted in this fair . . ." (ibid.).
57. Marion White Singleton, *God's Courtier: Configuring a Different Grace in George Herbert's The Temple* (Cambridge: Cambridge University Press, 1987), 87.
58. Frederic Jameson, *Postmodernism, or The Cultural Logic of Late Capitalism* (Durham NC: Duke University Press, 1991), 6.
59. Tuve, *A Reading,* 187.
60. See also Julia Guernsey, in *Essays in Literature* 22. no.2 (September 1995), 196–215. Elizabeth Clarke has recently reminded us that "On the whole, Herbert operates as if his human rhetoric is sanctioned, and indeed, uses rhetorical strategies which give the impression of validating the poetry." *Theory and Theology in George Herbert's Poetry*

(Oxford: Clarendon Press, 1997), 274. For a different view, which holds that Herbert's poems extinguish the speaking voice, and therefore the self, altogether, see Stanley Fish, *Self-Consuming Artifacts: The Experience of Seventeenth-Century Literature* (Berkeley: University of California Press, 1972), 156–223.
61. Shakespeare, sonnet 102, 3–4.

CHAPTER 6

1. Johann Wolfgang von Goethe, *Faust I & II* trans. Stuart Atkins (Princeton: Princeton University Press, 1984).
2. Marco Polo, *The Description of the World,* trans. A. C. Moule and Paul Pelliott (London: G. Routledge, 1938), 240.
3. Edward Taylor, *Sacramental Meditations I,* ed. Donald E. Stanford (New Haven: Yale University Press, 1956).
4. References to Donne's poetry are to John Donne, *The Complete English Poems,* ed. C. A. Patrides, (London: Dent, 1994).
5. In the twentieth century, alchemy has performed a similar function in the work of such thinkers as Carl Gustav Jung and Mircea Eliade. See especially Jung, *Jung on Alchemy,* selected and introduced by Nathan Schwartz-Salant (Princeton: Princeton University Press, 1995), and Eliade, *The Forge and the Crucible,* trans. Stephen Corrin (London: Rider, 1962). For an exhaustive psychoanalytical account of alchemy, see Johannes Fabricius, *Alchemy: the Medieval Alchemists and their Royal Art* (Copenhagan: Rosenkilde and Bagger, 1976). For recent accounts of alchemy's status in the early modern period, see especially Lyndy Abraham, *Marvell and Alchemy* (Aldershot: Scolar Press, 1990), and Piyo Rattansi and Antonio Clericuzio, eds., *Alchemy and Chemistry in the Sixteenth and Seventeenth Centuries* (Boston: Kluwer Academic Publishers, 1994). Older but still useful studies of alchemy are F. Sherwood Taylor, *The Alchemists, Founders of Modern Chemistry* (New York: Schuman, 1949); J. E. Mercer, *Alchemy, its Science and Romance* (New York: Macmillan and Co., 1921); Arthur John Hopkins, *Alchemy, Child of Greek Philosophy* (New York: Columbia University Press, 1934), and John Read, *Prelude to Chemistry: An Outline of Alchemy, its Literature and Relationships* (New York: Macmillan, 1937).
6. The prominence of alchemical figures in Donne's verse was first noted by Joseph Anthony Mazzeo, in *Renaissance and Seventeenth-Century Studies* (New York: Columbia University Press, 1964), 60–89.
7. Hans Christoph Binswanger, *Money and Magic: A Critique of the Modern Economy in the Light of Goethe's Faust,* trans. J. E. Harrison (Chicago: University of Chicago Press, 1994), 33.
8. Ibid., 9.

9. Jean-Joseph Goux, *The Coiners of Language,* trans. Jennifer Curtiss Gage (Norman: University of Oklahoma Press, 1994), 110.
10. Cited in Christopher Hill, *Antichrist in Seventeenth-Century England* (London: Verso, 1990), 119. Hill reports that Isaac Newton scribbled marginalia on almost every page of his copy of this pamphlet.
11. T. S. Eliot, *The Varieties of Metaphysical Poetry: the Clark Lectures at Trinity College, Cambridge, 1926, and the Turnbull Lectures at The Johns Hopkins University, 1933,* ed. Ronald Schuchard (London: Faber and Faber, 1993), 138.
12. E. M. W. Tillyard, *The Elizabethan World-Picture* (New York: Vintage Books, 1960), 92–3.
13. Marjorie Hope Nicolson, *The Breaking of the Circle: Studies in the Effect of the "New Science" upon Seventeenth-Century Poetry* (New York: Columbia University Press, 1960), 126.
14. Jonathan Dollimore, "Introduction: Shakespeare, Cultural Materialism and the New Historicism" in *Political Shakespeare: New Essays in Cultural Materialism,* edited by Jonathan Dollimore and Alan Sinfield (Ithaca: Cornell University Press, 1985), 5.
15. Robert Boyle, for example, seems to assume that the new learning will actually advance the cause of alchemy when, in his *Dialogue on Transmutation,* he has the character Zosimus defend alchemy from the charge that it cannot be rationally explained: "just because no chymist steeped in the narrow and lean principles of the Peripatetic Schoolmen has yet given an explanation, that one could not be given in the future when a deeper investigation into chymistry is carried out by rational philosophers . . ." (Appendix I in Lawrence M. Principe, *The Aspiring Adept: Robert Boyle and his Alchemical Quest* [Princeton: Princeton University Press, 1998], 255).
16. Herbert's poems are cited from *The English Poems of George Herbert,* edited by C. A. Patrides (London: J. M. Dent, 1974).
17. Francis Bacon, *Novum Organon* 45, trans. R. Ellis and James Spedding (London: George Routledge and Sons, 1959), 173.
18. Ibid., aphorism 85, 358–9. For Bacon's critical attitude to alchemy see Perez Zagorin, *Francis Bacon* (Princeton: Princeton University Press, 1998), 34–35, 42–43.
19. Hermes Trismegistus, in *The Mirror of Alchemy,* ed. Stanton J. Linden (New York: Garland Publishers, 1992), 16.
20. Cited in Abraham, *Marvell,* 167. See Walter Pagel, *Paracelsus: An Introduction to Philosophical Medicine in the Era of the Renaissance* (New York: S. Karger, 1958), Allen Debus, ed., *Science, Medicine and Society in the Renaissance: Essays to Honor Walter Pagel* (New York: Science History Publications, 1972) and Henry M. Pachter, *Magic into Science: the Story of Paracelsus* (New York: Schuman, 1951).

21. Aristotle. *Poetics*, trans. Ingram Bywater (Oxford: Clarendon Press, 1909), 22.1458b39–43.
22. Cited in Brian Vickers, "Analogy and Identity: The Rejection of Occult Symbolism 1580–1680," in *Occult and Scientific Mentalities in the Renaissance*, edited by Brian Vickers (Cambridge: Cambridge University Press, 1984), 95–163, quotation from 112.
23. Retrieved from *McMaster University Archive for the History of Economic Thought*, available 5/1/01: http://www.socsci.mcmaster.ca/~econ/ugcm/3113/locke/consid.txt.
24. Donne's poetry is cited from John Donne, *Complete English Poems*, ed. C. A. Patrides (London: J. M. Dent, 1994).
25. Cited in Nicolson, *Breaking of the Circle*, 25.
26. Cited in Vickers, "Analogy and Identity," 141.
27. Cited in ibid., 153.
28. Cited in ibid., 146. See also Brian Vickers, "On the Function of Analogy in the Occult" in *Hermeticism and the Renaissance: Intellectual History and the Occult in Early Modern Europe*, edited by Ingrid Merkel and Allan Debus (Washington D.C.: Folger Shakespeare Library, 1988), 265–92.
29. See Charles Nicholl, *The Chemical Theater* (London: Routledge & Kegan Paul, 1980), 25–6.
30. Cited in Betty Jo Teeter Dobbs *The Janus Faces of Genius: The Role of Alchemy in Newton's Thought* (Cambridge: Cambridge University Press, 1991), 162.
31. Retrieved from Chadwick-Healey's *Literature On Line*, available 5/1/00: http://lion.chadwick.com/home.cgi?source=config2.cfg.
32. John Gower, *Confessio Amantis* 4:457–61. Cited in Stanton J. Linden, *Dark Hierogliphicks: Alchemy from Chaucer to the Restoration* (Lexington: University Press of Kentucky, 1996), 57.
33. Cited in Linden, *Dark Hierogliphicks*, 64.
34. Cited in Linden, ibid., 79. Compare the alchemical language of Marx's observation that

> Since money does not reveal what has been transformed into it, everything, commodity or not, is convertible into money. Everything becomes saleable and purchaseable. Circulation becomes the great social retort into which everything is thrown, to come out again as the money crystal. Nothing is immune from this alchemy, the bones of saints cannot withstand it, let alone more delicate res sacrosanctae, extra commercium hominum. . . . (229)

35. *The Ecologues of Alexander Barclay*, ed. Beatrice White (Oxford: Oxford University Press, 1928), 2:601–2.
36. Cited in Linden, *Dark Hierogliphicks*, 82.

37. Cited in Linden, ibid., 56.
38. As Nicholas Barbon observed in 1690, the attempt to realize financial value through alchemy rests upon a fundamental misunderstanding of the nature of money:

> How greatly would those Gentlemen be disappointed, that are searching after the Philosopher's Stone, if they should at last happen to find it? For, if they should make but so great a quantity of Gold and Silver, as they, and their Predecessors have spent in search after it, it would so alter, and bring down the Price of those Metals, that it might be a Question, whether they would get so much Over-plus by it, as would pay for the Metal they change into Gold and Silver. (*A Discourse of Trade* [London: 1690, reprinted Baltimore: Johns Hopkins Press, 1905], 17).

39. *The Hermetic Museum,* ed. A. E. Waite (York Beach, MA: S. Weiser, 1990), 35.
40. In later alchemical texts, the concept of the philosopher's stone grows more and more abstract, less and less empirical. Isaac Newton conceives of it as coterminous with the ability to value things correctly: "'Tis unknown to the whole world, and yet the whole world has it before their eyes. Tis despised as dirt by the vulgar ignorant and sold at a vile price, but is precious to the Philosopher who knows its value because it contains all which he desires" (Dobbs, *Janus Faces of Genius,* 281–2).
41. Of course, this is true *a fortiori* in postmodernity. This leads the financier George Soros to compare capital to alchemy, on the grounds that financial value is free-floating and lacks any ultimate referent, whether gold or banknotes: "it is credit that matters, not money." George Soros, *The Alchemy of Finance: Reading the Mind of the Market* (New York: Simon and Schuster, 1987), 20.
42. Gerard de Malynes, *The Maintenance of Free Trade* (London, 1622), 17.
43. See Linden, *Dark Hierogliphicks,* 200, and Abraham, *Marvell and Alchemy,* 24.
44. L. C. Knights, *Drama and Society in the Age of Jonson* (London: Chatto & Windus, 1937), 107.
45. Ben Jonson, *Mercury Vindicated from the Alchemists at Court,* in *Ben Jonson: Selected Masques,* ed. Stephen Orgel (New Haven: Yale University Press, 1970), 131–32.
46. Quotations from *The Alchemist* are from *The Alchemist and Other Plays,* ed. Gordon Campbell (Oxford: Oxford University Press, 1998), this quotation from 213.
47. In fact, the whole notion of the mental conversion of physical stimuli into ideas could itself be thought of as a kind of alchemy, as John

Davies's *Nosce Teipsum* indicates. Our mind's capacity to form ideas, he writes:

> ... could not be, but that she turns
> Bodies to spirits, by *sublimation* strange;
> As fire converts to fire, the thinge it burnes,
> As we our meates into our nature change.
> From their grosse *matter* she abstracts the *formes*,
> And drawes a kind of *Quintessence* from things;
> Which to her proper nature she transformes
> Cited in Linden, *Dark Hierogliphicks*, 94.

48. Cited in Richard Strier, *Love Known: Theology and Experience in George Herbert's Poetry* (Chicago: University of Chicago Press, 1983), 208.
49. See Clarence H. Miller, "Christ as the philosopher's stone in George Herbert's 'The Elixir,'" *Notes and Queries* 45:1, 39–41 (1998).
50. This alchemical understanding of *telos* leads Louis Martz to describe "The Elixir," rightly in my view, as "the key to the entire *Temple*" (Louis Martz, *The Poetry of Meditation* [New Haven: Yale University Press, 1962] 257).
51. For recent considerations of Donne's understanding of the interaction between ideal and material spheres, see Theresa M. DiPasquale, *Literature and Sacrament: the Sacred and the Secular in John Donne* (Pittsburgh: Duquesne University Press, 1999) and Elizabeth M. A. Hodgson, *Gender and the Sacred Self in John Donne* (Newark: University of Delaware Press, 1999).
52. William Empson, *English Pastoral Poetry,* (New York: W. W. Norton, 1938), 84.
53. Andrew Marvell, "Upon Appleton House," 761. Cited from *Andrew Marvell: The Complete Poems,* ed. Elizabeth Story Donno (London: Penguin Books, 1972).

Chapter 7

1. John Weemse, *A Treatise ot the Foure Degenerate Sonnes* (London, 1636), 168.
2. *Complete Prose Works of John Milton,* ed. Don M. Wolfe (New Haven, CT: Yale University Press, 1959), 2:628–9. Subsequent in-text references to Milton's prose are from this edition.
3. See for example David Norbrook, *Writing the English Republic: Poetry, Rhetoric and Politics 1627–1660* (Cambridge: Cambridge University Press, 1999); William Kolbrener, *Milton's Warring Angels: A Study in Critical Engagements* (Cambridge: Cambridge University Press, 1997); David Armitage, Armand Himy, and Quentin Skinner, eds., *Milton and Republicanism* (Cambridge: Cambridge University

Press, 1996); Sharon Achinstein, *Milton and the Revolutionary Reader* (Princeton: Princeton University Press, 1994); Nigel Smith, *Literature and Revolution in England, 1640–60* (New Haven: Yale University Press, 1994).

4. J. G. A. Pocock, *The Machiavellian Moment: Florentine Political Thought and the Atlantic Republican Tradition* (Princeton: Princeton University Press, 1975), 373–4.
5. Aristotle, *The Nicomachean Ethics*, trans. J. E. C. Welldon (Buffalo, NY: Prometheus Books, 1987), bk.1, ch.8, p.24. I cite Welldon's translation here because I prefer "virtue" to "excellence" (e.g., at 1098a1, 17; 1102a1, 6), which is used by the revised Oxford translation. "Virtue" is the English term generally employed by writers in the sixteenth and seventeenth centuries.
6. Achinstein, *Milton*, 58.
7. Nigel Smith, "Popular Republicanism in the 1650s: John Streater's 'Heroick Mechanicks,'" in Armitage, Hiny, and Skinner, *Milton and Republicanism*, 144.
8. Like Milton, Augustine figured the opposition in terms of servitude and freedom: "how can a man who removes himself from the overlordship of God who made him and goes into the service of wicked spirits be just?" *The City of God*, trans. Gerald G. Walsh S. J., Demetrius B. Zema S. J., Grace Monahan O. S. U., and David J. Honan; ed. Vernon J, Bourke (New York: Doubleday, 1958), bk.10, ch.21, p.469.
9. This point is frequently reiterated: "It is neither fitting nor proper for a man to be king unless he be far superior to all the rest. . . . Everyone agrees that it is most improper for all to be slaves of one who is their equal, often their inferior, and usually a fool" (4:1.366–7).
10. See also Milton's reference in the *Commonplace Book* to

    the Romans who after their infancy were ripe for a more free government than monarchy, beeing in a manner all fit to be K[ing]s. afterward growne unruly, and impotent with overmuch prosperity were either for thire profit, or thire punishment fit to be curb'd with a lordly and dreadfull monarchy; w[hi]ch was the error of the noble Brutus and Cassius who felt themselves of spirit to free a nation but consider'd not that the nation was not fit to be free, whilst forgetting thire old justice and fortitude which was made to rule, they became slaves to thire owne ambition and luxury. (1:420)

11. See also *Paradise Lost* 12:97–101. Quotations from Milton's poetry are from Merrit Y. Hughes, ed., *Complete Poems and Major Prose* (New York: Macmillan, 1957). The Wisdom of Solomon connects this idea of the appropriate punishment more explicitly to idol worship:

11:15 In return for their foolish and wicked thoughts, which led them astray to worship irrational serpents and worthless animals, [God] didst send upon them a multitude of irrational creatures to punish them,

11:16 That they might learn that one is punished by the very things by which he sins.

12. The relative degree of influence exercised by the Hebraic and the Hellenic traditions on Milton's understanding of the opposition between flesh and spirit has been hotly argued, although usually with regard to Plato rather than Aristotle. Perez Zagorin finds the youthful Milton "fusing in his artist's imagination the didactic aims of the Puritan with the idealism of Plato" (*The Court and the Country: The Beginning of the English Revolution,* [London: Routledge & K. Paul, 1969], 175). Stephen Fallon stresses Plato's influence on the divorce tracts, and this leads him to see Milton's argument as confused and contradictory. Fallon plots a trajectory of progress in Milton's career, so that while "In the early 1640s Milton oscillates between Platonist and Pauline conceptions of the relation of soul and body" (*Milton Among the Philosophers: Poetry and Materialism in Seventeenth-Century England* [Ithaca: Cornell University Press, 1991], 84) and therefore "the early prose works reveal the influence of both Plato and Saint Paul, often in the same passages" (83), by the time of his maturity "Milton was able to work his way out of this incoherence with a materialism that allowed him to literalize Paul's figurative economy of the will and to eliminate the Platonists' ontological gap between soul and body" (85). Elsewhere, Fallon writes that the divorce tracts "reveal Milton experimenting with an early and not fully rationalized version of the monism informing *De Doctrina Christiana* and *Paradise Lost,*" and that as a result of this immaturity, "the dissonance between competing metaphysical systems threatens to break the harmony of the works" ("The Metaphysics of Milton's Divorce Tracts," in *Politics, Poetics and Hermeneutics in Milton's Prose,* ed. David Lowenstein and James Grantham Turner [Cambridge: Cambridge University Press, 1997], 67).

13. Milton seems to refer especially to *Nicomachean Ethics,* trans. J. E. C. Welldon (Buffalo, NY: Prometheus Books, 1987) bk.1, ch.2, 1094b7–11, p.13. Unless otherwise specified, references to the *Nicomachean Ethics* are from this edition. Aristotle makes the same point in *Magna Moralia:* "If therefore one is to act successfully in affairs of state, one must be of a good charatcter. The treatment of charatcer then is, as it seems, a branch and starting-point of statecraft." Trans. St. G. Stock, in *Complete Works of Aristotle,* vol. 2, edited by Jonathan Barnes (Princeton: Princeton University Press, 1984), bk.1, ch.1, 1181b25–27, p.1868.

14. Aristotle, *Politics,* tr. Carnes Lord (Chicago: University of Chicago Press, 1984). Subsequent in-text references to the *Politics* are from this edition.
15. *Nicomachean Ethics* bk.8, ch.10, 1160b29–31, p.15.
16. Aristotle, *Nicomachean Ethics* trans. W. D. Ross, revised by J. O. Umson, in *The Complete Works of Aristotle,* 1834.
17. United Provinces Declaration of Independence (1581), retrieved 7/4/01 from *The Internet Modern History Sourcebook:* http://www.fordham.edu/halsall/mod/1581dutch.html.
18. Aquinas, *Sentences* IV, d.44, q.1., a.3. c. Cit. Winston Ashley, *The Theory of Natural Slavery According to Aristotle and St. Thomas* (Ph.D. dissertation, Notre Dame, IN: 1941), 5.
19. *Nicomachean Ethics,* bk. 8, ch. 11, 1161a31–1161b4.
20. *Nicomachean Ethics,* bk. 8, ch. 10; 1160b1, 1–9.
21. Aquinas: *Summa Contra Gentiles* III, 81. Cit. Ashley, *The Theory of Natural Selection,* 39.
22. See *Tetrachordon's* insistence that "man is not to hold her [i.e., his wife] as a servant" (2:589).
23. See also Romans 7:14: "I am carnal, sold under sin."
24. Martin Luther, *Commentary on Galatians,* in *Martin Luther: Selections from His Writings,* ed. John Dillenberger (New York: Doubleday, 1961), 103.
25. See for example Arthur Barker, "Christian Liberty in Milton's Divorce Pamphlets," *Modern Language Review* 35 (1940): 153–161; Don M. Wolfe, *Milton in the Puritan Revolution* (New York: T. Nelson and Sons, 1941); Christopher Hill, *Milton and the English Revolution* (New York: St. Martin's Press, 1978); Timothy J. O'Keefe, *Milton and the Pauline Tradition* (Washington D.C.: University Press of America, 1982), 99–162; Stanley Fish, "Driving from the Letter: Truth and Indeterminacy in Milton's *Areopagitica,*" in *Re-Membering Milton: Essays on the Texts and Traditions,* edited by Mary Nyquist and Margaret W. Ferguson (New York: Methun, 1988), 234–54; James Grantham Turner, *One Flesh: Paradisal Marriage and Sexual Relations in the Age of Milton* (Oxford: Clarendon Press, 1987), 92–3.
26. See *Nicomachean Ethics,* bk.1, 1095b1, p.19–20 (1984): "Now the mass of mankind are evidently quite slavish in their tastes, preferring a life suitable for beasts."
27. I use the word "man" advisedly. In the divorce tracts as in his later poetry, Milton uses femininity as a synecdoche for sensuality in general, so that as Stephen Fallon puts it, "Enslavement to unfit marriage is interchangeable with enslavement to the woman and to the body" ("The Metaphysics of Milton's Divorce Tracts," in Loewenstein and Turner, *Politics, Poetics and Hermeneutics in Milton's Prose,* 69–84, 77–8). This use of the female as a trope for the flesh, which in Chris-

tianity derives from Origen's allegorical interpretation of Genesis, seems to me more relevant to Milton's concerns than any desire to bolster patriarchy, especially in the light of *Tetrachordon*'s advice that "the wiser should govern the lesse wise, whether male or female" (2:589). In *Paradise Lost,* Eve is an object of idolatry to both Adam and the serpent; however, as Raphael reminds Adam, this does not impute blame to the idol but to the idolater. For recent alternative views see Charles Hatten, "The Politics of Marital Reform and the Rationalization of Romance in *The Doctrine and Discipline of Divorce,*" *Milton Studies* 27 (1991): 95–114; Olga Lucia Valbuena, "Milton's 'Divorsive' Interpretation and the Gendered Reader," *Milton Studies* 27 (1991): 115–138; Elizabeth Hodgson, "When God Proposes: Theology and Gender in *Tetrachordon,*" *Milton Studies* 31 (1994): 133–154; Matthew Biberman: "Milton, Marriage and a Woman's Right to Divorce," *SEL* 39 no.1 (1999): 131–153; and Matthew Jordan, *Milton and Modernity: Politics, Masculinity and Paradise Lost* (New York: Palgrave, forthcoming).

28. Most famously, William Prynne worried about "the late dangerous increase of many Anabaptisticall, Antinomian, hereticall, Atheisticall opinions, as of the soules mortality, divorce at pleasure &c" (cit. J. Milton French, *The Life Records of John Milton* [New York: Gordian Press, 1966], 2:108). Ephraim Pagitt believed that "Mr. Milton permits a man to put away his wife upon his meere pleasure, without any fault in her, but for any dislike, or disparity of nature" (*Heresiography* [1647], 87, cit. French, *Life Records,* 171). Clement Walker considered Milton "a Libertine that thinketh his Wife a Manacle ... one that (after the Independent fashion) will be tied by no obligation to God or Man," (*Anarchia Anglicana: or, the History of Independency. The Second Part* [1649] 199, cit. William Riley Parker, *Milton's Contemporary Reputation* [Columbus: Ohio State University Press, 1940], 82). The author of *The Character of the Rump* (1660) thought him "an old Heretick both in Religion and Manners, that by his will would shake off his Governours as he doth his Wives, foure in a Fourtnight" (cit. Parker, *Milton's,* 98–9), while Robert Baillie fretted that

> Concerning Divorces, some of them goe farre beyond any of the Brownists, not to speake of Mr. Milton, who in a large Treatise hath pleaded for a full liberty for any man to put away his wife, when ever he pleaseth, without any fault in her at all, but for dislike or dyspathy of humour ... (*A Disuasive from the Errours of the Time* [1645] 116, cit. French, *Life Records,* 132).

29. For a different reading of Milton's typology in these tracts, see Jason P. Rosenblatt, "Milton's Chief Rabbi," *Milton Studies* 24 (1988):

43–71. Rosenblatt sees Milton as advocating the Mosaic dispensation over the Christian in *The Doctrine and Discipline*.
30. The association of license with tyranny was often drawn from Livy's account of the dissolute young Roman aristocrats who, finding their pursuit of pleasure hampered under the republic, enter into a plot for the restoration of the Tarquins.
31. *An Answer to a Book, intituled The Doctrine and Discipline of Divorce* (London, 1644), 5; reprinted in Parker, *Milton's*, 170–217.
32. On Milton's Pauline hermeneutics, see especially Theodore L. Huguelot, "The Rule of Charity in Milton's Divorce Tracts," *Milton Studies* 6 (1974): 199–214. See also William Kolbrener's argument that, in Milton's major works, "ontology gives way to a perspectivism which parallels the epistemological method of Milton's scriptural hermeneutics." (*Milton's Warring Angels*, 93). Kolbrener does not discuss the divorce tracts, but his observation offers an apposite description of their technique. It is worth remarking, however, that in these works "the epistemological method of Milton's scriptural hermeneutics" is solidly based upon the spirit/matter dichotomy, which his contemporaries such as Hobbes and Descartes understood to be ontological. Milton thus makes a startling and confusing gesture when he wrests the issue away from metaphysics and locates it in the realm of epistemology. He is implicitly claiming that the struggle within the self between opposed modes of consciousness is more fundamental than ontological questions about the nature of the human condition. While the later Milton undoubtedly espouses a monist ontology, this fact is less influential on his politics, philosophy, and theology than his epistemological, ethical, and hermeneutical dualism. Far from being immature or contradictory, the subjective dualism that Milton develops in the divorce tracts provides the basis from which he extrapolates his lifelong politics of church and state.
33. Here he follows Matthew 19:11: "All men cannot receive all sayings," which Milton cites in *Tetrachordon* (2:679). As Joseph Wittreich notes, "What distinguishes Milton from his epic predecessors is the fact that his 'fit' audience is finally a moral rather than a social category" ("'The Crown of Eloquence': The Figure of the Orator in Milton's Prose Works," in *Achievements of the Left Hand: Essays on the Prose of John Milton*, edited by Michael Lieb and John T. Shawcross (Amherst: University of Massachusetts Press, 1974), 47.
34. Compare John Weemse:

> There are some sinnes that are carnall sinnes; and some spirituall, Ephes. 6.12 and these are greater then carnall sinnes; Idolatrie is a spirituall sinne, and adulterie is a carnall sinne; The spirit being delighted with Idolatrie is a greater sinne then when the flesh is delighted with Adultery, and there is a greater aversion from God in Idolatry, then the conversion

and adhaering to sinne in Adulterie. (*A Treatise of the Four Degenerate Sonnes* [London, 1636], 192).

35. Cedric C. Brown has remarked on "Milton's wide sense of incompatibility leading to divorce, where unfitness of spirit in the wife can be treated *as if it were* a case of idolatry in the wife of a true believer" ("Milton and the Idolatrous Consort," *Criticism* 35 no.13 [summer 1993]: 419–39, 425). On "fornication," see Lana Cable's observation that "Milton spurns the definition that says sexual adultery or 'fornication' is the highest breach of marriage, and instead argues that the highest breach of an individual marriage—whatever that breach might be—is 'fornication'" ("Coupling Logic and Milton's Doctrine of Divorce," *Milton Studies* 15 [1981]: 143–59, 157), and Jason P. Rosenblatt's contention that in rabbinic readings the scriptural words "uncleanness" and "fornication," "which appear at first to restrict the grounds of divorce to unchastity and sexual offence, widen their meaning to include any kind of obnoxious behavior" ("Milton's Chief Rabbi," *Milton Studies* 24 [1988]: 43–71, 60).

36. Compare *De Doctrina:*

    ... the word "fornication," if it is considered in the light of the idiom of oriental languages, does not mean only adultery. It can mean also either what is called "some shameful thing" (i.e., the lack of some quality which might reasonably be required in a wife), Deut.xxiv.1, or it can signify anything which is found to be persistently at variance with love, fidelity, help and society (i.e., with the original institution of marriage). (6:378)

Chapter 8

1. Karl Marx, *Capital* vol. 1, trans. Ben Fowkes (London: Penguin Books, 1976), 126n4.
2. Rice Vaughan, *Of Coins and Coinage* (pub. 1675, written before 1672), retrieved from *The McMaster University Archive for the History of Economic Thought,* available 5/1/01: http://www.socsci.mcmaster.ca/~econ/ugcm/3113/vaughan.coin.
3. As J. G. A. Pocock puts it, "the Western moral tradition displays an astonishing unity and solidarity in the uneasiness and mistrust it evinces towards money as the medium of exchange." (*Virtue, Commerce and History: Essays on Political Thought and History, Chiefly in the Eighteenth Century* [Cambridge: Cambridge University Press, 1985], 103–104).
4. Christopher Hill, "Thomas Traherne," in *The Collected Essays of Christopher Hill* (Amherst: University of Massachusetts Press, 1985) 1:234.

5. Thomas Traherne, *Centuries of Meditation* 2 vols., ed. H. M. Margoliouth (Oxford: Clarendon Press, 1958) 1:142. Subsequent in-text references are from this edition. Traherne may be thinking here of Thomas More's *Utopia*, in which

> ... gold and silver, of which money is made, are so treated by [the inhabitants] that no-one values them more highly than their true nature deserves. Who does not see that they are far inferior to iron in usefulness since without iron mortals cannot live, any more than without fire or water? To gold and silver, however, nature has given no use that we cannot dispense with, if the folly of men had not made them valuable because they are rare. On the other hand, like a most kind and indulgent mother, she has exposed to view all that is best, like air and water and earth itself, but has removed as far as possible all vain and unprofitable things. (Thomas More, *Utopia*, ed. Edward Surtz, S. J. [New Haven: Yale University Press, 1964], 85).

6. Graham Dowell, *Enjoying the World: The Rediscovery of Thomas Traherne* (London: Mowbray, 1990), 75. Leigh A. DeNeef raises the question of value in *Traherne in Dialogue: Heidegger, Lacan and Derrida* (Durham NC: Duke University Press, 1988), but he is interested in its semiological rather than financial significance.
7. T. O. Beachcroft, "Thomas Traherne and the Cambridge Platonists," *Dublin Review* 186 (1930): 278–289.
8. Carol L. Marks, "Thomas Traherne and Cambridge Platonism," *PMLA* 81(1966): 521.
9. Carol L. Marks, introduction to Traherne's *Christian Ethics* (Ithaca: Cornell University Press, 1968), xliv. See also Carol L. Marks, "Thomas Traherne's Commonplace Book," *PBSA* 63 (1964): 458–465). For more general studies of Platonism among Traherne's contemporaries, see Ernst Cassirer, *The Platonic Renaissance in England* trans. James P. Pettegrove (New York: Gordian Press, 1970); Rosalind L. Colie, *Light and Enlightenment: A Study of the Cambridge Platonists and the Dutch Arminians* (Cambridge: Cambridge University Press, 1957); and James Deotis Roberts, *From Puritanism to Platonism in Seventeenth-Century England* (The Hague: Martinus Nijhoff, 1968).
10. Rosalie L. Colie, "Thomas Traherne and the Infinite: The Ethical Compromise," in *The Huntington Library Quarterly* 21 no.1 (1957–58):75.
11. Donald R. Dickson, *The Fountain of Living Waters: the Typology of the Waters of Life in Herbert, Vaughan and Traherne* (Columbia: University of Missouri Press, 1987), 172–173.
12. Barbara K. Lewalski, *Protestant Poetics and the Seventeenth-Century Religious Lyric* (Princeton: Princeton University Press, 1979), 229.

13. Marjorie Hope Nicolson, *The Breaking of the Circle: Studies in the Effect of the "New Science" upon Seventeenth-Century Poetry* (New York: Columbia University Press, 1960), 196.
14. It is interesting to wonder whether Traherne's peculiar sensitivity to the various nuances of these words may result from the fact that, as with Henry Vaughan, his first language was not English but Welsh. A. M. Allichin has speculated on this in *Profitable Wonders: Aspects of Thomas Traherne* (with Anne Ridler and Julia Smith, [Harrisburg PA: Morehouse Pub., 1989], 23), but the thesis, though probable, is unprovable. Regarding the influence of meditative techniques on Traherne, see especially Richard Douglas Jordan, "Thomas Traherne and the Art of Meditation," *Journal of the History of Ideas* 46 no.3 (1985): 381–403 and Louis L. Martz *The Paradise Within: Studies in Vaughan, Traherne and Milton* (New Haven: Yale University Press, 1964).
15. Aristotle, *Magna Moralia* bk. 2, 1203b, in *The Complete Works of Aristotle* (the revised Oxford translation), ed. Jonathan Barnes (Princeton: Princeton University Press, 1984), 2:31.
16. Thomas Traherne, *Christian Ethics*, ed. Carol L. Marks and George Robert Guffey (Ithaca: Cornell University Press, 1968), 26. Subsequent in-text references are from this edition.
17. Aristotle, *Politics* 1257a1, 7–10, trans. Carnes Lord (Chicago: University of Chicago Press, 1984), 46.
18. Aristotle, *Nicomachean Ethics*, trans. J. C. Welldon (Buffalo, NY: Prometheus Books), 1987, 161.
19. *A Discourse Upon Coins by Bernardo Davanzati, A Gentleman of Florence; Being publickly spoken in the Academy there, Anno 1588,* trans. John Toland (London,1696), 1.
20. Francis Bacon, "Of Riches," in *Francis Bacon*, ed. Brian Vickers (Oxford: Oxford University Press), 1.
21. Edward Misselden, *Free Trade or, The Means to Make Trade Flourish* (London, 1622), 6–7. Facsimile reprint in *The English Experience*, no. 267 (New York: Da Capo Press, 1970).
22. William Petty, *The Economic Writing of Sir William Petty*, 2 vols., ed. Charles Henry Hull (Cambridge: Cambridge University Press, 1899), 1:50–51.
23. Ibid., 2:439–440.
24. The phrase is from P. G. M. Dickson, *The Financial Revolution in England: A Study in the Development of Public Credit, 1688–1756* (London: Macmillan, 1967).
25. Petty, *Economic Writing*, 1:183.
26. Nicholas Barbon, *A Discourse of Trade* (London, 1690; reprinted, Baltimore: Johns Hopkins Press, 1905), 13.
27. Ibid., 13–14.
28. Ibid., 14.

29. Ibid., 14.
30. Ibid., 15.
31. Ibid., 18.
32. John Locke, *Considerations of the Consequences of Lowering Interest* (London, 1691; reprinted New York: Augustus M. Kelley, 1968), 31.
33. Joyce Oldham Appleby, *Economic Thought and Ideology in Seventeenth-Century England* (Princeton: Princeton University Press, 1978), 20. See also Albert O. Hirshman, *The Passions and the Interests: Political Arguments for Capitalism before its Triumph* (Princeton: Princeton University Press, 1977).
34. Edward Ford, *Experimented Proposals how the King may have Money* (London, 1666), cited in Appleby, *Economic Thought*, 213.
35. Thomas Hobbes, *Leviathan*, ed. C. B. MacPherson (London: Penguin Books, 1968), 208.
36. Compare Thomas Lodge's *An Alarum Against Usurers* (London, 1584): "Doe we buie ought for the fairenesse or goodness? Spangled Hobbie horses are for children, but men must respecte things which be of value indeede" (6).
37. R. H. Tawney, *Religion and the Rise of Capitalism* (Gloucester, MA: P. Smith, 1962), 36.

Chapter 9

1. Colin Nicholson, *Writing and the Rise of Finance: Capital Satires of the Early Eighteenth Century* (Cambridge: Cambridge University Press, 1994), xii.
2. Walter Benn Michaels, *The Gold Standard and the Logic of Naturalism: American Literature at the Turn of the Century* (Berkeley: University of California Press, 1987), 58.
3. Marc Shell, *Money, Language and Thought: Literary and Philosophical Economies from the Medieval to the Modern Era* (Berkeley: University of California Press, 1982), 4.
4. James Thompson, *Models of Value: Eighteenth-Century Political Economy and the Novel* (Durham, NC: Duke University Press, 1996), 3.
5. Ibid., 17.
6. The concept of "reification" was first developed by Georg Lukacs in *History and Class-Consciousness*, trans. Rodney Livingstone (Cambridge, MA: M. I. T. Press, 1922), and it has been most famously applied to the analysis of psychology and ideology by the thinkers of the Frankfurt School. It designates the condition of objectification—the reduction of ideas, relations and representations to material things—when that condition has become *total*, affecting every sphere of human existence. Under such a condition signs, whether monetary or linguistic, are treated as though they were the objective things to which they refer. See David Hawkes, *Ideology* (New York: Routledge, 1996), 109–114.

7. Michael McKeon, *The Origins of the English Novel: 1600–1740* (Baltimore: Johns Hopkins University Press, 1987), 312.
8. Sandra Sherman, *Finance and Fictionality in the Early Eighteenth Century: Accounting for Defoe* (Cambridge: Cambridge University Press, 1996), 10.
9. Ibid., 100.
10. As Carolynn Van Dyke notes, there is an important distinction to be made between *prosopopeia* and other allegorical modes. In a personification, an abstract concept is embodied in a human being, and this automatically involves a commentary on the relationship between ideal forms and the mind of the individual subject. It is in the nature of personification allegory, Van Dyke claims, that it "always invites speculation about the status of abstractions." This speculation allows the allegorist to use his formal figures to remark upon the moral status of his characters. In Prudentius's *Psychomachia,* for example, Van Dyke finds that:

    Each embodied Virtue is defined by a slightly different compound of universal with concretions; each survives because the compound remains stable, surrendering neither its immortal identity nor its force in the world. In contrast, the Vices are defeated by identification with material existence: they can be destroyed physically. In such ways, the interplay of universals and concretions—that is, the allegorical form itself—shapes and differentiates the first five episodes. (*The Fiction of Truth: Structures of Meaning in Narrative and Dramatic Allegory* [Ithaca: Cornell University Press, 1985], 53.)

    In similar fashion, Deborah Madsen argues that *Piers Plowman* invokes allegorical meaning to indicate the presence of spiritual significance in material experience—this is the revelation experienced by the Dreamer, whose "dream" reveals to him the fact that the empirical world is in fact an allegory for an imperceptible spiritual dimension. The "worldly" majority remain blind to this dimension and thus unconscious of their own allegorical status:

    The reader is taken through a bewildering sequence of interpretive modes as the dreamer, Will, attempts to discover a perceptual form that will make his dream-vision intelligible. The landscape that confronts him takes the form of a tableau: the "tour on a toft" and a "deep dale bynehte, a dongeon theinne" represent, in the manner of a romance emblem, a spiritual condition. Wandering between the two and oblivious to them is a "feeld ful of folk" who, in their realistic appearance and bustling variety, resist any such emblematic schematization. (*Re-Reading Allegory: A Narrative Approach to Genre* [New York: St. Martin's Press, 1994], 84.)

As Michael Murrin points out, the medieval or Renaissance allegorist necessarily "recognized the fact that morality followed inevitably from his tropological medium." (*The Allegorical Epic: Essays in its Rise and Decline,* [Chicago: University of Chicago Press, 1980], 196.) But in Murrin's view, the kind of moral commentary that allegory was able to offer seemed increasingly inappropriate to the modern world, so that allegory was "rapidly dying" as early as the late sixteenth century. Rosemund Tuve connects this development to the decline of the Aristotelian world picture, with its intricate correspondences between the levels of creation, finding "a belief in a principle of analogy, under Spenser's presentation of allegory (quite vanished by Bunyan's time)" (*Allegorical Imagery: Some Medieval Books and their Posterity,* [Princeton: Princeton University Press, 1966], 8), and Gay Clifford links it to an Eliotian dissociation of sensibility that evacuated spiritual significance from the world of sensuous experience *(The Transformations of Allegory* [London: Routledge, 1974], 8). Certainly, Renaissance allegorists frequently prefaced their work with apologies for their formal mode. But as Spenser does in his preface to *The Faerie Queene,* they often excuse their allegorical practice by claiming that it corresponds to the condition of empirical reality:

> To some I know this Methode will seeme displeasaunt, which had rather have good discipline delivered plainly in way of precepts, or sermoned at large, as they use, then thus clowdily enwrapped in Allegoricall devises. But such, me seeme, should be satisfide with the use of these dayes, seeing all things accounted by their showes, and nothing esteemed of, that is not delightfull and pleasing to commune sence.

Bunyan prefaces each of his major works with similar assertions of the correspondence between his chosen literary form and the world on which he is commenting.

11. Joan Webber, *The Eloquent "I": Style and Self in Seventeenth-Century Prose* (Madison: University of Wisconsin Press, 1968), 22.
12. John Bunyan, *The Pilgrim's Progress,* ed. Roger Sharrock and James Blanton Wharey (Oxford: Clarendon Press, 1960), 1. Subsequent in-text references are from this edition.
13. Thomas Luxon, *Literal Figures: Puritan Allegory and the Reformation Crisis in Representation* (Chicago: University of Chicago Press, 1995), 32.
14. Ibid., 171.
15. Samuel Taylor Coleridge, *Collected Works,* ed. Kathleen Coburn (Princeton: Princeton University Press, 1987), 7:103.
16. Compare Milton, addressing Parliament in *The Doctrine and Discipline of Divorce:* "who among ye . . . hath not been often traduc't to be the agent of his own by-ends, under pretext of Reformation . . ."

Complete Works of John Milton ed. Ernest Sirluck et al. (New Haven: Yale University Press, 2:225).

17. John Bunyan, *The Holy War*, ed. James F. Forrest (New York: New York University Press, 1967), 11. Subsequent in-text references are from this edition.
18. Stanley Fish, *Self-consuming Artefacts: The Experience of Seventeenth-Century Literature* (Berkeley: University of California Press, 1972), 237.
19. Van Dyke, *Fiction of Truth*, 171.
20. John Bunyan, *The Life and Death of Mr. Badman*, ed. James F. Forrest and Roger Sharrock (Oxford: Clarendon Press, 1988), 1. Subsequent in-text references are from this edition.
21. As Gay Clifford notes in *The Transformations of Allegory*, when Faithful is executed in Vanity Fair, we are not to take this as indicating that Christian has lost *his* faith (19). Edwin Honig, in *Dark Conceit: The Making of Allegory* (Evanston, IL: Northwestern University Press, 1959), and Jon Whitman, in *Allegory: The Dynamics of an Ancient and Medieval Technique* (Oxford: Clarendon Press, 1987), have argued that allegories convey their messages by manipulating the relationship between an abstract concept and its personified representation. See also Paul de Man, "The Rhetoric of Temporality," in *Interpretation: Theory and Practice*, ed. Charles S. Singleton, (Baltimore: Johns Hopkins University Press, 1969). In *Towards an Aesthetics of Reception*, trans. Timothy Bahti (Brighton: Harvester Press, 1982), Hans Robert Jauss suggests that allegory represents the self's alienation from the objective world which characterizes the experience of modernity. Certainly, there is a long literary history of employing personification to represent money. In *Models of Value*, James Thompson provides early modern examples from Richard Barnfield's *Lady Pecunia* (1605) to Charles Johnstone's *Chrysal: or, the Adventures of a Guinea* (1760), and Simon Schama has shown how large the figure of "Queen Money" loomed in the imagination of the seventeenth-century Dutch in his *The Embarrassment of Riches: An Interpretation of Dutch Culture in the Golden Age* (Berkeley: University of California Press 1988), 323–43.
22. As Patrick Collinson mentions, many Renaissance emblem books portrayed the various vices through realistic images while reverting to allegorical abstractions for the depictions of virtues. (*From Iconoclasm to Iconophobia: the Cultural Impact of the Second English Reformation* [Reading: University of Reading Press, 1986], 22).
23. Stuart Sim goes so far as to claim that Badman "is designed to symbolize the Restoration society Bunyan so despised" in "'Safe for Those for Whom It Is to Be Safe': Salvation and Damnation in Bunyan's Fiction," in *John Bunyan and his England, 1628–88* ed. Anne Laurence, W. R. Owens, and Stuart Sim (London: Hambledon Press, London, 1990), 154.

24. On the generic status of Bunyan's work in general, see Ian P. Watt, *The Rise of the Novel; Studies in Defoe, Richardson and Fielding* (London: Chatto and Windus, 1957), 80. It is generally agreed that Bunyan's figural mode represents a decisive departure from the established, Spenserian allegorical tradition. Michael McKeon sees Bunyan as "straining" towards the novel form through the compelling nature of his plot, which threatens to subsume its allegorical significance (*Origins of the English Novel*, 297). McKeon builds on the argument of Stanley Fish in *Self-consuming Artefacts*. See also Maureen Qulligan, *The Language of Allegory* (Ithaca: Cornell University Press, 1979), 129; E. Beatrice Batson, *John Bunyan: Allegory and Imagination* (London: Croom Helm, 1984); and Michael Mullett's comments on *Badman* in *John Bunyan in Context* (Keele: Keele University Press, 1996), 211.

25. See Phillip Rinson, *Classical Theories of Allegory and Christian Culture* (Pittsburgh: Dusquesne University Press, 1981), 160, and Valentine Cunningham, "Glossing and Glozing: Bunyan and Allegory," *John Bunyan: Conventicle and Parnassus: Tercentenary Essays* ed. N. H. Keeble (Oxford: Clarendon Press, 1988), 221.

26. The connection between allegorical personification and the commodity form was first explored by Walter Benjamin in *The Origin of German Tragic Drama*, trans. John Osborne (New York: Verso, 1977). Terry Eagleton extrapolates from Benjamin's ideas in *Walter Benjamin, or Towards a Revolutionary Criticism* (London: Routledge, 1981). See also Frederic Jameson's comment that "allegory is precisely the dominant mode of expression of a world in which things have been for whatever reason utterly sundered from meanings, from spirit, from genuine human existence," in *Marxism and Form: Twentieth-century Dialectical Theories of Literature* (Princeton: Princeton University Press, 1971), 71; and Ellen Cantarow, "A Wilderness of Opinions Confounded: Allegory and Ideology," *College English* 34: no.2 (November 1972): 215–255. It is interesting to recall in this context that the literal meaning of "allegory" is "other-speaking for the market-place." This point provides the basis of Angus Fletcher's groundbreaking argument in *Allegory: The Theory of a Symbolic Mode* (Ithaca: Cornell University Press, 1964), 2n1.

27. On the influence of Aristotle, see especially John T. Noonan, *The Scholastic Analysis of Usury* (Cambridge, MA: Harvard University Press, 1957), and Odd Langholm, *The Aristotelian Analysis of Usury* (Oslo: Universitetforlaget AS, Oslo, 1984). On the influence of Deuteronomy, see especially Benjamin Nelson, *The Idea of Usury: from Tribal Brotherhood to Universal Otherhood* (Princeton: Princeton University Press, 1949), and Norman Jones, *God and the Money-Lenders: Usury and Law in Early Modern England* (Oxford: B. Blackwell, 1989).

28. Compare Martin Luther, who Bunyan informs us in *Grace Abounding,* was among his favorite authors:

> Among themselves the merchants have a common rule which is their chief maxim and the basis of all their sharp practices, where they say: "I may sell my goods as dear as I can." They think this is their right. Thus occasion is given for avarice, and every window and door to hell is opened.... If we were to tolerate and accept the principle that everyone may sell his wares as dear as he can, approving the practice of borrowing and forced lending and standing surety, and yet try to advise and teach men how to act the part of Christians and keep a good and clear conscience in the matter, that would be the same as teaching men how wrong could be right and bad good. (Luther, "Of Trade and Usury," in *Selected Writings,* ed. Theodore G. Tappert, trans. Charles M. Jacobs, revised by Walther I. Brandt (Philadelphia: Westminster Press, 1967), 2:87, 100–1.)

Luther and Bunyan adhere strictly to the doctrine of the just price. For an example of a less stringent analysis, compare Thomas Cooper's *Wilie Beguile ye* (London, 1621). Although Cooper is willing to permit some degree of market manipulation, he takes for granted the distinction between a commodity's "price" and its "worth":

> 1. Touching those ordinary sleights of tendering, pressing, sliking, garbeling, washing &c of our wares; thought there be much deciet in them: yet there may bee also some lawfull use thereof, with these conditions. 2. That hereby only our Wares may be made more saleable, and yet so as the glasse and stretching of them, diminish not the substance and goodnesse therefor. 3. Be not a means to enhance the price, about the worth thereof: by making them seeme hereby finer and sounder then they are indeed. (66)

29. Arthur Dent, *The Plaine Mans Pathway to Heaven* (London, 1601), 154–155, emphasis in the original. Compare Thomas Becon: "What craft, deceit, subtility, and falsehood use merchants in buying and selling! How rejoice they when they have beguiled their christian brother!" (Cit. Neal Wood, *Foundations of Political Economy: Some Early Tudor Views of State and Society* [Berkeley: University of California Press, 1994], 181). An obvious influence on Bunyan is Richard Bernard's *The Isle of Man* (London, 1627), in which the reprobate figures are again characterized by their carnality.

30. See also Richard Corbett, "Satira 2 (Against Shams)," in *The Time's Whistle* (London, 1647; reprint London, 1871), 24:

> Mechanico, reputed by moste men
> An honest tradesman & grave citisen,
> When thou dost come into his shop to buy,
> Although it be the least commodity,
> With kind salutes & good wordes will receave thee;
> But trust him not, in 's deeds he will deceave thee. (lines 655–60)

And Benjamin Keach, *Sion in Distress: or, the Groans of the Protestant Church* (London, 1681), 29:

> What lying, cheating, couz'ning and deceit
> Do Traders use? O! how they over-rate
> What they would sell? but if they be to buy,
> They undervalue each Commodity. (lines 799–802)

We can trace the subtle and gradual amelioration of the market's ethical status by comparing such passages with Defoe's *The Compleat English Tradesman* (1725–27):

> a talking rattling mercer or draper, or milliner, beyond his counter, would be worth nothing if he should confine himself to that mean silly thing called *Truth;* they must Lie, it is in support of their business, and some think they cannot live without it: but I deny that part, and recommend it, I mean, to the tradesman I am speaking of, to consider what a scandal it is upon trade, to pretend to say that a Tradesman cannot live without lying. (cit. Sherman, *Fiction and Fictionality,* 116)

31. Thomas Hobbes, *Leviathan* (London: Penguin Books, 1985), 209.
32. Ibid., 208.
33. Joyce Oldham Appleby, *Economic Thought and Ideology in Seventeenth-Century England* (Princeton: Princeton University Press, 1978), 247. See also Barry Supple, "The Nature of Enterprise," in *The Cambridge Economic History of Europe* vol. 5, ed. E. E. Rich and C. H. Wilson (Cambridge: Cambridge University Press, 1977), 405:

> The regard for one's "own commoditie," the self-interest which by the eighteenth century had been incorporated into the powerful and approving body of impersonal economic theory, eroded the link between entrepreneurial activity and non-economic criteria of behaviour.

Pierre Bourdieu makes a similar point:

> Economic theory which acknowledges only the rational responses of an indeterminate, interchangeable agent to "potential opportunities," or more precisely to average chances (like the "average rates of profit" offered by the different

markets), converts the immanent law of the economy into a universal norm of proper economic behavior. (*The Logic of Practice*, trans. Richard Nice, [Stanford: Stanford University Press, 1990], 63.)

34. William Petty, *The Political Anatomy of Ireland* (1691), in *The Economic Writings of Sir William Petty*, 2 vols., ed. Charles Henry Hull (Cambridge: The University Press, 1899), 1:181.
35. Petty sums up his methodological principle in a letter of 1687:

    [Algebra] came out of Arabia by the Moores into Spaine and from thence hither, and W[illiam] P[etty] hath applied it to other than purely mathematical matters, viz: to policy by the name of *Political Arithmetick* by reducing many termes of matter to termes of number, weight, and measure, in order to be handled Mathematically.

    Cited in Alessandro Roncaglia, *Petty: The Origins of Political Economy*, trans. Isabella Cherubini (Armonck, NY: M. E. Sharpe, 1985), 19–20. See also Richard Olson's summary of Petty's technique of abstraction from human behavior, on the assumption that "There are quantifiable regularities in aggregate behaviors (we now call these statistical laws) which can be empirically discovered even if we cannot know precisely how each individual event is caused" (*The Emergence of the Social Sciences, 1642–1792* [New York: Twayne, 1993], 62).

36. Compare Adam Smith's comment that, following the division of labor, "Every man thus lives by exchanging, or becomes in some measure a merchant..." (*The Wealth of Nations* [New York: Random House, 1994], 24). Smith is, of course, responsible for the most famous personified figure for market forces: the "invisible hand."
37. Nicholas Barbon, *A Discourse of Trade* (London, 1690, reprinted Baltimore: Johns Hopkins Press, 1905), 14.
38. Sir Dudley North, *Discourses Upon Trade* (London, 1691, reprinted Baltimore: Johns Hopkins Press, 1907), 27.
39. Ibid., 12.
40. Bernard Mandeville, *The Fable of the Bees and Other Writings*, ed. E. J. Hundert (Indianapolis: Hackett, 1997), 56.
41. Cit. E. G. Hundert, *The Enlightenment's Fable: Bernard Mandeville and the Discovery of Society* (Cambridge: Cambridge University Press, 1994), 38.
42. Mandeville, *Fable of the Bees*, 137.
43. Ibid., 146.
44. John Asgill, *Several Assertions Proved* (London, 1696, reprinted Baltimore: Johns Hopkins Press, 1906), 20.
45. Nicholas Barbon, *A Discourse Concerning Coining the New Money Lighter* (London, 1696, reprinted Westmead: Gregg International, 1971), 43.

46. It is salutary to compare this passage from *Mr. Badman* with Defoe's advice to *The Compleat English Tradesman* (1725–27): "he must be all soft and smooth; nay, if his real temper be all fiery and hot, he must shew none of it in his shop; he must be a perfect *complete hypocrite,* if he will be a *complete tradesman*" (cit. Sherman, *Finance and Fictionality,* 102, original emphases).
47. Barbon, *Discourse Concerning Coining,* 53.
48. Bernard Mandeville, *An Enquiry into the Origin of Honour and the Usefulness of Christianity in War* (London: Frank Cass, 1971), 89. See also the chapter on Defoe's *The Compleat English Tradesman,* 91–128.
49. Christopher Hill, *A Tinker and a Poor Man: John Bunyan and his Church 1628–1688* (New York: Alfred A. Knopf, 1989), 225.
50. Compare John Winthrop's journal for September 1639, in which the Massachusetts governor records his trial of Robert Keane for extortion. Winthrop admits that "a certain rule could not be found out for an equal rate between buyer and seller, though much labor had been bestowed in it, and divers laws had been made, which, upon experience, were repealed, as being neither safe nor equal." Despite this, Winthrop ruled that the idea "That a man might sell as dear as he can, and buy as cheap as he can" was a "false principle" (*The Journal of John Winthrop,* ed. Richard S. Dean, James Savage and Laetitia Yeandle [Cambridge, MA: Belknap Press of Harvard University Press, 1996], 307–8).

Index

Abraham, Lyndy, 159, 165
abuse, 23, 69, 78–95, 98, 102–3, 112–13, 119, 127, 140, 150, 173, 180, 186–7, 201
Achinstein, Sharon, 170
Agnew, Jean-Christophe, 81
alchemy, 7, 137, 143–67
allegory, 213–30
Althusser, Louis, 11
Amariglio, Jack, 19–20
Anabaptists, 171, 182–3
Anglicanism, 74, 177
Anderson, Perry, 11–12, 15–16
　Lineages of the Absolutist State, 11–12
Antichrist, 67, 70, 98
antifoundationalists, 22
antinomianism, 170–1, 178–9, 181–4, 187–8, 197
antisemitism, 116, 122–9
antitheatricalism, 77–96, 157
Appleby, Joyce Oldham, 204, 225
Aquinas, St. Thomas, 28–9, 57, 70, 96–9, 101, 113–14, 175–6
Arianism, 61, 63
aristocracy, 11, 12, 15
Aristotle, 6, 8, 10, 23, 28–33, 36, 40–2, 46, 53, 58–9, 65, 68, 70–1, 77, 79, 82, 85–6, 96–9, 101, 103, 105, 107, 109, 114, 119, 145–7, 149–52, 155–6, 158–9, 162–3, 169–71, 173–80, 184, 187, 189, 192, 194–5, 197–203, 211, 216, 222–3, 229–30
　Magna Moralia, 28, 198
　Metaphysics, 28
　Nicomachean Ethics, 28, 31, 171, 173–6
　On the Generation of Animals, 28
　Poetics, 149
　Politics, 30, 32, 99, 114, 171, 173–6, 222
Arminius, 57
Asgill, John, 227
Ashmole, Elias, 154–5
Athanasius, 65
Augustine, St., 55–6, 60, 82, 86–7, 99–100, 125, 131, 171
　Christian Doctrine, 82
　City of God, 131, 171
avarice, 16, 23, 56, 68, 82–3, 119, 121–2, 125
Aylett, Robert, 126

Babylon, 3, 54, 70, 89, 178
Bacon, Francis, 9–10, 29–30, 33–6, 71, 77, 97, 122–3, 136–8, 144–51, 200–1, 204
　Novum Organon, 33, 148–9
Bacon, Nicholas, 57–8
Bale, John, 98
Bancroft, Thomas, 98
Barasch, Moshe, 65
Barbon, Nicholas, 36, 44–5, 192, 202–5, 208, 226–8
　A Discourse Concerning Coining the New Money Lighter, 227
　A Discourse of Trade, 36, 202–3, 226
Barclay, Alexander, 154
Baudrillard, Jean, 53
Bell, Thomas, 123
ben Israel, Menassah, 115–16
Bernard, Richard, 57
　The Isle of Man, 57
Bernard, St., 123
Besancon, Alain, 59, 77

Bible, 5–6, 8, 109, 129–30, 165, 199
   Chronicles, 132
   Colossians, 55, 57
   1 Corinthians, 38, 58, 159, 187
   2 Corinthians, 132–3
   Deuteronomy, 54, 108, 110, 114, 181–3, 192, 222
   Ephesians, 55, 57, 179
   Exodus, 54, 134
   Ezekiel, 133
   Galatians, 178
   Genesis, 178–9, 194
   Isaiah, 54
   Matthew, 56, 66, 136, 181–2, 184
   Psalms, 54–5
   Jeremiah, 124, 133
   John, 71, 135, 178
   Judges, 171
   1 Kings, 132
   Revelation, 3
   Romans, 56, 133
   Wisdom of Solomon, 54, 188
Binswanger, Hans-Christophe, 145
Blake, William, 206
Boccaccio, 100
Booth, Stephen, 102, 111
bourgeoisie, 9, 10, 11, 12–13, 15–16
Brenner, Robert, 11
Bucer, Martin, 97
bullionism, 22, 35–7, 39–40, 50–1, 151, 201–2
Bunyan, John, 5, 6, 25, 139, 213–30
   The Holy War, 217, 229
   The Life and Death of Mr. Badman, 7, 213–30
   The Pilgrim's Progress, 139, 215–9, 229
Burghley, Lord, 97
Burton, Robert, 24
   Anatomy of Melancholy, 24
Byzantium, 17, 59–66, 72

Caesar, Julius, 173
Calvert, Thomas, 115–16
Calvin, John, 35, 49, 55, 57, 73–5, 77, 127, 133, 143–4, 194, 196, 215, 219–20, 225, 227
   Institutes of the Christian Religion, 49, 73–4

Catholicism, 6, 30, 50–1, 57, 72–3, 87–8, 98–9, 132, 134, 182
Cato the younger, 171
causality, 28–30, 33–5
Chaucer, Geoffrey, 154
Chettle, Henry, 80
Chrysostom, St. John, 100
Cicero, 87, 103, 169, 171, 173
Clark, William, 24, 152–3
Clarke, Henry, 82
class struggle, 12, 15, 19
classical economics, 45–7, 49–51, 64
classical republicanism, 170–1, 177, 187
Coleridge, Samuel Taylor, 216
concupiscence, 55–7, 98–9, 101, 103, 116, 157
Constantine, 60, 62
Cooke, Alexander, 67
Cooper, Thomas, 82
Copernicus, 37–8
Copronymus, Constantine, 62
Cosmopolita, Eyraeneus Philalethes, 146
covetousness, 6, 9, 55–8, 66, 91, 98, 111–12, 153
Crawshaw, Richard, 134
Cromwell, Oliver, 173
Cudworth, Ralph, 194, 196
custom, 5, 23, 30, 38, 40–1, 46, 59, 126, 143, 155, 162, 166, 177, 187, 198–9, 206–7, 210
   see also nomos

Dante, 100
   Inferno, 100
Davanzati, Bernardo, 200
Davenant, George, 39
Defoe, Daniel, 214
   The Complete English Tradesman, 214
Dekker, Thomas, 80
Dent, Arthur, 223–4
   The Plaine Man's Pathway to Heaven, 223–4
Derrida, Jacques, 22, 52
Descartes, Rene, 29, 34
devil, the, *see* Satan
Dionysus Areopagitica, 59, 77
dissociation of sensibility, 17, 146–7
divorce, 5, 7, 30, 169–90
Dobb, Maurice, 11, 15

Dollimore, Jonathan, 147
Donne, John, 4, 6, 81, 143–67

Eck, Johannes, 62
eidola, 5, 58, 70
eikon, 58–9
Eliot, T. S., 146–7
empiricism, 9, 10, 28–9, 33, 95, 136–9, 148, 150, 153, 158, 217
Empson, William, 165
Emser, Hieronymous, 72
Engels, Freidrich, 9
Ephesus, 59
equivalence, 30
Erasmus, 101–2
Eucharist, 21, 23, 33, 60, 68–75, 87–8, 98, 188
Eusebius, 62
exchange value, 8, 31–2, 46, 79, 85–6, 118–19, 123–4, 126, 141, 144, 156, 162, 192–4, 196–211, 229

Fenner, Dudley, 80
Fenton, Roger, 107, 112
Feuerbach, Ludwig, 14, 51, 66
  The Essence of Christianity, 51
Fish, Stanley, 128, 141, 217
Ford, Edward, 204
fornication, 181, 184, 188–9
Foucault, Michel, 22, 96
  History of Sexuality, 96
Fuggers, 37, 68

Gager, John, 80
Gervaise, Isaac, 35–6
Gnostics, 61, 171
Goethe, Johann Wolfgang von, 143, 145–6
gold, 15, 21, 24, 35–47, 50, 54–6, 100, 109, 119, 121, 123, 129, 132, 143–67, 192–4, 198, 200–5, 207–10
Gosson, Stephen, 24, 78, 80–1, 85, 87, 90
Goux, Jean-Joseph, 21–2, 145–6
Gower, John, 154
Gregory II, Pope, 62
Gregory of Nyssa, 63
Gresham, Sir Thomas, 38
Guernsey, Julia, 140–1

Hegel, G. W. F., 66
Herbert, George, 4, 6–7, 56, 115–42, 147–8, 159–60, 163
  The Priest to the Temple, 118–19, 134
  The Temple, 115–42
Heywood, Thomas, 78
Hilarie, Hugh, 70, 98
Hill, Christopher, 9–10, 11, 15, 16, 193
Hobbes, Thomas, 204, 224, 230
Holstun, James, 7
  Ehud's Dagger, 7
Homer, 58, 137
Howard, Jean, 81
Howson, John, 86
Hume, David, 45
Hutchinson, John, 3–4
Hutchinson, Lucy, 3–4
hyper-real, 60, 74, 77, 230

Incarnation, 61, 63, 88, 123, 132, 167, 194
indulgences, 66–8
inflation, 37–8
Irene, Empress, 62, 66

Jameson, Frederic, 140
Jonson, Ben, 7, 23–4, 89–91, 94, 101, 156–8, 165
  The Alchemist, 157–8
  Bartholomew Fair, 89
  Epigrams, 101
  Mercury Vindicated from the Alchemists at Court, 156–7
  Volpone, 23–4
Judaism, 30, 100, 108–10, 116, 122–33, 135–6

Karlstadt, Andreas, 71–3, 75, 116
Knieger, Bernard, 116
Knights, L. C., 156
Koritz, Amy, 18
Koritz, Douglas, 18

LaBlanc, Gregory, 18
labor power, 8, 12–14
labor theory of value, 13
Langland, William, 100
latitudinarians, 216
Law, John, 35–7, 64, 75
  Money and Trade Considered, 45

Law, William, 227
legalism, 30, 109–10, 116, 123, 125–8, 131, 136, 180–5
Leo the Armenian, 63
Leo the Isaurian, 62
Lewalski, Barbara, 127–8, 195
licence, 181–4, 186–7
Linden, Stanton J., 156
literalism, 25, 30, 56, 73, 108–10, 114, 116, 123–8, 131–2, 135, 180–8
Locke, John, 44, 150, 192, 203–5, 208
  Considerations of the Consequences of the Lowering of Interest, 203–4
Lodge, Thomas, 79
logocentrism, 22, 128
logos, 22, 53, 165
Lombards, 100
Lollards, 171
Luther, Martin, 23, 50, 62, 66–73, 77, 116, 171, 179
  Appeal to the Ruling Class of the German Nationality, 67
  The Babylonian Captivity of the Church, 70
  Commentary on Galatians, 69, 179
Luxon, Thomas, 215
Lyotard, Jean-Francois, 20

Machiavelli, 171
Mallarme, Stephane, 145–6
Malynes, Gerard de, 39, 41–3, 155–6, 191
  The Maintenance of Free Trade, 41–3, 155–6
Mandeville, Bernard, 227–9
  An Enquiry into the Origin of Honour, 229
  The Fable of the Bees, 227
Manichees, 61, 72, 99, 171
Marlowe, Christopher, 123, 128
  The Jew of Malta, 123
Marston, John, 81, 89–94
Martyr, Justin, 124
  Dialogue with Trypho, 124
Marvell, Andrew, 146, 159, 165–6
Marx, Karl, 8, 9, 10, 13–15, 49–52, 66, 94, 96, 123–4, 129, 191, 205, 211, 213
  Capital, 13–14, 191
  Comments on James Mill, 50

The Communist Manifesto, 9
Economic and Philosophical Manuscripts, 14, 49–50, 94
Grundrisse, 50
On the Jewish Question, 124, 129
materialism, 6, 8, 11, 16, 19, 28, 118, 127, 146, 153–4, 185, 191, 196, 217, 230
McClosky, Dierdre, 19
mercantilism, 39–45, 49–51
Meres, Francis, 100
Milton, John, 5–8, 56, 169–90, 197
  Areopagitica, 182, 187
  Of Christian Doctrine, 178–9, 182
  Colasterion, 180, 185
  Defence of the English People, 172, 186
  The Doctrine and Discipline of Divorce, 176–7, 180–90
  Eikonoklastes, 170
  Paradise Lost, 170, 172
  Of Reformation, 173, 184–5
  Tetrachordon, 170, 177, 179, 187, 189
Misselden, Edward, 39–42, 191, 201
  Free Trade, 40–1
monophysitism, 61, 71
Moses, 178, 181–3, 186
Mosse, Miles, 101, 107
Mun, Thomas, 39, 43–5, 50, 191
  England's Treasure by Foreign Trade, 43–4
Munday, Anthony, 79, 87, 91

Nairn, Tom, 15–16
Nashe, Thomas, 78
Nestorianism, 61, 63
neoclassicism, 20
neoplatonism, 59, 193–6
neopragmatists, 22
new economic criticism, 18–19
Newton, Isaac, 39, 145, 147, 152
Nicarus, 155
Nicolson, Marjorie Hope, 146–7, 195
nomos, 5–6, 30–1, 38, 46, 51, 54, 66, 126, 135–6, 141, 144, 155–6
  see custom
Norbrook, David, 179
North, Sir Dudley, 44–5, 226–7
  Discourses of Trade, 44, 226

Northbrooke, John, 78–9, 85, 90
Norton, Thomas, 154

objectification, 4, 6, 25, 53, 55, 58, 73, 87, 94, 115–42, 171, 175, 187, 190
Origen, 127
Orphism, 60
Osteen, Mark, 18

Paracelsus, 149, 151
Paul, St., 38, 55–8, 127–8, 133, 135, 171, 173, 178–80, 184, 188–9
 see Bible
Pepys, Samuel, 39
Perkins, William, 138
Petrarch, 171
Petty, William, 192, 201–2, 204, 208, 225, 227
 Political Anatomy of Ireland, 201–2
 Quantulumcunque, 201
 A Treatise of Taxes, 201
Pharisees, 66, 181–3
Philo of Alexandria, 100
phusis, 5, 30–1, 51, 54, 61, 66, 126, 141, 144, 155–6
Plato, 58–9, 63–5, 77, 127, 141, 150, 157, 161, 164, 166, 197
 Cratylus, 77
 Symposium, 58
 Timaeus, 59, 150
Plotinus, 59, 128
Pocock, J. G. A., 170
Polo, Marco, 143
Pope, Alexander, 139
Popery, *see* Catholicism
Pound, Ezra, 95
Presbyterians, 183
proletariat, 8, 12–13
Prynne, William, 7, 80, 87–8, 92

Rainoldes, John, 80
Rankins, William, 80
Ricardo, David, 13
Rochester, Earl of, 67
Rossi-Landi, Feruccio, 19
Rous, Francis, 78, 81, 87
Ruskin, John, 1
Russo, David F., 19–20

Salmasius, 173, 180, 186
Sander, Nicholas, 103
Satan, 23, 63, 68, 72, 81, 84–6, 88, 119
Saussure, Ferdinand de, 17, 21–2
scholasticism, 28, 95, 97, 99, 101, 112, 114, 161, 163, 211, 213
Scot, Reginald, 154
Scott, Gregory, 74
Seldon, John, 105
Seneca, 60
Sennert, Daniel, 151
sensuality, 6, 22, 30, 82, 126, 137, 158, 176, 180, 182, 185, 187
Shakespeare, William, 6, 8, 93–114, 141
 King John, 93–4
 Measure for Measure, 101
 The Merchant of Venice, 97, 109–10, 112, 114, 125–7
 Sonnets, 7, 95–114
 Timon of Athens, 93, 101
 Twelfth Night, 101
Shell, Marc, 19–20, 23, 110, 214
 Money, Language and Thought, 20
Sibbes, Richard, 159
Singleton, Marion White, 139
Skinner, Quentin, 179
slavery, 173–90
Smith, Adam, 13, 45, 49–50, 64
Smith, Nigel, 170
sodomy, 7, 95–114
Spengler, Oswald, 3
Spenser, Edmund, 23
 The Faerie Queene, 23
Stockwood, John, 81
Strier, Richard, 130
Stubbes, Phillip, 5
Sweezy, Paul, 15

Tawney, R. H., 8–9, 37, 211
 Religion and the Rise of Capitalism, 8–9
Taylor, Edward, 143–4
Taylor, John, 78
Taylor, Thomas, 3
teleology, 5, 7, 8, 22, 24, 28–29, 31–6, 42, 47, 57–9, 64, 85–6, 97, 99, 103–6, 114, 116, 127–8, 136, 138, 156, 158–9, 165, 170, 176–7, 184, 187, 197, 203, 211, 216, 230

telos, 5–7, 24, 28–29, 31, 45–7, 50, 53, 58, 82, 86, 97–9, 101, 103, 132, 152–5, 160, 175, 177, 182–3, 187, 197, 205–6, 230
Tertullian, 57, 83–7
   The Apparel of Women, 84–5
   Idolatry, 84
   Spectacles, 84
Theodora, Empress, 60, 66
Theodore the Studite, 63–5
Tillyard, E. M. W., 146–7
Toliver, Harold, 128, 136
totality, 11, 20
totalization, 22
Traherne, Thomas, 6–7, 191–211
   Centuries of Meditation, 193–4, 197–211
   Christian Ethics, 198, 200
Traheron, Bartholomew, 87, 98
Trismegistus, Hermes, 149
Tuve, Rosemund, 130, 136, 140–1
typology, 7, 115–42, 178, 181, 184, 189
tyranny, 172–90

United Provinces, 174
use value, 31–2, 46, 86, 118–19, 126, 141, 144, 156, 194, 196–211, 230
usury, 7, 8, 9, 16, 23, 31–2, 35, 39, 43, 79, 95–114, 116–18, 122–5, 154, 230

value, financial, 13–14, 21–3, 27, 35–52, 66, 84–5, 116, 118–19, 121, 123, 129, 143–67, 191, 193–4, 196–211
van der Wee, Hermann, 38
Vaughan, Rice, 42, 150–1, 192–3
   A Discourse of Coins and Coinage, 42–3, 150, 192–3
Vendler, Helen, 122, 128, 138
Violet, Thomas, 38, 40
Virgil, 100, 157

Wallerstein, Immanuel, 15, 17, 27
Walton, Izaac, 133
war of the theaters, 89
Warhol, Andy, 140, 142
Weber, Max, 9, 96
Weemse, John, 81, 98, 127, 169
Wheeler, John, 55
   A Treatise of Commerce, 55
Whichcote, Benjamin, 194, 196
Wilson, Thomas, 101
Wing, John, 116–17
Winstanley, Gerrard, 8
Wood, Ellen Meiksins, 16
   The Pristine Culture of Capitalism, 16
Wood, Neal, 16, 97
Woodmansee, Martha, 18
works righteousness, 69, 72, 125, 134, 136, 179, 225

Yahweh, 53–4
Yazid, Caliph, 62